HOUSE OF LORDS

El Narco

The Bloody Rise of Mexican Drug Cartels

IOAN GRILLO

BLOOMSBURY

LONDON • NEW DELHI • NEW YORK • SYDNEY

First published in Great Britain 2012

Copyright © 2011 by Ioan Grillo

The author has asserted his moral rights

Bloomsbury Publishing Plc
50 Bedford Square
London WC1B 3DP

www.bloomsbury.com

Bloomsbury Publishing, London, New Delhi, New York and Sydney

A CIP catalogue record for this book is available from the British Library

UK trade paperback ISBN 978 1 4088 2433 7
Australian trade paperback ISBN 978 1 4088 2634 8

10 9 8 7 6 5 4 3

Typeset by Westchester Book Group
Printed and bound by CPI Group (UK) Ltd, Croydon CR0 4YY

Contents

Map: The Golden Triangle   vii

1. Ghosts   1

Part I: History

2. Poppies   17

3. Hippies   38

4. Cartels   55

5. Tycoons   73

6. Democrats   89

7. Warlords   109

Part II: Anatomy

8. Traffic   133

9. Murder   152

10. Culture   169

11. Faith   186

12. Insurgency   202

Part III: Destiny

13. Prosecution   225

14. Expansion   241

15. Diversification 259

16. Peace 274

Acknowledgments 293
Books 295
Notes 297
Index 311

The Golden Triangle

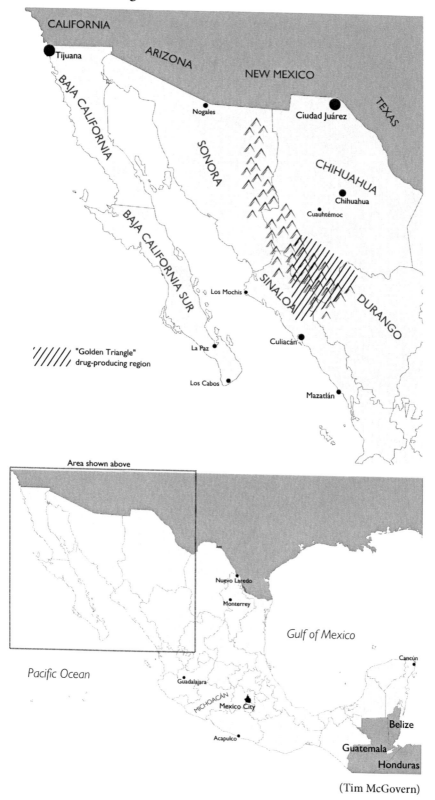

(Tim McGovern)

CHAPTER 1

Ghosts

It all seemed like a bad dream.

It may have been vivid and raw. But it felt somehow surreal, as if Gonzalo were watching these terrible acts from above. As if it were someone else who had firefights with ski-masked federal police in broad daylight. Someone else who stormed into homes and dragged away men from crying wives and mothers. Someone else who duct-taped victims to chairs and starved and beat them for days. Someone else who clasped a machete and began to hack off their craniums while they were still living.

But it was all real.

He was a different man when he did those things, Gonzalo tells me. He had smoked crack cocaine and drunk whiskey every day, had enjoyed power in a country where the poor are so powerless, had a latest-model truck and could pay for houses in cash, had four wives and children scattered all over . . . had no God.

"In those days, I had no fear. I felt nothing. I had no compassion for anybody," he says, speaking slowly, swallowing some words.

His voice is high and nasal after police smashed his teeth out until he confessed. His face betrays little emotion. I can't take in the gravity of what he is saying—until I play back a video of the interview later and transcribe his words. Then as I wallow over the things he told me, I pause and shudder inside.

I talk to Gonzalo in a prison cell he shares with eight others on a sunny Tuesday morning in Ciudad Juárez, the most murderous city on the planet. We are less than seven miles from the United States and the Rio Grande, which slices through North America like a line dividing a palm. Gonzalo sits on his bed in the corner clasping his hands together on his lap. He wears a simple white T-shirt that reveals a protruding belly under broad shoulders and bulging muscles that he built as a teenage American football star and are still in shape at his age thirty-eight. Standing six feet two, he cuts an imposing figure and exhibits an air of authority over his cellmates. But as he talks to me, he is modest and forthcoming. He wears a goatee, gray hairs on his chin below a curved, black mustache. His eyes are focused and intense, looking ruthless and intimidating but also revealing an inner pain.

Gonzalo spent seventeen years working as a soldier, kidnapper, and murderer for Mexican drug gangs. In that time he took the lives of many, many more people than he can count. In most countries, he would be viewed as a dangerous serial killer and locked up in a top-security prison. But Mexico today has thousands of serial murderers. Overwhelmed jails have themselves become scenes of bloody massacres: twenty slain in one riot; twenty-one murdered in another; twenty-three in yet another—all in penitentiaries close to this same cursed border.

Within these sanguine pens, we are in a kind of sanctuary—an entire wing of born-again Christians. This is the realm of Jesus, they tell me, a place where they abide by laws of their own "ecclesiastical government." Other wings in this jail are segregated between gangs: one controlled by the Barrio Azteca, which works for the Juárez Cartel; another controlled by their sworn enemies, the Artist Assassins, who murder for the Sinaloa Cartel.

The three hundred Christians try to live outside this war. Baptized Libres en Cristo, or Free Through Christ, the sect founded in the prison borrows some of the radical and rowdy elements of Southern American evangelicalism to save these souls. I visit a jail block mass before I sit down with Gonzalo. The pastor, a convicted drug trafficker, mixes stories of ancient Jerusalem with his hard-core street experiences, using slang and addressing the flock as the "homeys from the barrio." A live band blends rock, rap, and *norteño* music into their hymns. The sinners let it all out, slam-dancing wildly to the chorus, praying with eyes closed tight, teeth gritted, sweat pouring from foreheads, hands raised to the heavens— using all their spiritual power to exorcise their heinous demons.

Gonzalo has more demons than most. He was incarcerated in the prison a year before I met him and bought his way into the Christian wing hoping it would be a quiet place where he could escape the war. But when I listen carefully to his interview, he sounds as if he has really given his heart to Christ, does really pray for redemption. And when he talks to me—a nosy British journalist prying into his past—he is really confessing to Jesus.

"You meet Christ and it is a totally different thing. You feel horror and start thinking about the things you have done. Because it was bad. You think about the people. It could have been a brother of mine I was doing these things to. I did bad things to a lot of people. A lot of parents suffered.

"When you belong to organized crime, you have to change. You could be the best person in the world, but the people you live with change you completely. You become somebody else. And then the drugs and liquor change you."

I have watched too many videos of the pain caused by killers like Gonzalo. I have seen a sobbing teenager tortured on a tape sent to his family; a bloodied old man confessing that he had talked to a rival cartel; a line of kneeling victims with bags over their heads being shot in the brain one by one. Does someone who has committed such crimes deserve redemption? Do they deserve a place in heaven?

Yet, I see a human side to Gonzalo. He is friendly and well-mannered. We chat about lighter issues. Perhaps in another time and place, he could have been a stand-up guy who worked hard and cared for his family—like his father, who, he says, was a lifelong electrician and union man.

I have known angry, violent men in my home country; hooligans who smash bottles into people's faces or stab people at soccer games. On the surface, those men seem more hateful and intimidating than Gonzalo as he talks to me in the prison cell. Yet they have killed nobody. Gonzalo has helped turn Mexico at the dawn of the twenty-first century into a bloodbath that has shocked the world.

In his seventeen years in the service of the mafia, Gonzalo witnessed extraordinary changes in the Mexican drug industry.

He began his career in Durango, the mountainous northern-Mexican state that is the proud birthplace of Mexican revolutionary Pancho Villa. It is also near the heartland of smugglers who have taken drugs to America since Washington first made them illegal. After dropping out of high school and abandoning his hopes of becoming an NFL quarterback, Gonzalo did what many young tough nuts in his town did: he joined the police force. Here he learned the highly marketable skills of kidnapping and torture.

The path from policeman to villain is alarmingly common in Mexico. Major drug lords, such as the 1980s "Boss of Bosses" Miguel Ángel Félix Gallardo, began as officers of the law, as did notorious kidnapper Daniel Arizmendi, alias the Ear Lopper. Like them, Gonzalo left the police after a reasonably short stint, deserting when he was twenty years old to pursue a full-time criminal career.

He arrived in Ciudad Juárez and did dirty work for an empire of traffickers who smuggled drugs along a thousand miles of border from east of Juárez to the Pacific Ocean. The year was 1992, glorious days for Mexico's drug mafias. A year earlier, the Soviet Union had collapsed and governments across the world were globalizing their economies. A year later, Colombian police shot dead cocaine king Pablo Escobar, signaling the beginning of the demise of that country's cartels. As the 1990s went on, Mexican traffickers flourished, moving tons of narcotics north and pumping back billions of dollars amid the surge in free trade created by NAFTA. They replaced Colombians as the dominant mafia in the Americas. Gonzalo provided muscle for these gangster entrepreneurs, pressuring (or kidnapping and murdering) people who didn't pay their bills. He became a rich man, earning hundreds of thousands of dollars.

But by the time of his arrest seventeen years later, his job and his industry had drastically changed. He was leading heavily armed troops in urban warfare against rival gangs. He was carrying out mass kidnappings and controlling safe houses with dozens of victims bound and gagged. He was working with high-ranking city police officers, but fighting pitched battles against federal agents. He was carrying out brutal terror, including countless decapitations. He had become, he tells me, a man he did not recognize when he stared in the mirror.

"You learn a lot of forms of torture. To a point you enjoy carrying them out. We laughed at people's pain—at the way we tortured them. There are many forms of torture. Cutting off arms, decapitating. This is a very strong thing. You decapitate someone and have no feeling, no fear."

This book is about the criminal networks that paid Gonzalo to hack off human heads. It tells the story of these groups' radical transformation from drug smugglers into paramilitary death squads who have killed tens of thousands and terrorized communities with car bombs, massacres, and grenade attacks. It is a look inside their hidden world and at the brutal mafia capitalism they perpetrate. It is the tale of many ordinary Mexicans sucked into their war or victimized by it.

This book is also an argument about the nature of this startling transformation. It contends—despite what some politicians and pundits say—that these gangsters have become a criminal insurgency that poses the biggest armed threat to Mexico since its 1910 revolution. It looks at how failures of the American war on drugs and Mexico's political and economic turmoil have triggered the insurgency. And it argues for a drastic rethinking of strategies to stop the conflict from spreading into a wider civil war on the United States' doorstep. That solution, this book argues, does not come from the barrel of a gun.

Understanding the Mexican Drug War is crucial not only because of morbid curiosity at heaps of severed brain cases, but because the problems in Mexico are being played out across the world. We hear little about communist guerrillas in the Americas these days, but criminal uprisings are spreading like bushfire. In El Salvador, the Mara Salvatrucha forced bus drivers into a national strike over antigang laws; in Brazil, the First Command torched eighty-two buses, seventeen banks, and killed forty-two policemen in one coordinated offensive; in Jamaica, police clashed with supporters of Christopher "Dudus" Coke, leaving seventy dead. Are pundits going to insist this is just cops and robbers? The Mexican Drug War is a frightening warning of how bad things could get in these other countries; it is a case study in criminal insurgency.

Many Salvadoran gangbangers are the sons of communist guerrillas—and call themselves combatants just like their fathers. But they don't care about Che Guevara and socialism, just money and power. In a globalized world, mafia capitalists and criminal insurgents have become the new dictators and the new rebels. Welcome to the twenty-first century.

Anyone on the planet with half an eye on the TV knows there is an orgy of butchery in Mexico. The country is so deep in blood, it is hard to shock anymore. Even the kidnapping and killing of nine policemen or a pile of craniums in a town plaza isn't big news. Only the most sensational atrocities now grab media attention: a grenade attack on a crowd of revelers celebrating Independence Day; the sewing of a murder victim's face onto a soccer ball; an old silver mine filled with fifty-six decaying corpses, some of the victims thrown in alive; the kidnapping and shooting of seventy-two migrants, including a pregnant woman. Mexico reels from massacres comparable to brutal war crimes.

And it's all because a few American college kids are getting high.

Or is it?

Anybody taking a closer look at the Mexican Drug War works out quickly that nothing is what it seems. Every view is clouded by deceit and rumors, every fact argued over by competing interest groups and agencies, all key personalities, shrouded in mystery and contradictions. A squad of men dressed in police uniforms are filmed kidnapping a mayor. Are they really police? Or are they gangsters in disguise? Or both? An arrested thug tells all, signs of torture evident on his taped confession. Then thugs capture a policeman and videotape the officer giving a contradictory version of events. Whom do you believe? A villain commits murders in Mexico, then becomes a protected witness in the United States. Can you trust his testimony?

Another bizarre element is how the conflict can be everywhere and nowhere. Millions of tourists sun themselves happily on Cancún's Caribbean beaches, oblivious that anything is amiss. The Mexican capital is less murderous than Chicago, Detroit, or New Orleans.[1] And even in the hardest-hit areas, all can appear perfectly normal.

I have arrived at a restaurant in Sinaloa state twenty minutes after a police commander was gunned down having breakfast. Within an hour, the corpse had been carted away and waiters were preparing tables for lunch; you could eat some tacos and have no clue there had been an early-morning murder. I have watched hundreds of soldiers sweep into a residential neighborhood and kick down doors—and suddenly vanish with the same speed they arrived.

Americans visit the colonial town of San Miguel de Allende or the Mayan pyramids of Palenque and wonder what all the fuss is about. They can't see any war or severed craniums. Why is the media hyping it? Others visit family over the Texas border in Tamaulipas state. They hear gunshots popping on the street like firecrackers at a carnival, and they wonder why these battles are not even mentioned in the next day's newspapers.

Politicians are lost for language to even describe the conflict. Mexican president Felipe Calderón dresses up in a military uniform and calls for no quarter on enemies who threaten the fatherland—then balks angrily at any notion Mexico is fighting an insurrection. The Obama administration is even more confused. Secretary of State Hillary Clinton assures people that Mexico is simply suffering from inner-city crime like the United States in the eighties. Then she later says Mexico has an insurgency akin to Colombia's. An embarrassed Obama implies that Clinton didn't mean what she said. Or did she? The head of the DEA cheers on Calderón for winning the war. Then a Pentagon analyst warns that Mexico is in danger of a Yugoslavia-style rapid collapse.[2]

Is it a "narco state"? Or a "captured state"? Or just in a right bloody state? Are there narco terrorists? Or is that phrase, as some conspiracy theorists claim, part of an American plot to invade Mexico? Or a CIA plot to steal budget from the DEA?

Perhaps such confusion should be expected from a Mexican Drug War. The fight against drugs is famously a game of smoke and mirrors;[3] Mexico is a modern classic in the conspiracy-theory genre; and war always emits fog. Put all three together and what do you get? Smoky, black murkiness so dense that you can't see your nose in front of your face. Confounded by such perplexity, many understandably throw their hands in the air and shrug that we just cannot comprehend what is going on.

But we must.

This is not a random explosion of violence. Residents of northern Mexico have not turned into psychotic killers overnight after drinking bad water. This violence exploded and escalated over a clear time frame. Identifiable factors have caused the conflict. Real people made of flesh and blood have pulled the strings of armies, made fortunes from the war, or pursued failed policies from government towers.

At the center of the whole dirty drama are the most mysterious figures of all: the drug smugglers. But who are they?

In Mexico, traffickers are described collectively by the Spanish word *El Narco*, using a singular proper noun. The term, which is shouted loudly in news reports and whispered quietly in cantinas, provokes the image of an enormous ghostlike form leering over society. Its capos are shadowy billionaires from ramshackle mountain villages, known from grainy, twenty-year-old photos and the verses of popular ballads. Its warriors are armies of ragged, mustachioed men who are thrust before the press like captured soldiers from a mysterious enemy state. It attacks like a wraith under the noses of thousands of police and soldiers patrolling city streets, and the vast majority of its murders are never solved. This ghost makes an estimated $30 billion every year smuggling cocaine, marijuana, heroin, and crystal meth into the United States. But the cash disappears like cosmic mist into the global economy.

In short, El Narco is the eight-hundred-pound gorilla in the room. But most people can't put much of a face on that gorilla.

On the streets where El Narco reigns, being in the drug underworld is referred to as being in "the movement." That word gives a sense of the broad meaning of organized crime on the ground; it is a whole way of life for a segment of society. Gangsters have even begotten their own genre of music, *narcocorridos*, lead their own fashion style, *buchones*, and nurture their own religious sects. These songs, styles, and sermons all build up an image of the drug lords as iconic heroes, celebrated by dwellers of Mexico's cinder-block barrios as rebels who have the guts to beat back the army and the DEA. El Narco has entrenched itself in these communities over a century. By following its development as a movement—rather than just sketching the police stories of the drug kingpins—we can get much closer to understanding the threat and figuring out how to deal with it.

My personal contact with the drug trade began more than two decades before I sat in a sweaty prison by the Rio Grande prying stories from a mass murderer—back on the green pastures of southeast England. I grew up near the seaside city of Brighton, where my dad taught anthropology. When I was a teenager in the 1980s, drugs flooded into the area like a tidal wave—despite the shouts of Nancy Reagan, La Toya Jackson, and spotty adolescents from a British show called *Grange Hill* to "Just Say No." The popular drugs were Moroccan hashish, known as rocky; Turkish heroin, known as smack; and later Dutch ecstasy, known as E's. Students or dropouts from my school could be found getting high, low, or "on one" all over the place—from public gardens to public toilets.

No one gave a moment's thought to the far-off lands that the mind-bending substances came from, or what the drug trade gave or took away from those countries. The farthest up the food chain anyone knew about was when a local dealer got busted by the DS (drug squad) and we chatted excitedly over the details of the raid and what prison time he got.

As I came out of these teenage years, many who had experimented with drugs went on to get good jobs and start families. Some still had the odd binge, many switching to Colombian cocaine, which became fashionable in nineties England. I also knew several who suffered addiction, mostly from heroin, and went through bad bouts of stealing from their parents' homes and drying out in rehabs. Most got over it in the end. Some are still burned-out addicts two decades later whom I find on trips home propping up bars of grimy local pubs.

Between the ages of sixteen and twenty-one, I also knew four young men who died of heroin overdoses. Two were brothers. One of them finished his days passed out in a public toilet. The fourth one, Paul, had stayed over at my house days before he injected the lethal dose into his bloodstream.

Paul was a brash, brawny fellow, with a mop of thick black hair and meaty hands, who would strike up conversations with strangers from bus stops to pubs. We stayed up all night as he rambled on about the girl he was seeing, his fights with his younger brother, and his philosophy on class struggle. Then he was gone. I don't personally blame the people who trafficked the heroin that caused Paul's death. I don't think he would either. But I do strive to understand the forces that led to it and search for a different world in which his death could have been avoided—and he would still be chatting to strangers at bus stops today.

I traveled to Latin America with a backpack, a one-way ticket, and a goal to be a foreign correspondent in exotic climes. The Oliver Stone movie *Salvador* inspired me with its story of reporters dodging bullets in the Central American civil wars. But by the turn of the millennium, the days of military dictators and communist insurgents were no more. We had passed through "the End of History," we were told, and were promised a golden age of democracy and free trade the world over.

I set foot in Mexico in 2000, the day before former Coca-Cola executive Vicente Fox was sworn into office as president, ending seventy-one years of rule by the Institutional Revolutionary Party or PRI. This was a titanic moment in Mexican history, a seismic shift in its political plates. It was a time of optimism and celebration. The PRI clique who'd ravaged the country and lined their pockets for most of the twentieth century had fallen from power. Its massacres of protesters and dirty wars against rebels were over, people cheered. Ordinary Mexicans looked forward to enjoying the fruit of their hard work along with freedom and human rights.

A decade later, downhearted Mexicans fought off accusations they lived in a failed state. Cartel gunmen scattered corpses in plazas; kidnappers brutally stole fortunes of successful entrepreneurs; and while the government no longer censored the press, gangsters dug graves for dozens of journalists and cowed newspapers into silence. What had gone wrong? Why had the dream soured so suddenly?

In the first years of the decade, no one saw the crisis ahead. The American media heaped high expectations on the cowboy-boot wearing Fox as he entertained Kofi Annan and became the first Mexican to address a joint session of the U.S. Congress. The other big Mexican story was Subcomandante Marcos, a postmodernist rebel who led the Mayans of Chiapas into a symbolic rebellion for indigenous rights. Marcos gave TV interviews smoking a pipe and wearing a ski mask, quoting poets and inspiring leftists across the world. When El Narco was mentioned, it was in the good news of soldiers rounding up wanted capos.

However, the jangle of gunfire and chops of executioners' axes began to sound in the background. The first wave of serious cartel warfare began in the fall of 2004 on the border with Texas and spread across the country. When President Felipe Calderón took power in 2006 and declared war on these gangs, the violence multiplied exponentially.

So why did cartels blossom during the first decade of Mexico's democracy? Tragically, the same system that promised hope was weak in controlling the most powerful mafias on the continent. The old regime may have been corrupt and authoritarian. But it had a surefire way of managing organized crime: taking down a token few gangsters and taxing the rest. This point is now recognized by most Mexican academics and is a central theme in this book: the Mexican Drug War is inextricably linked to the democratic transition.

Just as the collapse of the Soviet Union ushered in an explosion of mafia capitalism, so did the demise of the PRI. Mexican special-force soldiers became mercenaries for gangsters. Businessmen who used to pay off corrupt officials had to pay off mobsters. Police forces turned on one another—sometimes breaking out into full-on interagency shoot-outs. When Calderón replaced Fox, he threw the entire military out to restore order. But rather than falling into line, as Calderón hoped, gangsters actually took on the government.

In the first four years of Calderón's administration, the Mexican Drug War claimed a stunning thirty-four thousand lives.[4] That tragic statistic is enough for everyone to realize it is a serious conflict—more casualties than in many declared wars. But it should also be taken in perspective. In a country of 112 million,[5] it is a low-intensity war. The Vietnam War claimed 3 million casualties; the American Civil War six hundred thousand; in Rwanda, militias massacred eight hundred thousand people in a hundred days.

Another hard fact in Mexico is the number of officials who have been murdered. In this four-year period, cartel gunmen slayed more than twenty-five hundred public servants, including twenty-two hundred policemen,[6] two hundred soldiers, judges, mayors, a leading gubernatorial candidate, the leader of a state legislature, and dozens of federal officials. Such a murder rate compares to the most lethal insurgent forces in the world, certainly more deadly to government than Hamas, ETA, or the Irish Republican Army in its entire three decades of armed struggle. It represents a huge threat to the Mexican state.

The nature of the attacks is even more intimidating. Mexican thugs regularly shower police stations with bullets and rocket-propelled grenades; they carry out mass kidnappings of officers and leave their mutilated bodies on public display; and they even kidnapped one mayor, tied him up, and stoned him to death on a main street. Who can claim with a straight face that is no challenge to authority?

Yet in Mexico, the phrase *insurgent* sets off an even bigger political bang than the narco's car bombs. Insurgents were the glorious founding fathers who rebelled against Spain. The biggest avenue in the country, which cuts across Mexico City, is called Insurgentes. To give criminals this label is to imply they could be heroes. These are psychotic criminals. How dare you compare them to honorable rebels?

Talk about insurgency, wars, and failed states also sends shivers down the spines of Mexican officials looking for tourist and investment dollars. Brand Mexico has been given a hiding in the last three years. Some officials are even convinced there is a gringo plot to divert tourists from Cancún to Florida.

Mexico is nothing like Somalia. Mexico is an advanced country with a trillion-dollar economy,[7] several world-class companies, and eleven billionaires.[8] It has an educated middle class with a quarter of young people going to university. It has some of the best beaches, resorts, and museums on the planet. But it is also experiencing an extraordinary criminal threat that we need to understand. As tens of thousands of bodies pile up, a strategy of silence won't make it go away. In Spanish, they call that "using your thumb to block out the sun."

From my early days in Mexico, I was fascinated by the riddle of El Narco. I wrote stories on busts and seizures. But I knew in my heart they were superficial, that the sources of police and "experts" were not good enough. I had to talk to narcos themselves. Where did they come from? How did their business function? What were their goals? And how was a limey going to answer this?

My search to solve this quandary took me through surreal and tragic ambiences over the decade. I stumbled up mountains where drugs are born as pretty flowers, I dined with lawyers who represent the biggest capos on the planet, and I got drunk with American undercover agents who infiltrated the cartels. I also sped through city streets to see too many bleeding corpses—and heard the words of too many mothers who had lost their sons, and with them their hearts. And I finally got to narcos. From peasant farmers who grow coca and ganja; to young assassins in the slums; to "mules" who carry drugs to hungry Americans; to damned gangsters seeking redemption—I searched for human stories in an inhuman war.

This book comes from this decade of investigation. Part I, "History," traces the radical transformation of El Narco, going back to its roots in the early twentieth century as mountain peasants through to the paramilitary forces today. The movement is a century in the making. This history does not intend to cover every capo and incident, but to explore the key developments that have shaped the beast and fortified it in Mexican communities. Part II, "Anatomy," looks at the different pillars of this narco-insurgent movement today through the eyes of the people who live them: the trafficking; the machine of murder and terror; and its peculiar culture and faith. Part III, "Destiny," looks at where the Mexican Drug War is headed and how the beast can be slain.

While centered on Mexico, this book follows the tentacles of El Narco over the Rio Grande into the United States and south to the Colombian Andes. Gangsters don't respect borders, and the drug trade has always been international. From its earnest beginning to today's bloody war, the growth of Mexico's mafias has intrinsically been linked to events in Washington, Bogotá, and beyond.

To dig deep into this story, I owe a huge debt to many Latin Americans who have spent decades laboring to understand the phenomenon.

In the last four years, more than thirty Mexican journalists digging up vital information have been shot dead. I am continually impressed by the bravery and talent of Latin American investigators and their generosity in sharing their knowledge and friendship. The list is endless, but I am particularly inspired by the work of Tijuana journalist Jesús Blancornelas, Sinaloan academic Luis Astorga, and Brazilian writer Paulo Lins, author of *City of God*.

I recorded or filmed many of the interviews that make up this book, so their words are verbatim. In other cases, I spent days prying into people's lives and relied on notes. Several sources asked me to avoid surnames or to change their names. With the current murder rate in Mexico, I couldn't challenge such requests. On one occasion, two gangsters gave an interview on Mexican television and were murdered within hours, inside a prison. Five sources whose interviews helped shaped this book were subsequently murdered or disappeared, although these killings almost certainly had nothing to do with my work. Those people are:

Police Chief Alejandro Dominguez: shot dead, Nuevo Laredo,
    June 8, 2005
Human-rights lawyer Sergio Dante: shot dead, Ciudad Juárez,
    January 25, 2006
Journalist Mauricio Estrada: disappeared, Apatzingan, July 2008
Criminal lawyer Americo Delgado: shot dead, Toluca, August 29,
    2009
Director of Honduran Anti-Drug Police Julian Aristides Gonzalez:
    shot dead, Tegucigalpa, December 8, 2009

The last on the list, Julian Aristides Gonzalez, gave me an interview in his office in the sweaty Honduran capital. The square-jawed officer chatted for several hours about the growth of Mexican drug gangs in Central America and the Colombians who provide them with narcotics. His office was crammed with 140 kilos of seized cocaine and piles of maps and photographs showing clandestine landing strips and narco mansions. I was impressed by how open and frank Gonzalez was about his investigations and the political corruption that showed up. Four days after the interview, he gave a press conference showing his latest discoveries. The following day he dropped his seven-year-old daughter off at school. Assassins drove past on a motorcycle and fired eleven bullets into his body. He had planned to retire in two months and move his family to Canada.

I don't know how much any mere books can help stop this relentless barrage of death. But literature on El Narco can at least contribute to a more complete understanding of this complex and deadly phenomenon. People and governments have to start making better sense of the mayhem and form more effective policies, so that other families, who may be closer to the homes and loved ones of readers, do not suffer the same tragedy.

PART I

History

CHAPTER 2

Poppies

Into the bowl in which their wine was mixed, she slipped a drug that had the power of robbing grief and anger of their sting and banishing all painful memories. No one who swallowed this dissolved in their wine could shed a single tear that day, even for the death of his mother or father, or if they put his brother or his own son to the sword and he were there to see it done.

—HOMER, *ODYSSEY*, CIRCA 800 B.C.

Under the blasting sunlight of Mexico's western Sierra Madre, the pink poppy takes on a slightly orange color, making the finely crumpled leaves stand out against red-brown earth and gnarly cacti. I'm staring at the opium poppies after driving up hours of dirt roads in a battered pickup truck. The path was so bumpy and vertical that I was thrown up and down as if I were on a fairground ride. I thought it was a miracle we never got a punctured tire or a rock smashing through the gas tank. Luckily, my driver—a local singer who goes by the stage name El Comandante—knew all the tricks for swerving round the sharpest debris.

Few outsiders come here. This is a place where they cut off heads and stick them on wooden poles, people warn, as they did a few days earlier in a nearby village. But I'm not seeing any severed craniums right now. I'm just staring at poppies and marveling at how beautiful they are.

What I'm looking at is not a whole opium crop, just few plants grown by a woman outside her village shop, which is across a dirt crossroads from a small army outpost. Matilde is a handsome lady in her fifties with bright, pretty eyes and skin worn like brown leather from the sun. Many people in these mountains speak with a drawl so thick I understand little of what they say. But Matilde pronounces her words carefully and looks me straight in the eyes to make sure I comprehend. "The poppies are beautiful, aren't they?" she says as she sees me admiring her flowers. Where did she get seeds for opium? I ask. From her brother, she tells me, adding that this is a village of *valientes* or brave ones—the term mountain folk use for drug traffickers, the men who pulled this community out of poverty. Meanwhile, she scorns the soldiers in the outpost as *guachos*, an old Indian word for servants.

Matilde is particularly angry at the *guachos* because of a recent shooting at this crossroads.[1] Four local young men were driving to a girl's fifteenth birthday in a shiny white Hummer. (It is a village of dirt shacks, but residents love their fancy cars.) The soldiers shouted at the Hummer to stop. But it was dark and the revelers were blaring music and they carried on. So the soldiers started blasting their assault rifles—and when they thought they were receiving fire, they blasted some more. After a few rounds, the Hummer had stopped and four young men were dead, as well as two soldiers.

The army first reported that brave troops had killed four cartel hit men. But then a different version came out. The men in the Hummer had not been armed. There had been no return fire; the soldiers had been shooting from two sides and killed their own troops. It was classic stupidity, reminiscent of the stumbling conscript armies who fought the First World War in Europe. And the mistake is still being made by these troops that America—through a $1.6 billion aid program—is underwriting to fight the war on drugs at the source.

"The *guachos* are idiots," Matilde tells me. "They should go home to their own stupid villages."

This is where it all began. In these mountains, Mexico's earliest drug traffickers grew opium more than a century ago. Over generations, these ramshackle communities churned out kingpin after kingpin. Barely literate men speaking the drawl of these highlands went out and set up sprawling international networks moving billions of dollars.

A few hours up dirt roads from Matilde's store is the family home of Joaquin "Chapo" Guzmán,[2] the five-foot-six drug lord that *Forbes* valued at $1 billion. Government agents say he is still hiding up in these jagged hills somewhere, protected by villagers who love and fear him. Close by is the house of his childhood friend Arturo Beltrán Leyva, alias the Beard. Hundreds of Mexican marines recently hunted down the Beard. They stormed an apartment block where he was holed up and kept shooting for two hours while his men hurled frag grenades and unleashed automatic rifle fire. Five of the Beard's bodyguards died before giving him up. Then the marines shot the drug lord to pieces and decorated his body with dollar bills.

In revenge, Beltrán Leyva loyalists identified the family of a marine who had died in the shoot-out. Gangsters went to the marine's wake and murdered his mother, brother, sister, and aunt. They used to just kill rival gangsters, now they massacre entire families. What is it about these mountains? What do they have that can yield men so creative, so entrepreneurial, and yet so cold-blooded?

The Sierra Madre Occidental stretches 932 miles from the U.S. border at Arizona deep into Mexico. It is a big and wild enough terrain to hide an entire army in, as Pancho Villa proved when he fled U.S. forces after raiding Columbus, New Mexico, during the Mexican Revolution. From the sky, the mountains look like a crumpled rug covered in yellow-green hair, decorated by a splattering of lakes and ragged ravines. They twist and spiral through the Mexican states of Sonora, Sinaloa, Durango, and Chihuahua. The latter three are known as Mexico's Golden Triangle for all the drugs they produce.

Every day, Mexican soldiers buzz over the Triangle in helicopters searching for the light green of marijuana crops or the pink of opium. The troops find crops and burn them; they are such experts now, they can rip up and torch an acre of marijuana in less than an hour. Then mountain farmers sow more marijuana and poppy seeds and raise more green and pink blobs to be spotted from the sky. And the ritual starts again.

The crossroads where I gawk at opium is on the southwest corner of this Golden Triangle in the state of Sinaloa. There are gangsters all over these mountains, but most of the top dogs come from here. While Sicily is the home of the Italian mafia, Sinaloa is the cradle of Mexican drug gangs, the birthplace of the nation's oldest and most powerful network of traffickers, known as the Sinaloa Cartel.

American agents only started using the name Sinaloa Cartel in indictments in the last couple of years. Before that they called it the Federation, and before that a host of other names such as the Guadalajara Cartel—named after Mexico's second city, which Sinaloan crime bosses used as a base of operations. But all these names are just approximations to describe a quarrelsome empire of traffickers that spans out from Sinaloa across half the U.S. border. Some capos of this empire are linked by blood or marriage to the very first peasants who grew opium in the heights a century ago. It is an unbroken dynasty.

Like Sicily, Sinaloa has geographical traits that are condusive to organized crime. The state is a little smaller than West Virginia, but anyone who wants to disappear can move rapidly into the Sierra Madre and slip over peaks into Sonora, Chihuahua, or Durango. Beneath the highlands, Sinaloa boasts four hundred miles of Pacific coastline, where contraband has been smuggled in and out for centuries. Silver, muskets, opium, and pseudophedrine pills to make crystal meth have all been sneaked across its shores. Between the sea and the mountains, Sinaloa has fertile valleys that have spawned great plantations—particularly in tomatoes and onions—and earth teeming with gold, silver, and copper. This natural wealth fueled the growth of the state capital, Culiacán, a lively city built where the gushing Tamazula and Humaya rivers meet, and the buzzing port of Mazatlán.

Commercial hubs are crucial for organized crime, providing headquarters and businesses to launder money. Again, such merchant centers mark a similarity between Sinaloa and other criminal hot spots. Sicily developed a mafia that bridged an unruly countryside and the commercial hub of Palermo, a port linking North Africa and Europe. Medellín in Colombia was a buzzing market city surrounded by bandit hills when its infamous son Pablo Escobar rose to be the world's number one cocaine trafficker. Criminal conspiracies do not spring up in certain regions by pure chance.

Sinaloa has a history of unruliness going back long before anyone talked about the Sinaloa Cartel. Pronounced *see-nah-loh-ah*, the name comes from the word for a local spiky plant in the language of the Cahita, one of six indigenous peoples that flourished in the region before the arrival of Europeans. Sinaloan tribes were mostly nomads who hunted and gathered for food, unlike the great empires of the Aztecs (Mexicas) and

Mayas to the south. But their resistance to European invaders was more ferocious and effective than that of the vast Aztec legions, who fell before Spanish conquistador Hernán Cortés in 1521. When Spanish swashbucklers tried to extend their empire into the northwest, Sinaloan tribes thwarted them, aided by the hostile terrain. One of the tribes' most noted triumphs was the murder of conquistador Pedro de Montoya in 1584 by Sinaloan indigenous Zuaques.[3]

Scarred Spaniards returned to Mexico City and wrote of ritual cannibalism among the ferocious Sinaloan tribes. Some historians dispute the claims as Spanish horror stories. But whether truth or myth, the idea has been taken on wholeheartedly by modern Sinaloans, who proudly boast that when the Spanish came, they were devoured. Whether they feasted on victims or not, indigenous resistance turned Sinaloa into a bloodstained frontier with only skeleton settlements by the end of the sixteenth century.

Jesuit missionaries found crucifixes were more effective than cannons at bringing tribesman into the Catholic empire. The conquest of Sinaloa was thus based more on faith than submission to the sword. The effect can be felt today, with Sierra Madre folk holding dear to their spiritual beliefs and folk saints. But the region continued to exist on the fringe of the law, serving as a hotbed for silver and gun contraband during the War of Independence from Spain from 1810 to 1821.

After banishing the Spanish Crown, Mexico suffered decades of civil strife and upheavals, allowing bandits to flourish in Sinaloa and elsewhere. One of the key issues Mexico has struggled with since independence is security. The inheritors of New Spain suddenly ruled a complicated country of competing fiefdoms and ethnic groups. The Spanish left the legacies of a corrupt bureaucracy, torturous police, and millions of dispossessed. The rulers needed a system to control this mess. But in the first decades of the nineteenth century, they were more concerned with who was top dog. Coup followed coup. Liberals battled with conservatives. Descendants of Spaniards clutched for power while indigenous tribes and bandits raided in frontier territories.

Internal disorder left Mexico weak against the ambitions of its powerful northern neighbor. Texan militias and then the full U.S. army defeated Mexican troops in two wars, and the United States strong-armed Mexico into selling the entire northern third of its territory. The possessions ceded in the 1848 Treaty of Guadalupe included huge chunks of Colorado, Arizona, New Mexico, and Wyoming, the whole of California, Nevada, and Utah, with political recognition of the loss of Texas.[4] In total, the ceded territory measured more than nine hundred thousand square miles, laying the foundations for the USA to become a twentieth-century superpower. Sinaloa lay some 360 miles south of this new line in the sand.

The Mexican-American War remains a burning-hot bone of contention between the two nations. Mexico annually commemorates a squad of young cadets shot dead by American troops (*los ninos héroes*), and politicians routinely bark about the imperial monster to the north. Meanwhile, the vast wave of Mexican migration to the United States is referred to as *la reconquista*—the reconquest. Many Texans or Arizonans, on the other hand, are bitterly incensed at accusations they stole the mammoth chunk of turf. The few inhabitants of the acquired territories, they argue, were liberated by the green-capped soldiers (at whom Mexicans are said to have shouted "Green, go"—the origin of the word *gringo*).

A 2009 billboard ad by Swedish vodka brewer Absolut illustrated how these wounds are still sore. Behind the slogan IN AN ABSOLUT WORLD, the ad showed an imaginary map in which a giant Mexico stretches close to the Canadian border and dwarfs the United States. The ad helped sell liquor and got some chuckles in Mexico. But Americans were so angry they bombarded the vodka brewer with thousands of complaints until Absolut withdrew the ad and apologized for causing offense. These attitudes all have a profound effect on the Mexican Drug War—and the knee-deep role of the United States.

Following loss of territory and pride, Mexico plunged into more civil strife and disorder—until dictator Porfirio Díaz took its reins. A muleteer of Mixtec origins, Don Porfirio was a war hero against the Americans and the French, before ruling Mexico with a big stick from 1876 to 1911. His domination of power was not all about force. He found an effective formula to control the wild Mexican beast—a network of local chieftains, or *caciques*, who all got their piece of the pie. But if anyone dared to defy his rule, Don Porfirio would smash back with brutality. Up in the Sierra Madre, this meant rivers of blood. The Yaqui tribe refused to give up their ancestral lands to make way for sprawling plantations. Díaz unleashed manhunts, transporting prisoners in chains to tobacco plantations in Mexico's swampy south. Most died from disease and inhumane conditions.

But amid heightened security, the dictator oversaw rapid industrialization and mass agriculture. In Sinaloa, Díaz's rich friends developed profitable plantations, while American and British companies built railroads and dynamited mine shafts. Industrialization brought Sinaloa into the international grid, beckoning steamers from across the globe. The plantations also swallowed the plots of small farmers, unleashing an army of landless peasants hungry for opportunity. The territory was ripe for trafficking. Now all Sinaloan bandits needed was a product. And in the reign of Don Porfirio, pretty pink opium poppies were first brought to the Sinaloan highlands.

A century after Porfirio, I stare at Matilde's poppies, which grow between surreal-shaped cacti that sprout out of the ground like tentacles. Stepping closer, I feel the petals are as soft as velvet and release a sweet aroma like an English garden on a spring morning. Such a pretty plant, yet the source of so much pain. Covering the fury of the drug war—the thousands of killings, beheadings, piles of seized dollar bills, the foreign aid, changing maps of cartel territory, and streams of refugees—we lose sight of the root of this whole conflict. It all starts with a simple flower on a hill.

The opium poppy, *Papaver somniferum*, is a flower with particularly potent properties. It contains one of the oldest drugs known to man, a substance that has been called "magical" and "godly," as well as "poisonous" and "evil." The plant's medicine is released when you scrape the buds with a knife, releasing a light brown mud. On the Sinaloan hills, they call it gum, and the people who scrape it are called gummers or, in Spanish, *gomeros*. Only a tiny amount of mud is released from each plant. Sinaloan gummers take a two-and-half-acre field with tens of thousands of poppies and harvest them to get just ten kilos of pure opium. I look at such a bag that has been seized by soldiers. The plant doesn't look or smell pretty anymore—it is a sticky, dark mess, with a toxic stench.

When this mush is eaten or smoked, it unleashes its miraculous effect: pain abruptly disappears. The consumer may have a gaping hole in the side of his head, but suddenly all he can feel is numbness. The incredible speed with which it works has epic consequences. Opium is one of the most effective anesthetics known to man. It was even once sold in the United States under the label GOD's OWN MEDICINE. But while curing agony, the mush also releases its infamous side effect: the consumer feels a sleepy euphoria.

I ask Matilde to describe the effect of these flowers. What is the magical property they have? What is it that makes them so valuable? She looks at me blankly for a moment, then answers in a slow, thoughtful tone.

"It is a medicine. And it cures pain. All pain. It cures the pain you have in your body and the pain in your heart. You feel like your body is mud. All mud. You feel like you could melt away and disappear. And it doesn't matter. Nothing matters. You are happy. But you are not laughing. This is a medicine, you understand?"

Such effects have inspired writers for three thousand years, from Homer to Edgar Allan Poe. They describe the opium buzz as feeling as if you were covered in cotton wool; being the happiest in your life; or feeling as if your head were a feather cushion that could burst open. Musicians croon about this blissful low in a hundred songs, looking for melancholy chords that conjure up glazed smiles in smoke-filled opium dens.

The scientific secrets of opium were uncovered by two physicists in Baltimore, Maryland, in 1973.[5] When opium is eaten or smoked, the scientists found, it stimulates groups of molecules called receptors in the central nervous system—the brain and the spinal cord. The whole drug war mess starts with chemical reactions.

Opium has an especially potent effect when it hits the brain's thalamus—an inch-long, ovoid mass that registers pain. To put it simply, when we have a toothache, messages rush to the thalamus and we feel discomfort. Opium's ingredients bond with receptors in the thalamus and make the pain messages it is receiving slow down to a crawl. Our tooth may still have a cavernous hole, but we only feel a dull twinge rather than seething agony. This same chemical bonding makes people feel euphoria. Their brains are slowed down, but this makes them overcome with bliss, in turn making them feel creative, philosophical, romantic.

The other opiates, such as morphine, codeine, and the queen of them all, heroin, work the same way. In the Sinaloan mountains, gummers now turn almost all their opium into heroin, including Mexican mud, which is light brown in color, and black tar, which is . . . well, black and looks like tar.

The chemistry that creates such "godly" effects also leads to the dreaded downside: addiction. The brain sends its own natural opiate-type signals to slow down pain. When people blast themselves with opium or heroin too regularly, these natural mechanisms stop functioning. Without their fix, people feel the notorious "cold turkey" withdrawal effects, such as diarrhea, depression, and paranoia. As a heroin addict I knew back in Britain said, "Imagine the worst flu and multiply it by ten. Then, know you can make it go away with one more hit."

Thousands of years before Sinaloan gummers made heroin, primitive humans had discovered opium's power. Poppy-seed capsules show that hunter-gatherers in Europe scraped gum four millennia before the birth of Jesus Christ. Around 3,400 B.C. in southern Mesopotamia (modern Iraq), the world's first farmers drew images of opium poppies on clay tablets under the name *Hul Gil* or the "joy plant." Two millennia later, ancient Egyptians wrote about our poppy in the Ebers Papyrus, one of humanity's oldest medical documents, as a remedy to prevent the excessive crying of children. As European civilization rose, opium was enjoyed from Constantinople to London. But the flower gained the most popularity in China, where poets deemed the mud "fit for Buddha,"[6] and the nation's army of opium smokers grew into the millions.

The Chinese finally saw the sour side to their favored flower by the end of the eighteenth century, with rising complaints of addiction. In 1810, the Qing Dynasty issued a decree banning the mud and putting sellers to death. "Opium is a poison, undermining our good customs and morality," screamed the first act of narcotics prohibition in the modern world.[7]

The ban created the first drug smugglers—in the form of polite, pipe-smoking gentlemen of the British Empire. Seeing a golden opportunity, British merchants in the East India Company smuggled thousands of tons of opium from India into the land of the dragon. When Qing soldiers stormed British ships, Queen Victoria's galleons showered the Chinese coast with cannon. If the East India Company was the first drug cartel, then the Royal Navy was the first band of violent cartel enforcers. After the two Opium Wars, the company won the right to traffic in 1860. The Chinese kept smoking and took the poppy with them in their diaspora round the planet.

Coolie laborers traveled on steamships to Sinaloa from the 1860s to toil on railroads and sweat in mine shafts. As was their custom, Chinese immigrants brought opium poppies, gum, and seeds on their long journey over the Pacific. The arid Sierra Madre provided an ideal climate for the Asian poppies to flourish. In 1886, the opium poppy was first noted as growing in Sinaloan flora by a Mexican government study. The flower had taken root.[8]

Sinaloan newspapers soon remarked on opium dens springing up in Culiacán and Mazatlán. Known as *fumaderos*, the haunts were described as dingy rooms above city-center shops where only Asians went. There are no known photos of these venues, but they were likely similar to an opium den documented in a classic journalistic photo from Chinatown Manila of the same period. In the black-and-white shot, Chinese men lie on mattresses and slump against the wall, their mouths on pipes up to two feet long. Their faces show blissful glazes, enjoying the magic euphoria of the brown mud.[9] Similar scenes of opium dens were documented in California and New York, where Chinese and curious Americans burned away their sorrows.

But then the U.S. government raised its hand and took an action with profound consequences: it outlawed the Herb of Joy. The story of El Narco is also the story of American drug policy.

Growing up with drug prohibition, it is easy to think of it as an age-old ban, such as the outlawing of robbery or murder. It seems almost like a law of nature: the earth circles the sun; gravity pulls objects down; and narcotics are illegal—facts of life, pure and simple. But scholars have shown that prohibition is a late-blooming policy that has always been tainted by discord, disagreement, and disinformation.

The basic challenge of drug policy is tough: the majority favor certain recreational drugs, such as alcohol, which causes death and addiction. Doctors and soldiers need other narcotics, such as opiates. Meanwhile, people from poor and broken communities are hammered by addiction to any mind-bending substances they can get their hands on.

But debate over drug laws has been clouded by emotive, unscientific forces, including racism. Weird myths become accepted truths. In the early days, American newspapers claimed that the Chinese used opium to systematically rape white women and that cocaine gave Southern Negroes superhuman strength. More recently, we have heard about generations of deranged subhumans called crack babies, or that LSD makes people think they can fly.

Amid fears of moral collapse, doctors and scientists are drowned out.

Shouting at the forefront is one of the great crusaders of modern times: the drug warrior. Politicians soon realized the drug issue was a useful platform, in which they fight an evil, alien force that can't answer back. They look both tough and moral and win support from that crucial group, the concerned middle class.

The father of American drug warriors is Hamilton Wright, appointed U.S. opium commissioner in 1908. An Ohio native, Wright was influenced by puritanical beliefs and sharp political ambition. He made his job a personal crusade to protect good Americans against a foreign menace and was the first person to envision the United States as leader in a global campaign to stop drug use. To later drug warriors, this made him a visionary; critics see him as starting policy on the wrong foot. Wright rang the alarm bells of an epidemic in a 1911 *New York Times* interview, under the headline UNCLE SAM IS THE WORST DRUG FIEND IN THE WORLD. As he told the *Times*:

"The habit has this Nation in its grip to an astonishing extent. Our prisons and our hospitals are full of victims of it, it has robbed ten thousand business men of moral sense and made them beasts who prey upon their fellows, unidentified it has become one of the most fertile causes of unhappiness and sin in the United States . . .

"The opium and morphine habits have become a National curse, and in some way they must certainly be checked, if we wish to maintain our high place among the nations of the world and any elevated standard of intelligence and morality among ourselves."[10]

There was indeed rising opium consumption in Wright's day, with an estimated one hundred thousand to three hundred thousand American users. Such a number is significant, but at about 0.25 percent of the population pales in comparison with contemporary drug use. While some "dope fiends" puffed opium in dark dens, many got hooked from doctors' prescriptions.

Wright was also concerned about another drug gaining popularity in the early-twentieth century: cocaine. He collected police reports on African-American cocaine use and pushed the angle the white powder was whipping uppity blacks into a frenzy. The story played big in the press. Among numerous articles about cocaine-crazed Negroes, the most infamous was printed in the *New York Times* in 1914. The piece of inflammatory racism is regrettable, verging on self-parody to modern readers. Under the headline NEGRO COCAINE "FIENDS" NEW SOUTHERN MENACE (a certain eye-catcher with your Sunday coffee), the piece opens with a rant about cocaine-crazed blacks murdering whites. It then follows with a spectacular tale about a police chief in North Carolina facing a black on blow:

"The Chief was informed that a hitherto inoffensive negro, with whom he was well acquainted, was 'running amuck' in a cocaine frenzy, had attempted to stab a storekeeper, and was at the moment engaged in 'beating up' various members of his own household . . .

"Knowing that he must kill this man or be killed himself, the Chief drew his revolver, placed the muzzle over the negro's heart, and fired— 'Intending to kill him right quick,' as the officer tells it, but the shot did not even stagger the man . . .

"He had only three cartridges remaining in his gun, and he might need these in a minute to stop the mob. So he saved his ammunition and 'finished the man with his club.' "[11]

A cocaine-crazed Negro turning into the Incredible Hulk! Chinamen using their foreign poison to seduce white women! It certainly rattled the white establishment. Wright finally got thirteen nations to sign an accord to rein in opiates and cocaine in 1914, and in December of that year the U.S. Congress passed the daddy of American drug laws: the Harrison Narcotics Act. It was not totally prohibitionist, aiming to control rather than wipe out drugs. A certain amount of legal opiates would be needed for medicine as they are today. But the Harrison Act did create an immediate black-market trade in opium and cocaine. El Narco was born.

Back in Sinaloa, it didn't take long to do the math. An unruly state, poppies in the mountains, and an illegal opium market 360 miles to the north. It was an easy equation: Sinaloan poppies could be turned into American dollars.

Chinese immigrants and their descendants had the vision and connections to kick-start Mexico's first drug trafficking. Over decades, they had grown into a community that spread from Sinaloa up to cities on Mexico's northwest border. Most were bilingual in Spanish and Mandarin and had Mexican Christian names. The list of early arrested traffickers includes Patricio Hong, Felipe Wong, and and Luis Siam. The Chinese built a network that could harvest the poppies, turn them into gum, and sell the opium to Chinese dealers on the U.S. side. As the British had defied Chinese prohibition, so the Chinese would defy American law.

The vast Mexican-U.S. border was ideal for trafficking—a problem that has confounded American authorities for the last century. It is one of the longest borders on the planet, stretching two thousand miles from the Pacific at San Diego to the Gulf of Mexico at Brownsville. The Mexican side has two major metropolises: Ciudad Juárez, smack in the middle of the line; and Tijuana (reportedly named after a madam of prostitutes named the Tía Juana). Many migrants in these cities are from the Sierra Madre states of Sinaloa and Durango, creating family links between the border and bandit mountains.

The border also boasts a dozen medium-size Mexican towns, including Mexicali, Nogales, Nuevo Laredo, Reynosa, and Matamoros. In between cities are vast stretches of wild land running through deserts and arid hills. Over the years, everything from ceremonial Aztec skulls to Browning machine guns to white tigers have been smuggled over the line in the sand. The first batches of opium slipped over the membrane like water through a sieve.

Washington called on Mexico to stop this traffic. But Mexico had more pressing concerns. After Porfirio Díaz had resisted democracy for thirty-five years, Mexicans finally rose up and overthrew him. But celebrations didn't last long, with the country descending into a bloody civil war involving four major armies. Much of the Mexican Revolution fighting took place in the northwestern territories close to the Sierra Madre, with famous battles in Ciudad Juárez and Parral. Many Sinaloans fought, including Pancho Villa's executioner, Rodolfo Fierro, who earned a reputation as one of the most sanguine murderers in the conflict. The immense violence claimed about a million casualties or 10 percent of the entire Mexican population, a legacy of blood loss that is still felt today in family and folk memory.

While Mexicans worried about surviving, Americans worried about opium smugglers. The Harrison Act created the Narcotics Board to police the drug trade, but it had no budget for real investigations. However, agents in customs, consulates, and the Treasury put their heads together to build the first big American probe into Mexican traffickers. Details of this case were later dug up by Sinaloan academic Luis Astorga, who pored through dusty documents all over Washington. It showed the agents ran straight into a snake pit.

The case was opened in September 1916 when a special agent in charge of customs at Los Angeles sent a report to Washington with dynamite implications.[12] His informants, he wrote, had tracked a syndicate of Chinese Mexicans who were smuggling opium through Tijuana into California. In Los Angeles, the syndicate sold the opium to a Chinese man called Wang Si Fee, who also had connections in San Francisco. Working with the traffickers was a shadowy figure called David Goldbaum, whose nationality is unclear. Goldbaum attended a meeting with none other than the governor of Baja California (Tijuana's state)—Colonel Esteban Cantú. After a heated negotiation, Goldbaum had agreed to pay Cantú $45,000 up front and $10,000 a month for immunity for the syndicate to traffic through northern Mexico.

The report shows that even back then, agents used a tactic that would characterize America's antidrug efforts for the next century: paid undercover informants. Furthermore, the amount of the bribe—$45,000 at the value of 1916 dollars—indicates that even in the earliest days decent profits were to be made in the junk trade. The report also mentions that a member of the crime syndicate was driving around in a Saxon Six, one of Detroit's most expensive automobiles. But the agents were most concerned about the central revelation—Mexico's politicians were in on the game.

More evidence was added to the Governor Cantú file. A customs agent reported that Baja California police made opium busts, such as four hundred tins of gum seized in the port of Ensenada—but the same drugs later reappeared for sale. Treasury officials stated that Cantú sold opium to a distributor named J. Uon in Mexicali, south of Calexico. Uon then dealt the opium out of a shop called Casa Colorada, which doubled as a Chinese employment agency.[13] A second Treasury report added that Cantú was himself a morphine addict. The governor had injected the opiate into his arms and legs so much they were black with bruises, the source said.

Stacked files of damning testimonies were sent to Washington. Both customs and Treasury officials urged the State Department to investigate and take up the issue with Mexico. The agents thought they had a red-hot case. And then . . . nothing. There are no records that Washington ever pressed Mexico over the issue, and Cantú served out his term untroubled. Maybe Cantú was on the side of the alliance that Washington approved of in the Mexican Revolution at that moment. Maybe the government was more concerned about war in Europe. Maybe officials just didn't care to stop the supply of opiates, which were being handed out in bucketloads to troops on all sides in the bleeding trenches of France.

Whatever the reasons, the Cantú case would set a precedent that American drug agents would be complaining about for the next century. Time after time, when agents built cases involving foreign political targets, the State Department would do nothing or even block their efforts. The drug war abroad and Washington's foreign diplomacy were two different missions with two very different priorities.

In the 1920s, the opium trade became an even lower priority when police focused on a new public devil: booze. As the "noble experiment" of alcohol prohibition gave birth to America's most infamous mobster, Al Capone, it also financed up-and-coming hoodlums on the Rio Grande. Mexican border cities were already popular for their brothels and table-dance clubs. Now the lure of alcohol spawned cantinas serving whiskey and tequila to thirsty Americans. Entrepreneurial Mexicans also smuggled liquor to the huge network of speakeasies across the United States. Just as the Chicago bootleggers shot back at police who tried to seize their booty, so the border smugglers retaliated.

A report in the *El Paso Times* in 1924 describes how one gang of bootleggers got into a firefight with customs agents after they seized three sacks of tequila bottles and sixty-three gallons of whiskey. The drama focuses on the heroic acts of a customs agent identified only as Officer Threepersons, who takes on sixteen bootleggers single-handedly and shoots one of the Mexicans dead. Or so he says. The thrilling action at the border begins:

"First indications of the battle were seen about midnight Saturday when Customs Officer Threepersons and Wadsworth 'pitched their camp' at the end of First Street to lie in wait for a cargo of liquor to be brought across the border.

"Shortly after their arrival near a large tree close to the monument, Wadsworth left Threepersons to bring their automobile closer to the scene of operations. No sooner had Wadsworth left when 16 Mexicans appeared . . .

"A man jumped in his path and pointed a pistol at him. Threepersons told the man to throw up his hands, but the man refused and fired his pistol point blank at the officer. Threepersons fired his 30-30 caliber rifle at the man, who dropped to the ground.

"The gun battle lasted for over an hour and was heard in practically every part of the city."[14]

A gunfight lasting an hour in the center of town! A gang of sixteen armed men! The story sounds like many that fill border newspapers today. Except this battle was on the American side—in the center of El Paso. At that time though, with daily shoot-outs and massacres in Chicago, the El Paso skirmish was small potatoes, relegated to page ten of the local rag.

As Prohibition ground to an end, Mexican bootleggers scrambled for a new product. They were quick to eye the handsome profits that Chinese made from their tins of opium and heroin. Bandits back in the Sinaloan highlands had also become jealous of the Asian gummers with their American cars and big homes. Mexicans wanted a piece of the pie. They soon realized they could take the whole lot.

Mexican villains expropriated the Chinese opium business amid a wave of racial violence against Asians. (It is not only American racism that has shaped the drug trade.) Antagonism had grown against the Chinese for several decades, with Mexicans slandering the immigrants for being immoral and filthy—and looking enviously at their successful shops and restaurants. Racism reached fever pitch, spurred on by prominent politicians.

Criminals also whipped up racism. In 1933, the American consul in Ensenada sent a report to Washington about the rising anti-Chinese tide. He cited an informant, a Mandarin-speaking American, saying that known villains were among the key anti-Chinese activists. Among them was a smuggler surnamed Segovia, who was moving round the states of Sonora, Sinaloa, and Baja California putting money into violent anti-Chinese groups. Segovia's aim, the report said, was to take over Chinese opium-poppy production.

Racial tension exploded onto the streets. Among those who joined the lynch mob was a university student named Manuel Lazcano. Born in a Sinaloan ranch in 1912, Lazcano would go on to to become a prominent figure in law enforcement and politics, serving three terms as Sinaloa's attorney general. He was later ashamed for taking part in racial attacks and claimed to be shocked by their cruelty. His memoirs are among the most open of any Mexican official's and provide one of the best sources on the early Mexican drug trade. Shown in a photo as a sharp, handsome young man smoking a pipe, Lazcano describes how an anti-Chinese mob marched into the central plaza of Culiacán to recruit followers.

"There were 150 people, which was a lot for those days in Culiacán. The banners were pathetic: Chinese shown eating rats; Chinese with sores in their heads (they used to say that the Orientals had endless diseases, were dirty and ate reptiles). There was a shower of attacks and insults . . . The boys started to push, to demand that we got involved. I remember their voices: 'Come on, Come on.' And I went in: I became anti-Chinese. It is something that still makes me feel bad."[15]

Lazcano describes how the mob would scour the streets to hunt Chinese. Finding their victims, he writes, they would drag them to a clandestine jail in a shuttered-up house and keep them prisoner with their arms and legs bound. When they had enough captives, they would pack them into boxcars, put them on cargo trains, and ship them out of state. Sinaloans then took over the Chinese homes and property. The ethnic cleansing in Sinaloa came as the Nazi regime was persecuting Jews in Europe. Lazcano didn't miss the comparison.

"We have seen films of the brutal repression that the Jews were subjected to and scenes of how they were transported like animals. Well, the same thing happened in Sinaloa but with the Chinese. Seeing the images in real life was overwhelming."[16]

Elsewhere, Mexican gangsters didn't bother with boxcars; they simply shot dead Chinese rivals. In Ciudad Juárez, a gunman known as El Veracruz is reported to have rounded up and murdered eleven Chinese men working in the opium trade. His boss was allegedly a woman from Durango called Ignacia Jasso, or La Nacha. Mexicans began to dominate the drug trade from the opium-growing Sierra Madre to the bubbling border cities.

Described as a short, robust woman with a black ponytail, La Nacha became the first famous female mobster in Mexico. By all accounts, she was a talented businesswoman. La Nacha recognized the changing demands of the market and expanded production of heroin, reportedly having her own makeshift labs to process the Sierra Madre poppies. Rather than smuggling her drugs over the border, she sold the packets of heroin out of her home in the center of Juárez. Americans, including many GIs from the base at El Paso, would cross the river to buy their fixes. Other customers came from as far as Albuquerque, New Mexico, for her famous mud.

The market was small by today's standards, and Mexican mud was considered inferior to the dominant Turkish heroin. But there was enough business to make La Nacha one of the wealthiest residents in Juárez. She sponsored an orphanage and a breakfast program for children, as well as having a flashy American car. She also had money to buy off police. As the local newspaper *El Continental* reported on the heroin queen on August 22, 1933:

"Ignacia Jasso, alias La Nacha, has still not been arrested by authorities for possession and sales of heroic drugs [heroin] which they say she has done for many years out of her own house in Degollado No. 218. We are informed that La Nacha travels tranquilly round the Juárez streets in her luxury car that she just bought. It seems she has some important influences and this is why she has not been captured."[17]

Again, as in the Cantu case, the first years of the drug trade bring up stories of corruption. But by the time of La Nacha, corruption was not by a renegade governor in the midst of civil war. The years of battle had finally subsided and an all-powerful party ruled Mexico.

The Institutional Revolutionary Party, or PRI, has been compared to the Soviet Communist Party for its grip on power, ruling Mexico almost as long the Bolsheviks ran Russia. It is also credited with giving Mexico the longest period of peace in its history and shielding it from the turbulent conflicts that wracked South America throughout the twentieth century.

PRI founding father General Plutarco Elias Calles created the party in 1929 after serving a term as president. He aimed to create peace and order by uniting all core sectors of society—trade unions, peasants, businessmen, and the military—all singing the same song and waving the same flag. Influenced by totalitarian Soviet communists and Italian fascists, Calles traveled to Europe to scrutinize politics. Curiously, he ended up spending more time looking at the British Labour Party and German Social Democrats. In any case, the PRI was a truly Mexican organization, even taking the green, white, and red of the Mexican flag as its colors. It aimed to embody the nation.

Some American journalists call the PRI a leftist party. They are way off the mark. While the PRI would produce some leftist presidents, such as Lázaro Cárdenas, it would also throw up some raving capitalists such as Carlos Salinas. Essentially the party was not about ideology but about power. Much of its system of control was taken straight from the play-book of Don Porfirio Díaz. It went back to a network of *caciques* or chiefs, who kept order in their turfs. In this patchwork of little kingdoms, thou-sands of police forces were created. However, a key difference with the Díaz regime was that the PRI would change its president every six years. Rule was by an institution instead of one strongman. The genius of this setup led to Nobel Prize–winning writer Mario Vargas Llosa calling it the "perfect dictatorship."[18]

The PRI system relied on corruption to keep ticking over smoothly. Businessmen could pay off small-town *caciques*, who could pay off gov-ernors, who could pay off the president. Money rose up like gas and power flowed down like water. Everybody was happy and stayed in line because everybody got paid. Historians have noted this paradox in Mexican politics—corruption was not a rot but rather the oil and glue of the ma-chine.[19] In this system, heroin money was just one more kickback flow-ing up. The drug market was a fraction of the size of today, and officials didn't see it as a huge deal. It was a misdemeanor—the way many people today view pirated music.

Manuel Lazcano—the student who had been in the race riots—remembers this attitude as he rose up in the PRI political machine in Sinaloa. He explains how he knew many of the people who took over the Chinese opium business.

"Things started slowly. I like to think that people were not conscious of the harm that they were doing. At the beginning it was like something normal, a minor crime, tolerable, passable. Similar to going to Nogales and bringing back a case of cognac."[20]

Sinaloan opium output rose dramatically in the 1940s, Lazcano remem-bers. Like many others, he says the growth was due to a mystery customer who paid in dollars for vast loads of poppies. The generous client, he says, could have been Uncle Sam himself.

The notion that the U.S. government systematically brought Sinaloan opium during the Second World War is the classic conspiracy theory in the early Mexican drug trade. In today's Sinaloa, politicians, police, and drug traffickers all talk about such a deal as pure fact. The Mexican De-fense Department also describes it in its official history of the drug trade printed on the wall at its Mexico City headquarters. However, U.S. officials vehemently denied the deal at the time.

The conspiracy theory goes that the U.S. government needed opium to make morphine for its soldiers in the Second World War. The American army was certainly handing out bucketloads of morphine as its troops bled from Japanese and German shells. The traditional supply of opium poppies for this U.S. medicine was Turkey. However, the war cut off supply lines, with German U-boats roaming the Atlantic sinking merchant vessels. The U.S. government thus turned to the Sinaloan gummers and cut a deal with the Mexican government to let them grow their poppies.

Lazcano remembers the ease with which friends shipped opium paste north in the period as indication that a deal was on.

"I knew several people from the mountains. They were friends of mine that grew opium poppies and after harvesting them they would go to Nogales dressed as peasants with four or five balls in a suitcase or in a rucksack. The curious thing is that at the border they would go through customs without any problem, without any danger—in sight of customs guards. They handed in their goods where they had to hand them in and returned completely calmly; it was obvious that they let them go past."[21]

An American journalist visited Sinaloa in 1950 and found that sources in business and local government all confirmed the pact. He wrote an inquiry about it to the U.S. Federal Bureau of Narcotics, the agency created in 1930 to better coordinate American antidrug efforts. The FBN's director for its first thirty-two years was Harry Anslinger, a hard-line drug warrior. Anslinger responded personally to inquiries about the pact, saying the theory is "utterly fantastic and goes beyond even the wildest imagination."[22] Mexico's finest narco-ologists have also been unable to dig up any conclusive evidence that the deal ever took place, and some question whether Mexican authorities made it up to ease their own conscience.

Whether Uncle Sam helped or not, the Sinaloan opium trade certainly bloomed. Sinaloans gained such a reputation for production of the mud that even their baseball team was known as the Gummers. In the 1950s, Lazcano went on government business to the same mountain municipality where I stare at the pretty poppies. Back then, there was no dirt road even as bad as the one I climbed up. He took a small plane. But in the highlands, Lazcano writes, he saw peasants with "radios, guns, cars and even gringo canned food"[23] from the opium business.

The descendants of cannibal tribes, bandits, and displaced peasants had found a crop that pulled them out of wretched poverty. The opium and heroin trade became ingrained in their culture, along with pickup trucks, folk saints, and later Kalashnikov rifles. El Narco had rooted itself in a community from where it could sprout like a hungry plant. It was into this environment, that Joaquin "Chapo" Guzmán and the "Beard" Beltrán Leyva were born in rough shacks in 1957 and 1961. As they grew up, a social phenomenon would explode onto the world that would transform their people's drug trade from a niche business supporting a few hill folk to a multibillion-dollar global market—the social revolution of the sixties.

CHAPTER 3

Hippies

You know, it's a funny thing. Every one of the bastards that are out for legalizing marijuana is Jewish. What the Christ is the matter with the Jews, Bob? What is the matter with them? I suppose it is because most of them are psychiatrists.

—PRESIDENT RICHARD NIXON, MAY 26, 1971,
WHITE HOUSE TAPES, RELEASED MARCH 2002

The Summer of Love is said to have kicked off on June 1, 1967, when the Beatles released their landmark album *Sgt. Pepper's Lonely Hearts Club Band*, with its iconic cover of the Liverpool lads in orange, blue, pink, and yellow suits. The album stayed at the top of the Billboard 200 for fifteen weeks straight, in part because American record buyers were so excited by its references to drugs. Looking back, the references were laughably tame. The nearest the album comes to even mentioning the name of a drug is in code in "Lucy in the Sky with Diamonds" (LSD for the few stragglers who were never told). Then the closing song says those oh-so-rebellious words "I'd love to turn you on," which was enough to get it banned on the BBC on the grounds it could "encourage a permissive attitude toward drug-taking." But drugs seemed so exciting that summer you only needed to hint at them and kids would come running. Suddenly, intoxicating herbs represented youth, revolution, and a brave new world. That same month, thousands puffed joints in front of TV cameras as Jimi Hendrix and Janis Joplin played weird new blends of rock at the Monterey festival in California. The world was turning on its head.

But not up in the Sierra Madre. In the summer of 1967, a teenager called Efrain Bautista was sleeping on the same dirt floor he had shared with eight brothers and sisters for all sixteen years of his life. In his village of mud and bamboo shacks, nobody had ever heard of Sgt. Pepper, the Beatles, LSD, Liverpool, or Monterey because nobody had a transistor radio or a record player, let alone a television set, and newspapers didn't get that far into Mexico's jagged highlands.

It would also be hard to have a summer of love because the folk in his part of the mountains were locked into a number of deadly feuds. His own extended family was at war with another clan because of some half-forgotten dispute his uncle had got into over a girl. His uncle had ended up killing a rival suitor, and the aggrieved clan had taken revenge by murdering another of Efrain's uncles as well as his cousin. Both clans sat tensely waiting for more bloodshed. These feuds had habits of annihilating whole generations of certain families.

But despite that Efrain and his village were a world apart from American hippies waving their long hair to Ravi Shankar, they became intrinsically connected by a light-green plant with sticky buds and an unforgettable bittersweet smell. As American lust for marijuana shot through the roof, the psychedelic herb roared through the Mexican countryside. Seasoned drug growers in Sinaloa couldn't begin to meet the demand, so farmers started raising it in neighboring Durango, then over in Jalisco, then in the southern–Sierra Madre states of Oaxaca and Guerrero, where Efrain lived. Efrain and his family went through a sudden conversion from being small farmers to producers on the bottom rung of the drug chain.

The meteoric rise of American drug taking in the 1960s and 1970s had dramatic impacts on a number of countries beyond Mexico, including Colombia, Morocco, Turkey, and Afghanistan. Within a decade, recreational drugs went from being a niche vice to a global commodity. In Mexico, the surge in demand transformed drug producers from a few Sinaloan peasants to a national industry in a dozen states. The government had to a respond to a much more widespread flouting of the law. But the industry began to pull in billions of dollars and politicians wanted to be in on the game. The raise in stakes led to Mexico's first kingpins and unleashed the first significant wave of drug-related bloodshed. El Narco went through a sudden and astounding adolescence.

Efrain's family became aware of the marijuana boom searing through the Mexican mountains when a cousin began growing it in a nearby village. Efrain's father and grandfather had always known about cannabis, with the enticing star-shaped leaves cropping up sporadically all over the Sierra Madre. Unlike opium poppies, which were imported in the late-nineteenth century, marijuana had been used in Mexico since at least the days of Spanish rule, with some people arguing that Aztecs consumed the psychedelic weed. During the bloody campaigns of the Mexican Revolution, marijuana helped many soldiers forget their sorrows in clouds of smoke. Ganja also inspired the most famous verse of the folk song "La Cucaracha," with the memorable lyrics "The cockroach, the cockroach, now he can't walk. Because he doesn't have, because he lacks, marijuana to smoke." In peacetime, cannabis was popular in Mexican prisons while enjoyed by cultural icons such as muralist Diego Rivera.[1]

When Efrain's father saw his cousin making good profits from marijuana, he asked him about growing weed himself. His cousin happily gave him seeds and introduced him to his buyer. Efrain explains the decision to step into the drug business:

"My father had four fields so we were a well-off family by the standards of those mountains. We had some cows and grew corn and limes and some other crops. But it was still hard to get enough money to feed everyone. We were nine brothers and sisters, and my dad also looked after the children of his brother, who had been killed in a feud. My dad was lazy, but clever. He would look for ways to make money that took less effort and brought in better rewards. So we tried marijuana."

Efrain smiles as he remembers his youth while we eat chili-laced eggs in a Mexico City diner. He has lived in the capital for decades now but still carries the mountain way: coarse but open and frank. He has weather-beaten skin with light eyes that he attributes to some French descendants way back over the centuries. But despite some European ancestry, he is proud of being a son of Guerrero—a state whose very name means "warrior" and has the reputation as one of the most violent regions of Mexico.

"First we grew marijuana in just half a field where we had been raising corn. Marijuana is an easy plant to grow—our mountains are perfect for it. We just left it out in the sun and the rain, and the earth did the work. In a few months, we had big plants shooting up. They were about one and half meters tall. My brothers and I harvested it, using our machetes. It was an easy plant to cut up. We filled a couple of sacks full of it. It smelled like crazy, so I guess it was good stuff. We took it down to the town to sell."

The nearest market town was Teloloapan, a mountain enclave of stone streets famous for its dishes of mole (chocolate and chili) and festivals where locals dress up in devil masks. Efrain and his father found his cousin's buyer, and he gave them a thousand pesos for the sacks stuffed with some twenty-five kilos of green. That was only worth about $5 per kilo and was a fraction of the price it would fetch on the quads of Berkeley. But to Efrain and his family, it seemed as if they had struck gold.

"It was the best crop we had sold, much better money than we got for corn or limes or anything. We had some great feasts with meat and all got new clothes and shoes. So we started growing marijuana in two of our fields, and then we sold harvests of marijuana every few months with up to a hundred kilos each. We were still not rich. But we didn't go hungry like before."

After Efrain and his family had been raising marijuana for two years, soldiers came through his mountain to destroy crops. Fortunately, their buyer warned about the troop maneuvers a week in advance—showing the organization moving the weed had some useful connections. As Efrain remembers:

"We cut up all the marijuana in a hurry. Some of it was ready, so we could hide it in sacks up in the mountains. Other crops were only half-grown and we had to throw them away. The soldiers came through our village but they didn't even check our fields. Then my dad was annoyed that we had wasted so much marijuana.

"At first we didn't even know where all our marijuana was going. All we knew is that we could go down to the town and sell it. But after we had been doing it for a while, we learned that it was going to El Norte [the United States]. Around the same time, some people from our mountains started heading up to El Norte to look for work. But I didn't want to go there. I loved the mountains too much."

Efrain and his family just called their product marijuana or by the Mexican slang *mota*. But in the United States, it was almost certainly sold by the attractive brand name Acapulco Gold. Teloloapan is in the same Guerrero state as Acapulco, where Elvis Presley and Tarzan actor

Johnny Weissmuller were sipping margaritas out of coconut shells in the 1960s. Over the years, tons of marijuana passed from the southern Sierra Madre into the beach resort, from where it could be shipped north on fishing boats. Years later, I would go to a federal police office in Acapulco to find a gold-chain-wearing officer sitting casually in front of a huge stack of three hundred kilos of seized Acapulco Gold pressed into compact bricks. The marijuana unleashed an odor so overpowering that it could be smelled right through the police station door. Up close, I could see it had a distinct brown-green color that is the source of its *gold* name.

Back in the 1960s, Acapulco Gold was a sought-after marijuana for American smokers, considered better quality than the weed growing in California or Texas. In any case, the U.S. marijuana market exploded so fast, dealers imported grass from wherever they could get it. By all accounts, Americans created the demand themselves and took to Mexico to supply it. Stoners rolled over the border to Tijuana in droves, buying ganja from anywhere they could. One group of students and their teacher from Coronado High School, San Diego, began sneaking marijuana into the United States off the Tijuana beach on surfboards. The so-called Coronado Company later graduated to yachts, before federal agents busted them.[2] Along the border in Texas, buyers would go down to the Rio Grande and wait for Mexicans to toss bags of marijuana over the river. Others would head down to seedy bars in El Paso or Laredo looking for any suspicious-looking Mexican who might be selling.

Marijuana on the border sold for about $60 per kilo compared to some $300 per kilo in East Coast universities. Some American entrepreneurs went deep into Mexico to get the product even cheaper. Among them was George Jung—a Boston stoner who began flying ganja across the country. Boston George later graduated to cocaine, had the hit movie *Blow* made about him, and has grown into a trafficker superstar with his own Web site, fan club, and T-shirt collection (Smuggler Wear).

A hippie with long blond hair, a big nose, and a thick Boston accent, George describes his exploits in numerous videos and memoirs written in his cell of La Tuna prison in Anthony, Texas, while serving a fifteen-year sentence. When he first looked for marijuana in Mexico, he says, he was inspired by the movie *Night of the Iguana* to go to the Pacific resort of Puerto Vallarta. Speaking only pidgin Spanish, he wandered round for two weeks before he scored. Soon he was making $100,000 a month, flying up ganja in light aircraft. Boston George bought from middlemen, who picked up the grass from thousands of peasant farmers like Efrain. These middlemen, he says, had connections with the Mexican military.

George eventually got arrested with a trunk full of marijuana at the Playboy Club in Chicago. Luckily (or unluckily) he shared a prison cell with Colombian Carlos Lehder, who introduced him to the Medellín Cartel and set him up to make millions in cocaine.

Shutting down George's Mexico operation had little effect on marijuana flowing north. The market just kept growing until, by 1978, a White House survey found that 37.8 percent of high school seniors admitted to having smoked weed. During the same period, use of heroin and later cocaine also shot up. Drug warriors jumped on this as evidence that ganja leads people down a slippery slope to darker vices. Maybe they're right. Or perhaps the bigger shifts in core social and economic factors triggered supply and demand in all three mind-bending substances.

Whatever the reasons, the period saw a radical change in America's drugs-taking habits. In 1966, the Federal Bureau of Narcotics said the most profitable drug in the United States was heroin and estimated its black market moved $600 million a year.[3] By 1980, reports said the American drug market was worth over $100 billion a year. This was a truly seismic shift that reshaped America from its universities to its inner cities; and Mexico from its mountains to its government palaces.

During America's drug-taking explosion, the president with the biggest impact on narcotics policy was unquestionably Richard Nixon. The feisty Californian declared the War on Drugs; browbeat foreign governments on drug production; and created the Drug Enforcement Administration. His thunderous actions defined American policy for the next forty years—and had a colossal impact on Mexico. However, as Nixon was so discredited by Watergate, later drug warriors prefer to downplay his titanic contributions. Meanwhile, drug-policy critics concede that while Nixon was confrontational, he gave more funding to rehab programs than some of his liberal successors.

Born in 1913, Nixon came to manhood during the antimarijuana drive of FBN director Harry Anslinger, who alleged that smoking weed caused repugnant, immoral behavior and drove people to kill. Such ideas are depicted in the classic 1936 exploitation film *Reefer Madness* (aka *Tell Your Children*), made at the height of Anslinger's fervent campaign. The movie follows a group of clean-living high school students who are lured by a drug pusher to smoke marijuana and go on to rape, murder, and descend into insanity. It has some fantastic moments, such as when a suited student puffs on a reefer and unleashes an evil Hollywood cackle.

The idea that marijuana drove people to rape and murder was discredited by the 1960s. But Nixon did still believe that weed made people immoral, alleging it was driving youth astray and causing the counter-cultural revolution he found so abhorrent. His ideas were revealed most clearly in the White House tapes that were declassified in 2002. Drugs, he said, were part of a communist conspiracy to destroy the United States. As he said in one recording:

"You see, homosexuality, dope, immorality in general. These are the enemies of strong societies. That's why the communists and the left-wingers are pushing the stuff. They're trying to destroy us."[4]

Nixon was also concerned about heroin, which he blamed for rising crime from Washington to Los Angeles. In his election campaign, he promised law and order. And when he took office in 1969, he wanted to take action that showed he was putting his money where his mouth was. His first sledgehammer move was to shut down the Mexican border.

Operation Intercept was born after Nixon's officials went to Mexico City in June 1969 to persuade Mexico to spray poison on marijuana and opium crops. Mexican officials refused, citing how Agent Orange sprayings in Vietnam were causing frightening side effects. As G. Gordon Liddy described the visit in his memoir, "The Mexicans, using diplomatic language of course, told us to go piss up a rope. The Nixon administration didn't believe in the United States taking crap from any foreign government. Its reply was Operation Intercept."[5]

Under Operation Intercept, customs inspectors thoroughly searched—or in agent talk *tossed*—every vehicle and pedestrian trying to enter the United States along the entire southern border. In between posts, the U.S. army set up mobile radar units, while drug agents patrolled in rented planes. The operation wreaked havoc, backing queues of cars deep into Tijuana and Ciudad Juárez. Mexicans with green cards couldn't get to their jobs; avocados rotted in gridlocked trucks; and Mexican expenditure plummeted in American cities. However, agents seized few actual drugs, with the smugglers waiting out the siege. After seventeen painful days and a barrage of complaints, Nixon called off the dogs. The

United States and Mexico agreed they would work together in a new Operation Cooperation.

Historians are mixed on the merits and failures of Nixon's aggressive experiment. On one side, it showed the United States could not afford the economic consequences of shutting down its southern border. Four decades later, with far greater trade between the two nations and the volatility of global markets, such a move is unthinkable. Customs agents have to contend with the reality that they can only search a fraction of cars and people coming from Mexico. However much they seize, a percentage of drugs will invariably slip through.

However, Nixon claimed it was a victory. He had shown his base that he meant business and strong-armed Mexico into fighting the drug trade. As part of Operation Cooperation, Mexico promised to crack down on drug crops, and American agents were allowed to work south of border. A new modus operandi was being developed for the drug war abroad—coercing countries to destroy narcotics at the source.

In 1971, Nixon extended the tactic to Turkey, where he pressured the government to clamp down on opium production under threat of cutting U.S. military and economic aid. He also worked with France to attack the so-called French connection of heroin labs. These actions had a serious impact on the Turkish product. But this was a blessing for Sinaloan producers, who expanded their own operations to fill the gap. Mexican mud and black tar were propelled from being a last resort for American junkies to a staple of their diet.

As he went into his 1972 election, Nixon focused on his fight against heroin as a cornerstone of his campaign. It was an easy target. Heroin was an evil, foreign enemy and it didn't answer back. Plus it diverted attention from the lost, real war in Vietnam and let him claim that he was helping inner-city blacks as well as his white base. Nixon defined the war in absolute terms, predicting the adversary would be completely annihilated:

"Our goal is the unconditional surrender of the merchants of death who traffic in heroin. Our goal is the total banishment of drug abuse from the American life. Our children's lives are what we are fighting for. Our children's future is the reason we must succeed."[6]

Nixon won the election with a stunning 60 percent of the vote. Of course, many other factors, such as a strong economy, helped his victory. But strategists the world over learned a valuable lesson: a drug war is good politics.

Nixon's 1973 creation of the DEA left an even bigger legacy. He set up the agency through an executive order, with a mission to "establish a single unified command to combat an all-out global war on the drug menace."[7] Now you had an entire agency whose very reason to exist was the war on drugs. Once installed in Washington, the DEA would successfully lobby for greater and greater funds over the decades. At its outset, it had 1,470 special agents and an annual budget of less than $75 million. Today, it has 5,235 special agents, offices in sixty-three countries, and a whopping budget of more than $2.3 billion.

In the optimistic early days, DEA agents thought they could really achieve Nixon's goal of the "total banishment" of drug traffickers. The mistake before, agents argued, was that they had gone after nickel-and-dime street busts. But the new outfit could go after the big conspiracies—and bring down the devil. Agents quickly opened such a case in Mexico. They stumbled into one of the most bizarre probes in DEA history—a case with the complexity of a John Le Carré spy novel and cast of characters including Cuban guerrillas, a lover of the Mexican president, and the Cosa Nostra.

The probe opened when San Diego DEA worked up through seizures to find who was moving major loads of drugs through Tijuana into California.[8] Using paid informants, they got to a palatial Tijuana residence known as the Roundhouse. Spying on the mansion, they saw well-tailored guests in expensive sports cars and an endless stream of call girls—and call boys. The wealth and extravagance suggested this was no simple street-level operation. Trailing the Roundhouse owner, they found he wasn't even Mexican but was a Cuban American named Alberto Sicilia Falcon.

A photo shows the young Falcon with slick black hair and film-star looks. He had been born in Matanzas, Cuba, in 1944 and fled to Miami with his family following the 1959 revolution of Fidel Castro. After a stint in the U.S. army, an arrest for sodomy, and a brief marriage and divorce, he was last seen in San Diego in 1968. Now just turning thirty years old, he had cropped up at the head of a Mexican trafficking organization. How on earth had he managed it?

DEA agents busted traffickers working for Falcon and, in agency speak, *flipped them*—or turned them into protected witnesses to rat out their boss. Based on their evidence, they said Falcon was buying heroin and marijuana by order from the producers in the Sinaloan mountains and flying it in light aircraft to the Tijuana area. He then moved it over the border with an army of so-called burros or donkeys—narco talk for paid smugglers—to a house in the luxury Coronado Cays neighborhood of San Diego. He was also pioneering the traffic of cocaine from South America. In total his operation was pulling in $3.6 million a week, the DEA estimated, making it the biggest trafficking organization they had ever seen out of Mexico.

DEA took their evidence to the Mexican federal police, who appeared surprisingly happy to get on the case. In July 1975, Falcon was busted in a Mexico City mansion. That was when things got really weird.

Police searched Falcon's house and found Cuban, American, and Mexican passports and Swiss bankbooks showing accounts of $260 million. It emerged the flamboyant bisexual moved in Mexican high society, hobnobbing with celebrities and politicians. He was particularly close to a glamorous film star named Irma Serrano, nicknamed the Tigress, known as the lover of a former Mexican president. But that was only the beginning. After Mexican police battered him and shoved electric shocks through his body, Falcon said he was an operative for the CIA, using his drug money to supply guns to rebels in Central America. Such a tale could be dismissed as the rantings of a villain under torture. However, he later repeated the claims in a jailhouse book that offers some substantiation.[9]

Falcon wrote he had been trained by the CIA at Fort Jackson, Florida, as a potential anti-Castro recruit. Furthermore, a man arrested with him was a fellow Cuban called José Egozi Bejar, who was in the 1961 Bay of Pigs attempt to topple Castro.[10] American officials also confirmed that Falcon indeed had his hand in weapons smuggling. ATF agents alleged an arms dealer in Brownsville, Texas, sold the Sicilia organization millions of rounds of ammunition.

Mexican police uncovered another curious connection. Fingerprints in a house that Sicilia visited matched those of Chicago mobster Sam Giancana. However, Giancana was shot dead thirteen days before Falcon's arrest. Later, declassified documents confirm that Giancana had himself worked with the CIA in a plot to assassinate Castro. A picture was being painted of Falcon living in a surreal twilight zone of mafias, politicians, and guerrillas.

The story took a last strange twist when Falcon and Egozi escaped from Mexican prison together through a tunnel complete with an electric light in 1976. They were nabbed three days later after Mexican police received an anonymous tip from the U.S. embassy. Falcon was convicted of racketeering, drug trafficking, arms trafficking, and fraud and rotted in a Mexican jail. The alleged CIA links were never followed up, and many grueling questions remain unanswered.

So what can the bizarre case of Alberto Sicilia Falcon tell us about the development of the Mexican drug trade? Who really was this mysterious character—a mastermind or just a fall guy? Conspiracy theorists claim it shows the drug trade was secretly controlled by American spooks—a recurring theme through the growth of El Narco. However, this lacks any concrete evidence. Even if the CIA had once funded Falcon and Egozi to fight Castro, that does not mean they were still operatives by the 1970s.

It is interesting though that the first major kingpin to be arrested in Mexico was a foreigner, whether he worked with spooks or not. Both Cuban and American gangsters had long experience in organized crime and knowledge of cross-border networks and money laundering needed for the expansive drug trade of the 1970s. If they had links to intelligence services at some point, all the better. The mountain bandits of Sinaloa were only beginning to understand the billion-dollar industry. Foreigners taught them how to make it work. Mexican newspapers depicted Falcon as an evil, alien crime boss who was sexually degenerate. But they also noted his immense fortune, a fact not lost on the Mexican public.

In Sinaloa, the influx of American dollars had transformed gummers into a richer and noisier clan. Since the 1950s, successful opium growers had moved down from the mountains to the outskirts of Culiacán. By the 1970s, they had created an entire neighborhood called Tierra Blanca, building ostentatious homes with brand-new pickup trucks on unpaved roads. The Sinaloa press began to increasingly call them *narcotraficantes* or narcos for short, as opposed to just gummers. The change in language implies a shift in status from mere poppy growers to international smugglers. Old Culiacán families looked with disdain at the uncouth narcos with their gold chains, mountain accents, and sandals. But they also eyed their stacks of dollar bills with interest.

The streets of Tierra Blanca echoed with the sound of gunfire as the sombrero-clad hillbillies blasted at each other, often in broad daylight. Throughout 1975, Sinaloan newspapers were packed with quotes from local politicians complaining about the rising narco threat, saying shootouts had become daily affairs and gangsters were driving in cars with no plates and blacked-out windows. SINALOA UNDER THE POWER OF

THE CRIMINAL MAFIA rattled one headline.[11] Officials were also concerned about reports of drug growers in the mountains "bearing enough firepower for a small revolution." Pressure mounted on Mexico's federal government.

The hammer finally came down in 1976, when Mexico launched its Operation Condor. Ten thousand soldiers stormed the Golden Triangle, new, hard-nosed police commanders arrived in Culiacán, and planes sprayed drug crops. The government's stated aim was to completely annihilate the narcos.

Operation Condor was the biggest government offensive against El Narco in the entire seventy-one history of the PRI. By all accounts it genuinely hit traffickers hard. DEA supplied planes for the crop spraying—they used 2.4-D acid on opium and the toxic herbicide paraquat on marijuana, and DEA agents were allowed verification flights to check the damage. One of these agents, Jerry Kelley, described missions over Sinaloa to *Time* correspondent Elaine Shannon:

"We flew every inch of the country and we knew what they were doing and what was there. It didn't matter who was corrupt. There was no way they could hide what was going on."[12]

This was the first American-backed spraying operation in the war on drugs and pioneered a tactic that would be replicated across the world, from Colombia to Afghanistan. History has now shown that spraying by itself cannot destroy a drug industry. But some Mexican traffickers apparently made a fatal mistake—they harvested poisoned marijuana and sent it to El Norte. Lab tests by the U.S. government found Mexican ganja with signs of paraquat. Who knows how much venomous weed was ever on the market. But mere talk of it was enough to rattle U.S. lawmakers, who were concerned their children at college could be shoving toxic salt into their system. The Health Department issued a public warning to marijuana smokers about poisonous weed, advising that it could cause irreversible lung damage.

The bad publicity pushed dealers to look for a new source of weed for millions of hungry hippies. It didn't take long to find a country with the land, laborers, and lawlessness to fill the gap—Colombia. Farmers had been growing weed in Colombia's Sierra Nevada since the early 1970s. As Mexico cracked down, the Colombians stepped up, creating a boom in their own marijuana industry known by local historians as the Bonanza Marimbera.[13] Soon DEA agents were uncovering Santa Marta Gold everywhere from Midwest rock festivals to Ivy League universities. This geographical movement of drugs production has become known as the balloon effect. In this analogy, when you grab one corner of the narco balloon, the air just rushes to bulge out the other side.

Back in Sinaloa, troops hammered narcos on the ground as well as from the air. Residents across the Sierra Madre still have painful memories of soldiers marauding through their villages, kicking down doors, and dragging hundreds of young men away. Reports came back of such ugly treatment of suspects that the Culiacán lawyers' association sent a team to investigate. They interviewed 457 prisoners locked up on drug charges and found that every single one complained of being beaten and tortured. The abuses against them included electric shocks, burns, and chili-laced water shot up the nasal passages. Other prisoners said they were raped by police. No officers were reprimanded.

The tactics may have been rough, but they were effective in slamming the narcos. The onslaught of soldiers in the mountains pushed many growers and other peasant farmers to flee their villages for city slums. Federal police also shot dead several key suspects including kingpin Pedro Avilés in 1978. Avilés's lieutenants ran from the heat in Sinaloa to reestablish themselves in Guadalajara. The poison of El Narco had spread. Now the Sinaloan narco tribe stretched from the mountains to Mexico's second-largest city.

So why did Mexico's government unleash Operation Condor? Had politicians suddenly seen the light that the drug trade was evil and dangerous?

One clear incentive was the American carrot. DEA bosses and the Jimmy Carter White House sang praises of Mexico's antidrug efforts calling it a "model program." More substantially, Mexico got to keep the hardware America supplied for the spraying. Within two years, Mexico had acquired thirty-nine Bell helicopters, twenty-two small aircraft, and one executive jet, giving it the largest police fleet in Latin America. Drug work became a new way for governments to gain aid and airpower from the United States.

The Mexican government also used Operation Condor to crack down on small bands of leftist insurgents. Students and disaffected workers had risen up in the 1960s to protest totalitarian rule. The PRI reacted in a calm and receiving way: in 1968, it ordered snipers to surround a demonstration and fire on the crowd from all sides. Drawings of the corpses can still be seen today in the somber Tlatelolco Plaza in Mexico City. Unable to challenge the system through protests, leftists formed guerrilla groups that carried out sporadic kidnappings and attacks on government installations. They were becoming quite a bother by the mid-1970s—just as Operation Condor kicked off.

Soldiers on drug operations rounded up suspected guerrillas, who happened to have a substantial presence in the Sierra Madre states of Sinaloa and Chihuahua, where Condor was concentrated. Often leftists would be arrested under the pretense of drug charges. Hundreds of activists were never seen again. Mexicans use the words *the disappeared* to refer to these lost souls. As antidrug operations spread to other states, so did the dirty war on leftists. Yet another modus operandi was established in the war on drugs—it could provide effective cover for anti-insurgency ops.

Coincidentally, the CIA had also code-named its own regional operation against communists in the 1970s Operation Condor. Observing Mexico's eradication campaign, the agency was sharply aware the Mexican government was using antidrug equipment for political work. As it said in a declassified memo to the White House:

"The army will also take advantage of the eradication campaign to uncover any arms trafficking and guerrilla activities ... Army eradication forces may devote as much effort to internal security as eradication. They do not however have their own airlift support capabilities and they may seek helicopters and other equipment from the Attorney General's limited eradication sources."[14]

The rest of the memo is blacked out with a felt pen. We can presume that has the really juicy parts. But don't worry. It is for our safety that we can't see it.

After two years of Operation Condor, it seems that the Mexican government had enough of battering the hell out of the narcos. In March 1978, Mexican officials informed DEA agents they would be making no more verification flights. The eradication campaign would officially continue—and still be praised by the White House—but without a bird's-eye view. President Carter raised no fuss, in line with his less confrontational attitude to drugs. But agents in the field moaned to their bosses there was a cover-up. DEA agents on the U.S. side also noticed that Mexican marijuana was flooding back in, the scare over venomous weed forgotten.

Another posthumous event left a stain on the legacy of Operation

Condor. Prosecutor Carlos Aguilar had led the head-busting in Culiacán and been lionized as a Mexican Eliot Ness. His reward was to head anti-drug operations in the whole of northeastern Mexico. However, after a few years, he left the force and splashed out on a hotel and several other businesses in the border city of Nuevo Laredo. In 1984, he was arrested with six kilos of heroin and cocaine but jumped bail. In 1989, Texas marshals arrested him in Harlingen and handed him to Mexican police, but he managed to maneuver his way out of any prison time. Then in 1993, he was shot in the head in his own house in an apparent drug-related hit.

So what really happened to Operation Condor? Had top Mexican officials been finally tempted by drug dollars? Had Mexico slipped back into an attitude that you can only bust so many dealers and accept that the traffic goes on? Or had the whole operation been an exercise to batter El Narco down to size and show who was boss? Once they had taken a beating, the gangsters went back to trafficking, knowing the politicians really ran the show.

The questions all highlight the complex nature of corruption and drug trafficking in Mexico. It is a delicate dance of bribes, busts, and switching sides. It is widely accepted that during decades of PRI rule, drug money flowed into the system like groundwater into a well. So much is proven by the constant stream of police and officials arrested for taking bribes. But there is still debate as to how far up the rot of corruption spread and how systematic and organized it was.

A popular saying in Mexico is "If you have God, why do you need the angels? And if you have the angels, why do you need God?" The adage applies to corruption and drug trafficking. In some instances, traffickers could have a local beat policeman paid off—an angel figure. In that case, they wouldn't need his bosses on their payroll. In other instances, they could have a police chief or a governor—a God figure—and they wouldn't need to pay off his subordinates. Sometimes, they could have both God and the angels and be sitting pretty.

Of course, the system was tenuous. Another policemen could arrest a man who was paying off his colleague, or officers could take down a villain paying their boss. But things were kept in check by the PRI power structure. Lower-ranking police would kick back money up the chain of command. Higher-ranking officials didn't even need to know where the bribes were coming from or have any contact with gangsters. Everyone respected the hierarchy, and if any official couldn't keep order, he could simply be replaced by another aspiring PRI member.

In the context of the PRI's elaborate corruption, the plaza system emerged to control trafficking. This plaza concept is crucial to understanding the modern Mexican Drug War. First mentions of it can be found in the late 1970s in border towns. By the 1990s, there are references to plazas all over Mexico, from the southern Caribbean coast to the peaks of the Sierra Madre.

The plaza in Mexico refers to the jurisdiction of a particular police authority, such as Tijuana or Ciudad Juárez. However, smugglers appropriated the term *plaza* to mean the valuable real estate of a particular trafficking corridor. As the trade through these territories moved from kilos to tons, it became a more complex operation to organize. In each plaza, a figure emerged who would coordinate the traffic and negotiate police protection. This plaza head could both move his own drugs and tax anyone else who smuggled through his corridor. In turn he would handle the kickbacks to police and soldiers, paying for his concession.

Accounts show that police were the top dogs in the deal.[15] Officers could smack gangsters around and, if they got too big for their boots—or showed up on the DEA radar—take them down. Police could also bust anyone who wasn't paying his dues, showing that they were fighting the war on drugs and clocking up seizures and arrests. The system ensured that crime was controlled and everyone got paid.

Up in the Sierra Madre, Efrain Bautista and his family survived through these shifting currents of the 1970s, quietly selling their crops of marijuana in the market town of Teloloapan. Efrain said no leftist guerrillas were in his village, so they avoided the military attacks aimed at insurgents. In the nearby community of El Quemado, troops stormed in looking for guerrillas and dragged away every able-bodied man. Many never returned. Efrain also said his crops were on remote highlands between jagged rocks and forests and avoided the paraquat spraying. However, the relentless feuds eventually forced him to flee.

As marijuana money oozed into his community, Efrain remembers, many of the young men bought more sophisticated weapons, particularly Kalashnikov rifles. Russian Mikhail Kalashnikov developed his AK-47 assault rifle during the Second World War as a weapon that Soviet peasants could easily maintain and use to defend the motherland against marauding foreign armies. Like Russians peasants, farmers in the Sierra Madre took to the rifle with enthusiasm, affectionately calling it the Goat's Horn because of the its curved ammunition clip. Efrain remembers when his family first got hold of one.

"In our mountains, people used to have shotguns or really old American Colts or Winchesters from the days of the Revolution. We used to fight our battles with those guns or even with machetes. But then we started seeing the Goat's Horns around. They were incredible weapons that could spray bullets in seconds and hit targets from five hundred meters away. We asked the people we sold the marijuana to and they said they would look into it. And then one day they had this brand-new AK-47—so we paid for it with our entire crop of marijuana. We took it up to the mountain and would hunt snakes or coyotes with it. But then we had to use it to defend our family."

Efrain's clan had endured various feuds over the years. Many of the participants sold marijuana, but the feuds were about unrelated beefs, such as women and disrespect. At the end of the 1970s, Efrain's family bit off more than they could chew. The feud began with argument over a drunken card game, but turned into a fight to the death.

"The family we were fighting had this guy who was a real killer. He had this innocent, boyish face that made you think he wouldn't hurt anyone. But he was an authentic murderer. He killed two of my cousins and a brother. I had to take my family and run for my life."

Efrain settled in a slum of tin-roof houses in the Mixcoac area of southern Mexico City. When he arrived, he was twenty-five years old and had a wife and three young children to support. He had sold marijuana for a decade, providing thousands of kilos to pot puffers across the United States. But he didn't have a peso of savings to show for it and had to start from scratch. He was one more of thousands who have drifted in and out of the drug business during its decades of growth.

"We were totally broke and had to sell chewing gum on the street just to get some money to eat. But we all worked hard and saved anything we could. I got jobs in construction and would work long hours carrying bricks and cement. After years, I got enough money to buy a taxi and we started to live okay. My youngest son could even finish high school and get a job in an office. But I miss the mountains. That is where my heart is."

CHAPTER 4

Cartels

Main Entry: car·tel
Etymology: French, letter of defiance, from Old Italian *cartello*, literally, placard, from *carta* leaf of paper.
Date: 1692

1 : a written agreement between belligerent nations
2 : a combination of independent commercial or industrial enterprises designed to limit competition or fix prices
3 : a combination of political groups for common action
—MERRIAM-WEBSTER'S COLLEGIATE DICTIONARY,

ELEVENTH EDITION, 2003

In the seething high desert of Colorado, nestled between lonely cacti and abandoned ranches, lies the most secure prison on the planet. Known as the Alcatraz of the Rockies or simply Supermax, the prison has a foolproof way of keeping its 475 inmates from murdering each other or escaping—they are kept in permanent lockdown, held twenty-three hours a day in twelve-by-seven-foot cells. Human rights groups complain the years of isolation drive the convicts mad. Officials say they get what was coming to them.

The list of inmates at Supermax reads like a who's who of the world's

most infamous terrorists and criminals. The September 11 attackers on
New York and Washington; Theodore Kaczynski, alias the Unabomber;
Barry Byron Mills, who founded the bloodthirsty prison gang the Aryan
Brotherhood; Salvatore "Sammy the Bull" Gravano, an underboss for
the New York mafia; Richard Reid, alias the shoe bomber; Ramzi Yousef,
of the 1993 World Trade Center explosion; and more killers, rapists,
arsonists, racketeers, and bombers fill the sterile desert hell.

Among this collection of the world's greatest villains is an aging
Latino with graying, curly hair and swarthy skin that earned him his old
nickname, El Negro. El Negro has survived more than two decades in
isolation and so only has only another 128 years to go before he com-
pletes his first century-and-a-half term and then can begin some multi-
ple sentences handed out at another trial. With such an insanely long
term, you may think prosecutors had a personal grudge against him. They
did. His unforgivable crime, they say, was conspiring to kidnap DEA agent
Enrique "Kiki" Camarena, who was then raped and murdered in Mexico
in 1985. This killing, the DEA said, was ordered to protect Mexico's first
drug cartel.

Funnily enough, the only kingpin of Mexico's first cartel to sit in an
American prison is not Mexican at all; he is a Honduran, Juan Ramón
Matta Ballesteros. To catch him, American marshals abducted him from
his home in Honduras in 1988, flew him out of the country, and threw
him before a U.S. judge. That didn't go down too well in Honduras. The
drug lord's supporters burned down the U.S. embassy in retaliation.

Matta was at the heart of the cocaine explosion in the 1970s and 1980s,
which meant he was also at the heart of a spiderweb of conspiracy
theories, coups, and revolutions connected to it. In those heady years,
cocaine spread across America like wildfire and swept over into ghettos
in the form of crack. The mind-bending chemical inflamed the much
talked about Miami crime wave, inspiring the 1983 classic movie *Scarface*; sparked L.A. gang wars, inspiring the 1991 classic *Boyz N the Hood*;
and fueled far worse violence in Colombia, which was too bloody and far
away to have any hit films made about it. It also financed U.S.-backed
guerrillas in Nicaragua, U.S.-backed generals in neighboring Honduras,
and the pineapple-faced dictator of Panama, Manuel Noriega. In fact, with
so many conspiracies, wars, gangsters, and side stories of cocaine in the
eighties, you can get lost in a dozen tangents.

But the story that is most crucial to the development of El Narco in
Mexico is the emergence of what people started calling cocaine cartels.

These conglomerates were billion-dollar operations that revolutionized the drug business. And Matta was a key player. His crucial role was to link up the biggest traffickers in Mexico with the biggest cocaine producers in Colombia, so it is apt that his homeland, Honduras, lies conveniently between the two nations.

I first got interested in Matta when I raced into Honduras hours after a military coup in 2009. The sweaty Central American country, which inspired the term *banana republic*,[1] has a long history of coups by mustachioed generals smoking cigars. But the 2009 coup grabbed special attention because after the end of the Cold War, politicians said we lived in a golden age of democracy where military takeovers by dubious Latin armies didn't happen. Watching troops shoot down protesters on the street, it was evident they did.

While covering this unhappy tale, I met a local journalist who said she knew the family of Honduras's most famous trafficker. I asked her to call them on my behalf, although I expected they would tell a meddling British reporter to get lost. But to my surprise, Ramón Matta, the son of the gangster slowly dying in the Alcatraz of the Rockies, came to meet me in my hotel lounge.

Ramón was a charismatic and smooth thirty-five-year-old with a finely trimmed goatee and stylish clothes. He cheerily answered my questions and chatted away for several hours over endless rounds of strong coffee. Ramón told me about the good sides of being the son of Latin drug lord—as a kid, he got flown to Spain to see the 1982 soccer World Cup—and the bad sides—it is hard to get a job or even car insurance. But he was mostly concerned about his father's health and the difficulty his family had in visiting him.

"It is so inhuman keeping my father there in isolation for so many years. Human beings just need contact with other humans. He is an old man now and doesn't pose any threat to anybody. But they still keep him in that hole in the desert, suffering."

Building on the interview with Ramón, I scoured dusty court documents, confidential reports, and aging newspapers. The gangster's name crops up in an incredible array of places. He is most commonly referred to as a member of Mexico's Guadalajara Cartel. But he is also considered to have been tight with top bosses in Colombia's Medellín Cartel and is sometimes referred to as a member of that crime syndicate. In his homeland, Matta is reported to have become the biggest private employer in the entire country. His name even springs up in a scandal over the CIA's working with drug traffickers to finance the contra rebels in Nicaragua. Damn, he was busy.

As with all drug lords, many details of Matta's life are hazy and contradictory. Starting with his name. While he is most commonly referred to as Matta Ballesteros, he is imprisoned in Supermax under the name Matta Lopez. He also surfaces on occasions as Matta del Pozo and Jose Campo. All reports feature the same black-and-white photo of him, taken in the late 1980s. He is shown sitting at a desk lifting his right hand in a powerful gesture. He has thick, curly hair above rough, strong features—a powerful forehead, deep-set eyes, and a broad nose.

Matta was born in 1945 in a poor neighborhood of the Honduran capital, Tegucigalpa, a chaotically built city that sprawls over mountains between jungles and banana plantations. He didn't fancy working for a dollar a day picking bananas. So at sixteen he did what many young Hondurans do and took the long trek north to search for the American Dream. Working as a supermarket clerk in New York City, he mixed in a cosmopolitan Latin ghetto with Cubans, Mexicans, Colombians, Nicaraguans, and many others attracted to the lights of the Big Apple. He married a Colombian woman, and when he was deported from the United States, he curiously claimed to be Colombian himself and was flown back to the Andean nation just as its cocaine industry was developing.

Since the 1914 Harrison Act banned cocaine in the United States, a variety of smugglers have brought blow to the noses of consumers who sniffed hard enough. These early cocaine traffickers came from a range of countries, including Peru—in the heartland of the coca-leaf country—Cuba, and Chile.[2] Just as Matta arrived, Colombians were building their own cocaine labs, particularly around the Medellín area.

Matta was soon sneaking back into the United States, where he got nabbed by police for a passport violation and locked up in a federal prison camp at Eglin Air Force Base. But the prison "camp" wasn't a great barrier to the young crook, and he escaped in 1971 to work with Colombians building up the budding U.S. cocaine market. One of Matta's early clients, the DEA say, was Cuban American Alberto Sicilia Falcon—the bisexual gangster in Tijuana. Matta supplied Falcon with Colombian cocaine, they allege, which he unloaded in California. The curly-haired Honduran realized it made better sense to stay in Central or South America and let others risk their liberty at U.S. ports.

Once the cocaine was in the United States, it was U.S. citizens who got it out to the biggest number of consumers. Neither Colombians nor Mexicans had any real reach into white suburban America. Among Americans who got rich off the blow explosion were Boston George Jung, Max Mermelstein, Jon Roberts, and Mickey Munday.

Cocaine was an easy sell. Unlike heroin or LSD, it didn't send people into an inward trance but sparked partying, prolonged sex, and didn't curse the user with a stinking hangover. In fact, it didn't do anything more than give a simple energy high for a couple of hours before the snorter would need another line. That is the great trick about cocaine: it really is nothing special. But the disco drug gained an image as being clean, glamorous, sexy, and fashionable. And it took America by storm. As Boston George remembers:

"I thought cocaine was a fantastic drug. A wonder drug, like everybody else. It gave you an energy burst. You could stay awake for days on end, and it was just marvelous and I didn't think it was evil at all. I put it almost in the same category as marijuana, only a hell of a lot better. It was a tremendous energy boost.

"It became an accepted product, just like marijuana. I mean Madison Avenue promoted cocaine. The movie industry. The record industry. I mean, if you were well-to-do and you were a jet-setter, it was okay to snort cocaine. I mean Studio 54 in New York, everybody was snorting cocaine, everybody was laughing and having a good time and snorting cocaine."[3]

Lines of white powder on mirrors were a staple of seventies America like *Saturday Night Fever* discos and blockbuster movies. Cinema audiences exploded with laughter when Woody Allen sneezed on a pile of coke in the 1977 flick *Annie Hall*. The front line of the Pittsburgh Steelers partied all night with cocaine dealer Jon Roberts, then went out two days later to win the 1979 Super Bowl. In 1981, *Time* magazine ran a front cover calling cocaine THE ALL AMERICAN DRUG.

All the hype about cocaine helped dealers sell it for an insanely high price. That is the simple beauty of *cocaina*—it is bloody expensive. From the seventies right through to the twenty-first century, the drug has retailed from $50 up to more than $150 for a single gram. Dealers make a much bigger markup on cocaine than on other mind-bending substances—and in turn traffickers make mind-boggling profits. The white lady churned out way more money than heroin and marijuana had ever come close to touching, billions upon billions of dollars.

Matta helped channel this money back to gangsters in Medellín, who fast became the richest criminals on the planet. No one ever knows how much drug kingpins really make, probably not even the gangsters themselves. But the Medellín traffickers were likely the first drug-smuggling billionaires. *Forbes* magazine later estimated the personal fortune of the number one Medellín smuggler, Pablo Escobar, to be $9 billion, making him the richest criminal of all time. The number two is estimated to be his colleague Carlos Lehder, at $2.7 billion. Who knows how the hell *Forbes* found data for those numbers. But they were certainly on the right track: the cocaine cowboys were stinking rich.

By the early eighties, Medellín mobsters had become visible and powerful figures. Escobar built an entire housing project for the homeless and was elected to Colombia's parliament in 1982, serving a short stint before being pushed out because of his trafficking. Around this time, the gangsters began to be called the Medellín Cartel, the first time the word *cartel* was used to describe drug smugglers. The term implied that traffickers had become an omnipotent political bloc. It was a frightening concept. But was it true?

The phrase *drug cartel* has won scorn from some academics, who argue it misleads people by giving an inaccurate description of traffickers engaged in price-fixing. But despite their moans, the word has firmly stuck for three decades, used by American agents, journalists, and, importantly, many traffickers themselves. Consequently, the cartel concept has had an immense influence on how the drug trade in Latin America is perceived, both by people inside it and out.

It is unclear who first coined the phrase. But it was certainly influenced by use of the term *cartel* to describe the Organization of Petroleum Exporting Countries, or OPEC, which was ever present in the media in the 1970s. OPEC represented the interests of exploited third-world countries who banded together to set oil prices and wield power over wealthy nations. In a similar vein, the Medellín Cartel cast an image of men from struggling Latin America who threatened the rich North. Escobar himself cultivated this idea, dressing up as revolutionary Pancho Villa[4] and calling cocaine an atomic bomb that he dropped on the United States.

For the DEA, the concept of cartels was highly useful to prosecute gangsters. Many early cases against Latin American smugglers were built using the so-called RICO laws, from the Racketeer Influenced and Corrupt Organizations Act, which had been designed to combat the Italian-American mafia. Under RICO, you need to prove suspects are part of an ongoing criminal organization. It is far easier to give that organization a name, especially one that sounds as threatening as the Medellín Cartel, than to say it is just a loose network of smugglers.

Later, prosecutors attacked traffickers with the law against conspiracy to distribute controlled substances. Again, it makes it easier if these conspiracies have names, and indictments against Mexican traffickers usually quote cartel titles. For example, court documents used to send Matta to the Supermax say, "The evidence showed that Matta-Ballesteros was a member of the Guadalajara cartel and that he participated in some of the meetings with other members of the cartel . . ."[5]

One man with explicit knowledge of the Medellín gangsters was their attorney Gustavo Salazar. Perhaps the most famous narco-lawyer of all time, Salazar has represented twenty major capos, including Pablo Escobar himself, and some fifty of their lieutenants. He has survived to tell the tale. He goes on today working with the latest generation of Colombian cocaine smugglers.

On a visit to Colombia, I called Salazar's office and left a message with his secretary saying I wanted to talk about drug cartels. Two days later, I got a surprise call from Salazar saying he would meet me in a Medellín café. When I asked how I would recognize him, he replied, "I look like Elton John." Sure enough, I arrived and found he was a dead ringer for the English pop icon. After some Colombian crepes, Salazar said the cartel concept was a fiction made up by American agents:

"Cartels don't exist. What you have is a collection of drug traffickers. Sometimes, they work together, and sometimes they don't. American prosecutors just call them cartels to make it easier to make their cases. It is all part of the game."

The media was also quick to jump on the cartel label. It is easier to give a group a name than some long-winded description. Hacks were also fond of the alliteration, Colombian cocaine cartels. It all made for lively copy.

Three decades later, the idea of cartels has taken on a definitive meaning on the bloody streets of Mexico. Corpses are found daily next to calling cards of organizations such as the Gulf Cartel—scrawled CDG in shorthand. These networks of killers and traffickers are far bigger than mere street gangs. And they certainly do try to limit competition, as in the dictionary definition of *cartel*. They are also federations of gangsters rather than monolithic organizations. Perhaps modern dictionaries need to define *drug cartel* or *criminal cartel* as a separate entry, to better reflect the way the word has come to be used.

In the early eighties, the Medellín cartel smuggled most of its cocaine straight over the Florida coast. It was a nine-hundred-mile run from the north coast of Colombia and was simply wide-open. The Colombians and their American counterparts would airdrop loads of blow out to sea, from where it would be rushed ashore in speedboats, or even fly it right onto the Florida mainland and let it crash down in the countryside.

Traffickers of the era smile over happy-go-lucky stories of those carefree days. In the documentary film *Cocaine Cowboys*,[6] smuggler Mickey Munday—a Florida redneck with an out-of-shape quiff—remembers driving in a speedboat loaded with 350 kilos of cocaine and giving a tow to a customs boat whose engine had blown out. On another occasion, an airdrop of cocaine crashed through the roof of a Florida church just as the preacher was giving an antidrug sermon. It was better than fiction.

The cocaine trade also rained dollars onto the Florida economy. No one will ever know quite how much of the white-stained money built Miami's skyline. But the financial storm left some obvious traces. In 1980, the Miami branch of the Federal Reserve Bank of Atlanta was the only branch bank in the U.S. reserve system to show a cash surplus—a whopping $4.75 billion![7] Authorities weren't too worried about these greenbacks. But they got uppity when the bullets flew.

Over the first five years of the cocaine boom, the homicide rate for Miami-Dade County almost tripled from just over two hundred in 1976 to over six hundred at its peak in 1981.[8] Violence wasn't just about blow. The influx of 120,000 Cuban immigrants, many from the island's jails, also sparked crime. Furthermore, the gangster killings had little to do with the Medellín bosses and more to do with local beefs of Colombian distributors, such as a psychotic female dealer called Griselda Blanco. The stocky Colombian had been a child prostitute and then teenage kidnapper in Medellín before moving to the United States to sell yayo. She snuffed anyone who pissed her off in any way, including three of her own husbands, earning her the nickname the Black Widow. It was certainly quicker than divorcing through the courts. But back in

Medellín, the bosses cursed her for bringing heat on their billion-dollar operation.

This heat rose all the way up to the White House of Ronald Reagan. Old Ronnie took the helm after his predecessor Jimmy Carter had taken a less confrontational policy to narcotics, focusing on treatment rather than war. Reagan's first move was to blame Carter for the cocaine explosion. The charges stuck, with drug warriors holding up Carter and the liberal 1970s as bugbears for decades to come. These bad years of permissive America were over, roared a triumphant Reagan. It was time to get tough on evil drug pushers. And Miami was ground zero.

In January 1982, Reagan created the South Florida Task Force to go toe-to-toe with the cocaine barons. Headed by Vice President George Bush, the task force brought in the FBI, army, and navy to the fight for the first time. This was a real war, Reagan said, so let's fight it with real soldiers. Suddenly, surveillance planes and helicopter gunships swarmed on Florida while FBI agents hit dirty banks. The state was so wide-open it didn't take long to haul in results. Within eight months, cocaine seizures were up 56 percent. Reagan and Bush sung their success and smiled for photo ops with confiscated tons of snow.

Back in Colombia, the kingpins felt the task force's bite. Seizures meant losses of hundreds of millions of dollars; the Medellín cartel needed to rethink its strategy. So it turned to Matta for a fix.

Matta had first used the Mexican "trampoline" to bounce drugs into the United States in the early 1970s, when he sold cocaine to Cuban American Alberto Sicilia Falcon. Since Falcon's imprisonment, Matta had cultivated relations with the rising stars among Sinaloan gangsters. These Mexicans could provide a great solution for the cocaine kings: why did they need to risk everything through Florida when they could spread it over another two thousand miles of land border? The Mexicans already had the smuggling routes, so for Matta and the Colombians it was just a question of handing them the cocaine and picking it up north of the river. DEA Andean regional director Jay Bergman describes the deal:

"The first stage of negotiations was 'We're the Colombians, we own this product, we own distribution of cocaine in the United States. Mexicans have got your weed and your black-tar heroin. Cocaine distribution from the sunny shores of Los Angeles to the mean streets of Baltimore, that is our territory. That is what we do. What we are going to do for you is we want to negotiate with you. We are going to provide you cocaine and you are going to deliver it from somewhere in Mexico to somewhere in the United States, and you are going to turn it back over to us, to our cartel emissaries.' That is the way it started out."

The historical importance of this deal cannot be overstated. Once billions of cocaine dollars poured into Mexico, its drug trafficking would become bigger and bloodier than anyone imagined. The Mexicans started off as paid couriers. But after they got a sniff, they would take the whole pie.

Matta's Mexican friends were old hands from the Sinaloan narco scene, many with blood connections to the earliest smugglers. Among them was Rafael Caro Quintero, a mountain cowboy who had been an outlaw since he was a teenager. Three of his uncles and one of his cousins had been heroin and marijuana traffickers. Caro Quintero outdid them all.

Above Caro Quintero and other hillbillies in belt buckles was a Culiacán native who wore slick white pants and designer-label shirts. Miguel Ángel Félix Gallardo became the most important connection for Matta and the Colombian drug lords. Many in Sinaloa consider Félix Gallardo to be Mexico's greatest capo ever—the unchallenged king of the Mexican underworld in his era. DEA also rated him as one of the biggest traffickers in the western hemisphere. It is widely believed that the song "Jefe de Jefes," or "Boss of Bosses," by the Tigres del Norte, perhaps the most celebrated drug ballad of all time, is about Félix Gallardo. However, as always in the murky world of Mexican gangsters, it is unclear if his real power and wealth were as great as his name.

Born in Culiacán in 1946, Félix Gallardo followed the path of many enterprising Sinaloan villains and joined the police force. An early photo of Félix Gallardo shows him slick and polished in a broad-topped officer's hat. A later photo shows him fresh out of the force, a smooth-looking mobster wearing fat 1970s sunglasses and sitting on a brand-new Honda motorcycle.[9] He is slim with sharp features and at six foot two is tall by Mexican standards.

When Operation Condor smashed Sinaloa, Félix Gallardo and other villains relocated to Guadalajara, Mexico's second-largest city. A pretty stretch of colonial plazas packed with mariachis and folkloric cantinas, Guadalajara was an ideal place for narcos to escape the heat and buy up

nice villas. Once Operation Condor petered out, they were soon organizing drugloads more ambitious than anything before.

To maximize profits, they did what any good businessmen do: went
for economy of scale. Instead of buying marijuana from small family farms,
they built enormous plantations. The DEA got wind of one such operation out of the Chihuahuan desert and pressured the Mexican army to
take it down. The bust set a worldwide record for marijuana farms that
hasn't been beaten since. Crops spread out across miles of desert and were
dried in more than twenty-five sheds, most bigger than football fields. In
total there was more than five thousand tons of psychedelic weed. Thousands of campesinos had worked on the plantation for wages of $6 a day.
When the army stormed in, the bosses had all disappeared, but the
campesinos were still wandering the desert, without food or water.[10]

Such colossal quantities of marijuana meant big bucks. But cocaine
profits were even bigger. Court documents allege Matta and his partner Félix Gallardo were personally raking in $5 million every single
week pumping cocaine through the Mexican pipeline. After Mexican
mobsters delivered the blow into the United States, documents say, Matta
was moving it though a network of distributors in Arizona, California,
and New York. The capo continued to use Anglo-Americans to get the
cocaine out to disco-dancing customers. Running the Arizona ring was
John Drummond, who eventually turned into a protected witness to rat
out the kingpin.[11]

It is likely Matta, Félix Gallardo, and the others never called themselves a cartel or gave their operations any particular name. In a later
prison diary Félix Gallardo wrote, "In 1989, the cartels didn't exist . . .
there started to be talk about 'cartels' from the authorities assigned to
combat them."[12]

But whatever the gangsters themselves said, DEA agents in Mexico
started to call the federation of gangsters the Guadalajara Cartel in dis-
patches back to Washington from 1984. As stated, it is much easier to prosecute an organization if it has a name. Furthermore, DEA agents in Mexico
were desperate to grab the attention of their bosses, who seemed to have let
the country drift off their radar to focus on Colombia and Florida. Agents
shouted that there were also kingpins in Mexico. To say there was "a
cartel" was to sum up an omnipotent threat just as in Medellín.

Despite the groans of these agents, the Mexican trampoline confounded the Reagan administration. While the task force showed off

gunboats in the Florida Keys, the price of cocaine on American streets actually went down. DEA agents complained that Reagan's war handed too much money to the military and not enough to seasoned operators who could really wound the cocaine cowboys.

By the mideighties, Matta and the Guadalajara gangsters felt invincible. The cocaine market was on fire, the Mexican trampoline pumped like the Trans Alaska Pipeline, and the Reagan administration was tied up in three Central American wars. It seemed as if nothing could go wrong. Then they overplayed their hand: in February 1985, thugs in Guadalajara kidnapped DEA agent Enrique "Kiki" Camarena, tortured him, raped him, and beat him to death.

For DEA agents, the murder of Camarena is the darkest chapter in the history of their work in Mexico. His photograph adorns DEA offices worldwide as a fallen hero, a muscular Hispanic in his late thirties with a smiling face that shows street smarts but perhaps a little naive optimism.

His story is told in most detail by Elaine Shannon in the 1988 book *Desperados.* Born in Mexicali and raised in California, Camarena had been a high school football star and marine before joining the DEA. After making major drug busts in the United States, he gained the nickname the Dark Rooster for his charisma and fight. On the Mexican streets, he was more of a sitting duck.

Arriving in Guadalajara in 1980, Camarena watched frustrated as traffickers grew in strength and power. To hit back, he wandered the rowdiest cantinas and grimiest back streets, sewing a web of informants. He followed their leads to the industrial marijuana-growing operations and took the brash move of going personally on Mexican army raids. His face started to get recognized. But he was still not happy. He and colleagues sent messages back to Washington complaining the Guadalajara gangsters had a network of police protection. Surely, the United States could not stand back and tolerate such corruption? He was seriously ruffling feathers. And he was seriously exposed.

Tension reached a boiling point in late 1984 when Mexican and U.S. authorities carried out several busts on the Guadalajara mob. Among them was the seizure of the record-breaking ganja farm. But there were also hits on the cocaine pipeline on the U.S. side of the border. In Yucca, Arizona, a vacationing detective spotted some fresh plane tracks on a

World War II–era airstrip. When he called it in, the police set up a desert roadblock and promptly netted seven hundred kilo bricks of cocaine in brightly colored Christmas tinfoil packets.[13]

The detective's luck had nothing to do with Kiki Camarena. But the mobsters didn't know that. To frustrated kingpins losing tens of millions of dollars, the DEA looked clever. And the gangsters got angry. According to court testimony, the major players, including Matta, the slickly dressed Félix Gallardo, and the cowboy gunslinger Caro Quintero, held meetings to decide what to do. The court documents state:

"Members of the enterprise, including Matta-Ballesteros, met and discussed the DEA seizures as well as a police report file covering one of the major marijuana seizures at Zacatecas, Mexico. The DEA agent responsible for the seizures was again discussed. The enterprise held yet another meeting [in which they] suggested that the DEA agent should be 'picked up' when his identity was discovered."[14]

As Kiki Camarena walked from the American consulate in Guadalajara one evening, five men jumped him, threw a jacket over his head, and shoved him into a Volkswagen van. A month later his body was dumped on a road hundreds of miles away. The decomposing corpse was in jockey shorts with his hands and legs bound. He had been beaten all over and had a stick forced into his rectum. The cause of death was a blow from a blunt instrument that caved in his skull.

American officials furiously called for justice. But the investigation descended into a tangle of botched crime scenes and scapegoats. Mexican police stormed a ranch of suspects and shot everyone dead—then charged the police on the raid for murder. Audiocassettes emerged of Camarena being tortured and interrogated. He was asked about corrupt police and politicians as well as drug deals.

U.S. agents tracked cowboy Rafael Caro Quintero down to Costa Rica, where he was busted by special forces and deported to Mexico. He has been in prison since. DEA agents then thought they had struck gold when they tracked Matta himself by a telephone wiretap to a house in Mexico City. "I have paid my taxes," Matta was heard saying, a presumed reference to paying off police. They passed the information to Mexican investigators, but the Mexicans stalled on going in. As DEA agents furiously watched the house on a Saturday night, four men drove off in a car. When the federal police finally kicked the door down Sunday morning, they found a lone woman. Matta had gone the night before, she said. DEA agents were livid.[15]

The curly-haired Matta next surfaced in the beach resort of Carta-
gena, Colombia. The DEA passed information to Colombian national
police, and this time a unit was in time to catch him. But not even prison
could stop Matta. The kingpin walked out of the Colombian jail through
seven locked doors after reportedly spreading millions of dollars round
the guards. "The doors opened for me, and I went through them," he was
later quoted as saying in a Honduran newspaper. Matta went back to his
homeland to live in a palatial home in the center of Tegucigalpa. Honduras had no extradition treaty with the United States.

As the Camarena case dragged on, America's war on drugs shot up to
fifth gear. First in 1986, two American sports stars, Len Bias and Don
Rogers, died of cocaine overdoses. Oh, God, cried newspapers, maybe
cocaine can kill after all. Then the media discovered crack. It wasn't a new
story. Use of cocaine freebase had been rising under a number of names
since it was developed in the Bahamas in the 1970s. But *Time* and *News-
week* ran cover stories, and CBS unleashed its special report "48 Hours
on Crack Street" to one of the highest ratings for any documentary in
TV history. Crack definitely sold.

Ronald Reagan jumped on the issue just as the 1986 midterm election
came up. "My generation will remember how Americans swung into action when we were attacked in World War Two," he cried. "Now we're in
another war for our freedom."[16] His war talk turned to a shooting gun in
the Anti Drug Abuse Act the same year. The law fought traffickers at the
beaches and the landing bays by making it easier to seize assets while
introducing mandatory minimum sentences, especially for crack dealers.
The administration also hiked resources for DEA and Customs. The war
on drugs went on steroids.

However, DEA still faced a major obstacle in Central America: the Cold
War. Throughout the eighties, the region served as a front line in the
fight on communism, an arena where spooks and conservatives believed
they battled the Soviet threat at America's doorstep. Within this conflict, the CIA invested most in the right-wing contra rebels of Nicaragua,
who were armed and trained in neighboring Honduras. Both contra
guerrillas and Honduran officers made money from cocaine.

CIA support of right-wing Central Americans linked to drug traffickers
has since been well documented and should be moved from conspiracy
theory to proven fact. However, some patriotic Americans still find it

hard to swallow. The connections are complicated. And to confuse the debate, some writers make other unproven accusations against the CIA, while others misrepresent the charges.

One can follow various strands but the most notorious was exposed by journalist Gary Webb in his 1996 series *Dark Alliance* published in the *San Jose Mercury News*.[17] Webb showed that a prominent Los Angeles crack dealer brought his product from two Nicaraguans, who in turn funded the contras. The story set off an atomic reaction. Suddenly, African-Americans were marching in Watts and shouting that the CIA was involved in the crack epidemic.

Dark Alliance was initially cheered as the scoop of the decade. But then major newspapers attacked it. Webb had made some mistakes. He said the Nicaraguan cocaine was the first major source of the drug into black Los Angeles. In reality, yayo had been dripping in for decades. Critics also attacked Webb for things he never said. They knocked him down for accusing the CIA of directly selling crack. He never wrote that. But with the conspiracy being a little confusing, it was easier just to say that the story was that CIA agents stood on corners selling rocks, then to accuse the writer of being stark raving mad.

The media pressure eventually forced Webb out of his newspaper, and in a sad final chapter, he committed suicide in 2004. Many have since vindicated Webb and said his media crucifixion was a dark moment in American journalism. While Webb may have made some errors, no one ever disproved the basic facts—that a major crack dealer brought drugs from men who gave money to a CIA-organized army. The *Los Angeles Times* and *New York Times* should have followed these leads rather than just looking for holes.

But however much it was shot down, *Dark Alliance* lit two major torches. First, it brought attention to an investigation by a Senate Foreign Relations subcommittee back in the eighties on connections between the contras and cocaine traffickers. Second, it forced the CIA to hold its own internal investigation, the findings of which were released in 1998. So now we have government-stated facts to guide our history. Both reports confirm that cocaine dealers indeed funneled money to contras paid by the CIA. And a certain name flashes up in both reports—Juan Ramón Matta Ballesteros, alias El Negro.

To bring guns to its contra army, the CIA hired the Honduran airline SETCO—allegedly established by none other than Matta himself. The Senate report states, "The payments made by the State Department . . . between

January and August 1986, were as follows: SETCO, for air transport service—$186,924.25." Then a few pages later, the report says, "U.S. law enforcement records state that SETCO was established by Honduran cocaine trafficker Juan Matta Ballesteros."[18]

Perhaps the CIA agents never knew they were working with drug traffickers. The agency's internal report says there is no conclusive proof that they did, thus clearing them of knowing. However, it does state, in long-winded, rambling terms, "CIA knowledge of allegations or information indicating that organizations or individuals had been involved in drug trafficking did not deter their use by the CIA. In other cases, CIA did not act to verify drug trafficking allegations or information when it had the opportunity to do so."[19]

In other words, see no evil, hear no evil.

What conclusions can we make about American spies and the development of the Mexican drug trade? To say that the CIA was the Dr. Frankenstein that invented the El Narco monster seems overblown. Market forces would create the Latin American cocaine trade, with or without the help of spooks. Furthermore, geography would ensure this trade would bounce through Mexico, whichever traffickers got a helping hand from smiling spies.

However, the role of the CIA is crucial in understanding the history of cocaine. It highlights how the U.S. government has failed to have a unified policy in its war on drugs abroad. While the DEA had a mission to fight trafficking, the CIA had a mission to bolster the contras, and they could not help but tread on each other's feet. Fears are that such a situation has been repeated in various theaters of conflict, such as Afghanistan, with members of the U.S. ally the Northern Alliance accused of trafficking drugs. Furthermore, the affair shows that where an illegal drug trade worth billions exists, rebel groups are going to tap into it. Sometimes, they can be allies of the United States, such as the contras or Northern Alliance; in other cases they can be enemies, such as Colombia's FARC or the Taliban. One day this money could fall into the hands of even more dangerous adversaries.

Unfortunately for the cocaine cowboys (and fortunately for Central America) the Cold War didn't go on forever. On March 23, 1988, the con-

tras and the Sandinista government in Nicaragua signed a cease-fire after some sixty thousand people had perished in fighting. Just twelve days
later, American agents arrived in Honduras for Matta. They couldn't arrest him legally because there was no extradition treaty. But they could
grab him illegally. A pact was made for Honduran special forces to work
with U.S. marshals to get the drug lord.

Just before dawn on April 5, Honduran "Cobras" and four U.S. marshals stormed Matta's palatial home in Tegucigalpa. It took six Cobras to
grab the squarely built forty-three-year-old drug lord, handcuff him, put
a black bag over his head, and throw him onto the floor of a waiting car.
Even while in the vehicle, Matta was still struggling, and a U.S. marshal
and Honduran officer pinned Matta down in the back as he was driven to
the huge U.S. military air base nearby. U.S. marshals then flew Matta
to the Dominican Republic and into the United States to be locked up in
Marion, Illinois. During the flight, marshals beat Matta and stuck stun
guns to his feet and genitals, he claimed. The quick kidnapping certainly
beat a lengthy extradition process. Matta went from his home in Honduras to an American federal penitentiary in less than twenty-four hours.

Back in Tegucigalpa, anger spread through barrios, where the beloved
Matta had built schools and handed out welfare. Students were also angry at their government's defying the Honduran constitution to help
the gringos. Two days after the arrest, about two thousand demonstrators massed at the U.S. embassy. After shouting "We want Matta in Honduras" and "Burn, burn," they hurled rocks and Molotov cocktails. Private
security guards from inside the embassy shot into the crowd, killing
four students. But that couldn't stop the blaze. The embassy burned to
the ground, with the fire also torching a car and killing a fifth person. The
Honduran government declared martial law throughout large sections
of the country.[20]

Once in the U.S. prison system, Matta got slammed with a cascade
of charges over cocaine trafficking, the Camarena kidnapping, and even
his escape from Eglin air base back in 1971. However, according to his
son Ramón, prosecutors offered him a deal. They said that if Matta became a witness against President Manuel Noriega of Panama, they would
give him an easy ride. Noriega, a former CIA asset, had blatantly been
aiding cocaine traffickers and was the target of a major operation. Matta
evidently refused any such deal. Whatever he was, he was not a snitch.

Judges acknowledged Matta had illegally been taken from his homeland. "The government does not dispute that he was forcibly abducted

from his home in Honduras," the court heard. But they said that didn't affect the trial. The Matta case is now cited as a precedent justifying kidnapping suspects from foreign countries. The charges against Matta also relied on dubious protected witnesses, including American cocaine dealers, who got various benefits for their testimonies.

Matta was nailed on several counts of conspiring to traffic cocaine and conspiring to kidnap a federal agent. However, he was acquitted of personally murdering Camarena. Rotting in the worst prison in the United States, he became a useful threat for U.S. prosecutors dealing with Latin traffickers. "If you don't make a deal," they could say, "you will end up like Matta." The architect of the Mexican trampoline disappeared into the seething Colorado desert. But back in Mexico, a new generation of traffickers inherited the billion-dollar trampoline and built bigger, bouncier, and bloodier springs.

CHAPTER 5

Tycoons

He is a journalist, the senor,
He writes what is happening,
He goes on with his mission,
Although the mafia attack him,
He condemns the cartel,
He criticizes the government,
He is a man of much faith,
He seeks peace for the people.

He is very brave, the senor,
There is no doubt about it,
He makes the nation tremble,
With a simple pen,
The journalist is king,
So say the analysts,
He is at the top level,
Of the narco-news.

—"EL PERIODISTA," LOS TUCANES DE TIJUANA, 2004[1]

Amid the cool seaside breeze of Tijuana, south of Revolution Avenue with its table-dance clubs, tequila bars, and sombrero shops, sits a converted house with barred windows and a reinforced door. While it looks like it could be a safe house or police installation, the building is actually a magazine office. Stepping inside, you see a rusty classic typewriter below a redwood-framed photograph of the founding editor, Jesús Blancornelas, an old man bearing a thin, gray beard, round, gold glasses, and an intense stare.

Upstairs, reporters hack on with the journalism that Blancornelas started, pushing harder than anyone else into the murky world of drug trafficking. The magazine he founded has paid a dear price for such coverage. Two of its editors were shot dead and Blancornelas himself survived four bullets before dying of cancer, possibly caused by the embedded caps, in 2006.

The story of the rise of El Narco is also the story of Mexican journalists who risk their lives to cover it. The American and British press could get nowhere with their special features or Pulitzer Prize pieces on Mexico without building on the work done day in, day out by Mexican reporters, photographers, and cameramen up and down the country. The grunts' digging and muckraking has even been the main source of investigations by Mexican police and American agents. For salaries as low as $400 a month, reporters resist attacks and intimidation to expose corruption and search for justice.

Of course, the story of Mexican media covering El Narco has not all been rosy. Some journalists take bribes from cartels. In return, they keep gangsters' names out of their paper, put their rivals' names in, or give special attention to narco propaganda. Some of these journalists are spotted riding round in new Jeeps and building plush extensions to their homes.

But in general, the Mexican media has been a crucial, critical check on the rise of drug traffickers and shown itself in a much more positive light than other Mexican institutions such as the police or politicians. No journalist embodies this critical spirit more than Jesús Blancornelas. Keeping his ear to the street, his nose to the halls of power, and his hands digging, Blancornelas churned out thousands of stories and several books on cartels, corruption, and carnage, setting the standard for Mexican reporting at the turn of the millennium. As well as getting him shot, his courage earned him a mass of international awards, including being named Hero of World Press Freedom by the International Press Institute. And how many journalists can boast they have a ballad about them?

Blancornelas covered the rise of drug cartels for thirty years, but his best work was during the 1990s. In this dynamic decade, the Cold War ended and Mexico jumped into globalized free trade. State companies were sold by the dozen, and a new batch of Mexican billionaires appeared from nowhere. This entrepreneurial spirit was strongest on the Mexico-U.S. border, where assembly plants mushroomed, NAFTA quadrupled the flow of goods, and vast new slums emerged. In this period, the power of drug traffickers shifted from Sinaloa and Guadalajara to this border, especially to three cartels: one in Tijuana; one in Juárez; and one by the Gulf of Mexico. El Narco consolidated its power amid the gold rush of globalization.

Blancornelas worked most closely on the Tijuana Cartel, pursuing the mafia relentlessly and exposing its capos, the Arellano Félix brothers. His stories were so crucial that almost every single account of the Tijuana Cartel cites him—and those that don't, should. In return, the Arellano Félix brothers ordered Blancornelas dead, sending ten gangbangers to wipe him off the map.

When I first arrived in Mexico in 2000, I worked in the shabby offices of the *Mexico City News*, an English-language daily run out of the capital's historic center. For a handsome salary of $600 a month, other hungry journalists and I hammered out stories for the declining readership on old, coffee-stained computers using telephone lines that beeped loudly every three seconds. It was the best job I had had in my life. I got to cover the Mexico City crime beat, which involved chasing a plump female crack dealer nicknamed Ma Barker and sitting through a weeklong court-martial of corrupt generals.

I soon found myself reading Blancornelas and called him for advice on stories. The veteran journalist was incredibly patient with a green British reporter asking dumb questions. He always took my weekly calls, despite his harassing deadlines, and would clarify all issues I battled to understand. When I phoned to ask about a particular trafficker, he would answer with his usual sport metaphors. "Grillo, if that trafficker you are writing about were playing baseball, he would be in the minor leagues." "What about this guy Ismael Zambada?" I asked dimly. "Now Zambada," he replied, "would be playing for the New York Yankees."

Such metaphors were natural to Blancornelas, as he spent years covering sports before he wrote about gangsters. After graduating college, he became sports editor of a local rag in his native state of San Luis Potosi in central Mexico before moving more than a thousand miles to the budding town of Tijuana. People can reinvent themselves on the border, and Blancornelas was one of many who found a new life in the city that Californians call TJ. In 1980, at forty-four years old, Blancornelas partnered with two other journalists to found the first Mexican newsmagazine to specialize in coverage of El Narco. They baptized it *Zeta*—the Mexican spelling of the letter *Z* (and nothing to do with the Zetas gang).

The first blood was spilled at *Zeta* in 1988. It was about power, rather than drugs. Coeditor Héctor Félix wrote columns criticizing Tijuana entrepreneur Jorge Hank, son of one of Mexico's most powerful politicians. Jorge Hank owned a popular racetrack and Félix wrote that Hank had fixed races and rigged bets. Hank's bodyguard and racetrack employees followed Félix from work on a rainy afternoon. One vehicle blocked Félix in and another pulled up beside him. Blancornelas wrote what happened next:

"From the Toyota pickup, Hank's bodyguard shot. Once, twice. Extremely accurate. Once near the neck, once in the ribs . . .

"This is not a soap opera line: his heart was completely destroyed.

"His gray Members Only jacket was shredded, smelling of gunpowder, soaked in blood and flesh."[2]

Blancornelas and his team uncovered the killers and got them arrested and jailed. But the journalist wanted Hank himself to go on trial. Prosecutors wouldn't touch the son of such a powerful politico, so *Zeta* printed a weekly letter on a black page demanding justice. "Jorge Hank. Why did your bodyguard kill me?" the letter starts, under Félix's name. *Zeta* still prints it today. Jorge Hank has since served a term as Tijuana mayor. He denies anything to do with the murder.

The year Félix was killed, Mexico elected a new president. As the big day approached it looked like the unthinkable could happen—leftist contender Cuauhtémoc Cárdenas could actually oust the PRI. Cárdenas wasn't really a revolutionary. His dad had been the iconic PRI president Lázaro Cárdenas in the 1930s, and he himself had been in the ruling party for many years. But feeling that the government had lost touch with the people, he had broken away and was now challenging the PRI in the first genuine two-horse race since 1929.

On election day, Mexicans couldn't believe their eyes; Cárdenas was ahead on the vote count. It seemed the election had not been rigged. It was too good to be true. Votes piled up in favor of Cárdenas. And then, *crash*.

There was a sudden computer failure. It had really been too good to be true. A month later it was declared that PRI candidate Carlos Salinas had won. Nothing had changed. Cárdenas told his supporters to stay off the streets. He didn't want bloodshed, and he didn't really want a revolution. There was bloodshed anyway, as gunmen killed dozens of leftist militants who supported Cárdenas. Within two years, they had murdered hundreds.

But despite a rigged election, PRI winner Salinas got good press in the United States. A short man with a trademark bald head, big ears, and straight-line mustache, President Salinas wooed American politicians with his perfect English and Ph.D. from Harvard. This was a new kind of PRI and a new Mexico. This PRI embraced free trade and modern capitalism even if it did carry out the odd electoral shenanigan to keep the communists out. Companies and assets long owned by the Mexican state were sold at bargain prices—telephone lines, railways, a TV network.

Suddenly, a new class of Mexican tycoons buzzed around in private jets. In 1987, when *Forbes* began its billionaire list, one Mexican was on it. In 1994, when Salinas left office, there were twenty-four *Forbes* billionaires. Where had this money come from? Salinas also negotiated the North American Free Trade Agreement with Bill Clinton, which produced some equally dramatic results. In 1989, cross-border trade between the United States and Mexico was at $49 billion; in 2000, it was at $247 billion![3] Mexicans flocked from country shacks to work in assembly plants on the border. Throughout the nineties, Tijuana and Juárez grew by a block a day, with new slums spreading over surrounding hills— slums that would later be the center of the drug war.

Salinas also went about reorganizing the narcotics trade. When he came into office, the undisputed godfather of Mexico was Miguel Ángel Félix Gallardo, the Sinaloan who partnered with Matta Ballesteros to traffic cocaine. In 1989, under orders from Salinas, police commander Guillermo González Calderoni nabbed the forty-three-year-old kingpin Félix Gallardo sitting quietly in a Guadalajara restaurant. Not a shot was fired.

Félix Gallardo later wrote in his prison diary how he had met with the commander Calderoni five times leading up to the arrest, and the officer had even given him some rare guacamaya birds as a present. On the day of his detention, Félix Gallardo wrote, he actually went to the restaurant to meet Calderoni to talk business.[4]

Whether or not the capo's account is true, that the Mexican government could take down the biggest gangster in the country without firing a shot was telling. In 1989, mobsters still relied on the police to operate, and these officers could take out narcos when they needed to. The detention of the head honcho reminded traffickers who was boss.

Following the arrest, Mexican capos held a gangster summit in the resort of Acapulco. It sounds like a scene from *The Godfather*. But these narco conferences really do happen. Journalist Blancornelas broke the news about the meeting, and it was later confirmed by a number of sources. Blancornelas said head honcho Félix Gallardo organized it from behind bars. However, Félix Gallardo wrote that police commander Calderoni set up the cozy get-together. Maybe it was both. Blancornelas describes the scene:

"They rented a chalet in Las Brisas. From it, you could see the beautiful Acapulco bay in cinemascope and bright colors, away from the relentless traffic of the seafront. No hawkers came up to the chalets, which were away from the annoyance of the blear of discos and the glare of the police. They managed to get the house sometimes used by the Shah of Iran. Who knows how they did it?"[5]

During a week's summit, the holidaying capos discussed the future of the Mexican underworld. Almost all guests were from the old Sinaloan narco tribe, a sprawl of families intertwined by marriages, friendships, and drug deals. At the meeting were several players who would be crucial in shaping trafficking over the next two decades. Among them was the Sierra Madre villain Joaquin "Chapo" Guzmán and his older friend Ismael "the Mayo" Zambada. Each capo was awarded a plaza where he could move his own drugs and tax any other smugglers on his turf.

It all sounded like a good idea. But the cozy arrangement didn't play out. Without the leadership of the imprisoned godfather, Félix Gallardo, the capos plotted and backstabbed to get a bigger piece of the pie. As Blancornelas wrote:

"Never in the history of Mexican drug trafficking could someone like Félix Gallardo operate again. He was a man of his word, of deals before shots, of convincing arguments before executions . . .

"If the capos had followed his instructions, then the most powerful cartel in the world would exist now. But the absence of a leader and the presence of several bosses, all feeling more superior than the next, caused a disorganized mess."[6]

Within this mess, three cartels rose to supremacy, in Tijuana, Juárez, and by the Gulf. While these cartels had their own hierarchies, trafficking from east of Juárez along a thousand miles of border to the Pacific was all controlled by Sinaloans. The Arellano Félix brothers who ran the Tijuana cartel, and Amado Carrillo Fuentes, who ran Juárez, were all from the Culiacán area and were deeply embedded in the old narco scene. Different bosses moved round the Sinaloan empire, chipping in together on loads, sharing corrupt cops, and passing around operatives. It is crucial to understand the links within this Sinaloan realm to make sense of the current Mexican Drug War.

The assassin Gonzalo, whom I interviewed in prison in Juárez, worked throughout the empire in the 1990s. He said he did jobs in Durango, Culiacán, Tijuana, Juárez, and other cities controlled by different cartels. He would simply be given recommendations by capos, who all knew each other. DEA agents also recognized the cooperation among all kinds of gangsters in northwest Mexico. A classified operational intelligence report back in the 1990s made the following observations about this system:

"The cartel scheme is widely accepted but distorts the real power and strength of Mexican drug traffickers. Recent examples of individuals who have the ability to transcend these 'cartel' boundaries include Amado Carrillo Fuentes.

"Joaquin Guzmán-Loera and Carrillo Fuentes jointly brokered multiton cocaine shipments from Bolivia and Colombia into Sonora, Mexico, and then into the United States through Arizona. During this time Carrillo Fuentes was also working closely with Ismael Zambada Garcia, establishing smuggling routes through Tijuana, Baja California."[7]

While the Sinaloan clan worked together, it was still quarrelsome. The biggest beef in the early nineties erupted between the Arellano Félix brothers and Joaquin "Chapo" Guzmán over traffic into California. The war was not as violent as those of the twenty-first century, fought with paramilitary hit squads. But thugs did clash in a series of shoot-outs and assassinations, leaving dozens of bodies.

Looking back, we can see the first signs that the Mexican government would prove unable to contain the beast of El Narco, that the bloodshed would spiral out of hand. But such an observation comes with the benefit of hindsight, knowing the bloodbath that would later drown Mexico. As professional historians say, it is always dangerous to read history backward. At the time, no one in the Mexican government seemed worried. "There is violence, but it is narcos killing narcos," politicians sighed. In any case, traffickers were not attacking the system, but rather competing with each other to see who could get the best of those to be bribed. The government could sit back and get paid, whoever won.

Amid this conflict, one particular murder shook Mexico, the killing of Cardinal Juan Jesús Posadas Ocampo in May 1993. The official explanation is familiar to many—the sixty-six-year-old man of the cloth went to Guadalajara airport to catch a plane when he drove into a firefight between Arellano Félix and Chapo Guzmán thugs. When Cardinal Posadas arrived in his white Grand Marquis car, gunmen attacked, thinking he was Chapo Guzmán himself. However, this explanation never washed with the robed men of Rome, who asked, how could hit men possibly confuse an elderly, tall cleric in a dog collar for a five-foot-six-inch gangster? Conspiracy theories emerged on how the cleric was assassinated because he had some explosive information on government corruption.

While the Posadas case is unlikely ever to be resolved, it is important as a landmark in bringing the drug mafia to public attention. For most Mexicans, it was the first time that they had ever heard of "drug cartels," and certainly the first time the Arellano Félix mafia and Chapo Guzmán got much mention. That these organizations could take out a top member of the age-old Catholic Church suggested that they were very powerful. However, many cynical Mexicans still thought these "cartels" were some imaginary scapegoat for government crimes. When one lives with a conspiratorial one-party state for seven decades, it easy to believe its hand is in every act. And a lot of the time, it is.

The media attention put pressure on the Mexican government to round up some capos. Then, as if by magic, two weeks after the cardinal killing, police in Guatemala nabbed Chapo Guzmán and swiftly deported him to Mexico, where he was locked up in a top-security prison. The Arellano Félix brothers had decisively outgunned and outbribed their rival.

A clan of seven brothers and four sisters, the Arellano Félix mob reinvented themselves in Tijuana like many others on the border; back in Sinaloa and Guadalajara, they had been employees; now they were capos. At the head of the mob were two of the brothers—Ramón Arellano Félix, a baby-faced psychotic who became the chief enforcer—and Benjamin Arellano Félix, the second-eldest brother, who was the brains of the operation. Blancornelas compared them all to brothers in the *God-*

father movies. Ramón, he said, was like the impulsive, violent Sonny Corleone, played by James Caan. Benjamin was the cold and calculating Michael Corleone, played by Al Pacino. Another brother, Francisco, was Fredo Corleone, weak in business and an incessant womanizer.

Blancornelas showed me an old family video of the Arellano Félixes at a Tijuana barbecue in their early days. They look a happy, festive bunch, the men with black hair molded into their own version of mullets and colorful Hawaian shirts tucked into their pants. They sip Tecate beer out of tins while a horde of young babies jump around on a trampoline. But on the streets they gained a grisly reputation.

Ramón Arellano Félix formed a notorious regiment of killers, recruiting Chicano gangbangers from San Diego and the bored sons of Tijuana's wealthy families—a cadre that became known as narco juniors. It was a funny mix: poor kids from America and rich kids from Mexico. But their victims were not laughing. The thugs were set on anyone who got in their bosses' way, not only killing but also devouring bodies in acid. The punishment was less about destroying evidence and more about devastating the victim's family psychologically. Ramón was even famed for throwing victims' corpses onto a fire, grilling up some steaks over it, and standing around with his goons, enjoying beef, beer, and cocaine. Who knows if that really went down. But on the street, word of such cruelty was a powerful deterrent.

Ramón also introduced a new bloody tactic—the *encobijado*. The word describes the practice of wrapping up a corpse in sheets and dumping it in a public place, often with a threatening note. Murder was on display for all the city to see. Ramón had created the first army of enforcers and pioneered Mexico's first gangster terror, an ominous development in the history of El Narco.

In modern capitalism, big corporations keep getting bigger, using their vast profits to expand their empires and eat up smaller competitors. In this way, Mexico's border cartels expanded in the nineties. Their wealth and power pushed them to the point where they could even usurp the original cartels in Colombia. By taking over from the Colombians, Mexican gangs would become the dominant criminal organizations in the whole of Latin America.

To get a better grasp on how Mexican traffickers got the upper hand over the Colombians, I talked to the DEA's Andean regional director, Jay

Bergman. The agent followed the seismic shift while working on dozens of huge busts and probes across the Americas. But Bergman didn't come across as the typical DEA agent trying to sell the company line or impress with stories of drug-busting bravado. In fact, Bergman appeared to be quite an intellectual who had read widely on economic theory to understand the smuggling mafias. When I sat down with him, he unleashed a tirade about the shift in power with the vigor of a writer with a book inside him struggling to get out. He explained, "What is interesting is that there was no hostile takeover or violence. At each progression, the Colombian cartels made a conscious decision to allocate more share to the Mexicans. And then it got to a time when the Mexicans started calling the shots."

Colombians first let Mexicans get their fingers into the cocaine pie after Reagan cracked down in Florida, which made cartels spread their smuggling risk along the Mexican-U.S. border. By 1990, Bergman explained, American agents had figured out how to shut down the Florida smuggling corridor completely, using naval vessels and aircraft to keep watch on a ninety-mile choke point. The Colombians were forced to hand almost all their merchandise to Mexican couriers, who would end up moving nine tenths of the cocaine that entered the United States. This shifted the white lady's routes to the East Pacific, a vast stretch of water with no natural choke points and a lesser U.S. navy presence. Typical of drug enforcement, solving one problem had created another bigger one.

U.S. agents then turned on Colombian head honcho Pablo Escobar to stop the flow of blow. The end of the Cold War aided them in their mission. With no communists to hunt, American spooks and soldiers were eager to fight drug traffickers for a brief moment (until they discovered Islamic militants). Rather than tripping each other up, the Pentagon, CIA, and DEA all worked together, feeding data from street informants and spook satellites to the Colombian police.[8]

Escobar had drawn particular attention to himself by his terrorist tactics—he even bombed an airliner, killing 110 passengers, as pressure to stop his being extradited to the United States. His brutal violence against rivals also created so many enemies that victims formed a paramilitary group to get him. A curious alliance was formed of Colombian police, soldiers, and criminals, and American spies, drug agents, and troops, all after the big guy. Escobar was just waiting to die. Colombian police finally caught up with him in a residential Medellín house, shot him dead, and posed smiling with his corpse. Drug warriors learned a new modus operandi—sometimes it is better to forget about an arrest and go for the clean kill.

Under pressure from all sides, Colombians started paying Mexican couriers in cocaine rather than cash. The Colombians had a huge markup. While a kilo of cocaine was worth $25,000 wholesale in the United States, it only cost Colombians $2,000 from a lab. But the Mexican border tycoons could see the huge business advantage of having product rather than money. They could sell it on the street for greater gain and build up their own distribution networks.

The DEA soon hit the Colombians again, arresting their sellers in New York and Miami and using the cases to indict kingpins back home on conspiracy charges. Faced with American jail time, Colombians took their deal with the Mexicans to a third phase, getting out of the United States altogether and letting Mexicans sell it there. Bergman explains their reasoning:

"They were thinking, 'How do I diminish my exposure to potential extradition? Why don't I just hand this whole thing to the Mexicans? I still make a huge amount of money and I lower my exposure to potential extradition as it's no longer my kilo. I get out of the business because it is getting too much pressure to do this in the United States. And concurrently I've got the European market, I'm making hand-over-fist money in Europe, I'm making tons of money in Mexico. Let the Mexican cartels deal with the DEA and the FBI and the U.S. customs.'"

However, Bergman goes on, U.S. laws were later changed so prosecutors could extradite Colombians even if they weren't directly connected to sellers in the United States. Someone selling drugs abroad could now be nailed just by knowing those drugs were headed to American soil. At the same time, the Colombian national police began to hammer the drug barons from behind.

"It completely backfired. Not only did the Colombians make less money, not only did the Mexicans take over, but the Colombians were being extradited left and right, and the cases being built against them were stronger and more powerful. The Colombians never quite got it. They always played checkers and never really played chess. They never really thought two steps ahead."

Up in Mexico, this meant cartels were raking in more money than ever before. Reports ebbed out of huge fiestas from Tijuana to the Gulf of

Mexico, with guests arriving on private jets, tigers displayed in cages, and beauty queens serving up cocaine. These were party years on the border. And in turn, bigger bribes than ever flowed into the system.

During seven decades of PRI rule, the loudest allegations of narco corruption at the top are shouted at President Salinas. Nothing has been conclusively proven. But investigations themselves highlight the depth of suspicion about the government's role in organized crime at the end of the twentieth century.

The Salinas conspiracy focuses on the president's brother, Raúl Salinas. During Carlos's 1988-to-1994 term, Raúl had a government job at $192,000 a year. That was tasty money in a country where the minimum wage is $5 a day. But Raúl also proved an especially good saver. In 1995, he was found to have $85 million in a Swiss bank account when his wife got arrested trying to withdraw it. That was only the tip of the iceberg. Investigators found he had a whopping 289 bank accounts in such veritable institutions as Citibank. Swiss police estimated he had upward of $500 million altogether.[9]

A Mexican politician has many ways besides drugs to skim money. However, Swiss police interviewed ninety Raúl Salinas associates, including convicted drug traffickers, and concluded that El Narco was the main source. Their report stated:

"When Carlos Salinas de Gortari became President of Mexico in 1988, Raúl Salinas de Gortari assumed control over practically all drug shipments through Mexico. Through his influence and bribes paid with drug money, officials of the army and the police supported and protected the flourishing drug business."

Raúl and his brother, President Carlos Salinas, have consistently denied all this as smears and misinformation. However, when Salinas finished his term in 1994, Raúl Salinas was arrested in Mexico for masterminding a murder and served a ten-year prison term before being acquitted. Money-laundering charges against him in Switzerland still drag on.

Carlos Salinas himself left Mexico after his term for a self-imposed exile in the Republic of Ireland. Apparently, he enjoys rain and thick black beer. Mexicans later vilified him as a puppet master akin to the evil emperor in the *Star Wars* movies and fear he is the hidden hand behind anything from guerrilla attacks to bad weather.

*   *   *

After Salinas left, his economic miracle collapsed like a paper tiger. In 1995, months into the new government of President Ernesto Zedillo, money poured out of the economy and the peso fell like a dead weight, triggering double-digit inflation. Overnight, the number of Mexican billionaires was halved from twenty-four to twelve. Down below, the middle class had their life savings wiped out, while many companies went out of business, costing millions of jobs. Bill Clinton, who had worked closely with Salinas, rushed faithfully to the rescue with a $50 billion bailout package to save Mexico from collapse.

This crisis sparked a surge in crime. Despite the steady rise of drug trafficking, modern Mexico had not been a dangerous country until then. Even in the eighties, mugging and robbery rates were relatively low, and Mexicans strolled the streets of big cities at all hours. But those good old days came to a rude end. Mugging, carjacking, and the heinous crime of kidnapping shot up, especially in the capital. Suddenly, everyone in Mexico City had a story about a family member getting a gun stuck to his head and turning out his pockets. Police failed to respond to this crime wave, creating an atmosphere of impunity that paved the way for the current criminal insurgency.

One Mexican industry wasn't affected by the peso crisis. Drug trafficking kept bringing in the billions, and as it got paid in dollars, the devaluation of the peso just gave El Narco more power. With an army of unemployed, the cartels could recruit foot soldiers more cheaply than before. El Narco became more deeply entrenched in slums across the country.

Another crucial transformation happened in this time: Mexicans in meaningful numbers started taking hard drugs. Mexicans had long seen cocaine and heroin as a gringo vice. "The Colombians make it, the Mexicans traffic it, and the Americans snort it," observers joked. But by the late nineties, Mexico had to concede it had its own army of heroin junkies and crackheads.

The spread of these drugs was directly linked to traffic. To maximize profits, Mexican capos started paying their lieutenants with bricks of cocaine and bags of heroin as well as cash. Many of these midranking hoods unloaded their products on Mexico's own streets to make a quick peso.

Tijuana developed the highest level of drug use in the country, with Arellano Félix affiliates setting up hundreds of *tienditas*, or little drug shops, especially in the center and eastside slums. The cartel's mob of hit men protected these drug retailers, adding an extra dimension to Mexican drug violence. Now it wasn't just about moving tons over the border; it was also about slinging crack to addicts.

Fighting over street corners drove violence to new highs with some three hundred homicides a year in Tijuana, and the same number in Juárez toward the end of the nineties. These were rates comparable to those of gang-infested U.S. cities such as Los Angeles, Washington, D.C., and New Orleans. The American media began to pick up on the bloodshed and, for the first time, talk about the danger of "Colombianization," or the prospect of a full-blown narco war exploding on the United States' doorstep. Most dismissed such naysayers as alarmist nut jobs. As it turns out, the alarmist nut jobs were right.

American media also picked up on the bubbly characters of the Arellano Félix brothers and their cocaine binges, disco dancing, and dissolving of victims in acid. *Time* magazine published a story on them,[10] and the movie *Traffic* even had characters based on them making cocaine deals with Catherine Zeta-Jones. Accompanying the media attention were a series of indictments and rewards in the United States. And anytime that anyone mentioned the Arellano Félix brothers, the name of journalist Blancornelas flashed up. He really pissed them off.

Blancornelas thinks the last straw for Ramón Arellano Félix wasn't even a story he wrote but a letter he printed. One day, a distraught woman came into the *Zeta* office and asked to publish an ad. When she was told how much it would cost, she said softly that she didn't have enough money. The curious *Zeta* worker asked to see what she wanted on display, and when he saw it, he immediately called Blancornelas. The journalist read the letter and was so moved he agreed to run it for free.

The woman had written a letter addressed directly to Ramón Arellano Félix, who'd ordered the murder of her two sons. The young men had been caught up in some street beef with one of Ramón's lieutenants. The mother wrote fearlessly out of love for her lost children:

"My beloved sons were the victims of the envy and cowardice of you, the Arellanos . . . You don't deserve to die yet. Death should not be your price or your punishment. I hope you live for many years and know the pain of losing children."[11]

The woman disappeared from Tijuana after publishing the letter. Blancornelas believes she ran before the mafia could execute her. The frustrated Ramón Arellano Félix thus turned his wrath on the journalist.

Ten hit men ambushed Blancornelas as he drove with his bodyguard Luis Valero. They sprayed their car with bullets, killing Valero instantly. But Blancornelas was still alive with four caps in him. The chief hit man than strolled up to the car to take the final shot. But as the assassin walked forward, he fired a bullet that ricocheted off the concrete and into his own eye, killing him instantly. The rest of the gang abandoned their chief in a pool of blood. Blancornelas was saved by a miracle.

"Ramón ordered me dead. God didn't want it . . . but disgracefully they killed my companion and protector Luis Valero."[12]

The chief hit man was identified as David Barron, a Chicano gangbanger from San Diego known to work with the Arellano Félixes. Barron had tattoos of fourteen skulls on his midriff and shoulders, reputedly one for each man he had killed. *Zeta* reporters identified six more of the attackers as fellow thugs of Barron's from the San Diego barrio of Logan Heights. But despite the fact that *Zeta* handed piles of evidence to Mexican police, the thugs were never indicted and they were seen moving freely in San Diego. Some are still there.

The three border tycoons of the nineties all went down eventually. Juan Garcia Ábrego of the Gulf Cartel was arrested in 1996. He gave himself up without a shot, nabbed in a ranch near Monterrey. As an old-school capo, he was ultimately respectful of the Mexican system, in which the government called the shots. A year later, Amado Carrillo Fuentes died of plastic-surgery complications in a Mexico City hospital. Or did he? A gangster of mythological proportions in life, he went out in his own puff of smoke. It was all a trick, people whisper on the Juárez streets; Amado is really kicking it in the Caribbean sipping margaritas. Or maybe he is working in a gas station in Texas alongside Elvis Presley.

The Arellano Félix brothers survived the longest. Ramón Arellano Félix, the baby-faced psycho who pioneered narco terror in Mexico, lived on until the twenty-first century. Then in 2002, he was shot dead in a traffic stop by a local policeman in the seaside resort of Mazatlán. It was quite an undramatic death for a legendary outlaw. Something had gone seriously wrong with his network of police protection. Blancornelas penned the story about the killing of the man who tried to kill him, noting,

"If some of his many victims could speak from the grave, maybe they would say to Ramón, 'As you are now, so once was I. As I am now, so you shall be.' "[13]

A month later, army special forces nabbed Benjamin Arellano Félix in a home where he kept his wife and children. The bosses' chief aides apparently failed to smell the trap. The capo is currently in Mexico's top-security prison, fighting extradition to the United States. Robbed of its two leaders, the Arellano Félix clan struggled on with the other brothers and sisters, but was severely weakened.

Blancornelas wasn't long celebrating the demise of his nemesis. In 2004, assassins shot dead Francisco Ortiz, the third founder of *Zeta* magazine. Ortiz was leaving a downtown clinic with his young son and daughter when gunmen fired four bullets into his neck and head. His two children shouted, "Papi! Papi!" as he died beside them, a witness said. This time, *Zeta* magazine was not even sure who was behind the hit.

Blancornelas despaired. While his reporting may have helped bring down one set of bad guys, cartels had only got more powerful and more violent. He was one of the few that saw the writing on the wall. As he said in an interview shortly before he died:

"El Narco used to be in certain states. But now its has grown across the whole of the Mexican republic. Soon El Narco will knock on the door of the presidential palace. It will knock on the door of the attorney general's office. And this will present a great danger."[14]

CHAPTER 6

Democrats

If the dog is tied up,
Although he barks all day,
You shouldn't let him free,
My grandma used to say.

But the fox broke the plates,
And the dog chewed on his leash,
And then the dog was freed,
To cause a bloody mess.

        —"LA GRANJA" (THE FARM), TIGRES DEL NORTE, 2009

The world threw up some intrepid and inspiring heroes of democracy at the end of the twentieth century. In Poland, there was Lech Walesa, the hardened union man who endured years of repression before leading his people to rise and defeat authoritarian communism. In South Africa, Nelson Mandela survived twenty-seven years on a prison island, then rid the world of the dastardly affliction of racist apartheid while avoiding a bloody vengeance that might have shattered his country. Then in Mexico there was . . . Senor Vicente Fox.

The man who led Mexico's final march from the authoritarian PRI to multiparty democracy was the unlikeliest of characters. He came from neither the socialist left nor Catholic right, the two factions that rose up to challenge PRI hegemony. Instead, he was a wealthy rancher and Coca-Cola executive who haphazardly stepped into politics at age forty-six and became governor of his native state of Guanajuato seven years later. While he joined the conservative National Action Party, he was never one of their true religionists. Rather than being ideological, he espoused his country values of hard work and forthrightness. He was known for his frank, rancherlike comments that could turn into gaffes. He once said, "Mexicans do the jobs in the United States that even blacks don't want to do,"[1] as well as calling women "washing machines with two flippers."

Fox had political talents suited for the moment in history. Mexicans were sick of conniving politicians who had sacked their country. Fox appeared an outsider, a straight shooter who would fix the broken political machine as if he were mending a tractor. In contrast to the tedious speeches of PRI presidents, he spoke in an everyday language that people understood. When he called for democracy, he sounded as if he believed in it from the bottom of his heart. Throughout the election cycle, both for his party's nomination, and then for the presidency, he was in a zone. He kept saying the right things at the right time. When he won, he was suddenly out of the zone. He looked like a cornered fox, overwhelmed and puzzled as to what to do.

Open with the press, Fox gave off a warm, familiar quality, appearing like the neighbor you used to chat to occasionally or an old friend from college. His tall, lanky body and mustache have a slightly comic air, akin to that of the English comedian John Cleese, although Fox wore cowboy boots and I never saw him in a bowler hat. His voice is deep and powerful, making him a charismatic speaker.

"I felt an incredible happiness to be at the head of this movement that liberated Mexico from the yoke of authoritarianism," Fox later told me, reflecting on his presidency in an interview in his native village.[2]

What was quite remarkable is that the PRI allowed Fox to win at all and didn't announce any computer failures in the middle of the vote count. The last PRI president, Ernesto Zedillo, was a curious character, a man from a poor family who became a Yale-educated technocrat and stepped into the Mexican presidency after the previous PRI candidate was assassinated. Zedillo, resistant to pressures from within his own party, was determined to allow the democratic transition. If Mexico were the Soviet Union, Zedillo was the reforming genius Mikhail Gorbachev and Fox the less sparkling Boris Yeltsin, who took the helm.

Zedillo made brave moves against his own corrupt establishment: he oversaw the arrest of Raúl Salinas for alleged murder; the arrest of the governor of Quintana Roo state on drug-trafficking charges; and even the arrest of his own drug czar General Jesús Gutiérrez Rebollo for being in league with mobsters. Zedillo also coaxed the PRI to loose its grip on power before it gave up the presidency. Mexico's federal electoral institute gained autonomy in 1996, and the PRI lost its majority in Congress in 1997. It would be harder to fix an election, even if the PRI wanted to.

These actions all shook up the drug underworld and its system of police and political protection. Gangsters nervously repositioned themselves and held tight to see what a democratic president would do. When Fox took office, the seismic lines of Mexican power shifted; the end of seventy-one years of PRI rule was a genuine political earthquake.

From his first days in office, Fox showed himself to be without a clear direction on most issues, drug trafficking included. Time and time again, he put forward plans, and when faced with resistance, he changed course or capitulated. He swore to convict officials from the old regime for their dirty war that "disappeared" five hundred leftists. But when the PRI wouldn't play ball, he left prosecutions hanging and just released a report about it. He promised sweeping modernizations of Mexico's economy and justice system. But when the opposition booed him in parliament, he avoided dealing with Congress as much as possible. He pushed hard for the rights of migrants, becoming the first Mexican to speak before a joint session of the U.S. Congress and urging a new guest-worker program. But then the September 11 attacks happened, and Americans put the immigration issue on the back burner.

Quite soon, it seemed, Fox abandoned trying to have much of a domestic program and spent time swanning round the world or entertaining visiting dignitaries. The United Nations, Organization of American States, World Trade Organization, and dozens more groups held summits in what critics started calling "Foxi-landia." Fox never looked happier than when he was hosting these events and cheering the wonders of multilateralism and the spread of democracy.

Fox had talked little about drugs in his election campaign—his focus had been on getting the PRI out of power. But when he took office, American drug warriors hoped that a democratic president could mean a new era of cooperation. The days of corrupt police conspiring to murder DEA agents were over. Now Mexico could help agents clock up arrests and busts the way the Colombians did. Fox keenly accepted the challenge, making a highly quotable promise in his first interview with American television following his victory. As he told ABC's *Nightline*, "We are going to give the mother of all battles against organized crime in Mexico. No doubt."[3]

Fox had promised to take the military out of the war on drugs. But after an initial meeting with American officials, who felt soldiers were the most reliable antidrug operatives, he switched course and said he would keep troops fighting traffickers after all. The Americans were happy. This was a guy they could work with.

The first sign that Fox's drug policy might not be as good as these Americans hoped came just two months into his administration. On January 21, 2001, arch-mafioso Chapo Guzmán escaped from a high-security prison in Guadalajara. The Sinaloan godfather was back in town.

According to data dug up by journalist José Reveles, Chapo built up his power in the prison over several years by throwing bribes at officials.[4] In return, he won the right to bring in different women to his cell; choose girls from the cleaning stuff to have sex with; and have relations with a female prisoner called Zulema Hernandez, a tall, blond armed robber in her thirties. Chapo also smuggled Viagra into the penitentiary. More pertinently, Guzmán used his network of corruption to break himself out. Zulema later gave journalist Julio Scherer a love letter from Chapo, in which the drug lord said his escape was imminent. As Chapo, or what some have guessed was a ghostwriter, penned:

"I want to give you a sweet kiss and feel you in my arms to conserve this memory every time I think of you, and withstand your absence so God can permit us to reunite in other conditions that will not be in this place."[5]

Two prison guards helped smuggle Chapo out of the pen. To get them on his side, the kingpin paid for the medical operation of the son of one and set up another with a beautiful Sinaloan girlfriend. This happy guard then personally drove Chapo out of the prison in a laundry truck.

As news of Chapo's escape broke, an embarrassed Fox published ads in newspapers and put up posters with a special hotline number to catch the kingpin. Almost a hundred calls came in every hour. But they all gave false or useless information, and in many of them laughter could be heard in the background. A naive president asking for help seemed hilarious both to children and adults. Mexicans hadn't quite caught on to the idea of citizen support for policing.[6]

So what can the escape of Guzmán really tell us about the Fox presidency? Conspiracy theorists cite it as evidence that the Fox administration allied with Guzmán and his Sinaloan gangster friends. Orders for the breakout, they say, must have come from upstairs. Fox's secret aim was to make a renewed Sinaloa Cartel the strongest mafia, with Guzmán as a national godfather, the way the eighties capo Miguel Ángel Félix Gallardo had been. After unleashing Chapo from his cage, Fox brought down his rivals, such as the Arellano Félix brothers, and allowed Chapo to expand across the country. This policy of supporting Guzmán, these theorists argue, carried on when Felipe Calderón took office.

Such a conspiracy theory, in various forms, has bugged both presidents in the democratic era. It has been written by gangsters on placards, shouted by politicians, and filled thousands of column inches.[7] But is there any truth to it?

Certainly no evidence has directly linked either Fox or Calderón to Chapo Guzmán. More substantiated than the conspiracy theory is the cock-up theory. Fox may have had nothing to do with Chapo Guzmán's escape and no power over his subsequent rise. Simply, Guzmán and his mafia partners were the most effective gangsters at building a network of corrupt officials from all wings of government. Neither Fox nor Calderón could really control the Mexican state. With the demise of the PRI, the basic system of power was gone. And this was the key to Mexico's breaking down.

With the benefit of hindsight, the escape of Chapo Guzmán appears to be a landmark event. But back in 2001, few saw it as an earthshaker. It was just one more gangster and one more example of bad Latin American prisons. Courts had indicted Chapo in Arizona in 1993 for racketeering, and in San Diego in 1995 for conspiracy to import cocaine. But there were not yet million-dollar rewards for him. Most observers of Mexico focused on a totally different agenda—looking at a convoy of Zapatista rebels driving peacefully to Mexico City and at ongoing investigations into the PRI's old dirty war. As Fox said in the later interview when I asked him about Chapo's escape:

"It is an important case, but it is not the hallmark of my government.

One swallow does not make a summer . . . Today, it is used by my opponents, by my political enemies, as an enigmatic issue."

Over the next three years, Fox's drug policy looked great to Americans. In 2002, municipal police shot dead Tijuana psycho Ramón Arellano Félix and the next month, soldiers seized his brainy brother Benjamin. Then in 2003, Mexican security forces nabbed kingpin Armando Valencia in Michoacán state and capo Osiel Cárdenas up in Tamaulipas. To American drug agents, who love busts and seizures, things had never looked better. I sat down with three DEA agents in the Mexico City embassy in early 2004. They said they were ecstatic with the Fox administration. An agent told me:

"Compared to the bad old days of Kiki Camarena, it is night and day. Mexico has really turned the corner in the fight against drug gangs. This country has a great future ahead."

And then the war started.

It began small, in the midsize border city of Nuevo Laredo, in the fall of 2004. Most media reports fudge this point to say that the Mexican Drug War started when Felipe Calderón took office in December 2006. That makes easy shorthand. While such simplifications help get the broad picture across, they can also create some dangerous misconceptions— namely that this war is entirely tied to the Calderón administration, and when he leaves office, it will magically disappear. The truth is that the conflict began before Calderón and will likely rage on after him.

Few saw the significance of the Nuevo Laredo turf war. But the conflict brought in a series of unprecedented tactics: the use of paramilitary hit squads; widespread attacks on police; and mass kidnappings. These tactics would spread across Mexico on a frightening scale, defining the way the conflict was fought.

At the heart of the Nuevo Laredo battle was Mexico's most bloodthirsty gang, the Zetas. The former special-force soldiers militarized the conflict, turning it from a "war on drugs" to a "drug war." Suddenly, the public saw captured criminals in combat fatigues with heavy weaponry. Where had these militias sprung from? To understand how the Zetas emerged, we need to shine a light on the radical evolution of drug trafficking in the Nuevo Laredo region.

* * *

Northeast Mexico has been a corridor for contraband since the days of Prohibition, when an enterprising criminal called Juan Nepomuceno bootlegged booze.[8] As Nepomuceno's crime syndicate transformed into the Gulf Cartel, the area known as the "little border" grew in strategic importance, aided by the rapid expansion of the American cities of Dallas and Houston. No huge metropolises were on the Mexican side of the little border, unlike upriver with Juárez. But more actual cargo flowed over. By 2004, Nuevo Laredo alone—with just 307,000 residents—saw $90 billion worth of legitimate goods heading north annually. That was more than double the $43 billion that went through sprawling Ciudad Juárez, and four times the $22 billion that went through Tijuana.

This volume of cargo meant ten thousand trucks and two thousand railcars passed through Nuevo Laredo daily. On the American side, Laredo opened straight into the I-35 highway speeding to Dallas. Drugs moved amid the vast volume of cargo and quickly shifted around Texas, then into the rest of the South and the Eastern seaboard. Laredo was a trafficking fire hose. And it was the only part of the border not controlled by Sinaloans.

By 1997, balding former car thief Osiel Cárdenas had murdered his way to the top of the Gulf Cartel. Cárdenas earned the nickname Mata amigos, or friend killer, for his Machiavellian moves to sieze power, stabbing his allies in the back. To secure himself as head honcho on the little border, Cárdenas had the notion of creating a special militia that would be more fearsome than any thugs that might come after him. He had seen the Arellano Félix brothers import Chicano gangbangers for their narco muscle. But he wanted to raise the stakes. So he turned to the Mexican army itself.

Cárdenas befriended a special forces commander called Arturo Guzmán Decena, who had been sent to Tamaulipas to clamp down on drug gangs. By all accounts, Guzmán was a talented and aggressive officer. A photo of him as a young enlistee shows him broad-shouldered, clean-shaven, and in trim shape, his right hand pinned to his chest in a Mexican national salute. His eyes stare sharply ahead with military focus, his face hinting at a certain innocence of youth. But something happened to convert this fresh recruit into a cold narco killer code-named Z-1.

Arturo Guzmán hailed from a humble village in Puebla, southern Mexico, and joined the military to escape poverty. His background is typical of the Mexican army. The corps is not controlled by adventuring upper-class officers like the British brass; nor is it an ideological right-wing brigade such as the Spanish; rather it is army of country boys from the poor south.

One of the best and brightest of recruits, Guzmán joined the elite Airmobile Special Forces Group or GAFE, the equivalent of the Green Berets. In the tradition of special forces, officers pushed recruits to their limits and instilled in them a die-hard attitude. The unit's motto: "Not even death will stop us, and if it surprises us, then it is welcome." Elite units from round the world provided GAFE training. Crack troops learned skills from the Israeli Defense Forces, whose experiences in Lebanon and the West Bank made them some of the best soldiers in urban combat. But the biggest influence on the GAFE came from closer to home, from American men of war.

The United States schooled Latin American soldiers throughout the late-twentieth century in warfare and anti-insurgency tactics at the infamous School of the Americas in Georgia and at Fort Bragg, North Carolina. When the manuals given to Latin American students were declassified in 1996, they sparked outrage. Printed only in Spanish, the instruction books explained the use of psychological warfare to break insurgencies. One particularly controversial manual entitled *Handling Sources* instructs Latin American officers on how to use informants. In cold, clinical terms, it details pressuring informants with violence against both them and their families. As it says on page 79:

"The Counter Insurgency agent could cause the arrest of the employee's [informant's] parents, imprison the employee or give him a beating as part of the placement plan of the said employee in the guerrilla organization."[9]

Back in Mexico, Guzmán and his comrades put their training into practice when the Zapatista uprising surprised the world in 1994. Led by the pipe-smoking revolutionary Subcomandante Marcos, some three thousand Zapatista rebels siezed town halls in the impoverished southern state of Chiapas. The insurrection was a largely symbolic protest against poverty and one-party rule; the rebels were poor, indigenous Mayans armed with old shotguns and .22-caliber rifles, and they beat a hasty retreat back into the jungle as soon as the army approached. But however hollow the military threat, the Mexican government was keen to hit back hard and flew in GAFE to hunt down Zapatistas.

Strike teams caught up with Zapatista rebels as they retreated through the ramshackle town of Ocosingo on the edge of the jungle. Within hours, thirty-four rebels lay dead. Subcomandante Marcos claimed in a communiqué that those killed had surrendered and been summarily executed, although the military insists they died fighting. The following day, soldiers captured three more rebels in the nearby community of Las Margaritas. Their corpses were dumped on a riverbank, their ears and noses sliced from their faces. The bloodshed shook the rebel movement, and Marcos was quick to sign a cease-fire twelve days after his rebellion began. From then on, Zapatistas turned to nonviolent protest, although they still maintained a small guerrilla army deep in the jungle.[10]

Now a highly trained and bloodied soldier, the rising star Guzmán transferred to the little border. Here, garish narco mansions stood on dirt streets hosting rowdy, all-night parties, and thousands of prostitutes danced in sprawling red-light zones. For the young officer who had spent his youth tramping around muddy jungles, it was a stunning change.

Investigators say Guzmán first worked with Cárdenas by taking bribes to turn the other cheek on Gulf Cartel drugloads. Such payoffs were typical. But while soldiers had long skimmed the profits of traffickers, it was unthinkable that they should actually defect to join them. Officers still saw themselves as protectors of the republic, who would no more easily join the narcos than a U.S. soldier would join insurgents in Iraq. Bribes were simply seen by soldiers as benefits of their job. But Guzmán shattered this model. He left the barracks for the last time and was reborn as a narco mercenary.

So what drove Guzmán to make this dramatic career move? It has been explained that he was tempted by the glitter of gold, seeing ostentatious gangsters earn more in a year than many professional soldiers in a lifetime. But he could also live well as a rising star in the army. By joining the cartel, he would become a fugitive who risked eventual death or imprisonment.

A crucial factor in his defection may have been the seismic change that was tearing the old order apart. The move to democracy made many in the army nervous about their place in the new Mexico. Badge-wearing officers were especially worried by demands to clean up abuses of the old regime. Families of the "disappeared" marched daily in the capital, and several officers were court-martialed for human rights abuses or drug corruption. As a judge sentenced General Gutiérrez Rebollo to fifty years in prison for taking narco bribes, all the army was watching. Amid this turmoil, Officer Guzmán decided he was better off outside the system.

When Osiel Cárdenas hired Guzmán, he didn't want just another gunslinger. Cárdenas asked his recruit to set up the most ferocious hit squad possible. A schemer, Cárdenas certainly had the imagination to envision an army-trained band of enforcers. But much of the initiative toward a full-fledged paramilitary likely came from Guzmán himself. Mexican federal agents later released a conversation they say an informant relayed to them about setting up the new unit:

Cárdenas: "I want the best men. The best."
Guzmán: "What type of people do you need?"
Cárdenas: "The best armed men that there are."
Guzmán: "These are only in the army."
Cárdenas: "I want them."[11]

Following orders, Guzmán recruited dozens of crack soldiers. Some media reports have described the formation of the Zetas as a mass defection of a single army unit. But military records show this is inaccurate. Soldiers left their barracks to work with Guzmán over some months and were from several units, including the Seventieth Infantry Battalion and Fifteenth Regiment of Motorized Cavalry. However, members of the GAFE special forces certainly made up a good number of the founding militia, which named itself the Zetas after a radio signal the GAFE used. Members were all given a Z code, starting with Guzmán as Z-1. Within months, Z-1 commanded thirty-eight former soldiers.

Backed by his new militia, Osiel Cárdenas felt more powerful than ever. This heady arrogance led him to a mistake that caused his downfall: threatening American officials. The agents—one from the DEA and one from the FBI—were driving through Matamoros in November 1999 with an informer pointing out narco real estate. Realizing they were being followed, they sped up in their car, which had consular plates, but were blocked in by a caravan of eight SUVs and trucks. About fifteen men, including several Zetas, poured out and surrounded their vehicle, training Kalashnikov rifles at them. Cárdenas himself then came out of the crowd and demanded the agents hand over their informer. The Americans refused, pleading with Cárdenas that he would never get away with killing

U.S. agents. According to the agents' testimonies, a furious Cárdenas shouted back, "You gringos. This is my territory. You can't control it. So get the hell out of here!"[12]

The agents drove straight to the U.S. border and got home unscathed. In March 2000, a federal grand jury in Brownsville indicted Cárdenas for assaulting the agents and on drug-trafficking charges, and the DEA put a $2 million bounty on his head. When Vicente Fox took power, Americans had Osiel Cárdenas at the top of the list of gangsters they wanted nailed.

However, unlike the old-school capos, Cárdenas refused to negotiate surrender. Instead, he called on his Zetas militia to protect his freedom through strength of arms. Cárdenas felt he could take the government on rather than submit to arrest—and became the first narco insurgent. The modus operandi that had regulated the Mexican drug trade for decades was dead, opening the curtains for the coming war.

The Zetas recruited more soldiers as well as former police and gang members to fill their ranks. Pitched battles between soldiers and Zetas burst out on the streets of Tamaulipas. Rattled by this resistance, the army sent in reinforcements to nab Cárdenas and encouraged them to shoot first and ask questions later. These gloves-off tactics succeeded in taking out Z-1. Guzmán was eating at a seafood restaurant with some of his entourage in November 2002. Soldiers burst through the door with guns blazing, and Arturo Guzmán was shot before he had a chance to respond. In total, fifty bullets hit Z-1 across his head, torso, arms, and legs. The promising young officer and founder of the first Mexican cartel paramilitary lay full of lead on a restaurant floor.

Soldiers then tracked Osiel Cárdenas himself to a safe house in March 2003. This time his Zeta bodyguards had a chance to shoot back, unloading thousands of rounds and fragmentation grenades at the besieging troops. But the gangsters were hopelessly outnumbered and surrounded on all sides. After half an hour, soldiers stormed through the door and seized the kingpin. The Zetas still didn't give up, with reinforcements launching attacks to try to free their commander in chief. Troops fought their way to the airport and flew Cárdenas to Mexico City. The arrest was radically different from the days when police would take capos down peacefully in restaurants. It became the new standard.

Osiel Cárdenas in handcuffs made a gleaming trophy for President Fox. But the implications of the Zetas were little understood. Most journalists saw them as an obscure drug gang, albeit with an exotic story. Rival traffickers also failed to see the threat that the militia posed. On the contrary, with Z-1 dead and Cárdenas in jail, the Sinaloan mob thought the Gulf Cartel was finished and moved in on its territory.

The Sinaloan mafia convened a narco summit to plan the expansion. Details of this landmark meeting have come from a trafficker turned protected witness who sat in on the get-together.[13] According to his account, Sinaloan mobsters, including the prison escapee Chapo Guzmán and "the Beard" Beltrán Leyva, sat down to discuss their plan of domination. Sinaloans already controlled the border from Juárez to the Pacific, they said. Now the mafia could take over the lucrative routes into East Texas. Who were the hicks of northeast Mexico to withstand them? Sinaloan gangbangers rolled into the northeast claiming the territory. The first phase of the Mexican Drug War pitted the might of the Sinaloa Cartel against the insurgent Zetas.

In 2004, just before the turf war broke out, I got a job covering Mexico for the *Houston Chronicle*. The Texan editor generously didn't mind working with a reporter with a daft British accent. I could always e-mail him if he didn't understand my slur. All I had to do was learn what Bubba, the typical Texan, liked and didn't like. "Bubba doesn't like the word *bourgeois*. Use a shorter one," he would say. I started writing on Mexico's transfer to democracy. Then corpses piled up on the Mexican side of the Texas border—soon there were twenty, then fifty, then a hundred murders. I was flown up to Nuevo Laredo. Bubba wanted to know what the hell was going on.

As the death toll rose into 2005, the three big Texan newspapers—the *Houston Chronicle, Dallas Morning News*, and *San Antonio Express*—all made splashes on the story. Suddenly, we were fighting a good old-fashioned newspaper battle for coverage. "Get up there and cover it like a war!" my editor screamed. I thought he was exaggerating. But in hindsight, we were at the front end of a conflict with serious implications.

I had the luck of working with two veterans who were some of the finest reporters the *Chronicle* ever had: Dudley Althaus and Jim Pinkerton. But even so, on the ground in Nuevo Laredo, I struggled to make sense of the turf war. It was frustratingly hard to get real information: police, prosecutors, the mayor, all spun suspect lines. So I tried different ways to get into the story. I had known plenty of degenerate drug addicts back home; surely, I could find some on the border who had an idea what was playing out. I trawled round drug rehabs, street corners, and cantinas. Sure enough, I soon found petty dealers and smugglers who described the battle from below.

I got close to a twenty-eight-year-old called Rolando. He was the wiry youngest of ten children born of a local police commander. Rolando had smuggled marijuana into the United States and served time in a Texas penitentiary, where he learned to speak perfect English. He also had two bad drug addictions: to heroin and to crack. We would sit in a small room of his friend's house, and he would inject heroin, then smoke a rock of crack straight after. I never understood why people got high and low at the same time. But Rolando seemed to function fine when on both and would ramble away about family, philosophy, or anything else that came up for discussion.

Rolando earned his living in Nuevo Laredo's red-light zone, known as Boys Town, a walled-off area of four blocks with wide dirt streets and lines of brothels and strip bars. As the story goes, Boys Town was first set up by American general John Pershing to keep all his whoring soldiers in one place. A century later, American truck drivers and teenage Texans looking to lose their virginity visited this den of sin. Rolando would use his English to guide these johns to the best bars and hook them up with the prettiest ladies in exchange for tips. He spent most of his money on drugs. But he also kept a girlfriend, who worked as a stripper. One day he had just discovered his girl was pregnant; we celebrated by drinking beer and listening to a jukebox in a grimy Boys Town cantina. The next time I saw him, he told me she had lost the baby. I watched him take his usual dose of crack and heroin to commemorate.

I went with Rolando when he brought his dope, both from dealers inside Boys Town or from *tienditas* in barrios. Back when he was growing up, he explained, people just sold drugs and kept the money. But now all the dealers had to pay their tax to the Zetas. He carefully pointed out Zetas operatives hanging around Boys Town. These well-built men stood close to the doors of nightclubs, chatting into cell phones or eyeing the street. Boys Town, like all Nuevo Laredo, was their turf.

When Sinaloans rolled into town, Rolando explained, they had also tried to tax dealers and smugglers. Some local thugs thought this was a good thing. The Zetas were a repressive mob. Perhaps they would be better off with new bosses. They helped the outsiders set up safe houses and get their paws into the city. Others were loyal to the Zetas and pointed a finger at anyone passing information to the invaders. People caught working with the wrong team were kidnapped, tortured, and thrown dead onto the street. A turf war is a filthy business.

The Sinaloans seriously underestimated their rivals. Many of the Sinaloans' recruits were thugs from the Mara Salvatrucha gangs of El Salvador and Honduras. The gangbangers had a fearsome reputation. But they were no match for the heavily armed and organized Zetas. Five cadavers of these Central American recruits, their arms and shoulders revealing MS tatooes, were thrown on the floor of a Nuevo Laredo safe house. A note lay next to the corpses, scrawled in the messy handwriting of narco assassins. "Chapo Guzmán and Beltrán Leyva. Send more *pendejos* like this for us to kill," it said. *Pendejos* is a Mexican swear word that literally means "pubic hairs." The Zetas were applying their military tactics, striking terror onto the Mexican street. Soon every gang in the country would be doing the same thing.[14]

President Fox ordered seven hundred soldiers and federal police into Nuevo Laredo to quell the violence. He called the offensive Operación México Seguro or Operation Secure Mexico, a campaign that Fox later incorporated into his antidrug efforts across the whole country. Nuevo Laredo was a laboratory for government strategy as well as cartel tactics.

Federal troops swiftly rounded up Zetas hit squads, lining up one group of seventeen gangster soldiers so the press could snap photos. This was meant to humiliate them, to show the government was on top. But it had the opposite effect. The thugs flashed across Mexican televisions, standing straight-backed and staring hard in front of automatic rifles, flak jackets, and radios. It let everyone know the Zetas were a gang to be feared.

Taking leadership of the Zetas was Heriberto Lazcano, or Z-3, known by his chilling nickname the Executioner. Hailing from the rural state of Hidalgo,[15] the muscular, thick-necked Lazcano shared a peasant background with his friend and mentor Guzmán, Z-1. Lazcano also joined the army as a teenager and gained promotion to the special forces. When Guzmán defected, the loyal Lazcano was quick to follow. However, Lazcano, who took control of the Zetas at age twenty-eight, proved he was more bloodthirsty than his teacher.

Guards at a penitentiary in Matamoros refused to smuggle in luxuries to some Zetas prisoners. So Lazcano applied pressure. One night, as six prison workers finished a late shift, waiting Zetas abducted them one by one. Hours later, a horrified guard at the prison gates found the bodies of the six employees in a Ford Explorer. They had been blindfolded, handcuffed, and shot in the head. The Zetas were showing a new approach for dealing with authorities. Police had once bullied criminals into paying up. Now the worm had turned.

One man in Nuevo Laredo willing to speak out against such terror was the head of the chamber of commerce, Alejandro Dominguez. I chatted with him in his office downtown, a few streets away from souvenir vendors and tequila bars long frequented by Texans. He was tall with a shock of silver hair and an affable manner. He argued the violence was oppressing residents, who needed to reclaim the city:

"The bloodshed takes away our freedom. It makes people too scared to walk on their own streets at night. But people have to take back those streets. They have to take back their parks. We cannot just hand the city over to criminals."

Six weeks later, the mayor named Dominguez as head of the Nuevo Laredo police force. He took the oath of office in a public ceremony, lifting his right hand above his chest and promising to protect and serve. A local journalist asked him if he was afraid of dying. He replied sternly, "I believe the corrupt officials are the ones who are scared. The only people I work for are the public."

That evening, Dominguez went to his downtown office, where I had interviewed him. Around seven o clock, he closed up and walked to his sports utility vehicle. Two gunmen opened fire, shooting forty bullets into his body. He had lasted just six hours in the job of city police chief. The assassination made international headlines, one of the first times the emerging drug war gained attention.[16]

Assassins started ambushing policemen all over Nuevo Laredo. Then federal and city police started shooting at each other. The rot in the Mexican state was rising to the surface.

I got a call about a firefight on a Saturday morning while I was having breakfast in my hotel. Rushing to the scene, I found a federal agent bleeding on a stretcher. He had been driving from the airport with other agents when city police stopped them and demanded to search their vehicles. First they argued, then broke into a fistfight, then started shooting. The federal agent survived various bullet wounds.

The next day, federal agents and soldiers swept on the city police station and arrested the entire force of seven hundred officers. Federal troops then stormed a safe house and found a horrific sight—forty-four prisoners bound, gagged, and bleeding. The prisoners said that city police had arrested them, then handed them over as captives of the dreaded Zetas.

Evidence of police working for the insurgent Zetas was startling, but would soon become depressingly typical in Mexico. Time and time again, federal troops rolled into cities and accused local police of being deeply entwined with gangsters. Officers no longer just turned a blind eye on smuggling, but worked as kidnappers and assassins in their own right, a grave fragmentation of the state. To aggravate this problem, many federal officers were also found working for gangsters, normally different factions of the Sinaloa Cartel. So as federal troops rounded up Zetas, observers asked whom they were serving: the public or Sinaloan capos?

These revelations underline a central problem in the Mexican Drug War. The PRI years featured a delicate dance of corruption; in the democratic years, it turned to a corrupt dance of death. In the old days, police officers were rotten, but at least they worked together. In democracy, police work for competing mafias and actively fight each other. Gangsters target both good police who get in their way and bad police who work for their rivals. For policy makers it becomes a Gordian knot.

Added to this thorny issue of corruption is a more fundamental problem of drug-law enforcement. Every time you arrest one trafficker, you are helping his rival. In this way, when the federal police stormed Zetas safe houses, they were scoring victories for Sinaloans, whether they liked it or not. Arrests did not subdue violence, but only inflamed it.

The Nuevo Laredo turf war raged on through a long, hot, bloody summer in 2005. That fall, violence spread to other parts of Mexico. While they were still battling for their own turf, Zetas expanded into many areas traditionally controlled by the Sinaloan mafia. The best form of defense is attack.

To beef up their army, they swelled their ranks with new recruits. Their bloody reputation helped them. Thousands of young thugs realized the name *Zetas* meant power and were keen to join the baddest team. But to encourage them, the Executioner audaciously put out job ads, which his men wrote on blankets and hung on bridges.

"The Zetas operations group wants you, soldier or ex-soldier," one banner said. "We offer you a good salary, food, and attention for your family. Don't suffer hunger and abuse anymore." Another said, "Join the ranks of the Gulf Cartel. We offer benefits, life insurance, a house for your family and children. Stop living in the slums and riding the bus. A new car or truck, your choice."

The Zetas also went abroad for talented killers. They found the most eager mercenaries in Guatemala, former members of the crack Kaibil commandos that tore through rebel villages in the nation's civil war. The hardened Kaibiles made the Mexican special forces look like Boy Scouts. With their motto, "If I retreat, kill me," they were trained to cut bullets out of their own bodies in combat. While the Mexican army killed hundreds of leftist insurgents, the Kaibiles massacred tens of thousands of rebels and their entire families.

The Gulf Cartel spent millions of drug dollars to finance the rapid growth of the Zetas. But to make the expansion more profitable, Zetas units generated their own income. Thugs with large arsenals of guns had a quick way of getting cash: extortion. At first, they taxed anyone in the drug business, including marijuana growers and street dealers. Later, they branched out to shake down anything in sight.

Efrain Bautsista, who grew marijuana for many years in the southern Sierra Madre, saw the changes in his old community. Although Efrain left the mountains for Mexico City in the early 1980s, he would go back to visit his family and had cousins and nephews still growing marijuana in the fields near Teloloapan in Guerrero state. He describes the entrance of the Zetas:

"There had never been fighting over marijuana in Teloloapan. If you wanted to grow *mota*, you just grew it and sold it in the town to smugglers. That is the way it had always been since back in the 1960s when we first started growing.

"Then these Zetas appeared and said that anyone who grew marijuana had to pay them. People in my part of the mountains are rough, and a lot of them told these men to fuck themselves. And then bodies started appearing on the streets. And people started paying up."

When police arrested regional Zetas soliders, they found many were local men who had enlisted with the northeastern mob. Mexican intelligence agents explain that Zetas cells are akin to franchises. As with McDonald's, local recruits get training and the best brand name in the business. Then a local leader, whom the Zetas called a second commander, can run his own outlet as long as he kicks back the payments to HQ. Paramilitary squads that sprung up in Colombia in the 1990s operated with a similar degree of local autonomy.

The new Zetas cells clashed with Sinaloans and their affiliates across Mexico. Suddenly violence hit the seaside resort of Acapulco; then bodies piled up in neighboring Michoacán state; then a convoy of Zetas drove hundreds of miles and carried out a massacre in Sonora state. As the war intensified, so did tactics. Decapitation was almost unheard of in modern Mexico. But in April 2006, the craniums of two Acapulco policemen were dumped by the town hall. The police officers had shot dead four thugs in a prolonged firefight, and the gangsters wanted to teach them a special lesson.

It is still unclear exactly what inspired such brutality. Many point to the influence of the Guatemalan Kaibiles working in the Zetas. In the Guatemalan civil war, troops cut off heads of captured rebels in front of villagers to terrify them from joining a leftist insurgency. Turning into mercenaries in Mexico, the Kaibiles might have reprised their trusted tactic to terrify enemies of the cartel. Others point to the influence of Al Qaeda decapitation videos from the Middle East, which were shown in full on some Mexican TV channels. Some anthropologists even point to the pre-Colombian use of beheadings and the way Mayans used them to show complete domination of their enemies.

The Zetas were not thinking like gangsters, but like a paramilitary group controlling territory. Their new way of fighting rapidly spread through the Mexican Drug War. In September the same year, La Familia gang—working with the Zetas in Michoacán state—rolled five human heads onto a disco dance floor. By the end of 2006, there had been dozens of decapitations. Over the next years, there were hundreds.

Gangsters throughout Mexico also copied the Zetas' paramilitary way of organizing. Sinaloans created their own cells of combatants with heavy weaponry and combat fatigues. They had to fight fire with fire. "The Beard" Beltrán Leyva led particularly well-armed death squads. One was later busted in a residential house in Mexico City. They had twenty automatic rifles, ten pistols, twelve M4 grenade launchers, and flak jackets that even had their own logo—FEDA—an acronym for Fuerzas Especiales de Arturo, or Arturo's Special Forces.

*   *   *

As corpses piled up from the border to beach resorts, reporters ran out to every scene of an execution-style killing or dumped body. The Mexican government had long been guarded about giving out homicide numbers. But the aggressive newspapers tallied up the killings and printed them in rather sanguine "execution meters." Some regional tabloids decorated these counts with graphics like sports scorecards. The tallies caught flak for being dehumanizing. But they served as the first crucial barometer of the violence. In 2005, fifteen hundred murders bore the hallmarks of organized crime across the country. In 2006, there were two thousand.

The rising death toll sparked concern. But on an international level, the conflict grabbed little attention, still being viewed as an internal crime problem, albeit with some juicy stories of bad guys rolling heads. Meanwhile, the foreign press focused on Mexico's first presidential election since the PRI had fallen—and how President Fox would pass the torch. By law, Fox was not allowed to stand for a second term.

The contest had promise as a great example of free franchise in action; it turned into a gripping two-horse race between conservative Felipe Calderón of Fox's National Action Party and the silver-haired Andrés Manuel López Obrador of the leftist Democratic Revolution Party. However, smears and political chicanery soured the contest and shook Mexico's young democracy.

López Obrador was a charismatic political animal with an extraordinary gift for public speaking, stirring up crowds with tirades against the unjust Mexico in which the poor toiled and the rich robbed. The establishment threw everything at him, including hidden videos of his aides taking bribes. But he just wouldn't go down. In a final attempt to shut López Obrador up, prosecutors charged him over an obscure land dispute, a case that would keep him off the ballot. It was clearly a political persecution. The feisty leftist rallied hundreds of thousands in protest, and editorials in London and Washington accused Fox of sabotaging Mexico's democracy. Realizing his very legacy was at risk, Fox fired his attorney general and dropped the charges.

The case had collapsed. But it left a terrible scar. In the next years, every politician accused of a crime said it was a political persecution. This made the job of cleaning up Mexico's rotten establishment that much harder. The left were right to defend López Obrador. But later, they rallied around politicians facing credible charges of working with the mafia. With police seen as a political tool, public confidence in the justice system plummeted.

As the presidential election approached, tensions reached fever pitch. López Obrador said the establishment was a gang of mafia capitalists. Calderón hit back by painting López Obrador as a mad, messianic populist who would plunge Mexico into crisis. His catchy slogan: "López Obrador—a Danger for Mexico." It was extremely effective in frightening a nation that had stumbled through crisis after crisis.

In the official count, Calderón won by 0.6 percent of the vote, making it the closest race in the nation's history. López Obrador shouted that the vote was rigged and set up protest camps in the capital. Meanwhile, in the southern state of Oaxaca, a teachers' strike transformed into an unarmed insurrection against the unpopular PRI governor. That crisis boiled on for five months, in which protesters burned buses and built barricades, and political violence killed at least fifteen people—mainly leftist demonstrators. After the murder of American Indymedia journalist Brad Will,[17] Fox finally sent in four thousand federal police to take Oaxaca city. To Calderón, Mexico looked a chaotic place. When he was sworn into power in December, the former lawyer was determined to restore order.

Leaving office, Fox retired to his ranch and carried on making frank comments to reporters. His presidency had seen the start of the Mexican Drug War. However, it is unfair to blame Fox for this (as some have). Fox dutifully followed the difficult law enforcement approach to drug cartels encouraged by the United States. Few foresaw that Mexico was on the edge of the abyss in 2006.

In an interesting footnote, Fox converted to the cause of drug legalization. "Legalizing in this sense does not mean drugs are good and don't harm those who consume them," he wrote from his ranch in 2010. "Rather we should look at it as a strategy to strike at and break the economic structure that allows gangs to generate huge profits in their trade, which feeds corruption and increases their areas of power."[18] The man whose "mother of all battles" was cheered by American agents had decided the fight was futile.

CHAPTER 7

Warlords

We have scorched the snake, not killed it.
She'll close and be herself whilst our poor malice
Remains in danger of her former tooth . . .
Ere we will eat our meal in fear, and sleep
In the affliction of these terrible dreams
That shake us nightly. Better be with the dead,
Whom we, to gain our peace, have sent to peace.
—*MACBETH*, WILLIAM SHAKESPEARE, CIRCA 1603

On December 1, 2006, federal deputies were brawling in Mexico's Congress hours before Felipe Calderón was due to enter the chamber to be sworn in as president. It was a fight for space. The leftist deputies claimed their candidate, Andrés Manuel López Obrador, had really won the election but been robbed of his rightful victory. They were trying to gain control of the podium to stop Calderón from taking the oath and assuming office. The conservative deputies were defending the podium to allow the presidential accession. The conservatives won the scrap. There were more of them, and they seemed to be better fed.

Among those attending the ceremony were former U.S. president George Bush (Bush the First) and California governor Arnold Schwarzenegger. I was covering the Congress door, snatching interviews as guests went in. The elderly Bush hobbled past with six bodyguards with bald heads and microphones at their mouths. I asked him what he thought about the ruckus in the chamber. "Well, I hope that Mexicans can resolve their differences," he replied diplomatically. Schwarzenegger strolled past with no bodyguards at all. I asked what he thought about the fisticuffs. The Terminator turned round, stared intensely, and uttered three words:

"It's good action!"

I phoned the quote back to headquarters and it went out on a wire story. Suddenly, Schwarznegger's statement was being bounced around California TV stations. Then the BBC led their newscast with it: "It takes a lot to impress Arnold Schwarznegger but today when he was in Mexico . . ." I got frantic phone calls from the governor's office in Los Angeles. Was his quote perhaps being used out of context? Well, I replied, I asked him straight and he told me straight.

For President Calderón, all this good action made a very testing first day on the job. He had to sneak into the chamber by the back door, rapidly get sworn into office while his deputies fought off leftists, then speed out again, defended by police in riot gear. However, he pulled it all off. With that he rapidly defused a complicated situation and killed any argument that he had not taken the proper vow of office. In a chaotic Mexico, he seemed like a man of decisiveness and action.

Ten days later, Calderon declared war on drug cartels. Wow, thought the public again. Here is a man of decisiveness and action.

Four years on, knowing that Calderón's war would lead to thirty-five thousand murders, car bombs, grenade attacks on revelers, scores of political assassinations, a single massacre of seventy-two people, and an endless list of other atrocities, the president's decision to attack cartels seems an earthshaking moment. Everyone figures that he must have had a grand plan. But it is so easy to read history backward. At the time, Calderon probably had no intention of still battling on with his offensive four years later, and he certainly didn't calculate on the country blowing up in his face. Like his pushing onto the Congress podium, his declaration of war was a reaction to events and a showing of strength and decisiveness. And like the swearing in, he hoped he would quickly resolve a messy situation. With the former, his bet was spot-on. But with the drug war, he seriously miscalculated.

*　*　*

Calderón is from the same conservative National Action Party as Vicente Fox, but they have little else in common. While Fox entered politics in middle age, Calderón was born into it. His father, Luis Calderón,
was a militant Roman Catholic who joined the Cristero rebellion in the
late 1920s to defend the Church against the repression of revolutionary
generals. The Cristero War claimed the lives of ninety thousand people
in three years, marking it as the last major conflict in Mexico before the
current drug war. It finished with a truce: Catholics could pray uninhib-
ited while the government would still be secular. In 1939, Luis Calderón
cofounded the National Action Party as a political force to fight for godly
values. The senior Calderón believed in a political Catholicism that demanded social justice as well as faith, a third line between the atheist
socialism and Protestant capitalism of the era.

With the PRI cheating National Action politicians out of office, Luis
Calderón brought up his children in a middle-class home in stark contrast to the vast haciendas of ruling-party stalwarts. The president described it as an intensely political environment, and four of five children
went into politics for the rising PAN. "My home was often a campaign
headquarters. We folded printed leaflets in what we called the 'paper train.'
In the kitchen we cooked up flour glue in big saucepans. My brothers
and I went out at night to put up the propaganda."[1]

Felipe Calderón, the youngest, won a scholarship to a Marist Catholic
school before studying law at a private university, then doing a master's
in economics and finally a second master's in public administration at
Harvard. Such an extensive education made him well qualified to be a
Latin American technocrat. He went into politics full-time at twenty-six,
became a federal deputy, PAN president, energy secretary, and was finally elected to the top job at the ripe age of forty-three.

Felipe Calderón's politics differed markedly from his father's in that
he largely kept his Catholicism private. As they climbed to power, National Action politicians decided they didn't want to appear like religious
zealots and focused on promoting free-market economic policies. Mexico's leftists unfairly accuse the PAN of being extreme right-wing fascists.
The PAN deny this, claiming to be centrists, and accuse the leftists of
being raving populists. Calderón spent his election campaign tarring
López Obrador as a messianic lunatic who would plunge the country
into crisis.

Calderón was little known to the public before the election, so there
was no track record for opponents to attack. Rivals turned to the oldest

slagging point in the book: physical appearance. Calderon is short, balding, and bespectacled. In the first presidential debate, PRI candidate Roberto Madrazo turned round to him and waved his hand in the air, signaling a low height. "You can't stand up to me," Madrazo smirked, "because you don't have the stature."[2]

The president's squat appearance soon became the central joke of political cartoonists. The short Calderón was shown struggling into an army uniform, trying desperately to look tough; he was drawn sitting in a tank, fighting to look over the steering wheel; and he was later depicted dwarfed by the tall gringo President Obama, who patted him on the head. The more he made tough war talk, the more cartoonists played on the joke. He was depicted as a little man going to battle—like other stumpy warmongers who have dotted history.

The declaration of war was made on December 11 by Calderón's new security cabinet, including the defense minister, attorney general, and public safety secretary. The first strike would be in Calderón's native state of Michoacán, where the Zetas-affiliated gang La Familia had left trails of headless corpses. Operation Michoacán, the team announced, would involve sixty-five hundred ground troops backed by helicopters and navy gunboats. The ministers threw around the phrase "reconquering territory" a lot. That was a key message of Calderón's campaign that was echoed again and again, a thrust to take back parts of Mexico where gangsters had got too strong. "It's about recovering the calm day-to-day life of Mexicans," Calderón said.[3]

I rushed with other reporters to follow troops into the battle, driving past the lush lakes of Michoacán and up to roughneck drug-producing communities in the mountains. The offensive certainly looked good. Long lines of military Humvees and jeeps full of masked federal police could be seen pouring down highways. In the hill town of Aguililla, long known as a hotbed of traffickers, pumped-up soldiers flooded streets, tossing pickup trucks and kicking down doors while helicopters buzzed relentlessly above. These images were flashed across the nation on daily newscasts. Here was a president who meant business, people remarked. The government was flexing its muscles.

Calderón rapidly spread the offensive to different states. Seven thousand troops rolled into the seaside resort of Acapulco, thirty-three hundred federal police and soldiers marched into Tijuana, six thousand more scoured the Sierra Madre. Soon, some fifty thousand men—including almost the entire federal police force and a substantial part of the effective military—were pulled into the war on drugs across half a dozen states.

Another early move was the mass extradition of kingpins. Just over a month into Calderón's presidency, a plane left Mexico City for Houston, Texas, with fifteen traffickers shackled and guarded by masked *federales*. Among them were the top American targets of Osiel Cárdenas, head of the Gulf Cartel, and Hector "Whitey" Palma of the Sinaloa cartel. It was another big action that flashed across TV screens and made a big point.

Calderon flew into a military base in Michoacán. Breaking tradition, he donned a soldier's cap and olive-green army jacket to salute the troops. Mexican presidents have shied away from wearing military colors since PRI civilian politicians took over from revolutionary generals in the 1940s. The photos of Calderón at the base became iconic Mexican political images—the president with his right hand raised and cap down to his spectacles, dwarfed by his muscular defense secretary. To make sure troops were on his side, Calderon pushed a pay hike for them through Congress and praised them as heroes of the republic at every opportunity. As he told the soldiers at Mexico's number one military base two months into his presidency:

"New pages of glory will be written. I instruct you to persevere until victory is achieved . . . We are not going to surrender, neither from provocation nor attacks on the safety of Mexicans. We will give no truce or quarter to the enemies of Mexico."[4]

It was certainly tough talk. But how different was Calderón's offensive from policies of the Fox administration? As the war dragged on, Calderón argued again and again that he had opened a new chapter. Previous presidents had let El Narco grow into a monster, he claimed, while he was the first to take it on. If there was violence, he retorted, that was the fault of those before him.

But in many ways, the differences between Calderón's and Fox's approaches to the drug war were more about style and scale rather than substance. Fox also sent soldiers to fight drug gangs, achieved major busts, and broke records for extraditions. Calderón's most novel actions were to increase military presence in urban areas and boost publicity for all his antidrug efforts. And he accompanied the blows with a much more confrontational rhetoric: it was a struggle of good against bad, he said; a fight against enemies of the nation; a battle in which you are with us or against us. His style made it all very much his war. He was bound to the fight.

Calderón had learned from the lessons of Nixon and Reagan that a drug war was good politics. Upon taking power, both those American presidents tuned up the rhetoric and made spectacular mobilizations, and voters loved them for it. Calderón also had the precedent of Operation Condor in the 1970s. In that offensive, the Mexican government beat the hell out of narcos for a year and they got into line. Calderón likely imagined it would be a short and swift campaign, a mistake common to so many drawn-out conflicts. British troops sailing out to the First World War were promised they would be home in time for their Christmas turkey.

Like in Operation Condor, Calderón could also use his drug war to send a message out to leftist militants. During the previous six years, Calderón had watched Fox fold his arms as leftist-led movements had embarrassed the government. In the town of San Salvador Atenco, a group protested plans to build an airport, kidnapping police and threatening to kill them until the government backed down; in Oaxaca, protesters seized the state capital for five months; and in Mexico City, López Obrador supporters blocked the center for two months. The leftists argued they were fighting an unjust system that favored the rich and screwed the poor. Calderón sneered at what he considered vestiges of a backward, anarchic Mexico. He wouldn't stand for such nonsense. In his first weeks in office, federal officials arrested a key Oaxaca rebel leader, while a judge handed an Atenco militant a hefty fifty-year sentence. Calderón spoke repeatedly about the need to restore order and reassert the power of the state. This message applied as much to street blockades and riots as drug decapitations.

As always, the American carrot was on offer. Three months into his presidency, Felipe Calderón sat down with U.S. president George W. Bush in the southwestern city of Mérida, and they bashed out the terms of their famous Mérida Initiative of American aid for the war. It was agreed that the United States would pitch in with $1.6 billion worth of hardware and training over three years.[5] The aid included thirteen Bell helicopters, eight Black Hawk helicopters, four transport aircraft, and the latest gamma scanners and phone-tap gear.

The initiative was quickly compared to Plan Colombia, which beefed up the Andean nation to fight cartels and guerrillas. However, there are some key differences. Plan Colombia was more money to a smaller country and helped transform Colombian security forces from the Keystone Kops to a regional power. The Mérida initiative meanwhile only gave about $500 million a year to Mexico, whose combined federal security budget was already $15 billion.[6] Such a sum from the Americans could not drastically change the balance of power. However, advocates argued the Mérida Initiative showed the United States was finally taking responsibility for all the gringo drug takers. Now, it was a U.S.-backed offensive, and whatever Mexican troops did on the ground became American business.

Calderón's offensive soon posted some whopping results in drug busts. Federal agents stormed a Mexico City mansion and nabbed $207 million of alleged meth money. It was the biggest cash bust anywhere in the world ever. In October 2007, Mexican marines broke another record. The troops made a surprise raid on the industrial port of Manzanillo halfway up Mexico's Pacific coastline. Steaming through the harbor, marines stormed a ship called *La Esmeralda*, a container boat with a Hong Kong flag that had traveled from the Colombian port of Buenaventura. The troops inspected the floor but it didn't feel right. So they ripped it open and . . . bingo. Bricks of cocaine were everywhere. It took them three days to count it. In the end they uncovered 23,562 kilo bricks or more than 23.5 metric tons of the white lady, the biggest cocaine bust in history. It was burned in the biggest cocaine bonfire the world has ever seen.

This enormous amount of cocaine is hard to comprehend. To put in more easily imaginable quantities, it is 23 million gram packets of yayo—or about 200 million white lines cut up on 200 million bathroom mirrors. Sold at gram level on the American street, it would be worth about $1.5 billion, and that is before it is cut up with flour. Calderón was earning his reputation as the Eliot Ness of Mexico. And gangsters were getting seriously pissed.

On the Mexican streets, violence raged on in Calderón's first year in office much as it had in Fox's last. The Zetas battled the Sinaloa cartel and its allies in half a dozen states. Both sides increasingly made snuff videos and put beheaded corpses on public display. But the total number of victims was only a little higher than it had been during 2006.

Then in August, some fantastic news arrived: the Zetas and Sinaloa cartel had agreed to a cease-fire. Like so many events in the Mexican

Drug War, the first sign of the truce was a rumor from an unnamed source, in this case a DEA agent. But Mexican officials, including the attorney general, soon corroborated it. And narco Édgar Valdéz, called the Barbie Doll because of his blond hair, later gave a videotaped confession in which he described details of the meeting where the truce was hammered out.[7]

The narco peace summit took place in the northern industrial city of Monterrey between the headquarters of the world's third-largest cement company and Sol beer factories. It is amazing how capos who had been cutting each other's head off could sit down for a nice chat. But business trumps bad blood. The two mafias agreed to stop massacring each other and redraw a map of their turf, the Barbie Doll related. The Gulf Cartel and its Zetas army would keep northeastern Mexico, including the city of Nuevo Laredo, as well as the eastern state of Veracruz; the Sinaloa cartel would keep their old territories including Acapulco and also acquire the Monterrey suburb of San Pedro Garza, the richest municipality in all Mexico. The Beard Beltrán Leyva was made the Sinaloan point man to keep peace with the Zetas.

As 2007 ended, I talked to an upbeat Attorney General Eduardo Medina Mora. Killings had finally gone down in the months following the truce; the year finished with twenty-five hundred drug-related murders. This was higher than 2006, Medina said, but finally the war had swung in the right direction. The government had made record seizures, extradited hot-potato kingpins, and was regaining control, he argued. American drug agents said they were working with the best Mexican president in history, and U.S. Black Hawk helicopters were due to arrive. After his first year in office, Calderón's war looked pretty damn good. The president said he would now start focusing on other issues, such as reforming the oil industry.

And then Mexico exploded.

In 2008, the Mexican Drug War intensified drastically and became a full-scale criminal insurgency. In 2007, an average of two hundred drug-related murders occurred per month. In 2008, this shot up to five hundred murders per month. The year saw an extraordinary rise in attacks on police and officials; and the conflict started to have a major impact on civilians, including the grenade attack on revelers during the 2008 Independence Day celebrations. Prolonged firefights in residential areas and massacres of fifteen or more victims at a time became widespread. As the year wore on, American TV networks jumped on the story, and newspapers started saying a real war was being fought in Mexico (although they still struggled to fathom what kind of war it was).

The geographical concentration of the 2008 fighting can also clearly be recognized. Nuevo Laredo was relatively peaceful, albeit under the iron grip of the Zetas. Meanwhile, 80 percent of all killings took place in three northwestern states that form a triangle from the Sierra Madre to the U.S. border: Sinaloa, Chihuahua, and Baja California. This was the region long controlled by the Sinaloan narco tribe. While the capos of this drug realm had always been at each other's throats, this was the first time that they sent whole armies at each other. Thus, while the first phase of the Mexican Drug War had been Sinaloans against Zetas, the second phase was a civil war in the Sinaloan empire.

The war between Sinaloan capos had three main flashpoints: Ciudad Juárez, Tijuana, and Culiacán. The kingpins of the Sinaloa Cartel, including Joaquin "Chapo" Guzmán and Ismael Zambada, were involved in all three of these fronts. In Juárez, they fought against Sinaloan Vicente Carrillo Fuentes; in Tijuana they backed Sinaloan Teodoro Garcia against the inheritors of the Arellano Félix cartel (also Sinaloans); and in the heartland of Sinaloa they fought against their longtime friend and ally "the Beard" Beltrán Leyva. It is easy to understand how this civil war could produce such massive casualties. But why did the empire blow up in 2008?

Two main arguments float around to explain the implosion. The first was put out by the Mexican government and supported by the DEA. According to this thesis, the war was a result of Calderón's intense pressure on cartels. With such record-breaking seizures as the 23.5 tons of cocaine,[8] they say, gangsters were all losing billions of dollars. This stress pushed them to argue over their plaza payments and who would cough up for lost tons of drugs. The Sinaloans had always been a quarrelsome clan, killing each other in mountain feuds or shooting each other in the Tierra Blanca ghetto. Under Calderón's push, these tensions boiled over into open warfare, both among themselves and in a desperate lash back against police. Violence was therefore a sign of success, the government argued, and signaled cartels were getting weaker.

The other argument was put out by gangsters themselves and supported by a substantial group of Mexican journalists and academics.

According to this critique, the war was linked to government corruption. The Sinaloan cartel of Chapo Guzmán and Mayo Zambada, they say, became emboldened by an alliance with federal officials to attempt a takeover of all of Mexico's trafficking supported by federal troops. Chapo Guzmán then helped arrest his rivals, such as the Beard's brother Alfredo Beltrán Leyva, whom soldiers nabbed in Culiacán on January 21, 2008. In reaction, the afflicted capos hit back against federal forces because they were working with Chapo. This accusation was put out on hundreds of messages, or *narcomantas*, written on blankets and dangled from bridges. A typical note, hung up in Juarez, said:

"This letter is for citizens so that they know that the federal government protects Chapo Guzmán, who is responsible for the massacre of innocent people . . . Chapo Guzmán is protected by the National Action Party since Vicente Fox, who came in and set him free. The deal is still on today . . . Why do they massacre innocent people? Why do they not fight with us face-to-face? What is their mentality? We invite the government to attack all the cartels."[9]

The government decries such accusations as the scrawling of ignorant gangsters who don't even sign their names. Calderón urges the media not to reprint such narco propaganda. And as I have said, no solid evidence links Calderón to the Sinaloa cartel.

But there is certainly evidence that some federal officials supported Chapo Guzmán's offensive. Toward the end of 2008, a government probe code-named Operation Clean House uncovered a network of twenty-five federal officials on the payroll of the Sinaloa Cartel. Among them were soldiers, federal police commanders, and detectives. However, contrary to the conspiracy theory, evidence suggests that some of these federal forces worked with Chapo Guzmán's rivals. As part of the same cleanup operation, police arrested fifty agents allegedly working for the Beard Beltrán Leyva.

As I have said, I prefer the cock-up theory to the conspiracy theory. Calderón may be honest, but he declared war on drug cartels with a rotten state apparatus, one that he could not fully control. Behind his push, police and soldiers hit gangsters harder than ever before, but these enforcers were still susceptible to bribes. As a result, Calderón's offensive just threw oil onto the fire. Drug violence had steadily been rising since 2004. And like water over a flame, this violence finally came to the boil.

*   *   *

Throughout 2008, my phone rang relentlessly with unknown numbers from round the globe. I would answer to hear the voices of anxious TV producers from Tokyo to Toronto eager to jet in and film the Mexican Drug War. "We want to ride around in a Mexican tank for a month getting action on the front line," they would demand. "We want an interview with Chapo Guzmán." At the same time, the nervous producers would demand absolute safety. "We have to make sure our crew is unharmed. Can you give us a hundred percent guarantee they will not be shot or kidnapped?"

Networks sent their seasoned war correspondents for the task. Veterans arrived with stories of running with Bosnian militias, escaping bombs in Chechnya, or riding through Kuwait as its oil fields burned. Many had just come from embeds with the American army in Iraq and Afghanistan. They wanted to organize such embeds with the Mexican army. But they soon realized the Mexican war was a totally different type of conflict. There was no elite Mexican squadron, such as Battle Company in Afghanistan, which they could follow in action, talking to its hard-bitten soldiers and filming its rocket attacks with a night-vision camera. They could not stare over valleys at insurgent outposts.

The Mexican army and police moved freely around the whole country; but then they could also be attacked everywhere. They were not hit by aerial bombings or rockets but Kalashnikov rifles and the odd grenade. One day seven federal police would be gunned down in Culiacán; the next, twenty bodies would be piled up in Tijuana; the next, a commander would be assassinated in his home in Mexico City. How could you be in the right place to catch the action?

I built up my strongest contacts in Sinaloa and focused on covering the war from there. Every month I would jet up to Culiacán with different TV crews to film thugs working for Chapo Guzmán and the Beard Beltrán Leyva blowing each other apart. Sinaloa tragically witnessed 1,162 homicides in 2008, the vast majority in Culiacán, so film crews were guaranteed to see at least a dozen corpses. It is a sad and dirty business covering death.

A Culiacán cartoonist was so bemused by the tall, white gringos running around in bulletproof jackets, he wrote a comic strip about it. "With the unexpected arrival of reporters, cameramen, journalists and photographers from the whole world to our state and their difficulty in decoding the particular slang of crime reporting, we have decided to lend them a hand and give them this guide for war correspondents to Culichi-English," he wrote in the Sinaloan comic *La Locha*. He then followed with amusing translations of Culiacán narco-speak such as the following:

Sicario: A very elegant way to call a killer for hire.
Cartel: A big family.
Ejecutado: The final outcome of the express method of judging
    and sentencing a member of the rival cartel.
Balacera or Tiroteo: Shooting or shoot-out. Run for your lives![10]

To get closer to the Culiacán action, I worked with seasoned Sinaloan crime photographer Fidel Duran. A bear of a man in his forties, Fidel had a bushy beard, gold chain of San Judas Tadeo, and thick Sinaloan drawl, making him very much a local macho. He had snapped pictures of mafia victims for decades and had a deep understanding of the conflict playing out. After filling the crime pages of various local papers, he and a colleague set up their own Web site called Culiacán AM, dominated by pictures of murder and gore. Some criticized it for being in poor taste. But it gained a huge number of hits, not only in Sinaloa but across all Mexico and in the United States. It also gained an enviable amount of advertising, hawking everything from cell phones to table-dance clubs.

Fidel seemed to know every Culiacán resident and state policeman and warmly greeted them with hugs and hand slaps before chatting with them about family and friends. However, the federal police and soldiers were all "foreigners" from other parts of Mexico. They treated Sinaloan crime photographers with suspicion; and in turn the photographers saw them as outsiders who wanted to loot the city. When the photographers followed federal operations, they would say they were keeping an eye to make sure the troops didn't rob homes or hurt people.

Fidel had also covered local mobsters. He even once trekked with reporters to the family home of Chapo Guzmán in the mountains to get an interview with his mother. She lived in the ramshackle village of La Tuna in a fairly simple house, although she did have a maid. Senora Guzmán railed against blaming so much destruction on her son and described his escape from jail as "taking a leave without permission." Then she made the journalists lunch.

Anytime a murder, shoot-out, or raid happened, Fidel was one of the first on the scene. His radio never stopped buzzing. Police officers, colleagues, or his enormous network of friends would all phone with news of gunshots, bodies, or grenades popping. Calls always seemed to come as we were eating; Fidel loved to devour enormous plates of food, and I would make sure visiting TV crews took us to the best Sinaloan seafood restaurants or charcoaled-chicken joints. As calls came about firefights, we would rush out, Fidel still grabbing prawns and marlin off the plates while they were taken away. Out on the road, he would burn the rubber as if he were a NASCAR racer. Mexican crime photographers are the most aggressive drivers I have ever seen, as moving fast is key to getting the photo. We would zoom through stoplights and arrive to see another crowd staring at bullets on the concrete, another bloody pile of corpses, another family crying.

While I had thought the 2005 turf war in Nuevo Laredo was bad, the 2008 fight in Culiacán was horrific. The rival capos hit back and forth across the urban area as if it were a game of toy soldiers. Gunmen for Chapo Guzmán would attack a Beltrán Leyva safe house with grenades and firebombs. Beltrán Leyva would strike back the next day, dumping cut-up bodies of Chapo employees in a car trunk. Chapo gunmen would shoot up a bar where the Beard's men drank. Beltrán Leyva killers would go into a car chop shop owned by a Chapo affiliate and massacre everybody inside.

Shorty versus the Beard! The two men had grown up together in the mountains, smuggled drugs together for years, gone to war against the Zetas together. Now they were fighting a war of annihilation. As they had worked in concert, they had crucial information on each other: they knew where each other's safe houses were; which police they had on their payroll; which front companies they owned. This was the key to why both sides could kill people at such a fast rate, why the fight was so bloody.

The rival gangsters were physical opposites: Chapo was small and mustachioed or clean-shaven; Beltrán Leyva was a hulk with his trademark wild-man beard. Chapo headed his own operations; Beltrán Leyva worked with his four brothers, who were all arch-villains. It was a family thing.

On May 9, Beltrán Leyva made the war even more personal—his men killed Chapo's son. Édgar Guzmán was a twenty-two-year-old university student who locals said wasn't particularly active in his father's organization. He was with two friends in a Culiacán mall parking lot, standing and talking in front of his bulletproof Ford Lobo. Fifteen gunmen attacked, spraying five hundred bullets on the three youngsters. A local cameraman arrived shortly after the murder and filmed the corpse of Édgar Guzmán sprawled over the concrete, his right hand grasping a Belgian-made pistol known as the cop-killer. When Culiacán residents saw the footage, they knew this would mean catastrophe.

Chapo Guzmán reportedly brought every rose in northwest Mexico to lay his son to rest, putting fifty thousand flowers on his tomb. A ballad was composed for the death of Édgar. Then Chapo went to war. Firefights broke out all over the center of Culiacán. On a May evening, guests were sitting in a restaurant in Culiacán's central plaza when a shoot-out broke out just one block away. They dove under tables for cover. Residents began a self-imposed curfew and stayed indoors at night throughout May and June, leaving the streets to the killers. Then people gradually returned to their old routines, absorbing the new level of violence into their lives.

Hours before gunmen had murdered the young Edgar Guzmán, a fellow narco assassin carried out another hit with deadly implications eight hundred miles away in Mexico City. Édgar Millán, the acting head of the federal police, walked into his home in the Guerrero neighborhood. The waiting assassin shot him at point-blank range. Millán's bodyguard fired back, wounding the assailant. The dying police chief used his last breath to start the interrogation. "Who sent you? Who sent you?" he demanded. Millán passed away before the assassin could answer.

Federal police rounded up suspects, including a corrupt officer who had given the assassin the keys to the house. After interrogations, *federales* announced that the mastermind of this killing was none other than Beltrán Leyva. The attack had been revenge for the arrest of his brother in January. The Beard was becoming an even bigger insurgent than the Zetas.

For the Mexican establishment, the murder of the federal police chief was a wake-up call. How could a high-ranking official be assassinated in his own home in the capital? This was no longer a crime problem; it was a national security problem.

Federal police stormed Culiacán, going after Beltrán Leyva thugs. A police unit got lured into a middle-class Culiacán neighborhood chasing a suspect. Then a gang of gunmen ambushed the officers with a barrage of automatic-rifle fire. Seven federal policemen were shot to pieces; the killers escaped into the night. Beltrán Leyva's rebellion was in full swing.

I went to the scene of the ambush. The gunmen had fired right through a metal garage door, using it as cover. It looked like a cheese grater with a hundred bullet holes in it. Other killers had fired from windows, raining caps down on the federal agents from above. The house was abandoned, so I walked in and snooped around. The assassins had left their garbage strewn over the building—old pizza boxes with half-eaten pies and heavily thumbed pornographic magazines. You could picture the scene: a dozen thugs holed up in the building, munching on pizza, staring at skin mags and waiting to kill *federales*.

Next door lived a fishmonger. He had thought the men going into the safe house were suspicious but sensibly kept his mouth shut. When the firefight broke out, he lay on his bedroom floor with his wife and two children, praying that no bullets would fly through his window.

As the turf war in Culiacán raged through a seething-hot summer, residents tried to get on with their lives. But bullets hit more and more civilians. Those who lost loved ones felt devastated, scared, isolated. They dreaded talking to the police or the press for fear of reprisals. But some mothers of murdered children started to meet and share their pain. Together, they felt stronger about denouncing the deaths and fighting for justice.

I met these families to try to persuade them to tell their stories to the TV crews I worked with. They were worried about being seen talking to foreign journalists. They wondered if they were being watched by gangsters, by police, by government spies. Could the cases of their dead sons upset someone in power? Could they put their other children at risk? I told them that we needed to document their cases to make the government do something about them. Only about 5 percent of these murders are ever solved, I said, media pressure will force the government to solve more. I was being half-truthful. I did want to get them crying on TV; but I didn't know if it would really make a difference to government investigations.

The bravest and most outspoken parent was Alma Herrera, a fifty-year-old businesswoman and single mother. Alma was in startlingly good shape for her age, looking fifteen years younger, her light brown skin immaculately cared for, her dresses elegant. Her first name means "soul" in Spanish. She spoke in a sweet, melodic Sinaloan tone, making such a powerful indictment of the situation that I felt scared for her just hearing her answer the questions. I was reminded of the brave mother in Tijuana who wrote the letter to *Zeta* magazine attacking the Arellano Félix for killing her sons. As Alma said:

"Our sons have been shot dead in their prime. Their lives have been stolen so early. And we see no justice. Are the authorities scared to discover the truth of these cases? Are they scared because so many police and politicians here in Sinaloa are involved with the mafia?"

Alma had lived with her two sons César, twenty-eight, and Cristóbal, sixteen. César, was a stocky, friendly young man with meaty hands and thick, black hair; Cristóbal, a slim, gregarious teenager.

One night, the brakes busted on the family SUV. César was good with cars but couldn't fix a brake system, so he promised to take it to the mechanic the next day. First thing in the morning, he and Cristóbal carefully drove the SUV down to the car shop. It was a blazing-hot Wednesday; a perfectly ordinary morning. There was a queue at the mechanics, and César and Cristóbal waited, talking and joking with other customers. In total, ten people were in the yard.

Suddenly, at eleven A.M., a commando troop of gunmen stormed the car shop. At the moment they entered, César was under his SUV, looking at the brakes. His brother, Cristóbal, and the other eight customers and mechanics were all exposed. *Bang. Bang. Bang.* The assassins sprayed everyone in sight, unleashing hundreds of bullets around the workshop. In seconds, nine people, including Cristóbal, were shot dead.

César was under the SUV so the assassins didn't see him. This saved his life. But he was hit by two bullets in his leg. He couldn't even feel the wounds. All he could think was, "If these assassins see me, I'm dead." He felt his cell phone in his pocket. If it rang, the gunmen would hear it and he would be dead. But if he tried to turn it off, it might make a bleep, and he would be dead. One of the assassins dropped a circular ammunition clip right next to the SUV. "If he ducks down to pick it up," Cesar thought, "I will be dead."

Minutes seemed like hours. The gunmen paced around the car shop, checking that there were no survivors who could identify them. By a miracle, they didn't see César. And they marched out.

César waited for more eternal minutes. Then he crawled out from under the SUV and stared at the corpses around him. There were nine bodies; two more than in the St. Valentine's Day massacre in Chicago. And this was just one forgotten incident in the Mexican Drug War. One of the corpses was Cristóbal. César could do nothing for his younger brother, the sibling that he saw grow from a baby to a sixteen-year-old.

César had two bullets in his leg but still had so much adrenaline in his blood that he couldn't feel them. He rushed out onto the street, managing to wander away before policemen arrived to seal the scene. The killers were causing more havoc, shooting at a local patrol car as they sped away through town.

César walked a few blocks into a swarm of people going about their daily routines—shopping, thinking about collecting kids from school, planning what they would have for lunch—oblivious to the massacre. The adrenaline started to go down. César stopped on the street. The first thing he thought about was not getting to hospital and saving his leg; it was about his brother, Cristóbal, and his mother, Alma. He phoned Alma. "Mama, there was a shooting in the mechanics shop. I am okay. But I don't know where Cristóbal is." It is hard to tell your mother that your brother is gone.

Alma picked César up and took him to hospital. A surgeon removed the bullets and he was in pretty good shape. He couldn't run fast anymore. But he could walk. One local newspaper erroneously reported that he was killed in the massacre. He didn't correct it; he didn't need to attract attention to his being there. He saw nothing from under the car. But some may have feared otherwise. His friends kept a distance. They worried that he could be hit and didn't want to be standing next to him to catch a bullet.

Alma had lost her youngest son. No one should have to bury his or her child, especially when he is sixteen and perfectly healthy. I have another friend who lost a young daughter and described it to me in the following way: "Once you have lost a child, there is nothing anyone can do to you that is worse." I filmed Alma crying by Cristóbal's grave, holding up a large framed photo of him, an image that flickered for a few seconds on television sets in far-off lands.

César and Alma later heard the mechanics shop was part of the financial network of a drug trafficker. A rival crew hit it as part of the turf war. You bring your enemy down by destroying their whole infrastructure: their police protection, their soldiers, and their assets. But did an innocent sixteen-year-old really need to die for that? Did that really bring a capo closer to victory?

After pressure from Alma and other families, the federal attorney general's office finally picked up the case. Two years later, they still had nothing on it. The government is dealing with thirty-five thousand drug-related murders, including the deaths of a leading gubernatorial candidate and dozens of mayors and police chiefs. The massacre in the Culiacán car shop is way down on its list of priorities. Alma and other mothers traveled to Mexico City and protested in the central plaza. They stood in a sea of people, one more rally in a swarming metropolis with demonstrations daily.

Chapo and Beltrán Leyva carried on blowing the hell out of each other throughout 2008. But by 2009, federal forces and American agents started to close in on the Beard. *Federales* raided a narco fiesta where famous musicians were playing, but the Beard narrowly escaped the sweep. Then in December 2009, American intelligence agents tracked Beltrán Leyva down to an apartment block in Cuernavaca, a spa town an hour's drive from Mexico City, where conquistador Hernán Cortés had built a huge plantation in the sixteenth century. The Beard used the area's green pastures to fly in cocaine.

American agents gave the address of the Beltrán Leyva safe house to Mexican marines, an elite force who had been trained with the U.S. Northern Command. Two hundred marines surrounded the building and a helicopter hovered overhead. Beltrán Leyva phoned his old friend and protégé Édgar Valdéz, the Barbie Doll, asking for hit men to break him out. The Barbie replied that the situation was hopeless and advised the Beard to give himself up. Beltrán Leyva said he would never go peacefully.

Marines tried to shoot their way in. Beltrán Leyva and his band of desperadoes fired back out of the windows and lobbed grenades. After two hours, marines stormed the apartment and blew away everything in sight. Beltrán Leyva and five of his aides were torn to pieces. The Beard had gone down like Al Pacino in *Scarface*, blasting his way to the next world. He was forty-eight years old.[11]

Someone decided to have some fun with the body. Perhaps it was the victorious marines, or maybe it was the forensics team. They pulled Beltrán Leyva's trousers around his ankles and decorated the bloody corpse with dollar bills. Gangsters played with the cadavers of dead policemen, so why shouldn't the good guys do the same to humiliate their victims? Photographers were invited in to snap pictures of the defiled body of the Beard. Within hours, it was all over the Internet.

Calderón's administration made the mistake of giving a public funeral to a marine who died in the raid. Uniformed men lowered his coffin into the earth and fired a salute into the sky. The next day, the marine's family held a wake in their swampy, southern hometown of El Paraiso—a name that means "paradise." Gunmen stormed into the candlelit vigil and killed the marine's mother, aunt, brother, and sister. Calderón called the assassins "cowards." But it was hard for a president to drown out a clear message: if you come after us, we will wipe out your entire family. Marines' identities were kept secret after that.

Family members buried the Beard in the Humaya cemetery in Culiacán, a graveyard packed with the grandiose tombs of generations of Sinaloan narcos. Police and soldiers stood by waiting for his villainous brothers to turn up. They all stayed away, with only women and children attending the funeral. A few weeks later, a severed head was stuck on the Beard's grave. A gruesome photo shows it in graphic detail; the victim is a mustachioed man in his thirties, the cranium between two enormous bouquets of flowers on the tomb. Even with death, the beef had not completely stopped.

The killing of the Beard, one of Mexico's most-powerful-ever traffickers, was a big victory for Calderón. But it did nothing to stop the violence. Instead it encouraged local mafias to try to seize Beltrán Leyva's lucrative territories, spreading the war from the Sinaloan empire of the northwest to Mexico's center and south. The warmongers switched alliances, betrayed each other, and wreaked bloody vengeance, exacerbating an already tangled conflict. The Mexican Drug War thus entered a third and even bloodier phase: fighting in a dozen states involving a dozen warlords.

Meanwhile, the ruckus between Sinaloan capos raged on in Ciudad Juárez, taking a city turf war to new depths. Thousands of gangbangers from the city's sprawling slums were pulled into the conflict, barrios warring against barrios. In 2009, Juárez famously became the most murderous city on the planet, overtaking Mogadishu, Baghdad, and Cape Town.[12] Tens of thousands who had papers fled over the border to live in El Paso. This exodus bled the economy, in turn leaving more jobless young men to fall into the ranks of the cartels. It was a vicious cycle. Juárez became a case study for urban failure.

By the end of 2009, things looked as if they couldn't get any worse. Then they did. While the army and the police had been dragged into the Sinaloan war in the northwest, the Zetas had multiplied across the whole of eastern Mexico, down into the southern states of Oaxaca and Chiapas and over the border into Guatemala. Many Zetas had been born poor country boys, and now they recruited thousands more of their ilk, forming cells in every small town, village, or barrio they touched. By 2010, the Zetas were estimated to have more than ten thousand soldiers.[13] Everywhere they went, they recklessly extorted, kidnapped, and looted. The old bosses in the Gulf Cartel could not restrain them; they were an army run by hit men such as Lazcano, the Executioner. Violence was no longer a way of control but a basic language of communication. They committed atrocities that made even seasoned cartel bosses sick, such as the massacre of the seventy-two migrants. They had gone beyond the pale.

Many in both the Mexican security services and the old cartels saw the Zetas as a psychotically antisocial movement that needed to be wiped out. Gangsters put out messages on blankets and Web sites calling for a national effort to destroy them. This unleashed some of the worst battles to date, particularly in the Zetas' heartland of the northeast. The Zetas fought off army units and rival cartel hit squads with heavy-caliber machine guns and rocket-propelled grenades. The fighting made the Mexican Drug War at last start to look like a more traditional war, with battles that lasted six hours and left dozens of bodies. In 2010, drug-related murders shot up drastically, to a stunning fifteen thousand over the year.

Calderón desperately threw more resources into his military offensive, repeating his mantra: "We won't back down against the enemies of Mexico." But as troops hit back, it only gave him another headache: they kept shooting civilians. When you unleash soldiers to fight criminals, you invariably end up breaking a few innocent heads. This has occurred in so-called peacekeeping missions in Afghanistan, Iraq, and Northern Ireland, to name a few. True, Mexican soldiers were not foreigners, such as Americans smashing their way through Fallujah. But they were from different states, normally hailing from Mexico's poor south and being sent on missions to its commercial north. They fought an enemy that blended into communities just as insurgents did in Baghdad, Kandahar, or Belfast. Soldiers quickly became an occupying force who eyed all locals as potential narco assassins. And many of those locals did indeed act as the eyes and ears of drug mafias.

Like troops in Iraq or Northern Ireland, Mexican security forces got hit with guerrilla tactics. Some of the worst attacks included the kidnapping and murder of ten soldiers in Monterrey; the ambush and killing of five soldiers in Michoacán; and a car bombing in Ciudad Juárez that killed a federal police officer and two others. More grinding were daily ambushes and kidnappings of agents in small groups. Troops were angry, scared, and aggressive. With itchy fingers, they opened fired on cars stopping too slow at checkpoints such as one in Sinaloa, in which they killed two women and three young children. On other occasions, they inadvertently shot civilians in the midst of running battles with cartel gunmen, such as two students killed in Monterrey. Worse still, soldiers were accused of premeditated abuses, including torture, rape, and murder. One case involved four teenage girls in Michoacán who said they were taken to a military barracks and repeatedly raped. After four years of Calderón's offensive, police and military bullets had killed more than a hundred innocent civilians.[14]

Calderón was in an impossible spot. The war he had promoted triumphantly in his first year had sprung rudely from his hands like a wild dog. On several occasions, he tried to push the drug war off the top of the agenda and say he was now focusing on other issues. But every time, a new massacre or atrocity would hit the headlines, pulling him back in. The conflict was compared to the Iraq War in its worst years, a fight that Calderón couldn't win but couldn't pull out of.

In 2011, four and a half years after his triumphant taking of power, Calderón looked concerned and exhausted. Soldiers and federal police kept nailing major kingpins, but violence only flared up more. Calderón backed away from his bellicose rhetoric, arguing it was a crime problem after all. He blamed the media for focusing too much on the bloodshed and giving Mexico a bad name. He promised unconvincingly that he would defeat El Narco by the time a new government took power in 2012. The constitution banned him from standing for a second term, and Mexican presidents generally become lame ducks toward the end of their term.

The Obama administration stumbled on with a befuddled agenda on Mexico. Publically, officials kept cheering on Calderón's campaign. But WikiLeaks showed that privately diplomats had serious concerns about where the drug war was headed. In January 2011, Secretary of State Hillary Clinton shot down to Mexico to say Calderón was winning the war—as part of a Wiki Leaks-damage-limitation tour. But then in February, the U.S. army's number two civilian leader, Joseph Westphal, contradicted her, saying criminal insurgents were in danger of controlling Mexico:

"This is about potentially the takeover of a government by individuals who are corrupt and have a different agenda . . . I don't want to see a situation in which we have to send soldiers to fight an insurgency on our border."[15]

The Mexican government reiterated its argument that it is not fighting an insurgency and Westphal retracted his statement. But the Obama adminsitration's flip-flop had sent a telling message—that it was increasingly confused on Mexico and shaky in its support for the current strategy.

America's stakes in the drug war were raised even higher with the February 2011 murder of U.S. agent Jaime Zapata in the state of San Luis Potosi. Zapata, working for Immigration and Customs Enforcement, or ICE, was attacked by alleged Zetas, who surrounded his SUV on the highway. When Zapata pointed to his diplomatic plates, a gunman retorted, "Me vale madre,"—a phrase that can be most closely translated as, "I don't give a fuck." Zetas shot Zapata and also wounded his partner with two bullets. It was unclear if the ICE agents were deliberately targeted or had just happened to drive into a Zeta area. But whatever the motive, the first murder of a U.S. agent in Mexico since Camarena put the spotlight on America's mission south of the river.

As presidential candidates vied to lead Mexico in 2012, political think tanks on both sides of the border questioned what a new drug-war strategy could be. Why did so many arrests and seizures only inflate violence? they asked. How could Mexico train better police? Why did drug gangs have an endless army of narco assassins? To answer these questions, one needs to look at the inner workings of the Mexican drug business and what drives it to the relentless killing. We now turn to this flesh and blood of El Narco.

PART II

Anatomy

CHAPTER 8
Traffic

Thus ended my career as a smuggler, —a career which however it may
be calculated to gratify a hard and enterprising spirit and to call forth
all the latent energies of the soul, is fraught with difficulty and danger;
in following which many and various have been the expedients to which
I have had recourse in order to escape detection, baffle pursuit and
elude the vigilance of those indefatigable picaroons which everywhere
line our coasts.

—JOHN RATTENBURY, *MEMOIRS OF A SMUGGLER*, 1837

To a hard-core drug aficionado, the evidence room on the Mexican army
base in Culiacán, Sinaloa, would be a wet dream; it has enough crystal
meth, cocaine, grass, pills, and heroin to keep a human being stoned, tripping, high, low, spun out, and seeing fairies for a million years. And then
some.

It is a fort within the fort, protected by barbed wire and closed-circuit
cameras, which, we are reminded, will be recording our journalist visit
one sunny December afternoon. While they call it an evidence "room," it
is actually the size of a warehouse, with no windows and one hefty steel
door. Every time this portcullis is opened, federal agents cut off special
seals, and when it is closed, they put on new ones, to make sure—and
show us—that no troops are pilfering the goodies. On the streets of

American cities, the treasure trove would be worth hundreds of millions of dollars.

General Eduardo Solórzano guides us through the chamber of sinful substances. He is a squat and square-jawed soldier in his fifties with glasses perched on the end of his nose and a black vest packed with beepers, radios, and cell phones that he keeps barking into in a curt, commanding tone. He accompanies his tour with comments in measured military language while occasionally getting excited at finding samples of rare types of narcotics amid the bags, bricks, and bundles.

As we step inside, a cocktail of mystic toxic smells greets us. To the left, towers of cling-wrapped marijuana loom above our heads. To the right are huge sacks of cut-up ganja plants and enough seeds to give birth to a forest of psychedelic weed. Walking forward, we stumble into a pile of giant, blue metal saucepans of the type Mexicans use in restaurants to cook up broths such as posole and consommé. General Solórzano lifts up a lid of one and flashes a knowing grin: "This is crystal." He smiles. The white sludge of raw methamphetamine fills the pan like a foul stew of ice and sour milk. In a corner, we catch sight of a much older Sinaloan product, black-tar heroin, which looks like jet-black Play-Doh, oozing out of yellow cans.

An inventory neatly lists the name of each type of drug next to a quantity in kilos; they currently total more than seven tons. Periodically, a bureaucrat in an office somewhere will sign the order for a certain batch of heroin or marijuana or crystal meth to be carted away and burned on a bonfire. But stocks are quickly replenished by a steady supply of new produce garnered in weekly raids on safe houses scattered all around Culiacán and in nearby villages and ranches.

On the afternoon of our visit, one such load conveniently arrives for us to photograph. A truck rolls up and young soldiers move with military orderliness to unload hundreds of brown packages into the warehouse. General Solórzano grabs one, reaches into his black vest for a box cutter, and carefully slices a triangle in the packaging to reveal white powder crammed into a brick shape. "Cocaina!" he says triumphantly. A lab technician quickly proves him right. The white-coated specialist conducts the test using a portable kit, which looks like a car toolbox. He selects a vial of pink solution, mixes it with a small sample of the captured blow, and it instantly turns blue—indicating a positive match.

General Solórzano, a foot lower than me but with shoulders twice as broad, turns round and stares me in the face. "Taste it," he says, unsmiling. "Go on." I look round at the other officers, agents, and technicians to see if he is joking. They all have sturdy straight faces. So I dab my little finger onto the cocaine brick and stick it into my mouth. Cocaine has an unforgettable bittersweet flavor, neither tasty nor disgusting, like a prescription medicine you cautiously swallow and are then relieved that it isn't so bad. "You will feel that your tongue falls asleep," General Solórzano says, a grin now spreading across his face. "This is pure, uncut cocaine." My tongue certainly does feel numb. And I also feel a little giddy. But then again, maybe that is from walking in the hot sun. Or maybe it is from earlier in the day when we watched soldiers cut up a whole field of captured marijuana and set fire to it, sparking a golden green blaze that unleashed clouds of ganja smoke wafting off into the horizon in these arid, jaggy mountains.

I once interviewed the chief FBI officer of a major city on the U.S. side of the Mexican border. Before I turned up, he had taken the trouble to read some of my articles. Speaking with a thick New York twang, he told me he had spent fifteen years by the Rio Grande making cases against drug traffickers. He went on, "I enjoyed your stories. When I get new recruits, I tell them that is exactly the way not to look at the drug business."

I betrayed a miffed look. What had I got wrong? I asked. He replied that it wasn't that I had got anything wrong. It was that the points I focused on were not going to help make cases. In our journalistic vision of the Mexican drug trade, we see stories of colorful kingpins and shifting maps of cartel territory. But on the ground level, the drug trade doesn't see that. It is about movement of narcotics, pure and simple. Drugs get produced, transported, sold, and snorted. Just follow those drugs and you make cases, he said. Forget about folk stories of kingpins and carefully drawn maps of cartel boundaries.

He made a good point. Stripped down its basics, El Narco—or Mexican drug trafficking—is just an industry. And like any industry, the mechanics of making and selling products are more fundamental than the companies and CEOs calling the shots. The evidence room in the army base in Culiacán is a fantastic display of this industry. It shows the colossal fruits of drug trafficking: tons of produce in hundreds of different packets and pans. Who knows how many different cartels or kingpins put money into these goods? And who cares? These mind-bending sub-stances have passed through thousands of hands in fields, laboratories, on ships, airplanes, and in trucks. And they all end up together in one room, being shown off to journalists to demonstrate Mexico's fight against trafficking, but having the reverse effect of illustrating how incredibly productive the country's industry is.

Mexico's drug industry never sleeps. Twenty-four hours a day, 365 days a year, somewhere new plants grow, chemicals react, transporters carry loads, burros cross the border. And every day, somewhere in the United States, Americans buy drugs that passed through Mexico and inhale them into their lungs, snort them up their noses, or inject them into their veins. Kingpins rise and fall, teenagers experiment, and old addicts overdose, and all the time the drug machine keeps ticking on with the steady rhythm of the earth circling the sun.

We all know the Mexican drug trade is so productive that it is one of the country's biggest industries. It rivals oil exports in helping stabilize the peso. It directly provides thousands of jobs, many in poor rural areas that most need them. Its profits spill over into a number of other sectors, par-ticularly hotels, cattle ranches, racehorses, record labels, football teams, and movie companies.

But as an industry we have little reliable data on it. Mostly we have estimates. Then we have more estimates based on estimates, x factors multiplied by y factors creating misty, doubtful numbers passed off as statistics. Both the media and officials help feed the misinformation machine. We all love to pack a story or press release with figures. *Forbes* magazine estimates that Chapo Guzmán is worth $1 billion—conveniently bang on the number with straight zeros. So what is their magic formula for that number? Pretty much, a wild guess. Back in the 1970s, DEA said that Mexicans temporarily controlled three quarters of the American heroin market after narcs hit the French Connection. A year later, it said that Colombian marijuana dealers controlled three quarters of the Amer-ican weed market after they hit the Mexicans. What a statistical coinci-dence! Or is three quarters just a standard estimate that really means a whole lot of drugs?

However, the Mexican drug industry is so important that we have to try to come to terms with its scale. The most solid figures are from busts on the United States' southern border. These are physical quantities of dope on the scales that can be compared year after year. And it is clearly being trafficked from Mexico to provide to American users.

The overall seizures confirm, just in case anyone doubted, that a shit-load of narcotics are moving north. In 2009, customs agents tossed cars and walkers going through the official ports of entry to nab a total of 298.6 metric tons of marijuana, heroin, cocaine, and crystal meth. Mean-while, border patrol agents who roam deserts and rivers seized a whop-ping 1,159 tons of marijuana, along with 10 tons of cocaine and 3 tons of heroin. These are enough drugs to get hundreds of millions of people wasted and would have been worth billions of dollars on street corners. But nobody can say how many tons of drugs they didn't catch. That number, the most important one, becomes another unknown.

These border seizures have held up year after year. Back in 2006, cus-toms nabbed 211 tons of drugs; in 2007, it to swung up to 262 tons; in 2008, it tilted back down to 242 tons; then in 2009, it shot up to 298 tons.[1] Cus-toms agents say the latest high may be the result of more agents, but they can't be sure; it could mean smugglers are busier. What is clear is that President Felipe Calderón's war on drugs and the thousands of shootings, busts, and massacres are not slowing the narcotics heading north.

On the border with Ciudad Juárez, drug seizures did fall as violence exploded—from 90 tons in 2007; to 75 tons in 2008; and 73 tons in 2009. But they were still higher than the 50 tons seized in 2006 when there was a fraction of the number of assassinations. Over on the San Diego–Tijuana crossings, seizures went up from 103 tons in 2007 to 108 tons in 2008, when fights between rival cartel factions left record piles of corpses.

This may seem all sound like masturbatory bean counting. It really isn't. These cold figures have frightening human implications: Mexican drug cartels can still operate at full capacity while they fight bloody bat-tles with each other and the government. In the drug business, it seems, a war economy functions perfectly well. Gangsters can go on having downtown shoot-outs with soldiers, leaving piles of severed heads, and still be trucking the same quantity of dope. That doesn't bode well for peace.

The formula for Mexicans to make drug money is hard to beat.

Take cocaine. A Colombian peasant can sell a bundle of coca leaves from a two-acre field for about $80. After it goes through its first simple chemical process, known as a *chagra*, it can be sold as a kilo of coca paste in the Colombian highlands for about $800. This paste will then be put through a crystallizing laboratory to become a kilo brick of pure cocaine—like that General Solórzano showed me. According to the United Nations, such a brick in 2009 was worth $2,147 in Colombian ports, rocketing up to $34,700 by the time it got over the U.S. border, and $120,000 when it was sold on the New York streets.[2] The traffic and distribution of the drug, the part run by Mexican gangsters, nets a 6,000 percent profit from the narco to the nose. If you calculate the cost all the way from the farm it is 150,000 percent. It is one of the most profitable businesses on the planet. Who else can offer that kind of return for your dollar?

Mexican cartels have emissaries in Colombia who place their cocaine orders. But Mexican gangs get Colombians to actually deliver the disco powder to them in Mexico or Central America, especially Panama and Honduras. The way the business has developed has made Mexicans traffickers the top dogs over the Colombian producers. DEA Andean Bureau chief Jay Bergman explained it to me using more great metaphors:

"Who really calls the shots in a global supply-and-demand economy? Is it Mexican cartels or Colombian cocaine suppliers? Is it the manufacturer or the distributor?

"In a legitimate economic model, is it Colgate or Walmart that calls the shots? It is actually Walmart who says, 'This is what we want to pay for it, this is a unit price, this is when we want it delivered, and this is how it's going to be,' and Colgate's position is, 'As long as we are making a profit, as long as we are not losing money, we are willing to work on those terms. And the more you can move my product, the bigger discount we will give you, and you get to really call the shots. Tell us where you want it, tell us how you want it, put it on the shelves where you want it, just get it sold.' . . . That is the evolved cocaine market we are dealing with."

From Central America, Mexican gangsters move cocaine on ships, submarines, or light aircraft. General Solórzano shows me the drug planes they have captured in Sinaloa. They are mostly single-engine Cessnas brought in the United States for about $50,000 a pop. The army now protects the seized aircraft because when they were in a police base, gangsters actually broke in and stole them back. In the last two years, soldiers have seized two hundred such planes. Driving around the airfield, the sheer size of the fleet makes a stunning sight. And these are only the ones they captured!

As drugs flow up into the United States, all kinds of people make money off them. People are subcontracted to ship, truck, warehouse, and finally smuggle the product over the border. To complicate this, drugs are often bought and sold many times on their journey. People actually handling these narcotics will often have no knowledge which so-called kingpin or cartel ever owned them, only knowing the direct contacts they are dealing with. Ask a New York cocaine dealer who smuggled his product into America. He would rarely have a clue.

All this helps explain why the Mexican drug trade is such a confusing web, which confounds both journalists and drug agents. Tracing exactly who touched a shipment on its entire journey is a hard task.

But this dynamic, moving industry has a solid center of gravity—turfs, or plazas. Drugs have to pass through a certain territory on the border to get into the United States, and whoever is running those plazas makes sure to tax everything that moves. The border plazas have thus become a choke point that is not seen in other drug-producing nations such as Colombia, Afghanistan, or Morocco. This is one of the key reasons why Mexican turf wars have become so bloody.

The vast profits attract all kinds to the Mexican drug trade: peasant farmers, slum teenagers, students, teachers, businessmen, idle rich kids, and countless others. It is often pointed out that in poor countries people turn to the drug trade in desperation. That is true. But plenty of middle-class or wealthy people also dabble. Growing up in the south of England, I knew dozens of people who moved and sold drugs, from private-school boys to kids from council estates (projects). The United States has never had a shortage of its own citizens willing to transport and sell drugs. The bottom line is that drugs are good money even to wealthy people, and plenty have no moral dilemmas about the business.

Iran Escandon is one of the thousands who have carried the white lady on her journey north. I find him in the municipal prison in Ciudad Juárez, playing keyboard in a jail-block church band. In my search to make sense of the Mexican drug trade, I have interviewed dozens of traffickers in cells, cantinas, and drug rehabs. But Iran stands out in my memory because he comes across as particularly innocent. That may sound like a funny word to use; he doesn't deny that he trafficked *cocaina*. But he seems innocent in the sense of being harmless or naive. He was a never a gang member or drug user like so many smugglers; never a policeman or murderer like so many others. He was caught with forty kilos of cocaine when he was just eighteen years old. In a flash, his youth disappeared and he got a ten-year sentence. When I meet him, he has four years left to go.

He speaks in a voice so soft that I have to crane my head forward to hear him. A beige puffer jacket covers his skinny frame, which contrasts with that of other inmates who show off bulky, tattooed torsos, built by bench-pressing concrete blocks in the scorching sun. His eyes are wide-open and warm. He balances delicately on the end of a bunk bed in the cell he shares with six others, telling me his story.

"It was cars that brought me here. I just loved cars. I loved to fix them, build them. I loved to race them. Cars were my passion."

Iran grew up in Cuauhtémoc, a city of a hundred thousand people set between cattle ranches and apple orchards, five hours south of Juárez. When he was seventeen, he dropped out of high school to work in a friend's car body shop near the marketplace. For fourteen-hour days, he would strip down fuel tanks, beef up motors, spray-paint bonnets.

"We would take old bangers and soup them up to turn them into machines that could race like bullets. I quickly learned to work on anything— sports cars, pickup trucks, Jeeps."

Happiness fills his eyes as he remembers good times past; times before he lived in a prison in the most murderous city on the planet; times that now seem an age away, like a distant memory, a dream he hopes one day to return to.

His family were caring but humble, his father a hardworking laborer and man of God, a convert to evangelical Protestant Christianity, which is spreading fast across Mexico. Like his father, Iran says he believes in a personal relationship with Jesus. He also believes in working hard and trying to make something of himself. That was what street races were about for him. On Saturday nights, Iran and his friends would take cars they had customized in their workshop and burn them up against machines from other crews. In Mexico, these illegal street contests are known as *arrancones*. When I mention *The Fast and the Furious*, Iran laughs.

"They were nothing like the races you see in the movies. There were no gangs with suitcases of money and Uzis. We were just a bunch of friends who loved car racing. We built up machines using anything we could find. It was a way to be creative, to be resourceful. And we could beat these teams with much more money than us. It was a great feeling."

One afternoon as Iran had his head in more filthy motors, a client turned up for some repairs on his vehicle. He was a well-dressed middle-aged man from Guadalajara who talked politely. When his car had been fixed, he offered the young guys some work—to drive a car upstate in exchange for ten thousand pesos, or about $900. The tires would be stuffed with pure Colombian cocaine.

"We thought, 'Wow. Ten thousand pesos just to drive a car upstate. Just think what kind of machine we can build with ten thousand pesos, and how we can win races with that.' It didn't even seem like we were doing something bad. We were just delivery boys."

After the first job, Iran and his friends celebrated like crazy. Then a week later, the man appeared again and asked for a second delivery. A few days later, a Sinaloan associate turned up with another package. Soon, they were moving several packages a week north. They had so much work, they started subcontracting other kids to drive packages. They were carrying up to 120 kilos of cocaine a shot in exchange for fifty thousand pesos or about $4,500. The money seemed like a small fortune to seventeen- and eighteen-year-olds. But it was a tiny fraction of what the white powder would fetch in American nightclubs.

"In a few months we went from being broke to having more cash than we could spend. As well as building great cars for the races, I would help my family out. I also changed my own car every month—I had an Escort, then a Jetta, then a Mustang. And as we had money, loads of girls were suddenly interested in us. I started living with my girlfriend. It all happened so fast."

The glory days were short-lived. Just after Escandon turned eighteen, he took on his most ambitious job yet: carrying forty kilos from Cuauhtémoc over the border and all the way to Colorado for a princely sum of $15,000. As he drove into Ciudad Juárez, soldiers stopped his car for a check. He took a deep breath while they felt under the hood and into the tires. Then they found the cargo.

"It was a nightmare moment. They pulled out the cocaine and my heart stopped. It had all been like a game, like a fantasy. In six months we went from nothing to riches. And then it was all over."

The smuggling organization never contacted Iran again or reprimanded him about losing the drugs. Maybe he was set up, he sighs, so that another, bigger load would get through, a classic technique of traffickers. While his crew moved drugs north, other teams they didn't know were certainly transporting cocaine on the same route for the same gangsters.

Juárez prison was terrifying and brutal for a skinny eighteen-year-old. In this ambience, he threw himself deeply into the evangelicalism of his father. He couldn't work on cars behind bars, so he put all his energy into learning to play the keyboard in the church band.

"I lost my family. I lost many things. I had to adapt to a hard and violent place. I had to grow up here and become a man. I can't look back and regret anymore. My years have gone. I have to look forward now. When I get out, I want to study music. I want to make music my life. At least I am still alive."

In Mexican border cities, everybody knows someone who has got mixed up in the drug trade: a cousin, a brother, a classmate, a neighbor. Everybody has a story. A taxidriver picked up a man who showed him ten kilos of cocaine he had stuffed up his sweater; a social worker's neighbor's house was raided and had a million dollars in cash; a waitress's brother and father are doing life sentences in American prisons for trafficking; a businessman's cousin started running drugs and got dissolved in a bath full of acid.

Everybody also knows that drugs are a fast way to make cash. If you are in between jobs, struggling with house payments, or desperate to get a new car, vacancies as a burro—someone hired to take drugs over the border—are always open. Making a film about youth in Ciudad Juárez, I talked to teenagers and young men from the barrios who had taken up the offer. The cartel offered a flat rate: $1,000 to drive sixty pounds of marijuana into the United States; more to take heroin, cocaine, or meth. You could use your own car or they lent you a vehicle. It was about three hours' work, then you got paid right away in cash—earning as much you would from a month sweating in a Juárez assembly plant. You could traffic once and never again. Or you could keep going back four, five times a week and start making some serious money.

Binationals or people with U.S. residency are particularly sought after. I interviewed a twenty-year-old living in El Paso who had made several shipments for the $1,000 fee, using the money to help his mom out and to buy studio equipment to record music. But then he got caught and sentenced to five years' probation, in which he had to stay indoors at night, wear a security tag, and was banned from going into Mexico. I asked him what was he most upset about. Being stuck in boring El Paso and not being able to go to Juárez and see his friends, he replied.

Mexican smugglers' endless ingenuity has made hours of entertaining reports for American television. A whole industry in Mexico builds so-called trap cars with secret compartments in tires, gas tanks, and under seats. Trucks are even specially made with sealed metal containers appearing like gas canisters that customs agents have to burn open with a blowtorch to look into. Ripping apart vehicles with fire is hard work in a place such as Laredo, where ten thousand trucks cross daily. And it is embarrassing for agents when they burn up a car with nothing in it.

Many traffickers avoid border posts altogether and walk right in over the desert. Gangs even manufacture their own hefty backpacks, designed to carry maximum loads of weed or cocaine. With hundreds of thousands of migrants walking over the border, it is easy for smugglers to slip in through the same routes—a point screamed out by America's "militarize the border" lobby.

Others don't go through or round the gates, but under. Mexican smugglers have built an extensive warren of tunnels that rivals that of the Gaza Strip. For Border Patrol agents, it is like playing *Space Invaders*—every time they fill one passage with concrete, another pops up. These are no mere rabbit holes. Cartels hire professional engineers, who build tunnels with wooden supports, concrete floors, electric lights, and even rail carts that carry dope. One passage that went into Otay Mesa, California, measured a colossal twenty-four hundred feet in length.[3] Another went on five hundred feet to come up behind an innocent-looking fireplace in Tecate, Mexico.

Then there is the art of disguise. Imagine any way you can camouflage narcotics, and you find that it has been done in an even weirder way in real life. Smugglers have hidden cocaine under the chocolate layer of candy bars, in the center of watermelons, mixed cocaine into fabricated fiberglass dolls, and even made yayo into an imitation of the soccer World Cup trophy. One smuggler went even further and put heroin into two artificial slabs of flesh that were plastered onto the end of his butt cheeks. The heroin leaked into his blood, causing his death.

In a hotel room in Culiacán, a twenty-one-year-old woman called Guadalupe shows off a new method of hiding marijuana. She works for some Sinaloan gangsters who agreed she could talk to journalists and even be filmed with the drugs—apparently for no recompense. Perhaps they like showing off how clever they are. Obviously, they don't fear they are giving away great secrets.

Guadalupe takes a green candle in a glass bottle and meticulously hollows out the wax, using a metal teaspoon. On her right side is big pile of green bud on a newspaper, which she sorts through and stuffs into transparent doggie bags. She then takes a roll of Fuji camera film, tears out the plastic filmstrip, and wraps it around one of the bags of ganja. She stuffs this bundle inside the candle and puts the wax back on top. Boom; there stands a regular-looking candle with drugs hidden inside. It was all done with the swiftness of a celebrity chef running through a recipe.

"This is a new technique. It is one of the most effective ones. The smell of the candle is very strong and police don't want to spend time digging away at the wax. It was created by a group of people whose only work is to think about new ways to transport merchandise."

I have heard about such figures before. They are referred to as *cerebros* or "brains"—people dedicated to dreaming up new ways for gangsters to smuggle their dope. In the corporate world, they would be like the masterminds who sit around drinking lattes and think up a genius way to package toothpaste or a catchy slogan for the Big Mac.

Guadalupe goes on, "When I first delivered this stuff, I got scared. But I learned to control the fear, so I don't betray myself and get caught. If I had been caught, then I wouldn't be here."

Guadalupe has a silky voice and glowing black hair. Many Sinaloan women dress ostentatiously in tight dresses and high heels and cover themselves in gold chains and jewels. But Guadalupe has modest clothes: simple black jeans and a red shirt with white circles on it. She says it is best to dress down to avoid attention. A high school friend first introduced her to the drug trade when she was seventeen.

"I told him I had certain economic problems. He said he was involved in all this, and he invited me to meet other friends of his and showed me that you can make good money fast. At first, I thought it was just men working in this business, but you see more and more women. This is probably because of the difficult economic situation in this country."

Pretty, young women have particular uses for the mafia. They are good at networking and setting up contacts, Guadalupe says, and experts in spying. As well as taking drugs down to a Sinaloan port, Guadalupe has been sent on many missions to collect information—about rivals, police, politicians, or anything the cartel wants to find out about. She was even once sent for a short stint to Russia to see how criminals there worked and assess if it was possible to do business with them.

"I went to observe all their mafia system—how the business moves there. We had contact with certain Russian gangsters. I observed to see if we could make a connection between them and the people here, to see if we could move drugs over there. But it was impossible. They have their own ways and their projects are very organized. We couldn't unite forces."

On another occasion back in Mexico, Guadalupe was ordered to seduce and sleep with a man, so as to spy on him and probe him for info.

"It was like an obligation. It is like a commitment you have to fulfill to be inside. This was the worst thing I have done in this business, for me personally; seducing someone just to get information."

Americans spend more on illegal drugs than the people of any other nation on the planet. That isn't surprising. They also spend more on Wrangler Jeeps, Big Macs, and Xboxes. But while Mexico can't cash in on American Xbox sales, the wretched gift of the drug trade goes straight over the Rio Grande.

The best indicator on American drug use is an annual survey by the Department of Health and Human Services, a cabinet-level agency.[4] Investigators knock on doors and ask people if they have smoked any crack recently or ever puffed on a reefer. After traipsing from Alaska to Brownsville over the whole year, they finish with answers from 67,500 respondents over the age of twelve. There is an obvious flaw in the method. You can't be sure that people are telling the truth; or whether the houseful of depraved junkies told the surveyors to get lost while Jehovah's Witnesses next door happily told all. But at least you can hope any margin of error is similar year on year.

According to this survey, overall American drug use was steady throughout the 2000s, in the period that the Mexican Drug War broke out and escalated. However, between 2008 and 2009, the number of people who said they had recently used drugs rose from 8 percent to 8.7 percent. In total, according to the survey, an estimated 21.8 million Americans were on some mind-bending substance in 2009. It seems unlikely that the bloodbath in Mexico is suppressing supply if more Americans are getting wasted.

The survey does, however, estimate that use of the most profitable drug, cocaine, has gone down: from 2.4 million American snorters in 2006 to 1.6 million in 2009. This has led some observers to argue that this shrinking market is one of the key causes of Mexico's butchery. Under pressure from decreased profits, the argument goes, the gangs have turned up the murders. The argument deals with a lot of unknown factors, but maybe this hypothesis is correct. If it is, it is a tough equation for Mexico to deal with: when drug profits swing up, gangsters get more powerful; when they swing down, they get more violent. It is the devil's logic.

We then have to guess what all this American drug taking is actually worth in cash. The most publicized estimates are in reports commissioned by the drug czar's office. When you first consider the challenges to experts compiling these studies, you wonder how on earth they can do it. So many factors are unknown: the amount of drug use varies enormously (you have cases such as Bill Clinton, who had one puff and didn't inhale, and then former New York Giants star Lawrence Taylor, who said he blew $1.4 million on blow in a year); and prices vary from city to city and even deal to deal. But the surveys, entitled "What America's Users Spend on Illegal Drugs," make some valiant efforts toward a plausible set of estimates.

The reports are packed with tables full of all kinds of riveting facts about drug use. We learn that in 1988, marijuana smokers puffed an average of 16.9 joints per month, the joints weighing an average of 0.0134 ounces; while in 2000 they smoked 18.7 reefers, which weighed on average 0.0136 ounces. Wow, that is exact stuff! The analysts also try to calculate their way round the fact that junkies and crackheads are famous for being lying, self-deceiving nut jobs. As the report says:

"Because drug users frequently deny their drug use, we need means to inflate self-reports to account for underreporting. This required an estimate of the probability that a chronic user would tell the truth when asked about his drug use. To develop that estimate we selected everyone in New York City who tested positive for cocaine, and we calculated the proportion that admitted to some illegal drug use during thirty days before being arrested . . . Truthful reporting rates differed from year-to-year and from site-to-site but generally, about 65 percent of cocaine users were considered truthful. Call this the provisional rate of truthfulness."

Or call it statistical sorcery. No mathematical equation can really compensate for the erratic behavior of drug addicts. But then these are only estimates.

The surveys have data on the drug market from 1988, when they estimate it was worth a whopping $154.3 billion, to 2000, when they calculate it was worth $63.7 billion. This steady decline is not only purported to reflect lowering American drug use in this period but also the undeniable fact that cocaine and heroin got much cheaper on American streets; in 2000, it cost less than half the price to shoot a bag of heroin into your arm than it would have in 1988.[5]

In the 2000s, the guesstimates have been incorporated into the United Nations drug report, which estimates that the American drug market has been fairly stable at about $60 billion. Analysts put this number through more statistical grinders to estimate that about half of the total, or $30 billion, goes to Mexican gangsters. Again, it is not an exact science. But everybody does agree that Mexican cartels are fighting for a prize with at least ten zeroes on the end.

So where does 30 billion in dirty drug dollars disappear?

Bankers believe it certainly helped keep the peso afloat during the world economic crisis from 2008 to 2009. It rivals Mexico's other big sources of foreign currency: in 2009, oil exports were worth $36.1 billion;[6] remittances sent home from Mexican migrants were $21.1 billion;[7] and foreign tourism brought in $11.3 billion. Drug money would be number two on this list.

But one shouldn't get carried away with its influence. Mexico is no Bangladesh. It has eleven billionaires, several world-class companies, and a total economy worth about $1 trillion. If the $30 billion figure is true, then drug trafficking accounts for some 3 percent of the gross domestic product.

The money does, however, constitute a much bigger percentage in certain communities and social groups. In the westside slums of Ciudad Juárez or the highlands of Sinaloa, the drug-trafficking mafia is likely the biggest employer. By falling most heavily in poor sectors, $30 billion has a particularly potent effect.

Thirty billion dollars also has the power to thoroughly corrupt Mexico's institutions. Public Safety Secretary Genaro Garcia Luna said in one speech that cartels could spend about $1.2 billion a year to triple the salaries of the nation's entire municipal police forces.[8] That is a true mathematical possibility. But it is also another X factor. No one can really say how many officers are on the cartel payroll, or whether the cop stopping you for speeding moonlights for the mafia or just takes bribes from motorists.

Physically, much of the cash moves back and forth over the border stuffed in suitcases or in the same secret compartments used to carry drugs. Mexican police and soldiers are often kicking down doors to find millions of dollar bills decorating lounges and kitchens. Overall, Calderón's troops nabbed over $400 million in the first four years of his offensive. That considerable chunk of cheese quickly made the Mexican government millions in interest. But it is only a tiny fraction of the estimated $120 billion in total that the cartels are estimated to have moved in the period. North of the river, in the same period, American police took another $80 million linked to Mexican cartels, an even smaller piss in the ocean.

Once in Mexico, billions are believed to go straight into bank vaults. Professor Guillermo Ibarra of the Autonomous University of Sinaloa crunched numbers on the money generated by the state's formal economy compared to what was in its banks. He found more than $680 million in bank deposits unaccounted for. And Sinaloa is a financial backwater compared to the economic whales of Mexico City, Guadalajara, and Monterrey.[9]

Gangsters' ostentatious tastes also spill much of the money over to local entrepreneurs. Culiacán boasts some of the highest sales of bulky SUVs and Jeeps in the hemisphere, helping keep up brands such as Hummer. Meanwhile, the garish mansions that line its hills employ any architects and builders who can keep up with capos' eccentric tastes and don't mind working for high-pressure clients.

But the real money sets up entire front companies. The U.S. Treasury has blacklisted more than two hundred Mexican firms it alleges launder drug money. They include everything from a prominent dairy in Sinaloa to car washes, flower shops, and clothing lines.[10]

I visited several businesses on this Treasury blacklist in Mexico City. My first stop was a spa and clinic in the upscale Lomas neighborhood. Walking through the door, I was greeted by friendly young women dressed in loose white uniforms, while middle-aged ladies sat in the waiting room reading glossy magazines. The manager said they knew nothing about drug cartels or U.S. Treasury blacklists but plenty about breast implants and liposuction. She asked me if I was after a weight-reducing massage, signaling that I was looking a bit portly myself. To add to this flab, I went to a second listed business, a gourmet taqueria in between the offices of some major Mexican and American corporations. The eatery specialized in food with the habanero chili pepper, the spiciest of all chiles. After gorging on three tacos, I felt the chili's burn—but learned little about mafia bosses.

The Treasury blacklist bans Americans from doing business with these places (I'm not American, so I didn't commit a crime). But it would be up to the Mexican government to shut them down. They evidently hadn't. And the alleged Laundromats kept on enlarging breasts and serving superspicy snacks.

This leads to a common reprimand of Calderón's mighty war. He may have smacked gangsters with a large hammer. But he hasn't followed the money. As long as cash keeps flowing, critics howl, bad guys will keep jumping to it.

Calderón has tried to remedy this, decreeing new measures to clamp down on dollar cash deposits and filing a major reform bill on money laundering in 2010. The bill would keep tight regulations on banks, investments, and funds; in short doing everything American critics call for. One can hope that if the law is approved, it will limit Mexico's gangster economy in the future.

However, on a globalized planet, Mexico is still limited in its scope to stop drug barons from moving cash. Even if it is pushed out of their banks, the money can easily flow elsewhere, such as the United States or offshore tax havens or China. A lot of it is in these places already. Reforms to make it easier to zap capital around the planet have made it harder to police that money. In 1979, some seventy-five banks were in offshore tax havens; today there are more than three thousand. Every day, seventy thousand international money transfers move a trillion dollars. The executive director of the United Nations Office on Drugs and Crime, Antonio Maria Costa, wrote:

"Money laundering is rampant and practically unopposed . . . At a time of major bank failures, if money doesn't smell, bankers seem to believe. Honest citizens, struggling in a time of economic hardship, wonder why the proceeds of crime—turned into ostentatious real estate, cars, boats and planes—are not seized."[11]

The Mexican dirty cash is but one slice in the world's vast money-laundering pie.

The rivers that connect Mexican drug dollars to bigger financial seas are illustrated in Technicolor by the curious case of Zhenli Ye Gon. Mr. Ye

Gon was born in China in the 1960s but became a naturalized Mexican in 2002. President Fox himself awarded him his citizenship papers, shaking the hand of a man who seemed to be an enterprising pharmaceutical entrepreneur. Ye Gon speaks Spanish with a strong Chinese accent, pronouncing the *l*'s too softly, which led to jokes about him in Mexico. Like many businessmen, he likes playing high-stakes poker. He also likes decorating his house with piles of dollar bills. Huge, mountainous piles.

Federales found this decor in 2007 when they stormed his mansion in the upscale Lomas de Chapultepec suburb of Mexico City: $205.6 million in hundred-dollar bills. It was so much money that the piles of notes spilled out of the lounge, down the corridors, and into the kitchen. DEA agents jumped triple cartwheels and categorized it as the biggest cash bust anywhere in the world ever.

There were also huge piles of peso notes. Mexican police said these pesos were worth $157,000, until journalists studied the photos and pointed out it looked like a lot more money. Oh, the police replied, you're right, and adjusted the peso amount to $1.5 million. The world's biggest-ever cash bust had just got bigger. It was finally counted in at worth more than $207 million.

Zhenli Ye Gon himself was spotted in Las Vegas at the time of the raid enjoying his favorite hobby—gambling. Mexican federal agents had got onto his case, and probably alerted his attention, after they busted tons of pseudoephedrine at a Mexican Pacific port in December. The businessman was importing these chemicals, they alleged, and selling them to Mexican mobsters to cook into crystal meth. Zhenli Ye Gon was buying the chemicals from a pharmaceutical company in the People's Republic of China.

Zhenli Ye Gon then gave an interview to the Associated Press in New York.[12] In a videotaped rant, Zhenli Ye Gon threw out some wild accusations in his defense. He confessed the money had been in his home but said that a Mexican politician had told him to stash it there under threat of death. He also said he was afraid that if he returned to Mexico, he would be killed. But some of his most startling statements concerned the United States. Zhenli Ye Gon said he had blown $126 million in Las Vegas, but been given 40 percent of his losses back as well as gifts of luxury cars. He was explaining a simple way to move suitcases full of dollar bills into the system: buy millions of dollars' worth of chips in a casino and get losses back in checks and cars.

American police nabbed Zhenli Ye Gon in a restaurant on the outskirts of Washington and charged him with conspiracy to import crystal meth. However, after a key Las Vegas witness recanted and the Chinese government refused to hand over documents, American prosecutors agreed to drop charges on the understanding that he would be extradited and tried in Mexico. Ye Gon was still fighting extradition in 2011 arguing that he wouldn't get a fair trial south of the border. He admitted he had imported chemicals from China, but argued that he had no knowledge that any of it would be used to cook up the kind of crystal stew that General Solórzano showed me.

The case shows that while the journey of a line of cocaine from farmer to nostril can be weird, the journey of a drug dollar can be even weirder. Imagine a Walmart–employee meth addict in Nebraska buying a bumper batch of crystal with five ten-dollar bills. The crisp notes travel from local dealers to Mexican distributors and float south over the border in a trap car. One ends up in the building of a narco mansion on the hills of Sinaloa; one ends up in a Mexico City mansion to line the floors for a record-breaking raid; one goes to China to pay for raw ingredients; one gets carried back up over the border and buys chips in Las Vegas.

Free trade in the twenty-first century can be surreal. This is mafia capitalism at its most spectacular. It's all about the money. That is why thugs are chopping off heads and rolling them into discos. And that is where our Nebraska addict's fifth bill goes: to pay for El Narco's second-biggest product after drugs: murder.

CHAPTER 9

Murder

A killer arrived in hell,
To inspect his work,
Without knowing that his dead,
Were already waiting for him,
He just went through the door,
And there began his end.

—GRUPO CARTEL, "A KILLER ARRIVED IN HELL," 2008

Twenty seconds of shooting. Four hundred and thirty-two bullets. Five dead policemen.

Four of the corpses sprawl over a shiny, new Dodge Ram pickup truck that has been pierced by so many caps it resembles a cheese grater. The cadavers are twisted and contorted in the unnatural poses of the dead; arms arch backward over spines, legs spread out sideways; the pattern of bodies that fall like rag dolls when bullets strike.

After arriving at too many murder scenes, I often felt numb staring at the lead-filled flesh spread out on the concrete, dirt roads, and car seats. The images all blur into one. But then little details come back: the twists of elbows over backs, heads over shoulders. These patterns come into my mind when I think about the murder scenes; and these patterns then filter into bad dreams when I am sleeping in a bed a thousand miles away.

This particular crime scene is on a sweaty December evening in Culiacán. The state policemen had hit a red stoplight next to a shopping center when the triggermen attacked. *Bang. Bang. Bang.* The assassins shot from the side and back, unleashing bullets in split seconds. A customized Kalashnikov with a circular clip can unload a hundred rounds in ten seconds. This is lightning war. People tend to shudder at Mexican gangsters having rocket-propelled grenades. But the AK is far more lethal.

The fifth dead policeman is a muscular, forty-eight-year-old commander laying ten feet away from the pickup, bathing in his own blood. His right hand is stretched upward clasping a 9 mm pistol, creating a death pose that could have been set up for a Hollywood movie. When the hit men sprayed, the commander had managed to jump out and run, pistol in hand. But the killers followed him with their shower of bullets, finishing him off by the edge of the sidewalk.

The commander has hard features, with high cheekbones and a broad nose over a finely trimmed mustache. His eyes are wide-open staring at the heavens. The left side of his face, just above his neck, was ripped open by a Kalashnikov bullet, distorting his visage with a gaping hole. Up close, it somehow looks like a rubber mask rather than the face of a real human being. Death is hard to comprehend.

We arrive ten minutes after the shooting and the police have yet to cordon off the area or cover the bodies with plastic sheets. Soon the block will be swarming with soldiers manning mounted machine guns, ski-masked homicide police, and forensic teams. But for now we can walk all over the bullet shells and stick our cameras to the faces of the victims.

A crowd of onlookers thickens on the street. Four young teenagers breathlessly analyze the attack. "That one is a Kalashnikov bullet. That one is from an AR-15," says a skinny kid in a baseball cap, pointing at a long, silvery shell next to a shorter, gold one. Beside them, middle-aged couples, old men, and mothers with small infants all gawk at the morbid display. The local press corps huddle together on the sidewalk, checking photos on viewfinders to make sure they have the best images for the police pages. They are relaxed, cheery; this is their daily bread.

Thirty minutes after the attack, a battered Ford Focus speeds through the crowd and screeches to a halt against the police tape. The wife of one of the victims jumps out and screams hysterically at the olive-clad soldiers guarding the scene. Her swinging arms are held back by her brother, his eyes red with tears. A few feet away, I grab the shoulder of my cameraman and pull him away to make sure he doesn't get a smack from an angry, grieving relative. Only when I see the pained look on their faces does the loss of human life really sink in. The screams show the suffering of those who knew the man in his best and worst moments, as a husband at the altar, as a father dancing with his daughter on her fifteenth birthday, as a lover in the dark of the night.

Another day. Another murder. In the Mexican Drug War, such violence has become so common that the slaying of five police at a stoplight was a brief tucked in local crime sections. The victims become more numbers for newspaper and government tallies, their human stories and struggling families soon forgotten.

These ambush-style killings account for the vast majority of deaths in the conflict. They are known as *ejecuciones*, or "executions." Even the name is chilling; it explains that someone has ordered a death sentence on the target. The gunmen rarely miss. Mexico has no death penalty, but the worst days have seen more than sixty executions—two dozen in Ciudad Juárez, more sprinkled over Michoacán, Guerrero, Tamaulipas, Sinaloa, Durango, Tijuana. The next-highest number of war victims are people who are kidnapped, murdered, and have their bodies dumped. Deaths in shootouts account for a small percentage. This is a war fought by assassins. Their hit-and-run tactics are extremely difficult to defend against.

In the mid-twentieth century, assassination was a lucrative and niche trade in Mexico. The killers were known as *gatilleros*, or "triggermen." They were skilled professionals who carried on their trade into middle age, using pistols and dispatching their victims at close range, often in the dark of the night.

One of the earliest *gatilleros* was Rodolfo Valdés, a Sinaloan known as the Gitano, or Gypsy. Valdes headed a gang of gunmen called the Dorados, the Golden Ones, who were paid by landowners to kill uppity peasants in the 1940s. This was the origin of many Sinaloan murder squads—to protect the crops and property of the wealthy against agrarian reform. El Gitano is reported to have taken the lives of more than fifty people. He is even alleged to have killed the governor of Sinaloa, who was gunned down in a carnival in Mazatlán in 1944. Governor Rodolfo Loaiza angered landowners by making too many expropriations. He is also reported to have annoyed opium growers by seizures of their crops.[1]

Other professional *gatilleros* worked in Mexico City in the employ of senior politicians and security officials. They did the dirty work that didn't go in the files. The most famous of these government hit men was José González, who wrote a book about his deeds in 1983. The son of Spaniards, Gonzalez claimed that he carried out more than fifty murders for various officials, but especially Mexico City police chief Arturo "Blackie" Durazo. Durazo was eventually imprisoned for extortion and other crimes.

González personifies the "professional" assassins of old. He had a university degree, didn't start murdering until he was twenty-eight, and carried on killing into his fifties. In his memoir, he attributes his ability to kill in cold blood to the murder of his own father in a bar brawl. "I believe that this incident sowed in my soul the disdain for the life of others and my eagerness for revenge," he wrote.[2]

In the 1980s, the Colombian mafia revolutionized the murder business. The architect of its killing machine was Isaac Guttnan Esternberg, a Colombian of German descent who worked for Medellín traffickers. Guttnan invented the "school of motorcycle assassins," to which young men from the slums enrolled in their thousands. He understood that alienated youth can be won by little more than a decent salary and sense of purpose. The assassins still used pistols, but they attacked on motorcycles, with one driver and one shooter. They became known as *sicarios*— from the ancient sicarii, Jewish Zealots who carried small daggers under their cloaks to stab Romans.

In 1986, Guttnan was himself assassinated by a *sicario*.[3]

I drive through Medellín to meet a *sicario*. It is a pleasant city. A cool breeze keeps the mountain valley fresh. Airy plazas are illuminated with sculptures of comically plump people based on the paintings of Medellín artist Fernando Botero. The most beautiful women in the world stroll down wide sidewalks.

Back in 1991, Medellín was the most murderous city per capita on the planet with some 6,500 homicides, among a population of 2 million. Now that crown has passed to Ciudad Juárez. But while Medellín has reduced the numbers of killings, it is still very violent, with 2,899 homicides in 2009.[4]

The man I am going to meet pulled the trigger on several of those hits. German photojournalist Oliver Schmieg arranges the interview. The Munich native has spent eleven years in Colombia and taken incredible photos of clandestine cocaine labs and guerrillas in combat with the army. I am blown away by how dogged and determined Oliver is. He works through his network of narcs, police informers, and street thugs. But the best contact is a former soldier who became chief of security for a prominent Medellín paramilitary leader. The contact pulls strings and Oliver is soon talking to the *sicario* on the telephone. The *sicario* first has to clear the interview with his direct boss, so he asks us to call back. Oliver phones again the next morning and the man says we can come over. We drive nervously to the address.

We arrive at an apartment block in Envigado, a middle-class neighborhood that has long been the heart of operations for the Medellín mafia. A doorman calls to the apartment and we are ushered upstairs. Our man opens the door and invites us to sit down at a large wooden table. The big apartment has little furniture, but a state-of-the-art plasma TV and a PlayStation 3 console.

Gustavo is twenty-four years old and strikingly thin, with light brown skin and crew-cut hair. He is dressed in a trendy green, short-sleeved shirt, Hawaiian shorts, and bright green canvas boots. A bulky childhood friend—and fellow *sicario*—shares the apartment and is pacing around with his shirt off, revealing tattoos on his back. Gustavo sits down with us and pins his elbows to the wooden table, fiddling around with a cigarette tin. At first he is a little nervous. But as we talk, he becomes more friendly and open. We talk for hours. The more we chat, the more I like him. He is clever and charismatic while being modest. I keep forgetting that he is a contract killer. Later I ask myself if it is wrong to like someone who robbed human lives. Can I really separate a human side of someone from the deeds they have done?

The flashy apartment we are in contrasts with the slum where Gustavo grew up. He was born in the *comunas* that snake up steep mountain slopes overlooking Medellín. The neighborhoods of unpainted breeze-block homes with tin roofs were squatted by thousands who swarmed to the city from Colombia's peaks, valleys, and jungles. Many had fled bombings and firefights between the government and communist guerrillas. Others just came looking for enough money to feed their families.

Gustavo was the second of three sons of a construction worker. His father made enough for them to eat most days, but not enough to get out of the ghetto. When Gustavo was a toddler, gunfire rattled daily in his *comuna*. When he was eight years old, Colombian police shot dead Pablo Escobar in Medellín.[5] Even as an infant, Gustavo knew all about the cocaine capo. "Up in the *comunas* Pablo was like a king. He was bigger than the Colombian president," Gustavo says.

The assassin speaks with the melodic accent of the Medellín slums and uses many terms from its mafia argot. He has words for pistols (irons), rifles (guitars), cocaine (parrot), and murder victims (little girls). But despite the slang, he pronounces his words carefully and holds back from swearing.

Following the death of King Escobar, top Medellín traffickers met to discuss business—in an underground garage in Envigado. From this infamous summit, the so-called Office of Envigado was born, an organization to oversee crime in Medellín. To avoid endless bloodshed, the office would make sure all debts between traffickers were paid—and collect 33 percent for the service.

At the head of the Office was Diego Murillo, alias Don Berna, who had been the chief of a gang of *sicarios*. Don Berna ruled that for anyone to commit murder, the Office had to authorize it. This was one of the key reasons for the decline in the Medellín murder rate. Each barrio had its "commander," who responded to the capo. On the street, the organization was also known as the mafia. American agents called it the Medellín Cartel.

As Gustavo became a teenager, his father tried hard to steer him and his brothers away from the mafia. But it was difficult to convince them an honest life paid off.

"You see your father sweating hard all day and just making a few pesos. And sometimes he was out of work for months. And then guys in the barrio working for the Office are driving brand-new cars and motorcycles and have five girlfriends."

Gustavo began to hang around on the street with older boys connected to the mafia, provoking his father's ire. Eventually, his father caught him smoking marijuana when he was thirteen and kicked him out of the family home. "It was a bit severe," Gustavo remembers. "Here we are in the cocaine capital of the world and my dad throws me out for smoking a spliff."

Gustavo slept on friends' floors and sometimes on the dirt streets of the slum, kept warm by the tropical heat. He also moved deeper into the arms of the mafia. As well as smuggling drugs, the Medellín gangsters ran protection rackets and sold stolen vehicles. Gustavo first made his name as an able car thief, the same trade that Pablo Escobar himself apprenticed in crime.

"I would go into the center of town and steal cars or motorcycles. I could find a way into anything. I used to love stealing. It became like an addiction."

Despite robbing day and night, Gustavo stayed in school until he was seventeen. By then, he was earning more than most adults in his *comuna*, and he dropped out to work full-time for the mob. Gaining the trust of the bosses, he would get jobs moving bricks of cocaine or packages of money, sometimes dollars and sometimes euros. The white powder came from plantations and labs to the north and west of Medellín. But the bosses in the city controlled it, and tons of it passed through the slums on its way to Pacific or Caribbean ports.

"I tried snorting cocaine but I never liked it that much. Some of my friends would love it. I always preferred smoking grass."

Gustavo drew closer to the top dogs in the Medellín mafia, and on one delivery he met kingpin Don Berna face-to-face. "He was very friendly. Obviously, he was a very powerful man. But he wasn't arrogant. He just acted like a regular guy," Gustavo remembers with a touch of awe in his voice. Soon after the meeting, Gustavo got the nod to start training as a *sicario*. He had just turned eighteen.

Gustavo stares intensely as he explains the assassination techniques: "We normally hit with one team on a motorcycle and another in a car. The bike has one driver and one shooter. The car blocks the victim in and the bike gets right beside the target. Then the shooter unloads fast and passes the gun into the car, where it is put in a secret compartment."

Gustavo first learned the art by driving a bike for his mentor, an older *sicario*. "He taught me how it was done, how you have to keep steady, keep focused, and above all not miss the target. How you shoot in the head and heart to make sure you kill.

"When I did my first hit, I got a little too close and shot too many bullets into the body. Then the blood and guts exploded out all over me. I had to throw away my clothes and wash hard to get it off. That night I had bad dreams. I kept remembering shooting the person and the blood spurting out."

Gustavo did more hits and the bad dreams stopped. Every few weeks he would be given a new target. Mostly he killed in Medellín, but he was also sent to take out victims in other cities across Colombia such as Bogotá and Cali. Soon he had killed ten, then fifteen, then twenty people. Then he lost count.

I ask him if he thinks about the victims. He shakes his head.

"I keep focused and do my work. Before I go out, I pray to Jesus and clear my mind. I never take drugs or drink before a job as I need my five senses. When I come back, I will relax and smoke a spliff and listen to music."

Gustavo says he doesn't know or ask who the victims are. A target is selected and another team will follow the person's movements to find the best time to strike. Then the *sicarios* will be called in.

"I get a call saying, 'There goes the little girl. Take care of her.' They will give me a photo of the target. And then we will go and hunt."

Gustavo says it is all about the money for him. He gets a base salary of about $600 a month plus a payment of between $2,000 to $4,000 for each hit he carries out. While such money is a far cry from that of the billionaire traffickers with their diamond-studded mansions and fleets of private planes, it makes him wealthy by the standards of the Medellín slums. Furthermore, with a 22 percent unemployment rate for Colombians under twenty-six years old, it is undoubtedly the best-paid job he could get.[6]

"Some people murder because they get pleasure out of it, because they actually enjoy killing and get addicted to the blood. But I do it out of need."

His blood money has taken him and his family out of the ghetto. As well as renting this apartment, Gustavo has bought his family a house in a lower-middle-class neighborhood. Teenage arguments he had with his parents are long forgotten, and he now sees them several times a week. His older brother is also in the mafia, but they are paying to put their younger brother through private school in the hope he will find a decent legitimate job.

Besides supporting his family, Gustavo likes to spend his earnings on designer-label clothes and high-tech Japanese motorbikes. He is also a big fan of English Premier League football and pays for cable TV to watch all the matches he can, as well as playing soccer video games on PlayStation 3.

"I support Wigan because they have Colombian striker Hugo Rodallega. I appreciate that Manchester United play good football as well. But I don't like Arsenal."

The references to British soccer teams seem a surreal connection from this Colombian hit man to the far-off reality of my homeland. Later, I publish the Gustavo interview in a British newspaper, and a Wigan fan group sticks the story on their Web page. They find it amusing that a Colombian assassin follows their team.

Gustavo tells me he likes romantic salsa music but avoids Medellín nightclubs in case he bumps into rival assassins. He is also a fan of electronic dance music and once went with a cousin in Bogotá to see London DJ Carl Cox.

"Everyone in the club was just drinking water and dancing like crazy. So I asked my cousin what was going on, and she said they were all taking the drug ecstasy. But I didn't want to take it as I was worried it might be too strong. I heard LSD is crazy as well. I have respect for people who take that, but I don't know if I want to risk it myself."

The reference to a British DJ strikes me as another surreal connection with the world that I come from. For Gustavo, being an assassin has given him the means into the consumer lifestyles enjoyed in the rich West: to watch soccer on cable, play video games, wear designer clothes, go to nightclubs; the same pastimes that any student, building worker, or office boy in my own country can enjoy. It also gives him a sense of achievement—to be a somebody in a barrio full of nobodies. It even gives him a status that makes these two dumb European journalists sit in front of him and lap up every word he says.

But whatever benefits it has, there is no easy way out of the mafia for Gustavo. Being a cartel hit man does not come with a retirement plan.

"The bosses don't let you leave because you know too much. When people try and get out, they can kill them. The only way is to just disappear without saying anything."

He claims he is not scared of prison and already did one short stint for being caught with a stolen car. His boss (commander) looked after him, sending him food, and he had conjugal visits from girlfriends every week. He also took his high school exams behind bars and passed with decent grades. I ask if there is any other job he would like to do with his qualifications. "I would like to be a police detective investigating murders," he says with a straight face. "But I can't because of my criminal record."

I ask him about his future, about the idea of marriage or children. He has several girlfriends but says he doesn't want to tie the knot yet.

"I might make a commitment when the time comes. The girls in Medellín love gangsters. They look for boyfriends in the mafia as they know they have money to spend."

Does he feel remorse about the people he has murdered? I ask. How can he square what he does with his Catholicism? "I know it is bad," he says. "But I do it out of need. I do it to support my family."

He also knows that his work may well lead to his own murder. But he tries to keep any fear tucked deep inside.

"I need to keep strong and focused. I can't spend all my time worrying if they are going to kill me or not. Everyone dies in the end."

Colombian assassins gained fame the world over, especially in Mexico. As Mexicans worked with their partners to move the white lady north, they also studied the notorious Colombian killing machine. The respect for Colombian hit men can be heard in many Sinaloan ballads, such as one called "De Oficio Pistolero," or "pistol-slinger by trade." "They are the Colombian mafiosi, they do not forgive mistakes," the song begins.[7]

Mexican assassins emulated many of the Colombian techniques and also began to call themselves *sicarios*. Like their partners, the capos recruited young men from the slums. They also used cars to block in their victims. However, while Colombians used motorcycles, Mexicans ambushed from Jeeps and SUVs. And while Colombians used pistols, Mexicans blasted with their beloved "goat horn" rifles.

As the Mexican Drug War escalated, the AK-47 ambushers began to spray with crazy amounts of bullets. Murder victims were often found with up to fifty caps inside them, while another three hundred spent bullets lay on the concrete. Such overkill helps ensure a hit. It also drastically raises the risk of hurting civilians. I began rolling up to an increasing number of murder scenes where bullets had struck bystanders: a businesswoman driving behind a target in her VW Beetle; the man making tacos on the side of the road; the mother walking along with her baby in a buggy. The Mexican press started calling them victims of "lost bullets." The civilian death toll hit the hundreds.

But *sicarios* always got their targets. And they almost always drove away unmolested. I was astounded how Mexican assassins could carry out simultaneous hits in three parts of Culiacán or Ciudad Juárez amid hundreds of police and soldiers and then disappear into thin air. And I was amazed how effective the gangsters were at kidnapping victims from their homes, workplaces, or restaurants—and dumping their bodies in public places later. Why do people give themselves up to a criminal commando they must suspect is going torture and kill them? Why don't they run for their lives?

Back in the prison in Ciudad Juárez, I ask these questions of Gonzalo, the cartel killer who orchestrated many of these kidnappings and assassinations. The thirty-eight-year-old operative sits on his bed in a wing of the prison run by evangelical Christians telling me about his brutal life in the mafia. His face shows little emotion as he recalls some of the techniques for sending people to their doom.

"We have all the points covered. We work like the police in the United States, you understand? In every job we have points. If someone tries to get away, there will be a point that will respond. To do a kidnapping, you have to think about it for a long time. You have to do it well, because if you mess up one time, that could be it for you."

He also elaborates how gangsters employ a large network of spies. And how, in many cases, victims are turned in by their own relatives.

"A lot of women move in this environment as well as kids, sixteen to eighteen years old. They can be very important points, watching things. A lot of the times, family members themselves will be involved in the jobs—brothers, uncles, cousins. And then it is easier as they know everything about the person, how they move. Sometimes they arrange to meet the person in some place. And then we turn up."

Finally, Gonzalo discusses the gangsters' biggest aid: support from police. Local officers working with the mafia will actually block off areas so *sicarios* can carry out a hit, then go in afterward once the commando is safely driving away. Furthermore, gangsters will often use codes to give to police officers that stop them to identify they are "protected." Such practices may seem terrifying revelations. But they have even been confirmed by many of the government's own publicized interrogations of thugs.

Prison itself does not even stop some killers. In Durango state penitentiary, it was uncovered that inmates would actually leave the jail at night, carry out murders, then return to their cells—all with the complicity of prison guards. They even traveled in prison vehicles and used the guards' guns.[8] In other cases, inmates have broken out en masse to join back with their cartel armies. In Zacatecas state prison, a convoy of Jeeps and SUVs pulled up, supported by a helicopter, and busted fifty-three convicts out. In Reynosa, eighty-five inmates simply put up ladders and poured over the wall before dawn. Even Hollywood movies would not tolerate such a simple escape scene.

Gonzalo himself says his old comrades have offered to get him out of jail. But he is not interested.

"My people, my friends, said to me, 'Let's sort this out. There are ways to get you out of there.' But I decided it was better to stay here, to look for peace and tranquillity, to leave the other man behind.

"I know Christ now. I know that he exists, that he is with us. I am not scared. If I am killed, amen. I am ready for whatever comes. For whatever."

The veteran killer finally wants to be out of the game. A new generation of *sicarios* are replacing the old, the dead, and the imprisoned. And while Gonzalo murdered and tortured to become a rich man, the young bloods take life for peanuts.

Five miles south of the Juárez jail where I talk to Gonzalo is the so-called Juárez School of Improvement—home to thirteen- to eighteen-year-olds. The name is a little ironic, as it is a penitentiary rather than a school and keeps dangerous criminals briefly off the streets rather than leading them to higher education. To drive home this point, the front of the "schoolhouse" is defended by soldiers with machine guns mounted on sandbags, and a series of cages mark the entrance. Behind the bars are dozens of "students" who aspire to be the next generation of drug lords.

Inside it is bare and ordered. In a dining area of stone tables, I find José Antonio, a cheery seventeen-year-old in baggy pants and a loose shirt. José Antonio stands just five feet six and has chocolate-colored skin, earning the classic nickname of the short and brown, *frijol*, or "bean." He has a mop of black, curly hair and bad acne, like many seventeen-year-olds you might see banging their heads at alternative-rock concerts in Seattle or Manchester. But despite his harmless demeanor, he has seen more firefights and murders than many soldiers serving in Iraq and Afghanistan.

Frijol came of age in a war zone. When the Zetas and the Sinaloa Cartel began their paramilitary fighting on the Texas border, he was just twelve years old—and in that year he joined a street gang in his Juárez slum. When Felipe Calderón declared war on drug cartels, Frijol was fourteen—and already had his hand in armed robberies, drug dealing, and regular gun battles with rival gangs. At sixteen, police nabbed Frijol for possession of a small arsenal of weapons—including two automatic rifles and an Uzi—and as an accessory to a drug-related murder.

The mass recruitment of Juárez gangbangers by drug cartels is one of the key causes of the bloodbath in the city. It produced a new generation of young, sanguine *sicarios* only loosely controlled by the crime bosses. It put the young people of entire neighborhoods into the line of fire—on their street corners, soccer fields, or house parties. High-school-age kids from Juárez would take part in—and be victims of—massacres that shocked the world.

Frijol is typical of the Juárez young lured into the ranks of the mafia. His parents hailed from a country village in Veracruz state but joined the wave of immigrants that flocked to work in Juárez assembly plants in the 1990s. They sweated on different production lines making Japanese televisions, American cosmetics, and mannequins for American stores, for an average of $6 a day. It was a step up from growing corn in their village, but it was also a radical change in their lives. Frijol's parents still celebrated peasant folk days and macho country values. But he grew up in a sprawling city of 1.3 million[9] where he could tune in to American TV channels and see the skyscrapers of El Paso over the river. Contraband goods and guns flooded south, and drugs went north. He was in between markets and in between worlds.

They lived in a huge slum that stretches up a mountain on the west side of Juarez. It is known as Bible Hill because higher up the slope is a message etched into the earth that says CIUDAD JUÁREZ: THE BIBLE IS THE TRUTH. READ IT. Americans can see the message—and the slum—from the comfort of El Paso. The neighborhoods on the hill are physically better than many in Latin America. It is not a shantytown. The homes are made of drab, unpainted cinder blocks. Almost everybody has water and electricity. But Bible Hill's slums are among the most violent barrios on the continent.

While Frijol's parents slaved for long days in the factories, he was left for hours at home alone. He soon found company on the street, in the community of teenagers hanging on the corner. They played soccer, laughed, shared stories, and looked after each other. And merely that—no elaborate initiation ceremony—made him part of a Juárez street gang. These gangs are known as barrios, the very word for "neighborhood." His barrio was called the Calaberas, or skulls, and had a hundred members, all from a few blocks on the hill.

"The gang becomes like your home, your family. It is a place where you find friendship and people to talk to. It is where you feel part of something. And you know the gang will back you up if you are in trouble."

The Calaberas were allied with a barrio to the south called El Silencio but bitter enemies of a barrio to the west called Chema 13. This shifting system of gang alliances spread like a confused spiderweb down the mountainside. Each territory bore the mark of its resident gang spray-painted on walls. Fights between rival barrios were common, often leading to deaths. For gang members, it was dangerous to wander into enemy territory. Most of the kids stayed safely within the few blocks of their territory and their people.

These barrios had been in Juárez for decades. New generations filled the ranks while veterans grew out of them. They had always fought—with sticks, stones, knives, and guns. There had always been deaths. I wrote a story on the Juárez barrios in 2004. In that year, police told me that about eighty murders were attributed to this street warfare. That is still a shocking number. But it was nothing compared to the blood that would flow in the streets at the end of the decade. The radical change happened when the barrios were swept up into the wider drug-cartel war.

Fríjol learned to use guns in the Calaberas. Arms moved around Juárez streets freely, and every barrio had its arsenal stashed round the homes of a few members. They would practice shooting in parks or up the mountain, then blood themselves in battles against enemy gangs. Then as the Sinaloa and Juárez cartels began to fight for the city, the mafias went to gangbangers for fresh cannon fodder.

"Men with connections started looking at who knew how to shoot. There was a guy who had been in the barrio a few years before and he was now working with the big people. And he started offering jobs to the youngsters. The first jobs were just as lookouts or guarding *tienditas* [little drug shops]. Then they started paying people to do the big jobs. They started paying people to kill."

I ask how much the mafia pays to carry out murders. Fríjol tells me without stopping for a moment. One thousand pesos. That is about $85. The figure seems so ludicrous that I check it out in several other interviews up in the barrios with former and active gang members. They all say the same thing. One thousand pesos to carry out a killing. The price of a human life in Juárez is just $85.

To traffic drugs is no huge step to the dark side. All kinds of people over the world move narcotics and don't feel they've crossed a red line. But to take a human life. That is a hard crime. I can at least comprehend assassins killing to jump from poverty to riches. But for someone to take a life for just $85—enough to eat some tacos and buy a few beers over the week—shows a terrifying degradation in society.

To try to get a handle on how this has happened, I talk to social worker Sandra Ramirez at a youth center in the westside slums. Sandra grew up in the barrios and worked on assembly lines before trying to steer young people away from crime. She says the teenage *sicarios* are the result of systematic alienation over the last two decades. The slums were a convenient place for factory workers but got nothing from the government. As the factory jobs slumped with the economy, the slums were left to rot. One 2010 study found that a stunning 120,000 Juárez youngsters aged thirteen to twenty-four—or 45 percent of the total—were not enrolled in any education nor had any formal employment.[10]

"The government offers nothing. It can't even compete with a thousand pesos. It is only the mafia that comes to these kids and offers them anything. They offer them money, cell phones, and guns to protect themselves. You think these kids are going to refuse? They have nothing to lose. They only see the day-to-day. They know they could die and they say so. But they don't care. Because they have lived this way all their lives."

As members of Fríjol's gang began working for the mafia, they were suddenly flush with more powerful weapons. They used to fight their gun battles with 9 mm pistols. Suddenly they had Kalashnikovs and Uzis. Giving an AK-47 to a bloodthirsty fifteen-year-old with no education is a ticket for disaster. Gangbangers killing under the name of cartels were involved in bloody massacres around the city.

Many barrio members were absorbed into two much larger gangs working for the drug cartels. One is the Barrio Azteca, a mob first formed by Chicano inmates in a Texas prison in the 1980s. The Aztecas have since mutated into a huge organization of thugs, drug dealers, and gunslingers in Mexico working for the Juárez Cartel. The other is the Artist Assassins, an organization that grew out of a Juárez street gang and mushroomed as it allied with the Sinaloa Cartel. On the streets, these two organizations are known as crews. As well as bloodthirsty teenagers, their number includes many adults in their twenties, thirties, or older who have grown into career criminals.

One of the founders of the Artist Assassins is a twenty-seven-year-old who goes by the nickname Saik. He is serving a sentence for doing a triple murder for the Sinaloa Cartel. Another gang member shows me a painting that Saik did; these thugs really are artists, hence the name. The morbid painting jumps out at me and keeps me staring hard. The basic idea is simple and common: a helmeted skeletal head smoking a reefer. But something in the depth and personality of this rotting cranium entrances me. It is as though the dark yellow skull stares right back into my eyes with a confident, almost smug expression in his green teeth. He is a mask of death. But the painting also emits a strong personality, showing off cockiness and ghetto panache.

The war between the Double A's and Aztecas has been catastrophic. Gunmen went into a drug rehab center in Juárez, lined up seventeen recovering addicts, and shot them all in the head. The killers were allegedly Double A members seeking to kill an Azteca leader hidden there. They exterminated everyone, leaving the world in stupefied horror.

In apparent revenge, Aztecas were allegedly behind the horrendous Salvarcar massacre in January 2010 that shook Mexico to the core. According to confessions, the gunmen went to a party to seek out three Double A members. The killers blocked off the entrances to the street and sprayed everyone they could see, murdering thirteen high school students and two adults. Victims included a high school football star and a straight-A student. Most, maybe all, had nothing to do with the drug war.

I ask Fríjol what it is like to be in firefights, to see your friends dead on the street and to be an accessory to a murder. He answers unblinkingly, "Being in shoot-outs in pure adrenaline. But you see dead bodies and you feel nothing. There is killing every day. Some days there are ten executions, others days there are thirty. It is just normal now."

Perhaps this teenager really is hardened to it. Or maybe he just puts up a shield. But it strikes me that adolescents experiencing such violence must go into adulthood with scars. What kind of man can this make you?

I ask about this to school psychologist Elizabeth Villegas. The teenagers she works with have murdered and raped, I say. How does this hurt them psychologically? She stares back at me as if she hasn't thought about it before. "They don't feel anything that they have murdered people," she replies. "They just don't understand the pain that they have caused others. Most come from broken families. They don't recognize rules or limits."

The teenage *sicarios* know the legal consequences for their crimes cannot be that grave. Under Mexican law, minors can only be sentenced to a maximum of five years in prison no matter how many murders, kidnappings, or rapes they have committed.[11] If they were over the border in Texas, they could be sentenced for up to forty years or life if they were tried as an adult. Many convicted killers in the school will be back on the streets before they turn twenty. Fríjol himself will be out when he is nineteen.

But the law is the least of their worries; the mafias administer their own justice. Juárez Cartel gunmen went to neighborhoods where gang members had been recruited for the Sinaloans. It didn't matter that only two or three kids from the barrio had joined the mob. A death sentence was passed on the whole barrio. The Sinaloan mafia returned the favor on barrios that had joined the Juárez Cartel. I went to a neighborhood where twenty teenagers and young men had hung out on a street corner a year ago. Fifteen of them had been gunned down in a spree of shootings, a bar they hung out in torched. A few of the survivors are incarcerated, the rest have fled the city, leaving their old neighborhood looking like a ghost town. Fríjol recognizes that youth prison may be hard, but it is a lot safer than the streets now.

"I keep hearing about friends who have been killed out there. Maybe I would be dead too. Prison could have saved my life."

God's own medicine. Opium poppies in the Sierra Madre Occidental.
(Fernando Brito)

Mixing up coca paste in a clandestine lab in Putumayo, Colombia.
(Oliver Schmieg)

The finished product. A kilo brick of pure cocaine. The markings indicate which cartel it belongs to. (Oliver Schmieg)

Economy of scale. Soldiers tear up an industrial-size marijuana plantation in Sinaloa.
(Fernando Brito)

Drug-ballad crooners Grupo Cartel pose outside the Humaya cemetery in Culiacán. The towering mausoleums are of deceased narcos. (Fernando Brito)

Holy Death. The faithful pray, dance, and smoke outside a shrine to the Santa Muerte in Tepito, Mexico City. (Keith Dannemiller)

Mexico's Eliot Ness. President Felipe Calderón explains his drug-war strategy. (Keith Dannemiller)

A soldier at the scene of a cartel killing in Sinaloa.
(Fernando Brito)

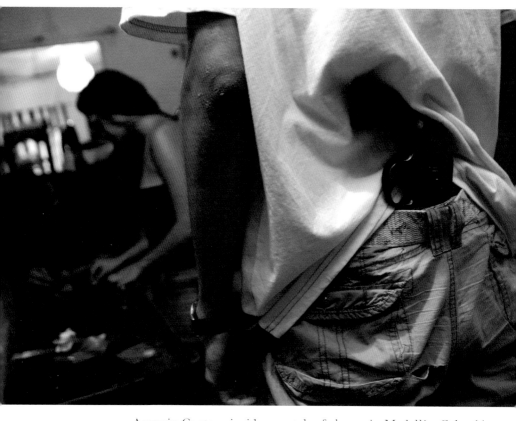

Assassin Gustavo inside a cartel safe house in Medellín, Colombia.
(Oliver Schmieg)

One move and you're dead. Colombian special forces bust a truckload of cocaine.
(Oliver Schmieg)

Urban war. Soldiers run to a crime scene in Culiacán.
(Fernando Brito)

A cartel murder victim in Sinaloa. (Fernando Brito)

Daily mourning. Family members lay to rest a murdered police officer in Sinaloa.
(Fernando Brito)

Body messaging. A corpse decorated by gangsters in Sinaloa.
(Fernando Brito)

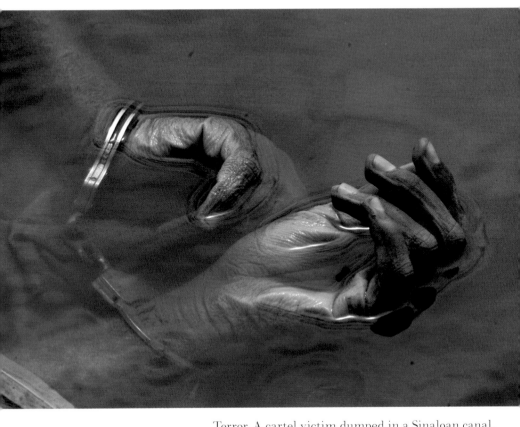

Terror. A cartel victim dumped in a Sinaloan canal.
(Fernando Brito)

Peace in the future? Schoolgirls in Culiacán march against violence. They carry photos of innocent victims. (Fernando Brito)

CHAPTER 10

Culture

A nation's culture resides in the hearts and in the soul of its people.
—MOHANDAS (MAHATMA) GANDHI

When Fausto "Tano" Castro suffered a near-death experience, he saw no pearly gates or angels. But, as may be expected from a musician, he did notice an abrupt transformation in the sound. As more than a hundred Kalashnikov bullets rained into his black Chevrolet Suburban and seven caps embedded in his arms, legs, and torso, he felt the noises around him become suddenly crystal clear, as if he were in a soundproof studio. Meanwhile, his body felt perfectly numb, registering no physical pain.

But when he realized he was indeed still alive and turned his head to inspect the damage, he burst into tears. Sprawled next to him on the passenger seat was his cousin and one of the most beloved singers in northern Mexico, Valentín Elizalde, alias the Golden Rooster. Elizalde had been ripped apart by twenty-eight shells and died instantly.

"I took him in my arms and kissed him. The moment felt unreal. Twenty minutes earlier we had been playing to this great crowd. They were going crazy for Valentin. Then there he was beside me, soaked in blood."

Castro recounts the story to me eighteen months after the ambush, which took place in November 2006 after a *palenque*, or cockfighting

event, in Reynosa, just over the border from McAllen, Texas. He has re-
covered surprisingly well. The bullet wounds have healed up to become
red, fleshy patches dotted up the right side of his body. After six months
in the hospital, he is walking around unaided and is even back playing
trumpet with his band—albeit with a replacement lead singer.

In fact, his group, Banda Guasaveña, has never been more in demand.
Elizalde has posthumously been nominated for a Latin Grammy and is
being compared to all-time great Mexican singers such as Pedro Infante.
Fans pack venues to hear the group play Valentín's most raucous numbers, including songs with such names as "118 Bullets" and "The Narco
Battalion." Meanwhile, in the year and a half since the shooting, fourteen
more Mexican musicians have been gunned down, burned, or suffocated
to death in murders that bear the hallmarks of organized crime.

To understand why *sicarios* would target crooners, composers, trumpet players, and drummers, one has to venture into the surreal world
known as *narcocultura* and its most emblematic form, the *narcocorrido,*
or drug ballad. Valentín Elizalde was one of the biggest stars the genre
has ever produced. While the music may have the folksy twang of accor-
dions and twelve-stringed guitars, the lyrics sing the glories of Kalashnikovs, cocaine kingpins, and contract killings.

Compared to gangster rap in the United States, the music is lambasted
by the Mexican government and banned on the radio. Critics say it glori-
fies drug traffickers and is part of the cause of so much violence. Whether
that is true or not, the incredible popularity of narco culture does illustrate just how entrenched traffickers are in society. *Narcocorridos* have
boomed in sales, rocking parties from the jungles of Central America to
the immigrant ghettos of Los Angeles. As gangsters haul tons of white
gold over the border and blow each other apart in turf wars, these balladeers provide the sound track.

But the crooners do more than just put earthy tunes to the carnage.
They also give it a script. Following a centuries-old tradition, the ballads
bring news to the street, describing prison escapes, massacres, new alliances, and broken pacts to a public that reads few newspapers. While
minstrels of nineteenth-century Mexico toured town squares, the contemporary balladeers emit their messages from pickup-truck stereos in
Brownsville to jukeboxes in Guatemalan cantinas.

The songs paint color onto the shady figures of the crime capos. King
of kingpins Ismael "the Mayo" Zambada was for a long time only known

from one grainy photo from the 1970s. But many on the street had vivid pictures of him from hundreds of songs detailing his exploits. The verses flatteringly speak about how he bribes top politicians, slaughters rivals, and has a fleet of planes to traffic his merchandise. One ode apparently dedicated to him even features on the 2007 album of the bestselling group Los Tucanes de Tijuana, released by Universal Music in the United States and Mexico.

His alias is the MZ,
Others call him the Godfather,
His name is well-known,
Even by newborn babies,
They look for him everywhere,
But he is not even hiding.
The dollars protect him,
And also the Goat Horns [Kalashnikovs].

At the heart of *narcocultura* is the figure of the mafia godfather. The personage is celebrated in mythological terms as the ragged peasant who rose to riches; the great outlaw who defies the Mexican army and the DEA; the benefactor who hands out rolls of dollar bills to hungry mothers; the scarlet pimpernel who disappears in a puff of smoke.

Mexico is not the only nation to idolize outlaws. England has celebrated the cult of Robin Hood in popular verse and literature from the thirteenth century. ("Robyn hode in scherewode stod.")[1] Sicily romanticizes peasant bandit Salvatore Giuliano in cinema and opera. And where would popular U.S. culture be without Jesse James, Pretty Boy Floyd, Al Capone, and John Dillinger? Or without the Notorious B.I.G. and Tupac Shakur?

But in the hinterlands of northern Mexico, the cult of the outlaw has a special ring. The region was a frontier conquered by tough adventurers far from the center of power—either in Mexico City, Washington, or Madrid. Added to this, many feel (and are) particularly hard done by in a land where rich politicians revel in palaces and keep several mistresses while the poor struggle to survive. Narcos are revered as rebels who have the balls to beat this system. On the streets of Sinaloa, people traditionally refer to gangsters as *los valientes*, "the brave ones."

The movie *The Godfather*—the zenith of cinema glorification of a capo—was a storming hit in Sinaloa. Even today, La Familia Cartel instructs all its followers to watch the trilogy. The films are particularly pertinent as Michael Corleone's godfather holds dear family values and loyalty, albeit in his own warped way (he kills his brother for being disloyal).

Al Pacino's other great gangster role, Scarface, is also a favorite south of the Rio Grande. I went to a prison in Nuevo Laredo after a criminal boss had been shot dead. Federal troops had stormed the penitentiary and were carting out all the luxury contraband the capo had stashed in his cell, including a pool table and disco sound system. (Incarceration was quite a party for him.) But the item that most grabbed my attention was an enormous framed photo of Al Pacino in *Scarface*. The fictional Cuban American Tony Montana is beloved by testosterone-filled men the world over. So it is natural that Latino gangsters themselves should find it easy to identify with the cocaine-snorting desperado who goes out with the words, "Say hello to my little friend!"

Mexico's own narco-cinema has churned out literally thousands of movies since the 1980s. The industry took off with the invention of home video, which allowed producers to make cheap B movies straight to VHS and later DVD. Known as video homes, productions are banged out in incredibly compact two-week shoots, often using genuine people in their roles—real campesinos, real prostitutes, and some real pistol-packing thugs. They have also turned out two superstars: Mario Almada, a lean Clint Eastwood–type gunslinger who normally plays cops; and Jorge Reynoso, alias El Senor de las Pistolas, a natural movie badass who plays bloodthirsty villains. Almada and Reynoso have made more than fifteen hundred narco movies between them and have many adoring aficionados, including lots of the traffickers. They also both confess to having met some of the top wanted capos, who are big fans of their flicks.

The violent, sexy tales have inspiring names such as *Coca Inc.*, *The Black Hummer*, and *Me Chingaron los Gringos* (The Gringos Fucked Me). Some of the most popular titles have up to seven sequels. As one may guess, they are packed with cocaine deals, scantily dressed women, crazy shoot-outs, and lots of big trucks burning through the desert.

I sit through hours of narco-movies, but find it hard to get into them. The plots seem too illogical and confused, the dialogue laughable. So

I ask about their appeal to Efrain Bautista, the native of the southern Sierra Madre who grew up in a marijuana-raising village. What do people see in these B movies? As soon as I mention them, Efrain flashes a grin from ear to ear.

"You have to see what my cousins in the mountains are like when they watch these films. They look at them like they are real life, like they are really happening at that moment. When the hero makes a bad decision, they curse at him, shouting at the TV. When the guns start firing, they crouch down, as if they could be hit by a bullet."

However, the biggest spenders on the movies and drug-ballad CDs are not in ramshackle Mexican villages but in Texas, California, Chicago, and other Latino parts of the United States. Immigrants identify with the struggles of the poor and enjoy a romanticized vision of their homeland. They also buy more originals, while in Mexico every market sells pirate copies.

However many films actually sell, narco-cinema producers have another special source of financing: drug dollars. Capos bankroll movies to launder money or get their own exploits immortalized on the silver screen. In a police interrogation, capo Édgar Valdéz, alias the Barbie Doll, said that he had given a producer $200,000 to make a biopic on him.[2] For broke, frustrated filmmakers, anybody throwing that kind of money seems like a fairy godmother (even if he is a mafia godfather).

Such spending by minted kingpins shapes all aspects of *narcocultura*. The capos' ostentatious homes have created their own architectural style, narco-tecture, which mixes Greek villas with Jacuzzis and tiger cages. They finance a whole industry of artisans bathing guns in gold and diamonds with elaborate engravings. And they pay for designer bulletproof clothes in the form of frilled cowboy jackets. Such spending makes capos like the lords of medieval Europe who patronized the arts and pioneered fashions that filtered down to the commoners. And the art form that capos favor most, the style that has the most impact on the streets, is the *narcocorrido*, or drug ballad.

Like so many elements of Mexican culture, the origin of the *corrido* stretches back to the blood-soaked Spanish conquest and the fusion of the European and indigenous worlds. Its base is in Iberian romance ballads, plucked on guitars by Spanish troubadours who followed in the footsteps of swashbuckling conquistadores. However, in the New World, poor mestizos—mixed-race Mexicans—inherited and developed this genre.

The ballads were especially popular in the ragged hinterlands of Chihuahua and Texas, in the days when the Lone Star State was in Mexican hands. Small communities separated by arid plains and thick forests were starved of newspapers, so wandering musicians were relied on to bring the news of conquests and coronations. Their role became crucial during the bloody war of independence in 1810. Tales of the priest Miguel Hidalgo ringing the church bells and crying, "*Viva México,*" were spread in rhyming verse. From these early days, the ballads were rebellious and subversive.

But the *corrido* really came into its own in Mexico's decade of sanguine revolutionary war from 1910 to 1920. Calls for land and freedom and the dynamiting of cities were transplanted into endless ballads sung from the firesides of militia camps to the caravans of refugees. In this period, the *corrido* found its modern and epic form. "The songs that were most genuine and best represented our popular sentiments flowered on the battlefield and in the bivouacs," wrote Vicente T. Mendoza, the foremost scholar of the genre.[3]

Showing remarkable folk memory, singers in the countryside of northern Mexico can still recite these rhymes of blood and betrayal, such as the popular "Corrido of the Revolution":

> *Wake up, Mexicans,*
> *Those who have been able to see,*
> *That they have been spilling blood,*
> *Just to get another tyrant to power,*
> *Look at my beloved homeland,*
> *How has it been left,*
> *And the men so brave,*
> *Have now all been betrayed.*

With the rise of radio and television, ballads lost importance as a media, leaving many crooners to focus on personal tales of hard work and lost love. But in one area they kept on the cutting edge of news: criminality. As early as the 1930s, balladeers sang about bandits and bootleggers. A popular verse of the era was the "The Ballad of Gregorio Cortez," about a Mexican Texan who shot a sheriff in self-defense and fled over the Rio

Grande. Celebrated folklorist Américo Paredes revived the verse in his 1958 book, *With His Pistol in Hand*, and it was eventually made into a movie in 1982.

> *Then said Gregorio Cortez,*
> *With his pistol in his hand,*
> *"Ah, so many mounted Rangers,*
> *Just to take one Mexican!"* [4]

When rock 'n' roll kick-started the modern recording industry, the door opened for Mexican music to hit the charts. Ritchie Valens (or rather Ricardo Valenzuela) turned a Mexican folk song into an international hit with "La Bamba" as early as 1958, followed by Carlos Santana's blend of Latin music and rock in the sixties. But *corridos* found their true expression from three brothers and a cousin who trekked north to work as ranch hands in Southern California in 1968. Taking their name from an immigration official who called them Little Tigers, Los Tigres del Norte were playing at Sunday congregations in a plaza in San Jose, California, when they were spotted by impresario Art Walker (a limey like myself) and signed to his upstart Fama Records. This deal set off the mammoth career that would see the Tigres churn out forty records, win almost every major award on both sides of the border, and tour nonstop for the next four decades, earning them the title of the Mexican Rolling Stones.

Just as Jamaican legend Bob Marley was given a rock touch to market his music, Walker encouraged Los Tigres to use a pumping electric bass and drums alongside the earthy accordion. The result was a raging success, defining the new *corrido* sound that still plays today; the Tigres tunes were catchy and danceable while retaining the luscious melancholy tone and polka rhythm of the Mexican ballad.

The Tigres soon discovered the popularity of songs about outlaws, with their third single, "Contraband and Treason," boosting them to success. The 1974 record, which is probably the first *narcocorrido* on vinyl, tells the tale of drug runners Emilio Varela and Camelia the Texan driving over the border at San Diego with pounds of marijuana stuffed into their car tires. After they arrive in a dark street in Los Angeles and hand over the herb for bags of cash, Camelia whips out a pistol and guns Emilio down, making away with the loot. The song shot to anthem status, inspiring covers from several rock bands and a 1977 movie. Listening to it now, it sounds like an innocent reminder of the good old days, like happy-go-lucky Mexican traffickers in Cheech and Chong films rather than psycho killers running around in ski masks.

While the Tigres were hesitant about showing off their narco side, an authentic gangster crooner emerged in Rosalino "Chalino" Sánchez. If the Tigres were the Rolling Stones of *corridos*, then Chalino was their Tupac Shakur—lovably crazy, proudly from the slums, and living a truly violent life. In and out of jail and caught up in various shootings, he was seen as a real villain, unlike the Tigres with their mullet haircuts and shiny suits. He unabashedly sang and swore about the trafficker lifestyle, pushing the limits of the genre, and became recognized as the godfather of the hard-core narco ballad.

In true outlaw style, Chalino's own bloody life and death is surrounded by myth. It has been most thoroughly documented by *Los Angeles Times* reporter Sam Quinones, who traipsed from village squares to prison records to pen Chalino's biography in the 2001 work *True Tales from Another Mexico*.[5] His story begins with an episode remarkably similar to that of Pancho Villa himself. When Chalino was an eleven-year-old growing up on a Sinaloan ranch, a local tough raped his sister. Four years later, Chalino stormed into a party, shot the rapist dead, exchanged fire with the rapists' two brothers, then fled to Los Angeles. For the rest of his teenage years, Chalino worked as a car washer, drug dealer, and coyote (migrant smuggler) before he was hit by the double trauma of seeing his brother murdered and getting tossed into Tijuana's notorious Mesa prison in 1984.

The death of his brother propelled Chalino on his path to fame. He composed his first *corrido* about his slain brother, then started charging fellow inmates to write ballads about them. Back on the streets of Los Angeles, he used his newfound talent to document the lives of the Mexican underworld, getting paid for ballads in cash as well as gold chains, watches, and embellished pistols. Seeing the success of his sound, he was soon dubbing his tapes and selling them out of a car trunk in true underground style. Word spread and suddenly he was performing in sold-out California clubs in front of thousands and signing with a major record label. It was the American Dream—for a glorious moment.

The bloody events of 1992 then turned him into a legend. First in a

January concert in the California desert city of Coachella, a drunken reveler clambered onstage with a gun and shot at Chalino. True to his reputation, Chalino pulled out a pistol and returned fire, starting a shoot-out that left seven people injured and at least one dead. The incident flashed on ABC News and his sales skyrocketed. Four months later, after playing to a roaring crowd in his home state of Sinaloa, he was detained by men in police uniforms. The next morning his body was found dumped by a canal with two bullets in his head—one more Sinaloan killing that has never been solved.

Chalino was gone, but the sound he created exploded. While music critics lambasted his cursing and nasally out-of-tune voice, he was a sensation among the roughnecks of Sinaloa and the Chicano gangbangers in California. Soon hundreds of imitators from both sides of the border churned out hard-core *narcocorridos*. Brought up on gangster rap, the U.S.-born crowd immediately identified with the drug lyrics, guns on album covers, and parental advisory stickers. Shaved-headed urban gangbangers even began to dress in Chalino's cowboy style—a white sombrero cocked to one side, a gaping belt buckle, crocodile-skin boots, and a pistol tucked in jeans. As Quinones sums up the crooner's influence: "In Chalino's hands, Mexican folk music had become dangerous urban dance music."

Two decades after Chalino, *narcocorridos* are more popular than ever. On the streets of Culiacán, market stalls sell hundreds of CDs whose covers show artists with Kalashnikovs, clad in cowboy hats, ski masks, or paramilitary uniforms. The music screams out of luxury pickup trucks and shiny, white Hummers with blacked-out windows, which speed down the road jumping stoplights. It rocks nightclubs full of women with inch-long synthetic nails embedded with precious stones, and men with alligator-skin boots who fire guns in the air to the beat. And it is plucked by quartets of musicians hanging out on street corners waiting to be hired to play a few tunes in the house of some drunken or coked-up revelers.

With ballads in such demand, thousands of young artists are trying to make their name as the next Chalino or Valentín Elizalde. Culiacán alone boasts five labels producing *corridos*, and each one has about two hundred balladeers on its books.

I visit the studio of Sol Records, which is built out of a two-room house in the Culiacán suburbs. As I stroll in on a midweek afternoon, it is packed with dozens of musicians clutching handfuls of their CDs and laying down tracks for their new wannabe hits. In the soundproof cabin, a band records a ballad about the latest bloodshed in one have-to-get-it-right take. The singer unleashes his lyrics, then swings his arms in the air, miming the firing of an automatic rifle.

Sol's producer, Conrado Lugo, is a chirpy, gargantuan man in his thirties who runs the label started by his father. He tells me about the surreal world of the Sinaloan *corrido* scene as an endless stream of musicians pass through. Conrado confesses that he personally preferred heavy metal as a teenager and didn't like producing drug ballads at first.

"I used to be depressed and hate my job. Then my dad said, 'Do you like having a brand-new pickup truck? Do you like having a gold watch? Then start liking *corridos*.' He was right, and over time I have learned to love this music."

It is certainly a good business for Sol Records. Rather than the label financing albums, the *narcocorrido* bands themselves or their patrons pay up front for the recording sessions. One of the bands' main sources of income is playing at private parties, bashes often held by the very villains they sing about. Even midlevel groups can make up to $10,000 for a night performing for these gold-chained clients. Big stars can charge an incredible $100,000 for an evening's entertainment.

But more crucially, traffickers actually pay composers to write songs about them. Every artist I talk to openly quotes the price they charge for penning a *corrido* about a gangster. While rookie composers ask for as little as $1,000 to write some verses about an up-and-coming thug, accomplished musicians can ask tens of thousands of dollars for a tune about a ranking cartel member. Though some traffickers have money to burn, they also see this as a good investment. A ballad in their name means prestige, and on the street this can mean respect and contracts.

"For the narcos, getting a ballad about them is like getting a doctorate," Conrado says.

Conrado tells me the story of one low-level trafficker who paid to get a particularly catchy ballad made about him. Soon everyone played it on his car stereo.

"The crime bosses were like, 'Bring me the guy from that song. I want him to do the job for me.' So he rose through the ranks because of the song."

"So what has happened to him now?" I asked.

"Oh, they killed him. He got too big. It was because of the song, really."

I ask Conrado if he feels bad glorifying gangsters, if the music promotes the bloodshed that is now killing these same musicians. He gives me the identical answer that I hear from dozens of composers and crooners: they are just storytellers describing the reality they see around them; and they are giving the public what it wants. The same arguments are used to defend gangster rap. Perhaps they have a good point. Songs don't kill people; guns kill people (although not according to the NRA).

"There is a lot of violence now. But musicians didn't invent it. In most of the cases of these singers who were shot, it had nothing to do with their music. They had beefs about a woman or money or something. Or they were in the wrong place or with the wrong people."

How about the singers with guns on their album covers? I ask him.

"That is just posing. That doesn't mean they are a gangster. Anybody can feel good posing with a gun. I do myself." He then yanks a cell phone out of his pocket showing a screen photo of him standing with an enormous high-tech-looking rifle.

Still, Conrado concedes, as the war has gotten bloodier, so have the songs. *Corridos* are released within days or even hours of breaking news stories, such as the killing of the Beard Beltrán Leyva or a major massacre. Several ballads tell the tale of a villain known as "the stew maker," who dissolved the bodies of three hundred victims of the Tijuana Cartel in acid. A popular tune called "Black Commando" describes the ski-masked hit squads that kidnap and torture. To keep up with this brutality, a new subgenre has emerged called *corridos enfermos*, or sick ballads. One such *corrido* graphically describes killers going into a house and mutilating a whole family.

Conrado introduces me to one of the most hard-core new bands on the scene. The group's name itself pulls no punches: Grupo Cartel de Sinaloa, or Grupo Cartel for short. It is not hard to guess their mafia affiliation.

"I wanted a name that said it like it is, with no disguise," the thirty-three-year-old composer César Jacobo tells me. "We are not hypocrites like some of these stars. This is the life we lead."

Grupo Cartel is not internationally known, but in Culiacán, it plays packed outdoor events with thousands of revelers. It is a classic *corrido* four-piece with a drummer, electric bass, twelve-stringed guitar, and accordion vocalist. The singer is just eighteen, with an incredibly powerful, melodic voice; the other musicians are in their twenties. When they turn up for us to take photos, they wear matching cream-colored suits and red shirts. César wears blue jeans and a trendy designer shirt beneath a well-trimmed goatee. He makes sure he is out of the photos. "Look mean for the camera," he tells the band with a grin.

César is clearly in charge. As well as writing the songs, he oversees the money, connections, concerts, and everything else. He also seems to be the figure of authority among another dozen tour managers, roadies, and hangers-on. As we travel from studios to seafood restaurants over a couple of days, he keeps answering a pair of cell phones in a hushed voice. But he gives me his full attention and is pleased that I will be putting the group in my story for a British Sunday magazine.

"You are going to make us famous in London. People will be listening to Robbie Williams and Grupo Cartel," he jokes.

The scene around Grupo Cartel illustrates the bizarre cross section of people in modern Sinaloan *narcocultura*. Kids from slums and poor ranches mix with private-school graduates. Sinaloan narcos have long sent their kids to expensive schools and mixed in high society. For other wealthy children it can be considered cool to dress up like hoodlums or hang around with the sons of capos. Just as in the United States, gangster culture has an allure that ascends class boundaries. In the new generation, you can find juniors from trafficking families looking like yuppies and the offspring of rich ranching families looking like traffickers.

Young Sinaloans in this hybrid narco culture are known as *buchones* and use a clothing style that mixes urban and rural, traditional and modern. *Buchones* like cowboy hats and ostrich-skin boots, but also sneakers and brightly colored baseball caps. *Buchona* girls typically dress in expensive tight dresses and boast ample jewels and breast operations, showing off the wealth of their gangster boyfriends.

César himself moved from rural poverty when he was ten to grow up in a Culiacán slum. He loves that middle-class and rich kids in Sinaloa listen to his music. "We played at this one mansion to the sons of a businessman. And they all treated us like celebrities." He smiles. "That makes me feel great. Like we have achieved something."

Over in more sophisticated Mexico City, wealthy kids are less interested in narco ballads, instead following rock and electronic music from the United States and Europe. They are more likely to be fans of U2 than Tigres del Norte. But narco ballads increasingly sound in Mexico City's vast slums. Pirate CDs of Valentín Elizalde, Chalino Sánchez, and the hard-core Grupo Cartel rock the capital's buses and taxis, house parties and cantinas, the melancholy sound and edgy lyrics appealing to everyone from teenagers to granddads.

César said his own father never listened to narco music, singing pure love songs in his home. But César was more interested in the ballads about the gunslingers and crime bosses in his barrio. The more time I spend with him, the more he admits he is close to this world. Childhood friends are *sicarios*. Others are traffickers. He prefers to write ballads about it.

His lyrics go deep into the inner lives of the assassins, describing their conflicts in choosing a path that in so many cases leads to their death. As well as using explicit lyrics, he mixes in fantasies and metaphors. In one ballad, he describes a hired killer arriving in hell to be confronted by his murder victims. As he talks, he bursts out into snippets of his songs.

"For me the words are the most important thing. Sometimes, I have all these weird ideas and I want to get them into the songs. I want to get the message right. Then I make it fit the rhythm."

He also wrote one love song. Sort of. It is about a friend who was shot dead over some beef with a lover. The song takes the voice of this friend apologizing to his wife for not being by her side, for being shot dead over some nonsense in an affair. It is called "Perdoname, Maria" (Forgive Me, Maria).

I want to ask your forgiveness,
That I won't see my children,
Crying clouds my conscience,
On the path I have taken,
I want you to know, Maria,
That I will always be by your side.

César has nine children by two women. That is quite fast work for a thirty-three-year-old. One of his young sons follows us around to the photo shoot, and César warmly shadowboxes with him on a dirt hill.

Most of Grupo Cartel's repertoire is about specific Sinaloan Cartel gangsters identified by their nicknames. He has songs about lieutenants called Indio, Cholo, Eddy, El Güero (Whitey), and verses about the big chief Mayo Zambada. They all describe the traffickers in classic narco glory. As the song "Indio" goes:

High-powered rifles,
Lots of money, in my pockets . . .
They used to send me kilos,
Now they send me tons.

Many Grupo Cartel songs are posted on the Internet along with photos of the famous gangsters they sing about. Some videos include grainy footage of Sinaloan assassins firing rounds in training or close-ups of their victims full of bullets, wrapped in tape, or cut into pieces. The videos are plastered together in amateur fashion and get hundreds of thousands of hits. I ask César who makes these clips. "I have no idea," he replies. "There are some sick people out there."

César admits the group's close links to the Sinaloa Cartel are potentially dangerous, making it a target for rival gangs. But he says to keep safe, they don't play much outside Sinaloa and some other "friendly" states. "There is always the risk of dying. But it is better to be a star for a few years"—he grins—"than live like a pauper for your whole life."

Maybe it was his closeness to the Sinaloa Cartel that provoked the hit on Valentín Elizalde, after the Reynosa concert. Or perhaps the reason was a splatter music video of one of his songs. Or did he mess with the woman of the wrong gangster? Or did a killer's girlfriend just make the mistake of saying that Valentín was attractive?

A lot of women in northern Mexico certainly thought the Golden Rooster was a sex symbol, with his broad nose and white cowboy hat tilted over his warm smile. But his voice was what won adoration from fans. As well as having the street cred of Chalino, he had a melancholy touch that conveyed both the joy and the struggles of his people, an epic quality like a John Lennon or a Ray Charles.

Valentín's music was also super-danceable thanks to the brass section of the Banda Guasaveña. Another great tradition in northern Mexico is Banda music, characterized by blaring trumpets and trombones. The sound came from German immigrants who set up beer breweries in Mazatlán port in the nineteenth century. Traditionally, no singers could shout loud enough to be heard over the wail of the Banda. But as *norteño* incorporated electric instruments and speaker stacks, crooners sang through microphones over the din.

Many of Valentín's songs were not even about gangsters. His most famous hit, "Como Me Duele" (How It Hurts Me), was a catchy dance number about amorous jealousy. But the Golden Rooster also wrote some of the hardest-hitting narco lyrics. One tune, "118 Balazos" (118 Bullets), chronicles a mafioso who survives three assassination attempts. As the song begins (above the sound of horns):

Now three times I have been saved,
From a certain death,
From pure Goat's Horns,
That have shot close to me,
118 bullets,
And God took them away.

Shortly before his murder, Valentín had a hit with a song called "A Mis Enemigos" (For My Enemies). The words had a vengeful tone, although to whom Valentín was talking was ambiguous. Was it another musician, a rival gangster, or even some politician? Videos appeared on the Internet with the song and images of murdered members of the Zetas gang. Some people interpreted the record as a taunt by the Sinaloan Cartel at their rivals. The tune became popular at the height of violence between the Sinaloa Cartel and Zetas, and some of the films were particularly brutal, including one snuff video of a Zeta who is tied to a chair and shot in the head.

As this video collected hundreds of thousands of hits, Valentín played in Reynosa, the heartland of the Zetas' territory. The concert was rowdier than ever and ended with the rain of bullets.[6]

Photographers arrived to take photos of the handsome twenty-seven-year-old lying on the car seat, riddled with lead. He is wearing a beige suit and black shirt, his eyes slightly open. The driver was also killed in the hit. Tano Castro's survival was a miracle. "I thank God every day that I am alive," he tells me.

Even in death, Valentín's enemies didn't leave him in peace. A video was taken of him lying naked in the autopsy room. Gaping bullet holes can be seen in his chest, his eyes are still slightly open, his tasseled jacket and cowboy boots beside the table covered in blood. The video was posted on the Internet with laughter dubbed over it. Police said they arrested two autopsy workers over the incident.

Following Valentín's murder, assassins killed a string of other musicians across Mexico. A band called Los Herederos de Sinaloa stepped out of a radio interview in Culiacán and were sprayed with a hundred bullets. Three group members and their manager died. In one week, three entertainers were killed in different incidents: a male singer was kidnapped, throttled, and dumped on a road; a trumpeter was found with a bag on his head; and a female singer was shot dead in her hospital bed. (She was being treated for bullet wounds from an earlier shooting.)

The Mexican public was particularly shocked by the slaying of Sergio Gómez, who founded his band K-Paz de la Sierra while he was an immigrant in Chicago. He shot to fame for a love hit called "Pero Te Vas a Arrepentir" (But You Will Have Regrets), a song so catchy that half of Mexico was singing it. Assailants abducted him after a concert in his native Michoacán state and tortured him for two days, burning his genitals with a blowtorch, before strangling him with a plastic cord. Sergio Gomez was also posthumously nominated for a Latin Grammy, competing with the deceased Valentín Elizalde for the prize in 2008. Neither of the dead men won.

In the vast majority of the musician slayings, police made no arrests and named no suspects. That is typical of the dismal clear-up rate of about 5 percent of murders during the Mexican Drug War. The killings had "all the marks of organized crime," police say in their standard comment after every murder. Why are they killing musicians? reporters asked. *Quien sabe* (Who knows).

However, police did make arrests in the Valentín Elizalde case. In November 2008, federal agents stormed a house and nabbed regional Zetas commander Jaime González, alias the Hummer. In press statements, officers said the Hummer organized and personally took part in silencing the Golden Rooster in retaliation for the music videos. The incident is still a little murky. While the Hummer was sentenced to sixteen years in prison for drugs and weapons charges, he has still not officially been charged for Valentín's killing.

*   *   *

As with with Jim Morrison, Tupac Shakur, and Kurt Cobain, the celebrity of the Golden Rooster grew with his death. Knowing his end, his songs sound sweeter, his melancholy voice sadder, his talk of killing more sinister.

"His presence is so strong. He still comes back to me in my dreams," Tano says. "And other people meet me all the time and say that Valentín is still with them. They are very sad that he is gone."

Corrido lovers from California to Colombia visit Valentín's grave in Sinaloa, keeping it covered in flowers.[7] And to keep the star alight, younger balladeers have even written tales about the life of the Rooster. Just like the kingpins he crooned about, the Golden Rooster has been immortalized in song.

CHAPTER 11

Faith

And the sea gave up the dead which were in it; and death and hell delivered up the dead which were in them: and they were judged every man according to their works.

And death and hell were cast into the lake of fire. This is the second death.

And whosoever was not found written in the book of life was cast into the lake of fire.

—REVELATIONS 20:13–15, KING JAMES BIBLE

The corpse of arch-gangster Arturo "the Beard" Beltrán Leyva lies below a two-story mausoleum in the Humaya Gardens cemetery on the southern edge of Culiacán. Nearby is the tomb of another powerful mobster, Ignacio "Nacho" Coronel, who was shot dead by soldiers in July 2010. Nacho Coronel was said to be close to Chapo Guzmán and fought against Beltrán Leyva. Thus in life, Nacho and the Beard were on opposite sides of the war; but in death they share the same earth.

Humaya Gardens has hundreds of other narco tombs in its sun-beaten soil. It is one of the most bizarre cemeteries in the world. Mausoleums are built of Italian marble and decorated with precious stones, and some even have air-conditioning. Many cost above $100,000 to build—more than most Culiacán homes. Inside are surreal biblical paintings next to photos of the deceased, normally in cowboy hats and often clasping guns. In some photos, they pose in fields of marijuana; in other tombs, small concrete planes indicate the buried mafioso was a pilot (transporting the good stuff).

As well as capos, many lieutenants or mere foot soldiers boast magnificent monuments. An alarming number are under twenty-five—and have died in recent years: 2009, 2010, 2011. On every trip I make to Culiacán, the graveyard expands exponentially, with new tombs appearing that are even more grandiose than the last.

One time I visit the Humaya just after Father's Day. Mountains of flowers fill the cemetery next to banners made by grieving wives. Photos of the young fathers are printed colorfully on the canvases with messages in the voices of their children. WE LOVE YOU, PAPA, YOU WILL ALWAYS BE WITH US says one banner. For these youngsters, the spectacular tombs are the best memory they will ever have of their fathers.

On several occasions, I find people visiting their loved ones. They often bring bands and sit with their whole family sipping beer and singing along to the dead person's favorite ballads. One time, I sit with three brothers mourning their father. One of them has brought along a voluptuous girlfriend dressed in jewels and revealing clothes. "Our dad was a farmer. And he grew the good stuff," the youngest brother tells me with a smile and a wink. They put bottles of the old man's preferred whiskey on his grave, in line with Mexican tradition. The deceased may have moved on, but they still have a presence.

But to what place have these dead traffickers traveled to? Did they ask God for forgiveness? Have they been allowed into heaven? Is there a special "gangster's paradise"?

Mexico's top Roman Catholic clerics say no. Violent narcos excommunicate themselves from God, the robed men shout from pulpits. They will not sit beside the lamb and the lion in the afterlife. Some priests in the countryside say otherwise. God forgives the sins of anyone who kneels down and makes his peace before death, they argue. And especially when capos give such generous donations to their country parishes—gifts that have historically been so common they even have their special term: *narco limosnas*, or narco alms.[1]

But as the drug war has escalated, many kingpins have said they don't care what Catholic cardinals say. If they are not allowed in Rome's house, they howl back, they will make their own.

The most virulent expression of narco religion is by La Familia Cartel in Michoacán. La Familia indoctrinates its followers in its own version of evangelical Christianity mixed with some peasant rebel politics. The gang's spiritual leader, Nazario Moreno, "El Mas Loco," or the Maddest One, actually wrote his own bible, which is compulsory reading for the troops. This sounds so nuts I thought it was another drug war myth. Until I got my hands on a copy of his "good" book. It is not an easy bedtime read.

But La Familia is only the most defined voice in a chorus of narco religion that has been rising in volume for decades. Other tones of the choir include some morphed rituals of Caribbean Santeria, the folk saint Jesús Malverde, and the wildly popular Santa Muerte, or Holy Death.

Many who follow these faiths are not drug traffickers or gun-toting assassins. The beliefs all have an appeal to poor Mexicans who feel the staid Catholic Church is not speaking to them and their problems. But gangsters definitely feel at home in these new sects and exert a powerful influence on them, giving a spiritual and semi-ideological backbone to narco clans. Such a backbone strengthens El Narco as an insurgent movement that is challenging the old order. Kingpins now fight for souls as well as turfs.

Jesús Malverde is the oldest religious symbol associated with El Narco. The real Malverde is renowned as a Sinaloan bandit executed a century ago. Images of his saintly face adorn amulets and statuettes from marijuana fields in the Sierra Madre to prison cells in San Quentin, cattle ranches in Jalisco to migrants' shelters in Arizona. But the most revered shrine of all is in the heart of Culiacán, right across the road from the grandiose state-government palace. Analysts have long observed this symbolism: the twin powers of Sinaloa—political and narco—are side by side.

The shrine lies inside a simple brick building painted dark green and decorated with green tiles. *Malverde* in Spanish literally means "bad green"; in Sinaloa, *verde* can also refer to the green of marijuana, as well as the green of dollar bills. The shrine's walls are plastered with photos of visitors that meld together like a mosaic wallpaper. The snaps show newlyweds and newborn babies, girls in white Communion dresses and tattooed teenagers with shaved heads, as well as plenty of rugged men in cowboy hats. Visitors also stick placards on the wall with messages of veneration. JESÚS MALVERDE. THANKS FOR THE FAVORS YOU HAVE GIVEN

ME says one plaque from Ventura, California. THANK YOU JESÚS MAL-
VERDE. FOR ILLUMINATING AND CLEANING OUR PATHS says another from
Zapopan, Jalisco. Many plaques illustrate how the faithful mix the folk
saint with orthodox Catholic symbols, addressing messages to Malverde
alongside the Virgin of Guadalupe and San Judas Tadeo, both popular
Catholic icons in Mexico.

In a small inner room of the shrine sits the main attraction: a painted
bust of Malverde surrounded by white and pink roses. He has pale skin,
jet-black hair, a finely trimmed mustache, and a traditional white Mexican suit. His face looks sad, in the godly, wise, suffering way that many
images show Jesus Christ looking sad. Visitors wait in the outer rooms
drinking and singing before praying silently next to the bust and touching Malverde's despondent face.

Shrine owner Jesús González has a room to one side jumbled with
crucifixes and Malverde paintings. He is in his thirties, the son of the
founder, who built the holy place with his own hands back in the 1970s. I
catch González on a summer afternoon so hot that the street feels like an
oven. He is sweating profusely in a white vest. We drink Coca-Cola from
plastic bottles and he tells me about the meaning of Malverde.

"Jesús Malverde loves and cares for the poor, for the humble. He knows
about their struggles. The rich exploit and the poor suffer today as they
did in the time when Malverde lived. Malverde understands what people
have to go through. He knows they have to fight. He doesn't discriminate
against those that are marginalized."

Again, a symbol of El Narco is associated with the idea of struggles of
the poor, of social rebellion. Gonzalez goes on, "Every country has its
Robin Hood. I'm sure in your country you have—"

"Robin Hood," I finish his sentence for him. "My country is where
Robin Hood comes from."

He smiles knowingly. "So you understand then."

Jesús Malverde was born in Sinaloa in 1870, González tells me. In that
time, the dictator Porfirio Diaz ruled Mexico with an iron fist, his friends
building huge haciendas in Sinaloa, while poor Indians were driven from
their ancestral land. In those wretched days, González goes on, Malverde's
parents were so poor they died of starvation. The young orphan struggled
to survive, taking dangerous jobs building railroads. After brushes with
cruel bosses and police, he was forced to be an outlaw. Malverde ran to the
hills and led a band of merry men who robbed from the rich and gave to
the poor. But the ruthless governor of Sinaloa put a price on his head and

one of his own men betrayed him for gold. Malverde fell before a firing squad in 1909, his head hung from a tree as a warning to other rebels.

The same story, with a few details changed here and there, can be heard far and wide in Sinaloa. The years Malverde reportedly lived coincide almost exactly with the reign of Don Porfirio, and the bandit saint died right before the Revolution. Typical of a saint story, documents confirming Malverde's life and death cannot be found, and it is not certain if he ever really lived at all. What is corroborated is that throughout the twentieth century, poor Sinaloans attributed miracles to the spirit of Malverde. The village cow was dry until people prayed to the bandit and suddenly the animal gave milk; a young boy was blinded, then one day woke up with the gift of sight; a man was dying of cancer and was unexpectedly cured. Stories spread from village to village, breeding more stories of miracles, and Malverde became a legend.

González plays down the association of Malverde with narcos, rightly pointing out that all kinds come to pray. On one visit, I find the owner of an Arizonan building company who is the son of Sinaloan immigrants. He tells me he drove fifteen hours to ask the bandit saint for the success of a medical operation on his son in Pheonix. On another occasion, I meet an elderly woman praying for her dying husband.

But drug traffickers certainly do venerate Malverde. Symbols are found in the hands of arrested kingpins and on corpses of gunslingers shot down on the street. On weekends, young *buchones* pack the Malverde shrine and hang outside in cars and trucks, narco *corridos* blaring out of stereos.

The Catholic Church does not recognize Malverde, but priests do not rail hard against him either. Folk saints have long been tolerated throughout Christiandom as a way for the faithful to reconcile their beliefs with local traditions. Malverde is just one figure rather than a new religion. Most Malverde believers still consider themselves Roman Catholics as they kiss the mustachioed bust.

Inside the shrine, a band plays ballads to the faithful for $5 a tune. I pay to hear as many Malverde *corridos* as they can remember and record them with a tape recorder, but I soon run out of money, and they say there are dozens more I haven't heard. Several ballads they play tell tales of the bandit fighting the governor's men. Others talk explicitly about gangsters praying to Malverde and becoming rich smuggling drugs. As one goes:

My hands full of gum [opium paste], I greeted Malverde,
Making promises to him, and he put his trust in me,
God doesn't get involved, he won't help you with the bad stuff.

I know drugs aren't good, but that is where the money is,
Don't blame Sinaloa, blame the whole of Mexico,
The business is growing, and in the whole world, my friends.

Today, I am going to Culiacán, driving a brand-new truck,
I'm going to a shrine because there I have a date,
It is with Jesús Malverde, to sing him happy birthday.[2]

The Santa Muerte, or Holy Death, is physically a much more aggressive symbol than that of Jesús Malverde. While the bandit is just a mustached man in a white suit, Santa Muerte looks like the grim reaper. The skeletal figure has hollowed eyes, sharp teeth, and a head-chopping halberd in its right hand. However, one marked difference from the reaper is that Santa Muerte is a woman, referred to by her devotees as *she.* She dresses up in a variety of clothes, from black capes to frilly pink dresses and often sports a colorful wig.

Catholic critics say veneration of Santa Muerte is the work of Satan. They accuse it of being a cult led by narcos and argue this diabolical figure has driven Mexico's orgy of violence. Assassins hack off craniums, they claim, in tribute to the death incarnate. But defenders of Santa Muerte retort she is just a popular spirit who cares for the poor and downtrodden. She existed in Mexico before the Spanish conquest, they claim, and is featured in the Bible. Her faithful also call her the Niña Blanca, or White Girl.

A big part of Santa Muerte's attraction is simply the power of her image. Statuettes and paintings of her cannot help but grab attention. There is now an entire art form of thousands upon thousands of images of the Santa Muerte, and they all look a little different. She is in huge statues and in tiny earrings; on the end of necklaces and tattooed on chests; printed on T-shirts and painted into murals; and even made into clocks and incense burners. But as well as being an art and fashion accessory, she has also become an influential religious figure, adorning street altars, shrines in houses, and her own special churches.

Her rise in popularity has been meteoric. Within a decade, Santa Muerte shot from an obscure symbol only a few people had seen to being in almost every city and neighborhood in Mexico, across Mexican communities in the United States, down in South America, and as far away as Spain and Australia. But the heart of her faith is in Tepito, in the center of Mexico City.

Also known as El Barrio Bravo, Tepito is a crowded quarter that dates back to before the Spanish conquest and is famous for street traders, boxers, and gunslingers.[3] Residents celebrate El Barrio for being a bulwark of street culture but admit the narrow alleys can be as forbidding as the casbah. Within Tepito's huge market, they say, you can find anything on the planet—the latest plasma TVs, surfer clothes, pirate copies of cinema blockbusters, guns, crack, and then quaint tea sets. There is also a never-ending collection of Santa Muerte memorabilia in stalls and entire shops devoted to her.

Two main points in the Barrio compete as Santa Muerte's spiritual center. The first is an altar near one of the main avenues, which may have been the first public worshipping place to Santa Muerte in its contemporary explosion. The owner is sixty-two-year-old Enriqueta Romero or Don Queta, who built the shrine outside her tenement block in 2001. Don Queta's altar is incredibly popular, and a constant stream of faithful turn up to give the White Girl presents of bouquets, candles, fruit, and even bottles of beer and cigarettes (Santa Muerte likes to drink and smoke). Hanging around the shrine, I find all types: a middle-aged street vendor praying for her troublesome son; a muscular, tattooed policemen who says the Holy Death protects him from bullets; a peroxide-blond prostitute who says La Santa shields her from aggressive clients. On the first day of every month, thousands of such believers pack the street around the altar for a special celebration, singing, dancing, glugging beer, puffing reefers, and showing their love for death.

A few blocks away, David Romo takes a more formal approach to the death cult. The swarthy, self-proclaimed bishop has built an indoor church, where he gives Communion and other quasi-Catholic rites beneath skeletal images of La Santa. He even blessed the marriage of one famous Mexican soap opera star (and former table dancer).[4] Romo claims to be a Catholic, but argues the conservative Vatican has lost touch with the people; gays, divorcées, and other sinners are all welcome at his temple. Santa Muerte is actually the Angel of Death as described in the Bible, he contends.

I film a mass in Romo's temple, which has a rather somber atmosphere. As I am staring through the camera lens, I feel a pinch on my leg; a viscious-looking black rooster that apparently lives in the church is trying to bite me. Some Christians say the black rooster is a sign of Lucifer. Then again, some have a grudge against goats as well.

Romo's cult has battled with the government as well as the Catholic Church. He registered his faith with the Interior Ministry, but under clerical pressure officials struck him off the list of recognized sects.[5] In answer, Romo led the faithful on protest marches through the capital bearing images of La Niña Blanca. He claims there are 2 million Santa Muerte faithful and says he is organizing affiliate churches all over Mexico and in the United States. Clerics then accused drug traffickers of funding Romo. Finally, in December 2010, police arrested Romo for banking the funds of a kidnapping gang linked to a cartel, and as of 2011 he was incarcerated awaiting trial. He continued to lead his sect from a prison cell.

It is hard for Romo or anyone else to dominate the Santa Muerte cult. The faith spreads fast and organically from town to town and barrio to barrio. Anyone can set up a congregation in his or her own style. It is a golden opportunity for wannabe messiahs.

In an industrial suburb to the north of Mexico City, a towering sixty-foot Santa Muerte overlooks warehouses, factories, and breeze-block homes. The skeletal titan, sculpted from fiberglass and painted in black and gray, is the child of a slim twenty-six-year-old called Jonathan Legaria. He constructed the statue in an empty lot and invited locals to pray with him beside it; hundreds now turn up every Sunday. The faithful fondly refer to Legaria as Comandante Pantera or Commander Panther.

Comandante Pantera wrote his life story in a self-published book he called *Son of the Santa Muerte*. He was born in Sinaloa, he wrote, but moved to Tepito as a baby. Abandoned by his parents, he became a champion teenage boxer while also witnessing bloody killings in El Barrio Bravo. After one murder, he saw a vision of the Santa Muerte and found a million pesos in the backpack of the victim. He discovered his mission, he wrote, and funded his faith. By 2008, his Santa Muerte congregation had become one of the most popular in Mexico.

But the son of death met his own death. As he drove his Cadillac SUV through the industrial sprawl, he was greeted by a rattle of gunfire. More than a hundred bullets covered his truck, killing him instantly. It had all the hallmarks of a classic organized-crime hit. Investigators said Comandante Pantera had probably been dealing drugs and had not paid off the mafia. He was a gang-funded preacher, they sighed, who died in the world of crime he perpetuated.

But was he really?

Legaria's mother gave a press conference and told a radically different version of events. The Pantera had never come from Sinaloa or lived in the Barrio, she said; he was really a rich kid, born in the plush Mexico City suburb of Satellite City. After he went to private schools, his father gave him a highly profitable business, verifying cars for their pollution levels. Legaria got into Santa Muerte after joining a motorcycle club and discovering he had a talent for ghetto preaching. Finding himself with a flock, he invented a new dynamic identity for himself. But, as he discovered to his peril, it was no game pretending to be a gangster during the Mexican Drug War.

His mother offered a reward for information to seek justice for her son. She got dozens of calls with an array of accusations: some said it was the Tepito Santa Muerte temple; others La Familia drug cartel; others even accused gunmen working for the Catholic Church. It was doomed to become yet one more Mexican murder mystery.[6]

I attend a mass in Pantera's temple a month after his killing. His common-law wife is presiding over the ceremony. It is a truly crazy party. Mariachis pluck out lively tunes and the faithful leap around as if they were possessed; one middle-aged woman is going particularly mad, dancing in frenetic circles. We then go through prayers reminiscent of New Age meditation. Hundreds of wide-eyed believers stare at the sky and claim to see the face of Pantera. A high school student tells me that the Santa Muerte cured her of cancer. Another tattooed young devotee claims they have severed heads buried under the temple grounds. I decide not to try looking.

Religious sects famously attract kooks, weirdos, and fantasists. But some really seriously dangerous people venerate Santa Muerte. Shrines dot the turfs of northern Mexico where the drug war rages. In the northeast, Mexican soldiers smashed up various Holy Death altars they said were built by the Zetas. Over in Sinaloa, I reported on a narco massacre of thirteen people in a village. Driving out, I ran into an altar of La Niña Blanca by the road. Seeing the image of death so close to bloody murder is unnerving.

In the southern state of Yucatan, killers left twelve severed craniums in piles on two ranches. Police arrested Zetas affiliates with the axes used for the beheadings. In their homes were shrines to the skeletal death queen.[7] These psychos seemingly feel the Holy Death condones such barbarity or is even pleased by it.

Catholic priests understandably rail hard against the heretical acts of Santa Muerte preachers. From the pulpit, they urge the faithful not to mess with the dark and diabolical. They argue that the reaperess encourages violence by making devotees believe she can deflect bullets. As Father Hugo Valdemar, the spokesman for the Mexico City diocese, told me, "Believers think they can act with impunity. They think they don't just have human strength, but also a divine protector. And of course for them she is strong and for them she is brave. This leads to more crime."

I personally follow neither Pope Benedict nor a skeletal incarnate of death. I was baptized under Roman law but stopped going to church when I was a teenager. If I were in segregated Northern Ireland (or North Texas), I would call myself an agnostic Catholic. In Mexico, I'm just agnostic.

However, I do find the idea of assassins cutting off heads and praying to a skulled she-deity discomforting. The cult helps villains justify barbaric actions, at least in their own minds. Of course, faithful adherents of many religions have justified atrocities in the name of their God. Maybe killers would commit exactly the same crimes without the cloaked skeleton. Maybe.

Anthropologists, meanwhile, have a field day with the explosion of Mexico's religious digressions. Santa Muerte, they say, reflects the nation's age-old fascination with the deceased, as shown in its Day of the Dead. The skeleton could even be a resurgence of an old Aztec deity called Mictecacihuatl or the Lady of the Land of the Dead.[8] An underground belief in pre-Hispanic deities, some argue, is proof of a continued resistance to colonial culture by Mexico's working class.

Others point to the postmodernist side of Santa Muerte. In many ways, she is an urban pop star. She has spread rapidly by the same media that demonize her, as well as via Web sites, pirate DVDs, printed T-shirts, and tattoos. She answers to the gripes of modern poverty, promising help in everyday struggles rather than in an afterlife.

Whatever the whys and wherefores, it is striking the Santa Muerte rocketed to prominence at the same time as the Mexican Drug War— and as the democratic transition. While traffickers fund some temples, the death saint spreads with her own energy. Perhaps the phenomena are different signs of rebellion against the old orders. At the dawn of the twenty-first century, Mexico stands at a crossroads on the path to both its judicial and spiritual futures.

Seizing the mad millennial moment, leaders of La Familia Cartel have taken steps to carve a Mexico in their own vision. They saw the way gangster foot soldiers grasped religious symbols. And the capos asked, why just finance other preachers when you can preach yourself? The result is a frightening evolution of narco religion.

Hailing from the western state of Michoacán, La Familia sprung to world attention with spectacular acts of violence, such as rolling five human heads onto a disco dance floor.[9] After one of its lieutenants was arrested in July 2009, the family also demonstrated a great capacity for small-town warfare, waging simultaneous attacks on a dozen police facilities and killing fifteen officers. Startled pundits dubbed it a kind of Tet Offensive. Arrested Familia hoods then claimed they had nine thousand men at arms, who had undergone religious indoctrination. Media barons swung their heads from the north to the west. Where had this upstart militia come from? How had they challenged the traditional narco powers of Sinaloa and the Gulf? Was it their religion that made them grow so fast?

The investigator best equipped to answer this sits in a heavily guarded office in Michoacán state capital, Morelia. Carlos has watched the rise of the ungodly gangsters throughout his career in law enforcement, in which he worked for a long time in the federal spy agency. He now heads a special state-federal unit that follows La Familia. Carlos has piles of documents, photos, and recordings of the gangsters stacked around him. He can't stop talking about his nemeses. His data sketches a grisly picture of how and why the happy family built its narco church.

La Familia was born in a roasting-hot mountain valley in Michoacán known as the Tierra Caliente. The expanse of lime orchards and agave spikes has long been a hotbed of outlaws and rather fundamentalist religion. Over the hill in grandiose Morelia, residents used to call the valley "hell." Wild criminals would be exiled to this inferno, where they had to scramble for a living in dirt villages. But the worm has turned. The roughnecks from hell now call the shots over the chattering political classes in Morelia. And if the politicians don't play ball, gangsters unleash their divine punishments.

La Familia had three chiefs who were all born of peasant farmers in the Tierra Caliente between the mid-1960s and 1970s. Nazario Moreno, "El Más Loco," also known as El Chayo; Servando Gómez, alias La Tuta; and José de Jesús Méndez, alias El Chango or the Monkey. Their share of power was considered equal, but Nazario headed the spiritual side of the clan. He is normally shown in a black-and-white photo so blurred it is made of gray squares sketching his thick neck, round face, and slim, black mustache.

Like many in the valley of hell, Nazario trekked up to the United States as a teenager, working jobs in California and Texas. But he was quickly lured from the life of a laborer to the luxuries of a drug smuggler. He stayed in the United States working with Mexican gangsters to distribute product.

Within godly America, Nazario came in touch with evangelical Christianity and was born-again to his new calling. As well as following Latino evangelical preachers, he became a huge fan of a Christian author called John Eldredge. In his book *Wild at Heart*, Eldredge paints a romantic idea of muscular Christianity; of man untamed but noble, struggling through a wilderness that can be Mesopotamia, the Sinai desert, or rural Colorado.[10] In this outback, man endures wounds and faces challenges that he must overcome like a warrior, with hard but holy acts. The metaphor found fertile terrain in El Más Loco. What could be closer to this wilderness than the Tierra Caliente, and what was a harder struggle than that of the poor Mexican peasant?

Nazario endured a wound that was no metaphor in 1998 when he almost died in a car accident. To cure a gaping head injury, doctors fixed a metal plate into his skull. The investigator Carlos says the shield made him even more loco. But Nazario felt like a visionary and began writing his rambling thoughts that would later shape into his "bible."

Back in Michoacán, the underworld was turned on its head with the 2003 arrest of regional strongman Armando Valencia.[11] During the ensuing upheavals, Nazario returned to Mexico and joined his old Tierra

Caliente buddies to vie for power. La Familia first allied with the Zetas and trained with their commandos in urban and rural warfare. But after they felt strong enough, they did a U-turn and started murdering Zetas to claim the territory as their own.

Under Nazario's direction, La Familia was quick to introduce religious indoctrination to its recruited fighters. The spiritual aspects were useful in providing a glue and discipline for its organization. As Carlos explains:

"These guys really do believe in their religion. They are genuine converts. But they also see the benefits of religion in running organized crime. If you have a kind of ideology, however bizarre, it gives a gang direction and justification for whatever it does. It is not just a war. It becomes a holy war."

La Familia financed certain evangelical churches and handed out copies of standard protestant Bibles in Spanish. Then Nazario printed his own good book. He called it *Pensamientos*, or *Thoughts*.

I get my hands on a copy of *Pensamientos* from a source in Morelia. The book is a hundred pages long and decorated with pictures of green lands and biblical images drawn by El Más Loco himself. He was not a bad artist. There is no price, as La Familia gives the book out free to troops. The copy I have claims to be the fourth edition, with a print run of 7,500. Overall, the book states that 26,500 copies have been churned out.

True to its name, *Pensamientos* is a splattering of individual thoughts as well as some anecdotes and moral lessons. Structurally, it is quite close to Mao Zedong's "little red book," which also jumps from short idea to short idea. Many passages are in the spirit of evangelical self-help that can be heard in sermons from Mississippi to Rio de Janeiro. As the narco prophet writes:

"I ask God for strength and he gives me challenges that make me strong; I ask him for wisdom and he gives me problems to resolve; I ask him for prosperity and he gives me brain and muscles to work."

However, on other pages, Nazario switches to phrases strikingly similar to those coined by revolutionary Emiliano Zapata—words of peasants fighting oppressors. As the Maddest One goes on, "It is better to be a master of one peso than a slave of two; it is better to die fighting head-on than on your knees and humiliated."

On other pages, Nazario talks in more concrete terms about building up La Familia's "movement":

"We are beginning an arduous, but very interesting, task: the building of consciousness. Today, we need to prepare to defend our ideals so that our struggle will bear fruit and organize so as to go down the best path, perhaps not the easiest, but the one that can offer the best results."

Pensamientos may not be a candidate for the Booker Prize. But Carlos assures me that the ideas hit home with uneducated peasants of the Tierra Caliente, as does the notion that they can carry out vengeful violence in the name of the Lord. The religion gives thugs, once recruited, a discipline that makes them more reliable soldiers. But if any of them mess up, they must themselves face the wrath of God. According to Familia declarations, employees who make a first mistake are tied up in a room; on a second, they are tortured; and a third mistake is their last.

An obvious gaping contradiction in all this is, how can drug traffickers and murderers claim to be devout Christians? To justify their actions, La Familia bosses argue they are bringing better-paying employment to Michoacán and, like many gangsters, act as benevolent godfathers, handing Christmas presents to poor kids in mass events. They also pose as vigilantes bringing divine justice to the lawless streets and say that while they sell narco poison to gringos, they won't deal to their own. To get out this message that they are really guardian angels, they have taken the brash step of going to the media. When they first burst on the scene in 2006, they placed an ad in several newspapers. The bravado text had a headline entitled MISSION and went on:

"Eradicate from the state of Michoacán kidnapping, extortion in person and by telephone, paid assassinations, express kidnapping, tractor-trailer and auto theft, home robberies done by people like those mentioned, who have made the state of Michoacán an unsafe place. Our sole motive is that we love our state and are no longer willing to see our people's dignity trampled on."[12]

Later, one Familia member gave an interview to Mexico's top-selling newsmagazine, *Proceso*, while La Tuta phoned up a Michoacán news show to rant about Familia's righteous defense of the homeland.[13] In another publicity stunt, Familia soldiers rounded up dozens of alleged rapists and muggers in the town of Zamora. Five were shot dead while others were whipped and then ordered to march down the streets with banners confessing their crimes. Old Testament justice was played out for real in the family's narco mission from God.

Carlos is adamant that La Familia's claim to be vigilantes is simply posturing. They may kill kidnappers and extortionists, he says, but only to go ahead and kidnap and extort in their place. However, in the Tierra Caliente, some residents openly support La Familia and argue they are better at getting a debt back or solving a dispute than the courts. When its gunmen ask for money, people rarely refuse.

La Familia also uses regional pride to rally farmers and small-town hoodlums. They claim to be good Michoacán men who have driven out "foreign" Sinaloans and Zetas and even seen the *federales* off. In this spirit, the Maddest One made all his troops watch the movie *Braveheart*. As La Familia gunmen shoot down soldiers, they can feel like Scottish barbarians beating out the bastard English (except La Familia assassins don't wear kilts). The *Godfather* trilogy was also compulsory viewing, educating men in loyalty and family values.

So what was Nazario? A deranged nut job on meth, or a religious visionary? One has to concede that there was a method to his madness. His religion and quasi ideology gave La Familia appeal and discipline, helping it become one of the fastest-growing outfits in the Mexican Drug War. As well as rapidly taking over Michoacán state, La Familia has pushed into Jalisco, Guanajuato, Guerrero, Puebla, and México state, including the slums around the capital. La Familia scripture may sound like a harebrained hodgepodge. But it is no more illogical than various loony religious or extreme nationalist movements that have sprung up around the globe—and sometimes claimed millions of followers. Having a quasi ideology adds punch. And in the experience of the Mexican Drug War, gangs imitate the successful techniques of their rivals. El Más Loco may not be the last Mexican capo to declare himself master of his own temple.

La Familia's success, however, put it bang on the police radar. American agents rounded up La Familia operatives in cities including Dallas and Atlanta, and the Mexican government offered a 30 million peso reward for Moreno's head. Someone close to the narco evangelist apparently went for this gold, informing the government he would be attending a Christmas party in the Tierra Caliente city of Apatzingán in December 2010. As federal police and soldiers stormed the city, the cartel rapidly responded by calling their foot soldiers to block roads and attack troops. Gunfights broke out on the streets, claiming eleven lives, including that of a baby hit in the cross fire. But federal police claimed they had killed their target, the Maddest One.[14]

However, Moreno had one last laugh—the federal police never captured his corpse. In the chaos of the shoot-out, federal police say, La

Familia operatives carried Moreno's cadaver into the mountains. The government released a tape of fellow kingpin La Tuta conceding that Moreno had died. But when there was no corpse, suspicion could always linger in people's minds. Moreno became another source of fables, such as Carrillo Fuentes, who died in the plastic surgery accident in 1997. The Maddest One still wanders in the Tierra Caliente dressed as a peasant, people whispered. He is disguised as a priest giving mass in Apatzingán, they muttered. The mystical narco preacher has become a legend, and his teachings still have a potent power in the seething hills of his birth.

CHAPTER 12

Insurgency

If someone attacks my father, my mother, or my brother, then they are going to hear from me . . . Our fight is with the federal police because they are attacking our families.

—SERVANDO GÓMEZ, ALIAS LA TUTA,
CAPO OF LA FAMILIA, 2009

The award-winning American TV series *Breaking Bad* has a scene in its second season set in the murder capital of Ciudad Juárez. In this episode, American and Mexican agents are lured to a patch of desert just south of the border looking for an informant. They discover the informant's head has been cut off and stuck on the body of a giant turtle. But as they approach, the severed cranium, turned into an IED, explodes, killing agents. The episode was released in 2009.[1] I thought it was unrealistic, a bit fantastic. Until July 15, 2010.

In the real Ciudad Juárez on that day, gangsters kidnapped a man, dressed him in a police uniform, shot him, and dumped him bleeding on a downtown street. A cameraman filmed what happened after federal police and paramedics got close. The video shows medics bent over the dumped man, checking for vital signs. Suddenly a bang rings out, and the image shakes vigorously as the cameraman runs for his life. Gangsters had used a cell phone to detonate twenty-two pounds of explosives packed into a nearby car. A minute later, the camera turns back around to reveal the burning car pouring smoke over screaming victims. A medic lies on the ground, covered in blood but still moving, a stunned look on his face. Panicked officers are scared to go near him. The medic dies minutes later along with a federal agent and a civilian.

I'm not suggesting that *Breaking Bad* inspired the murders. TV shows don't kill people. Car bombs kill people. The point of the story is that the Mexican Drug War is saturated with stranger-than-fiction violence. Mexican writer Alejandro Almazán suffered from a similar dilemma. As he was writing his novel *Among Dogs*,[2] he envisioned a scene in which thugs decapitate a man and stick a hound's head on his corpse. It seemed pretty out there. But then in real life some gangsters did exactly that, only with a pig's head. It is just hard to compete with the sanguine criminal imagination. Cartel thugs have put a severed head in a cooler and delivered it to a newspaper; they have dressed up a murdered policeman in a comedy sombrero and carved a smile on his cheeks; and they have even sewn a human face onto a soccer ball.

Many reports have gone into the social impact of such terror. But a central question is still hotly debated: Why? Why do cartel soldiers hack off heads, ambush policemen, and set off car bombs? And why do they throw grenades into crowds of revelers or massacre innocent teenagers at parties? What do they stand to gain by such bloodshed? Whom are they fighting? What do they want?

This puzzle goes to the heart of the debate about what El Narco has become. For the gangsters' motivations in many ways define what they are. If they deliberately kill civilians to make a point, that would make them, by many definitions, terrorists. If they are trying to win the monopoly of violence in a certain territory, that would make them warlords. And if they are fighting a full-on war against the government, many would argue it would make them insurgents.

It's a touchy issue. Words such as *terrorists* and *insurgents* set off alarm bells, scare away investment dollars, and wake up American spooks at night. The language influences how you deal with the Mexican Drug War, and how many drones and Black Hawk helicopters you fly in.

Journalists first started throwing the term *narco insurgents* into stories in 2008, as the war escalated and Beltrán Leyva's hit squads assassinated the chief of federal police and dozens of agents. The term was then analyzed in greater detail in journals and think tanks with loose links to the American law enforcement and military community, including in a series of articles published in *Small Wars Journal*, which looks at low-intensity conflicts the globe over. As it said in one story by John Sullivan and Adam Elkus entitled "Cartel v. Cartel: Mexico's Criminal Insurgency":

"From the beginning, the criminal insurgency was never a unified project. Cartels fought each other as well as the government for control of crucial drug smuggling routes, the plazas. The fragmented and post ideological quality of the struggle often confused American commentators used to the idea of a unified and ideological Maoist-type insurgency. Yet the essential character of the insurgency is something that Clausewitz [a German military genius] were he around today and tuning into gangster-promoting narco corrido music pumping out of Tijuana radios, could definitely understand."[3]

The concept soon filtered into the Pentagon, appearing in a December 2008 report by the United States Joint Forces Command. Among military concerns over the next decades, it said, was the worry that Mexican drug violence could trigger a rapid collapse, comparable to that of Yugoslavia. "Any descent by Mexico into chaos would demand an American response based on the serious implications for homeland security alone," it said.[4] This was incendiary stuff. Not only was the report suggesting the drug war could actually push Mexico over the brink, it was actually imagining a scenario in which U.S. troops would cross the Rio Grande for the first time since the Mexican Revolution. It was only in a speculative report in the Pentagon's darkest depths. But as violence intensified, the concept shot to the top of the administration in the voice of Secretary of State Hillary Clinton. As Clinton said in now infamous comments in September 2010:

"We face an increasing threat from a well-organized network, drug-trafficking threat that is, in some cases, morphing into or making common cause with what we would consider an insurgency, in Mexico and in Central America . . . And these drug cartels are now showing more and more indices of insurgency—you know, all of a sudden car bombs show up, which weren't there before. So it's becoming—it's looking more and more like Colombia looked twenty years ago."[5]

The declaration sparked a whirlwind of indignant responses. Mexico retorted that the Colombia comparison was misleading and that its security forces were not seriously threatened. Any suggestion that the government is losing control is of course disastrous for Brand Mexico.

But there were also critiques from liberal academics and NGOs in the

United States. These voices argue that Mexican drug cartels are not insurgents because they do not, like Islamic or communist insurgents, want to take power (and sit in the presidential palace, run schools, etc.). More pertinently, they rail against the expansion of military, anti-insurgency tactics used in Colombia or Afghanistan, and particularly the idea of American soldiers pushing into the Sierra Madre the way they reclaimed the Korengal Valley from the Taliban.

They have some real fears. Counterinsurgency campaigns have historically been disastrous for human rights—in Colombia, Iraq, Peru, El Salvador, Algeria, and dozens of other countries. And American troops pushing over the Rio Grande in the coming years is a genuine possibility. The narco-insurgency concept also plays into the hands of some in America's extreme right-wing circles. Islamic radicals, communist guerrillas, drug traffickers, narco terrorists, insurgent narcos—all get thrown into one toxic cauldron of anti-Americans. The war on drugs gets tied up neatly with the war on terror—and the use of any means necessary to fight a conceptual devil.

The Mexican conflict cuts through politics in strange ways, sparking responses from everyone from gun lobbyists and anti-immigrant groups to foreign policy critics and drug legalization activists. Phrases such as "criminal insurgency" invariably anger, or gratify, certain interest groups in the debate. But whatever the politics, the threat in Mexico needs to be understood. Mexican cartels have clearly morphed into organizations with a capacity for violence that goes way beyond the bounds of criminals—and into the realm of national security. The argument that gangsters do not want to seize the presidential palace does little to diminish their threat. Many classical insurgent groups have not tried to seize power. Al Qaeda in Iraq is only estimated to have a thousand fighters and no realistic chance of defeating the government. But it bombs soldiers and civilians with global goals in mind. The Irish Republican Army or the Basque-separatist ETA also had no chance of taking power, but fought as a form of pressure. Even Mexico's great insurgents Pancho Villa and Emiliano Zapata did not want to take the throne themselves, only to defeat tyrants to get a president more suited to their interests.

Merriam-Webster's dictionary defines *insurgent* as "a person who revolts against civil authority or an established government."[6] We can presume that to qualify as a real "revolt," it must be by force of arms rather than peaceful protest. So does El Narco fulfill this definition? Some gangsters surely do. They are not regular outlaws who shoot it out with a couple of police and run. Their revolt against civil authority includes attacks by more than fifty men on army barracks; assassination of high-ranking police and politicians; and mass kidnappings of ten or more policemen and soldiers. Who can say with a straight face that these are not serious challenges to the state?

Cartels also use more traditional political tactics in their insurgency. From Monterrey to Michoacán, gangs have organized marches against the army, some in which demonstrators held placards in support of specific cartels, such as La Familia. And to add pressure, gangsters increasingly block main streets with burning trucks, a measure that costs the economy dearly and terrifies the general public. These tactics are copied from opposition groups across Latin America and illustrate a clear politicization of the rebellion.

The other big gripe with the insurgency label is about ideology. The Mexican government itself has said in statements that the cartels are not insurgents because "they do not have a political agenda."[7] Surely, insurgents have to believe in some higher principle, critics argue, whether it be Marxism, a national flag, or Allah and the seventy-two virgins. The word *insurgent*, and even more so the Latin American word *guerrilla*, is synonymous with people who are fanatical about a cause, even if they are violent nut jobs. Mexico's narcos, these naysayers argue, believe in little other than laundering their millions, buying gold chains, and having a dozen girlfriends. At best they are "primitive rebels" in the sense of historian Eric Hobsbawm's work on bandits.[8] At worst, they aren't rebels at all, just psychotic entrepreneurs.

However, analysts have pointed out that various modern insurgencies have nothing to do with ideology. Back in 1993, Steven Metz of the U.S. Strategic Studies Institute wrote an essay called "The Future of Insurgency," in which he looked at uprisings in the post–Cold War era. Certain rebellions, he concluded, were solely about economic assets and could be better classified as "commercial insurgencies" or full-on "criminal insurgencies."[9] Another example of a commercial/criminal insurgency that analysts point to is the rebellion in the Niger Delta over oil fields.

The motives of Mexican capos vary from cartel to cartel and change over time. In 2011, Mexico had seven major cartels. All have thousands of men at arms organized in paramilitary squads. (The definition of *paramilitary* is "of, relating to, being, or characteristic of a force formed on a military pattern.") Four of the cartels use these troops to regularly attack federal forces. These are the Zetas, La Familia, the Juárez Cartel, and the Beltrán Leyva organization. The most insurgent of all are the Zetas, who fight daily battles with soldiers.

Attacks often have a specific motive and objective. Marco Vinicio Cobo, alias the Nut Job, was part of a Zetas cell that kidnapped and decapitated a solider in the southern state of Oaxaca. In his videotaped interrogation, he describes how the murder was ordered because the victim was a military intelligence officer who was getting too close to Zetas activities.[10] Across the country in Michoacán, La Familia gunmen attacked a dozen police bases and killed fifteen officers in response to the arrest of one of their lieutenants. Following that offensive, Familia capo Servando Gómez took the brash step of phoning a TV station. Talking to a startled anchor, he said La Familia responds to the harassment of gangsters and their families but offered a truce. "What we want is peace and tranquility," he said. "We want to achieve a national pact."[11]

In these cases, narco violence is a reaction to concrete strikes on criminal organizations. They are pressuring the state to back off and signaling they want a soft government who will not mess with their business.

However, in other cases, they are more aggressive in actually controlling parts of the state. An example is to attack political candidates. The contenders are not even in office, so have not had the opportunity to hurt cartels' business. But gangsters want to make sure the politicians are already in their pocket and hit those who refuse to make a deal or side with rivals. Of numerous attacks on candidates, the most high profile was on Rodolfo Torre, who ran for governor of Tamaulipas state in 2010. The physician, running on a PRI ticket, was predicted to win the race with a landslide margin of more than thirty points. But a week before the vote, gunmen showered his campaign convoy with rifle fire, killing him and four aides.[12] The ability to choose whether electoral front-runners live sends an ominous message to politicians about the power of El Narco.

But what prize is El Narco fighting for? If gangsters simply want the right to smuggle drugs, observers argue, it doesn't pose such an destructive insurgent threat to society. However, as the Mexican Drug War has escalated, gangsters have got increasingly ambitious. Certain cartels now extort every business in sight. Moreover, they have muscled into industries traditionally shaken down by the Mexican government. The Zetas dominate the east of Mexico, where the oil industry is strongest. They "tax" as much as they can from it, both by extorting the union and stealing gas to sell off as contraband. Over in Michoacán, La Familia shakes down both the mining industry and illegal logging—both assets the government used to benefit from. Such activities vary from gang to gang. The Sinaloa Cartel is largely limited to the traditional traffic of drugs. Meanwhile, the criminal groups that have branched out most are the very same that attack federal forces hardest. When gangs can "tax" industry, there is a serious weakening of the state.

Where cartels are strongest, their power seeps from politics into the private sector and media. In Juárez, business leaders argued that if they have to pay protection money to the mafia, they shouldn't have to cough up taxes to the federal government. It was a telling argument. The city's main newspaper, *El Diario de Juárez*, made the point even harder following the mafia murder of a twenty-one-year-old photographer on his lunch break. In a front-page editorial entitled "What Do You Want from Us?" *El Diario* addressed the cartels directly—and touched nerves in the Calderón government:

"You are at this time the de facto authorities in this city because the legal authorities have not been able to stop our colleagues from falling, despite the fact that we've repeatedly demanded it from them . . . Even war has rules. In any outbreak of violence protocols or guarantees exist for the groups in conflict, in order to safeguard the integrity of the journalists who cover it. This is why we reiterate, gentlemen of the various narco-trafficking organizations, that you explain what it is you want from us so we don't have to pay tribute with the lives of our colleagues."[13]

What does such narco power mean for the future of Mexico? The frightening prospect of a "failed state" is thrown around. But when broken down, the failed-state concept is not very useful in understanding the Mexican Drug War. The Fund for Peace and *Foreign Policy* magazine compile a Failed States Index every year. In 2010, Somalia was listed as number one, as the most failing state of all. Mexico was up at ninety-six, better off than such powers as India and China. A key factor is that Mexico has better public services and a wealthier middle class than much of the developing world. China or Cuba may have stronger governments, but wealth per capita is relatively low in both those countries. Meanwhile, violence has not stopped Mexico's ability to provide electricity, water, and schooling to most of its citizens. Yet.

More useful is the concept of "state capture." The idea emerged to describe how oligarchs and mafia capitalists seized control of chunks of state apparatus in Eastern Europe following the fall of communism. In Mexico, cartels definitely battle over hunks of the state, particularly regional police forces. When a cartel controls a territory, it becomes a shadow local government, one that officials and businessmen have to answer to. If you are being shaken down in such a realm, you don't know which police commanders are in the pockets of the mafia and usually prefer to pay up—or run for your life. It is a frightening reality.

The other big gauge of Mexico's degradation is by now an old chestnut: the Colombia comparison. Talk of Colombianization and the Andean narco insurgency has long dogged the discussion on Mexico, sliding into Clinton's comments. Colombia's experience of cocaine-funded guerrillas and paramilitaries is certainly worth learning from. In all the world, Colombia is the country that has faced a criminal insurgency most similar to Mexico's.

But in many ways, the comparison is a red herring. Colombia is Colombia; Mexico is Mexico. The nations have different histories and dynamics, and their drug wars play out in different ways. Thankfully, the Mexican Drug War has not yet slid to the depths of the Colombian Civil War in the mid-1990s, which displaced some 2 million people and cut off swathes of the country from the capital. Colombia has a Marxist guerrilla army larger than any in Mexico's history. But that doesn't mean Mexico is not dealing with a serious armed conflict. In South American countries, they now talk about the Mexicanization of their own drug industries and the use of *sicarios* and paramilitary hit squads. Mexico is becoming the new point of comparison for a criminal insurgency.

Miguel Ortiz ran La Familia's operations in the Michoacán state capital, Morelia, until his arrest in 2010. Before working as a mob lieutenant, he was a Familia operator for five years within the Michoacán state police. He was involved in various attacks on federal forces, including the offensive that killed fifteen officers, and hits on state officials. After his arrest, his interrogation video was released to the public.[14]

It's chilling viewing. He graphically describes techniques for cutting up corpses as well as assassinating functionaries. When it was shown on Mexican television, gasps were released from sofas and dining seats as families watched the 10:30 P.M. news. What a psychopath, people groaned. Thank God he is behind bars. That is the point of federal officials releasing such videos, to show the public they are arresting highly dangerous criminals. But interrogation films demonstrate a rather rough and skewed version of the justice system. They also tend to frighten the public more than making them feel safe, as they think about all the other psychos who are not behind bars. However, Ortiz reveals some startling insights into cartel guerrilla tactics, and his testimony is a great illustration of how the insurgency functions.

The video shows Ortiz at twenty-eight years wearing a dark shirt buttoned up to the top. He has a squat face with a slight double chin and muscular neck that gives him a bulldog look that earned him his nickname: Tyson. He talks in cold military terms about the bloodshed, using a language that has become common in cartel paramilitaries: execution victims are *targets*; kidnapped people tied up in safe houses are *cargo*.

Ortiz joined the police force when he was eighteen in 1999. At twenty-one, he says, he began to moonlight for La Familia, just as the mob was establishing itself in Michoacán. He picked the winning team. In the next few years, La Familia would mushroom in power to dominate the region. Working in the police force, he could arrest targets and hand them to Familia gunmen or even dispose of victims himself. This shows the classic modus operandi developed by gangs such as the Zetas and Juárez Cartels—where the local police once shook down crooks, the officers now work as executioners for the mob. It's state capture in action.

Ortiz left the police force in 2008 to work full-time for La Familia. But he would still ride around in police cars, wear a uniform, and work with other officers, he says. The benefits of owning a member of the police force were too good for the mafia to give away.

In July 2009, La Familia launched a major attack on federal police bases. Ortiz was called at five in the morning and told he had to work. Familia gunmen from the countryside drove into Morelia for the insurgent attack, and Ortiz supported them with as many state police vehicles as he could move. State police backing for an assault on *federales* is a startling example of the fragmentation of the Mexican state. After the insurgents had shot up the federal police base, one Mitsubishi minivan full of *sicarios* got a punctured tire. So Ortiz quickly transferred the hit men into patrol cars, drove them to a Walmart, and put them in taxis. The *sicarios* got away to fight another day.

The next month, Ortiz was rewarded with the powerful job of head of the Morelia plaza, a position known in Spanish as *encargado de la plaza*. Familia operatives took him deep into the Tierra Caliente countryside for the promotion ceremony on a burning-hot August weekend. He passed through the city of Apatzingán and onto the winding mountain road up to Aguililla, where they stopped the car and walked for two hours into the mountains. Arriving at a ranch, he was greeted by La Familia's top brass, including Nazario "El Más Loco" Moreno and Servando "La Tuta" Gómez themselves.

"It was very brief. They say the less you see them the better; we lasted at the most ten, fifteen minutes in the talk. They said what they had to say and said from this moment you are the *encargado de la plaza* of Morelia and your direct commander is Chuke [another code-named operative]."

This organizational structure of La Familia, described by Ortiz, is derived from that of the Zetas, who trained them. Plaza heads run cells, which are semiautonomous. They make money in their turf and kick back to the commander, who in turn deals with the capos. Lower down the ranks are the *sicarios*, and below them *halcones*, or hawks, who work as the eyes and ears of the cartel. Everyone is given nicknames to limit the information they have on each other. When *sicarios* are given a job, they normally have no idea why the person is targeted. They just carry out orders.

The Zetas initially modeled this chain of command based on the Mexican army they came from. Ranks included first commanders and second commanders, just as in the military. But the war evolved their structure to become closer to Latin America's guerrilla armies or right-wing paramilitaries, who use autonomous cells to coordinate thousands of men at arms. The Zetas trained La Familia members in this guerrilla warfare in 2005 and 2006, before the Michoacán mob betrayed them to claim the turf.

Ortiz instructed new recruits in his cell in the use of terror. He describes one night when about forty Familia mobsters gathered on a hill outside Morelia. Captured prisoners were brought up so rookies could be blooded.

"That is how we put the new people to the test. We made them kill.

Then we made them quarter the bodies, because the new people coming in lose their fear by cutting off an arm or a leg or something. It is not easy. You have to cut through the bone and everything. But we need them to suffer a bit so they lose fear little by little. We used butcher's knives or little machetes about thirty cm [ten inches] long. It would take the new people about ten minutes to cut off an arm, as some of them were nervous. But I could do it in three or four."

Carlos, the intelligence officer who follows La Familia, says the gangsters are particularly adept at cutting up bodies because many of the original members were butchers. More recent recruits, he says, often worked in taco joints. Their skills for cutting up sizzling pork are applied to human flesh.

When Ortiz's *sicarios* carried out killings, they would leave a message signed "La Resistencia," or the Resistance, a title used by certain cells in La Familia. The name celebrates rebellion, but for authorities it was a mark of intimidation. Ortiz confesses to being personally involved in the murder of a Michoacán state undersecretary for security. That attack was ordered because the official angered La Familia by messing with its system of police protection, Ortiz says. He then went higher up the chain after the State Security Secretary Minerva Bautista. First he put a hawk on her trail.

"We put a trustworthy lad to follow her for ten days—where she ate, where she slept, what time she went to the office and everything. We found the best day for the attack."

As Bautista left a state fair with her entourage, Ortiz and his assassins blocked a narrow highway passage with a disabled truck and opened fire from two sides. An incredible twenty-seven hundred bullets were shot at Bautista's heavily armored SUV. Two of Baustista's bodyguards died and the secretary took a bullet. The gunmen left believing the target was dead. But Bautista miraculously survived the hit.[15] Shortly after the bungled attack, federal agents nabbed Ortiz in a Morelia safe house.

"I heard rumors that they were getting close to me. Then they got me. I always had it in my mind that one day I was going to be arrested."

To try to make sure gunmen do hit their targets, cartels have developed training camps. The first such camps were discovered in northeast Mexico and linked to the Zetas, but they have since been found all across the country and even over the border in Guatemala. Most are built on ranches and farmlands, such as one discovered in the community of Camargo just south of the Texas border. They are equipped with shooting ranges and makeshift assault courses and have been found storing arsenals of heavy weaponry, including boxes of grenades.

Arrested gangsters have described courses as lasting two months and involving the use of grenade launchers and .50-caliber machine guns. A training video captured by police in 2011 shows recruits running across a field, taking cover on the grass, and firing assault rifles.[16] Sometimes training can be deadly. One recruit drowned during an exercise that required him to swim carrying his backpack and rifle. The discovery of these camps has sparked the obvious comparison to Al Qaeda training grounds in Afghanistan.

But however much schooling they give, cartels still love gunslingers with real military experience. In the first decade of democracy, up until 2010, one hundred thousand soldiers had deserted from the Mexican military.[17] There is a startling implication: country and ghetto boys sign up for the army, get the government to pay for their training, then make real money with the mob.

A crucial ingredient to sustain paramilitaries is access to military-grade weaponry. This has been no problem for cartels, which keep themselves supplied with an insane abundance of assault rifles and bullets. Who can fire two thousand seven hundred rounds in a hit unless they have more ammo than sense? Browning machine guns keep spitting fat .50-caliber shells while hundreds of grenades have been thrown in single battles. Where is all this firepower coming from? Mexican officials point their fingers straight north over the Rio Grande. Uncle Sam, they say, arms to the teeth the same narco insurgents it pays the Mexican government to fight. It is a seething indictment. But is it true?

The gun trade from America to Mexico has been a bone of contention for decades that has heated up through the Mexican Drug War. Mexican officials scream again and again that the United States needs to clamp down on illegal weapons sales. America promises new measures that will miraculously stop the flow of firepower. They fail. As bodies keep piling up, and the media keeps highlighting the role of American guns, U.S. authorities have been incapable of stopping the trade.

America's gun lobby is supersensitive about the issue. Why should American gun enthusiasts suffer because of Mexico's problems? they cry.

Guns don't kill people. People kill people. Reports on the issue are posted on pro-gun Web sites along with angry comments, sometimes personally insulting the journalists.

I followed this gun trail closely from seizures in Sinaloa to gun shops in Texas and Arizona. In the United States, I met some upstanding gun-shop owners and enthusiasts who make some valid points. The war in Mexico, they point out, is sustained by many factors besides guns, such as corruption in Mexican police forces. They are absolutely right.

But the ugly truth is that a huge number of weapons made or sold in the United States go to Mexican cartels. This is an irrefutable fact. Mexico itself has almost no gun stores and weapons factories and gives away few licenses. Almost all weapons in the hands of cartel armies are illegal. In 2008, Mexico submitted the serial numbers from close to six thousand guns they had seized from gangsters to the U.S. Bureau of Alcohol, Tobacco, and Firearms. About 90 percent, or 5,114 of the weapons, were traced to American gun sellers.

The ATF and Obama administration acknowledged America's responsibility in this tragedy. But the gun lobby still refused to concede the point. What about tens of thousands of other seized weapons in Mexico that hadn't been traced? gun activists said. The Mexican government, they alleged, was only tracing guns that looked as if they had come from America to sway the debate. So to make it easier to trace weapons seized in Mexico, the ATF introduced a new computer system. Between 2009 and April 2010, this traced another 63,700 firearms to U.S. gun stores.[18] And those are only the ones they have captured. People can argue endlessly about the exact percentages, but the underlying fact is that tens of thousands of guns go from American stores to Mexican gangsters. However much anyone supports the right to bear arms, they must admit this is a pressing problem.

American stores are not the only source of weapons for Mexico's mafias. They also steal them from the Mexican security forces and have been found taking huge caches from the Guatemalan military. International arms traffickers have also long moved guns through Central America and the Caribbean. If Mexican cartels didn't buy firearms from America, gun advocates argue, they would just get them from these sources. Maybe. But a flow of weapons into seaports or up through Central America would be slower and easier to fight, making guns and ammo more expensive. The flood of guns over the two-thousand-mile border from the United States is a tide as tough to stop as the drugs and migrants going north.

Global production and sale of small arms is a key factor making modern criminal insurgents so lethal. America is a big part of this. The AR-15 assault rifle, the civilian version of the M16, is one of the preferred weapons of Mexican mobsters. The gun is built by Colt and sold freely in Texas and Arizona, among other states.

The preferred cartel gun is of course the Kalashnikov, or AK-47, fondly known as the Goat's Horn. That is not American, gun enthusiasts point out, it is Russian. Actually, the Kalashnikov is now manufactured in at least fifteen countries, including the United States, by firms such as Arsenal Inc. in Las Vegas. Gun stores in Arizona and Texas also sell a huge quantity of imported Kalashnikovs from China, Hungary, and other countries. Guns, like drugs and dollars, go through their own surreal journeys in modern commerce: weapons are built in Beijing, sold in San Antonio, and used to murder in Matamoros. American stores only sell semiautomatic versions of the AK. But these are easy for Mexican mobsters to customize into fully automatic weapons. The vast majority of killings in the Mexican Drug War are committed with assault rifles.

Many versions of these weapons were prohibited by the assault weapons ban, which came in under Bill Clinton in 1994. That ban was lifted under George W. Bush in September 2004—exactly the time the Mexican Drug War erupted on the Texas border. Relaxed gun control was not the main cause of the conflict, but it surely threw oil on the fire.

In downtown Phoenix, Arizona, I walk into glass-paneled ATF offices to meet Peter Forcelli, who runs the anti-firearms-trafficking squad. Forcelli is a lively New Yorker with an accent as broad as it is long. "Can I speak Spanish?" he says. "No, I can't even speak English." He takes me down in the elevator to the basement vault where all the guns captured from smugglers are kept. It is arsenal fit for a militia.

Kalashnikovs and AR-15s in all shapes and sizes line racks or are shoved into huge buckets. In one corner sit some ultramodern rifles that look like something out of *Starship Troopers*, which are made by Belgium's Fabrique Nationale and sold in Arizona stores. There are also some

Fabrique Nationale 5.7 pistols, known as cop killers because of their ability to fire armor-piercing ammunition. The same type of gun was in the
hand of Chapo Guzmán's son when he lay bleeding dead on the Culiacán
concrete. Overall, the Phoenix stash is one of the biggest stockpiles of captured weapons in all America. "I saw more Kalashnikovs here my first
week than in fifteen years in the New York police," Forcelli tells me.

To buy guns in Arizona, you need to be a resident, Forcelli explains.
So, gun traffickers pay American citizens to walk into the shops and buy
the weapons for them. These are known as straw purchases. A straw pur-
chaser can be paid about $100 to buy a firearm, Forcelli says. The traf-
fickers can always find someone willing to do it. Gun sellers are meant to
report suspicious customers, such as when you get a pallid woman coming in and ordering half a dozen Kalashnikovs. Forcelli's squad will then
follow up the intelligence to bust safe houses and grab key players. They
have made many successful raids, netting the huge arsenal below. But
Forcelli concedes that the ATF is only capturing a fraction of the guns
going south. "We have twenty dedicated firearms investigators in a city
with thousands of gun sellers," he says. "Some shops don't get inspected
for years."

The Obama administration's big move was to put troops on Arizona
and Texas roads to catch the gunrunners as they drive their purchases to
Mexico. But the money might have been better spent on ATF intelligence, as random stops are ineffective at catching the guns amid the thousands of vehicles. The vast majority of traffic into Mexico cruises straight
over the border without any check. This is another gripe of the gun lobby.
If Mexico doesn't want firearms smuggled into its country, they ask, why
doesn't it police its border better? It is a valid point. Perhaps more of the
Mexican soldiers burning marijuana fields would be better off guarding
the American border.

Many of the same trap cars used to smuggle drugs north carry the
guns south, with weapons filling the hidden compartments. Some guns
filter down in ones and twos, known as ant traffic. But as the war has
intensified, increasingly bigger loads have shown up. One bumper seizure
came in May 2010, when the Laredo police, acting on intelligence, stopped
a truck heading to Mexico. The truck carried 175 brand-new, boxed assault rifles, 200 high-capacity magazines, 53 bayonets, and 10,000 rounds
of ammunition—an arsenal fit for a potent death squad.[19]

*   *   *

When the ATF raided one gunrunner's house in Yuma, Arizona, they found gangsters had left behind a rather foolish piece of evidence, a video of themselves trying out a weapon bought from an Arizona seller. It was such a nice piece of hardware, they couldn't resist. The film, recorded onto a laptop, shows the two thugs taking shots with a top-of-the-range Barret .50 caliber. It is such a big gun it has been mounted on a tripod, while the shooters sit down and use both hands to fire it. The bullets are 13.8 cm long, the size of small knives. The men are firing the weapon in what appears to be a patch of Arizona desert. Shots scream out, making the cameraman shake before panning round to a metal sheet that the bullets have torn through. One of those shown was arrested and charged, with some evidence provided by the video. The other man, and the gun, were believed to be in Mexico, waging war.

By most people's definition, .50-caliber guns are weapons of war and should only be in military hands. But they are available in Arizona stores, and they are increasingly favored by drug gangs. Gun enthusiasts insist their shells can't really fire through armored vehicles. But a Mexican officer I talk to insists they can and says he has faced them on the battlefield. When cartels set up ambushes on groups of soldiers, he says, they will often open fire with .50-caliber guns, set up on mountain paths or country roads. They then follow up with rocket-propelled grenades.

Grenades are not available in American stores, so that is one weapon the gun lobby doesn't need to defend. But many were still made in America. ATF agents have identified some captured grenades as M67 explosives that the United States supplied to Central American forces during the Cold War a generation ago. They have been traced to Guatemala, El Salvador, Honduras, and Nicaragua. Plenty of them are around. Some 266,000 M67 grenades went to El Salvador alone between 1980 and 1993.[20] That nation's civil war is now long forgotten in America. But agents say the grenades sell on the black market from $100 to $500 apiece. The first four years of Calderón's government saw more than a hundred grenade attacks. Furthermore, in one single battle—when marines shot dead kingpin Ezequiel Cárdenas, alias Tony Tormenta, in Matamoros—more than three hundred grenades were set off.[21]

Car bombs are less common. Up until 2010, a few IEDs scattered around the country caused damage and injury but no deaths. But after the Juárez bomb exploded killing three people in July 2010, fear surged through

Mexico about more carnage. Sure enough, in January 2011 another car
bomb exploded in Hidalgo state, killing a policeman and injuring three
others. The big worry about car bombs is that they are less discriminat-
ing about whom they kill then guns and often take down civilians. ATF
agents explain the Juárez bomb was a remote-operated device set off by a
cell phone and was of a similar complexity to the IEDs that blow up on
American troops in Iraq and Afghanistan.

The explosive itself was an industrial material called Tovex. A report
by the United States Bomb Data Center could shed light as to where it
came from, and American manufacturers could be involved yet again,
although not of their own will. The report explains that a Texas-based
company had suffered a raid on its installations at an explosives magazine down in Durango state, Mexico. A father-and-son team were guarding the gates, the report says, when two Suburban SUVs rolled up and
fifteen to twenty masked men stepped out bearing automatic rifles. They
snatched a whopping 267.75 pounds or 900 cartridges of the explosives as
well as 230 electric detonators. (The attack used just 22 pounds to make
the bomb.) It is dangerous storing explosive materials in a region swarming with cartel paramilitaries.[22]

Federal agents nabbed several men whom they accused of being behind the bomb, including one who they said made the cell phone call to
set it off. The bombers, the agents allege, were a cell of thugs from the
Juárez Cartel, using the terror tactic in reaction to arrests. As bombs
spread fear, they cause more pressure than mere guns and are a natural
escalation. It is the same logic that led Pablo Ecobar to use bombs; or the
Irish Republican Army; or Spanish separatists; or Al Qaeda: bombs make
a big bang.

Graffiti on city walls indicate the Juárez Cartel was indeed behind the
bomb. But the mafia scrawlings add an extra dimension. They weren't just
hitting *federales* because they busted their dope, they claim, but because
the *federales* were allied with their rival Chapo Guzmán. As one graffiti
said, FBI AND DEA. INVESTIGATE AUTHORITIES WHO ARE SUPPORTING
THE SINALOA CARTEL OR ELSE WE WILL SET OFF MORE CAR BOMBS.

Calderón tells us not to read the scrawlings of mafia murderers. But
whether you want to consider whether federal agents are corrupt or not,
the line of thinking expressed in the graffiti fits in with the twisted reasoning of Mexican drug cartels. The enemies they see first and foremost
are rival cartels. When they hit police or civilians, it is often to hurt these

rivals by breaking their system of protection. This logic helps explain the motivations behind many assaults in the drug war.

A similar thinking surrounds the grenade attack that killed eight civilians celebrating Independence Day in 2008. The explosives were lobbed into the main square of Morelia shortly after the state governor had rung the bell for independence. Revelers thought they were fire-crackers at first, then saw dozens of men, women, and children fall over covered in blood. If you want to use the word *terrorism* to describe the drug war, this is a solid place.

Federales captured one man who confessed to tossing a grenade. He said he was paid by the Zetas for the work of terror. But true to the strength of the command structure, he had no idea why the attack had been ordered. Cartel paramilitaries are experts at keeping information on a need-to-know basis.

However, Mexican intelligence officer Carlos explains the motivation of the grenade attack. The Zetas hit Michoacán state as it was the home of La Familia, he says, who had betrayed them. By hurting civilians, they were putting their finger up at La Familia's Michoacán regionalism. More crucially, they were also forcing the government to crack down on the area—and hurt La Familia's drug operations. In Spanish they call this *calentar la plaza*, or heat up the territory. As in Juárez, the first thought is for cartels. Civilians are collateral.

Severed heads; grenades; car bombs—the terror tactics get bloodier each time. It's as if the cartels were playing poker and have to keep raising the stakes to buy the pot. The bets just keep getting bigger. You have killed five of my men; I'll kill ten of yours. You assassinate a federal police of-ficer on my payroll; I'll kidnap and kill fifteen on yours. You throw gre-nades; I'll drop a bomb. No one feels he can stand down, or he will lose all the chips he has already thrown in.

Attacks are designed to be as sanguine as possible for maximum me-dia impact. Sometimes, killers will phone up newsrooms and tell them about a pile of corpses or severed heads to make sure it gets in the paper. It is unnerving when you get to a crime scene before the police. A Juárez thug arrested for the car bomb attack said atrocities will also be timed around the media schedules. "A lot of the attacks are made an hour be-fore news bulletins so they get out to the public," Noe Fuentes said on an interrogation video, "so people know what problem they are involved in."[23] Blaring out on plasma-TV sets, this carnage tells different stories to different audiences: the general public learns to fear El Narco; but young thugs on the street see who is the winning team.

Mexican media are caught up in a difficult discussion about how to handle this. In 2011, many editors have toned down coverage of the violence so as not to play into El Narco's game of terror. At the same time, they don't want to censor reporting on the conflict, which obviously involves a huge public interest.

In front-line states, these decisions are often taken out of journalists' hands. Gangsters will instruct newspapers not to cover a certain massacre or battle. For the safety of their staff and families, editors have to concede. Other times, the drug mafia will tell a newspaper specifically to cover certain murders. Again, it is best to do what they say. Sometimes, one gang will tell a paper to cover something and the rivals will tell them not to. Then editors are stuck between a rock and a hard place and often think the best move is to run for their lives.

Under such intense pressures, the mainstream media are getting less relevant in front-line states. Residents will often go to Twitter to find out if there are any shoot-outs on their way to work or log on to YouTube to see amateur video of them. New Web sites have emerged purely to cover narco violence. The most well-known is the notorious Blog del Narco. It is run from an unknown location, reportedly by a student, and airs no-holds-barred videos from all cartels as well as citizen journalists. The government tells people not to watch narco propaganda, but federal agents carefully study all content coming on the blog. It gets millions of hits and its advertising sales are booming.

Some of the first narco snuff videos looked almost frame for frame like Al Qaeda execution videos: a victim strapped to a chair; a ski-masked man grasping a sword; a head sliced off. As the poker pot heated up, so did the videos. A Zetas cell in Tabasco put twelve bleeding heads on YouTube. From the close-up shot, the faces look peaceful, death having drained the tension from their cheeks, their eyes shut above thick mustaches and square jaws. But as the shot pans out, the horror of their end is revealed: the necks reach stubs where they have roughly been cut off, the corpses hang upside down across the room on meat hooks, their blood draining away onto white floor tiles. "This is your responsibility for not respecting the deals you have made with us," reads a handwritten note in Spanish by the craniums.[24]

Snuff videos have got increasingly common as the conflict burns on. Tortured victims often reveal names of corrupt officials working for rival cartels before the ax falls. First it was just hit men tied with duct tape to the chair; then captured policemen; then politicians. Some videotaped confessions spark startling scandals, such as the revelation that prisoners were leaving their cells to commit massacres and then returning to the jail to sleep. Other times they just spread more suspicion that is not corroborated. Many narco videos look painfully similar to the government's own footage of interrogations of captured cartel thugs. Grainy shots of blood and torture have become a sanguine backdrop to Mexican political life.

One video really stuck in my head. From part of the babbling it looks to be by the Zetas. They have four prisoners on their knees, blindfolded, with their hands tied behind their backs. The prisoners are wearing military uniforms but they are not soldiers; a Zetas interrogator indicates they are a squad who worked for the Gulf Cartel whom the Zetas are fighting. The interrogator curses them for being fooled into murdering for the wrong side. Then the executions begin. "We are going to kill three and let one live," says the interrogator. *Bang.* They shoot the first prisoner in the head. He falls down like a sack of potatoes. The other three are still. They all pray to be the one who will be spared. *Bang.* They shoot a second prisoner. "We are going to leave one," the interrogator says again. The last two prisoners kneel still. They calculate they have a fifty-fifty chance of being the one survivor. *Bang.* They shoot a third prisoner and he hits the ground like a rag doll. Wow, the last prisoner is thinking. I am the one who has been spared. *Bang.* They kill him as well. The interrogator was lying. They had planned to massacre the four all along. Maybe the interrogator lied so the victims would be still while they were shot in the skull. Maybe he wanted to fuck with their heads. Maybe he just played the sick game to give the video an extra punch.

It is psychotic and hateful behavior. But such behaviour is typical in many war zones. Cartel thugs have gone beyond the pale because they are completely immersed in a violent conflict, living like soldiers in the trenches. Imagine the life of Zetas thugs in the war-torn northeast of Mexico, fighting daily with soldiers and rival gangs, moving from safe house to safe house, completely divorced from the reality of normal citizens. In these ghastly conditions they commit atrocities that the world finds so hard to comprehend. For many of these cartel soldiers on the front line, war and insurgency have become their central mission. While thugs have traditionally talked about fighting over drug smuggling, now many are talking about smuggling drugs to finance their war.

However much Calderón argues that the government is winning, the widening of the criminal insurgency is seriously shaking power brokers from Mexico City to Washington. Intelligence officers in the Pentagon continue to brainstorm about the prospects of the conflict on U.S. security. Their reports all pose a fundamental question: Where is the Mexican Drug War going? Will police and soliders, they ask, knock El Narco down to size as Calderón and the DEA claim? Or is the beast going to keep expanding in Mexico, the United States, and around the world? And could the criminal insurgency even explode into a wider civil war? It is to this destiny of El Narco that we now turn.

PART III

Destiny

CHAPTER 13

Prosecution

All my life I've tried to be the good guy, the guy in the white fucking hat. And for what? For nothing. I'm not becoming like them; I am them.

—JOHNNY DEPP IN *DONNIE BRASCO*, 1997

When DEA agent Daniel saw the movie *Miami Vice* at a cinema in Panama City, Panama, his heart jumped through his mouth. In the film, a remake of the iconic eighties cop series, detectives Crockett and Tubbs run an elaborate sting operation on Colombian cocaine traffickers. Wearing their trademark white suits and T-shirts, they pose as freelance drug transporters so they can arrange to move a cargo of the white lady, then seize it. It sounds like a funny contradiction: cops transporting drugs so they can bust them. But that is exactly the same sting Daniel was trying to set up in Panama in real life.

Daniel was also meeting Colombian cocaine barons, and he was also posing as a freelance drug transporter. After months of careful infiltration he was close to convincing the gangsters to put three tons of cocaine on a DEA-controlled ship sailing out of Panama City. It was the bust of a lifetime. Then *Miami Vice* hit the theaters. If those gangsters saw it, Daniel thought, he was dead.

"That was bad. I saw it and I was like 'Ain't that a motherfucker.' We were completely compromised. This is bullshit. This is the same fucking thing we are selling. Because agents made that movie. That it is why it is so fucking solid. It is very, very close.

"Then you have to grow some balls. Fuck the movie. This is me. I don't fucking care. That is the way I saw it at that time: make or break."

Such a sting may sound like rather sordid business. It is. Drug busting is a grimy game. And in the modern drug war, it has become downright filthy. Agents have to get down in the trenches with psychotic criminals to get ahead of them. They have to recruit informants close to these villains. And they have to know how to use them to stick the knife in.

The huge drug busts aren't made by luck and brute force. They are about intelligence, about knowing where the shipment is going to be or which safe house the capo will be hiding in next Tuesday. Only then you can send in the marines to start blasting. This intelligence, as drug agents have found after four decades in the war, usually comes from infiltrators or informants.

Many narco kingpins are behind bars or on the concrete full of bullets because of treachery. This makes gangsters extremely violent toward suspected turncoats. In Mexico, they call informants *soplones*, or blabbermouths, and like to slice their fingers off and stick them in their mouths; in Colombia, they call them toads.

But once kingpins are extradited to the United States, many become toads themselves, supertoads. They broker deals to give up other kingpins and tens of millions of dollars in assets. Then drug agents can make more busts and bring in more villains; and the jailed capos can write their memoirs and become movie stars.

This prickly prosecution process, developed over four decades of the war on drugs, is crucial to understanding the future of El Narco in Mexico, because a key question is whether Mexican and American agents can beat the beast of drug trafficking down by arrests and busts. DEA chiefs and the Calderón government keep pursuing this tactic. It has been hard and there have been a lot of casualties, they argue, but if they keep at it, then justice will prevail.

With their reign of terror, cartels often appear like invincible organizations, impervious to attacks from anything that police or soldiers throw at them. But if agents really got their act together, would cartels collapse like paper tigers? Can the good guys actually win the Mexican Drug War and lock El Narco safely behind bars? Or at least if the police arrest enough kingpins, will drug smugglers stop being a criminal insurgency threatening national security and go back to being a regular crime problem?

DEA agent Daniel's career offers startling insights into the attempt to put El Narco in jail. He has personally infiltrated a major Mexican drug cartel and a Colombian cartel. And he has lived to tell the tale. His story shows what the drug war strategy formed in Washington means on the streets of Mexican border cities.

Like many soldiers, Daniel comes from the rough end of town. DEA undercover agents are the coarse cousins of well-heeled CIA spooks. A Harvard-educated Anglo-Saxon is unlikely to be any good setting up cocaine deals with the Medellín Cartel. So the DEA needs people like Daniel, who was born in Tijuana, hung round with a California street gang affiliated with the Crips, and spent his teenage years beating the hell out of anyone who got too close. He was saved from a life of crime, he says, by joining the U.S. marines. He went to Kuwait and fired a machine gun in the First Gulf War before going to the trenches in the drug war.

I meet Daniel in an apartment and he tells me his story over Tecate beer and pizza. He is powerfully built, wears a suit and tie, and uses precise militaristic terms, common of veterans and cops. But his wayward youth also shines through and I catch him reciting old hip-hop and punk songs from the eighties, from Suicidal Tendencies to Niggaz With Attitude. He also loves the 1983 gangster movie *Scarface*. It helps to have the same cinematic taste as the mobsters you are dealing with.

"*Scarface* was the best movie ever. It was the American Dream, especially to an immigrant; the dream of coming to America and being successful."

Daniel already knew something of the world of drug trafficking when he watched *Scarface* as a kid in Imperial Beach, San Diego. He had spent his infancy over the line in Tijuana when the marijuana trade boomed in the seventies. One of his first memories was seeing his father invite strange men to their family home and pull stashes of money out of a secret compartment in a mahogany center table. Looking back, he believes his father was himself running weed. Then at age ten, his mother passed away and Daniel went to live with his grandparents in the United States.

"My mother was very hard with me and then she died five days before my birthday and I harbored a lot of resentment. That was one of the demons that haunted me throughout my life. I did a lot of things and I didn't fucking care."

Moving home and country was a tough challenge for a preadolescent. Daniel couldn't speak fluent English until he was fourteen, and by that time he was a troublesome kid and got thrown out of three high schools because of fighting and other misbehavior. Some of his friends were stealing cars or motorcycles and bringing drugs over the border, and Daniel was smoking weed and getting drunk a lot, especially on peppermint and schnapps.

"I was one of those bad drunks who ruined the party. Every time I was about to get in a fight, I stripped off my shirt. I was very into lifting weights and I did wrestling in high school. I wanted to show off and say, 'Are you sure you want to fuck with me?' It was a ritual."

Daniel finally got his high school diploma at a last-chance school in San Diego. Then it was straight into the Marine Corps. He enjoyed the physical training and left behind the weed-smoking wastoid. Talented at a number of sports, he was selected for an elite unit within the marines, and the military seemed to be a lot of fun. Then Saddam Hussein invaded Kuwait and it wasn't such fun anymore. After training in Oman, Daniel went into a hole in the desert and fired a SAW at Iraqi troops as they poured out of Kuwait City, probably killing many.

"It was sad because people surrendered. But some of them fought, especially the Republican Guard, so they got what they got.

"I froze my ass off. They said it was going to be hot so they threw all our cold-weather gear away. Then it was fucking freezing. It poured and rained the whole time, and the holes would fill up with water. It was miserable."

After four years in the marines, Daniel went back to civvy street carrying some of his misery home in the form of Gulf War syndrome, a condition believed to be caused by exposure to toxic chemicals, whose symptoms range from headaches to birth defects in the children of veterans. His military experience got him his first job busting traffickers, in California's antidrug task force. Alongside other veterans, Daniel would buzz around the state in a helicopter carrying an M16 automatic rifle and raiding marijuana plantations. Most were run by Mexicans and located inside national parks and forests and included some huge farms with up to twelve thousand plants. During one bust, some thugs from Michoacán fired at them with Kalashnikovs.

"I was getting close to the plantation and they fired. We hit the ground first, kneeling down, and we fired back, and they were gone. These people have balls, they are crazy."

Daniel's next job was in the U.S. Customs Service busting runners as they came over the border. Because of the huge quantity of traffic at Tijuana–San Diego, agents can only toss a tiny percentage of vehicles. So the key for Daniel and other agents was to try to read people and smell who was dirty. Daniel found he had a special talent for spotting smugglers.

"It is like a sense. I look at them and see if the person that is driving does not match the car or the car does not match the person. I get close up to their face and say, 'How are you doing?' And if you're carrying a bunch of money or drugs, I'm going to get all over your ass.

"The problem was, people on the streets knew me because I grew up there. They would say, 'This is a contradiction. We used to smoke grass together.' Well, that was then, this is now. To avoid retribution, I had to segregate myself and move way up north."

As Daniel scored big results busting marijuana, crystal meth, cocaine, and heroin, DEA agents spotted his talent and invited him over. Suddenly, he was a federal agent on a higher salary and working on the big investigations; his career had rocketed. First he would stay at the border and be called in when customs agents had made a bust. His job was to flip the smuggler and persuade him to work for the DEA. He found his knowledge of border culture gave him a special talent at turning suspects into informants.

"I don't even need a bad cop. I just need me because I sell the product. You did what you did. That is on you. How can I help you go forward? I can't go back and erase your fucking life. If you want to move forward, let's do it. I sell myself, I sell myself the way I reach people and the way I talk to them.

"I don't lie to them. I already know what is in the car. I know where you are going. Either you take it and I'll arrest the people who it really belongs to, or you can just sit on this shit for a while and just do your fucking time. If it's coke, heroin, or ice you are fucked. You are fucking fucked. Don't worry about it. The only way I can help you is if you fucking take it where you need to go. I'm not lying about any of the things, they are all true. If you have got five or ten keys [kilos] you are fucked. If you have got more than that, you are fucking destroyed."

Daniel would persuade the smugglers to take the drugs to their delivery point, followed by agents. Then they could bust a whole drug warehouse—in San Diego or often up in Los Angeles. Or they could keep following the gang and bust a whole smuggling operation.

Daniel also learned the art of cultivating informants and training them to get deeper into the cartels. As the "rats" get closer to the DEA, they can be used for a whole range of tasks, such as introducing other infiltrators to higher-ranking mobsters.

"Informants are a big key. They can say they are my buddy, say they went to school with me for ten years. They can make a whole bunch of stuff up. As long as you treat each other like it is true, the gangsters will believe it. You have got to believe it too."

Use of informants is ethically questionable. The DEA ends up paying money to dubious characters, albeit toward busting bigger drug loads and bigger criminals. In theory, agents cannot pay informants actively involved in criminal activities. In practice, agents try not to know what their informants are up to. As they admit, "these guys are not choirboys." Agents are also worried the informant could be a double agent who is feeding info to the cartel. Or a triple agent. Daniel discovered you have to push into an informant's mind to make sure he is playing straight.

"I've got to make sure they are not fucking lying and setting me up so I can fail. Who wants to fucking die for nothing? I can't do that.

"Informants are all dirty. All of them. Except maybe they are clean for a moment. They are like a dirty person who took a shower that day. Guess what? He's clean for that day. Tomorrow he is dirty again."

During the Mexican Drug War, two high-profile cases of bad informants have caused scandals for American law enforcement. They didn't involve the DEA, but Immigrations and Customs Enforcement, an agency that is part of the Bush-created Homeland Security department and has also moved into fighting drug gangs. ICE agents broke the rules and hired informants who carried out murders in Ciudad Juárez. It caused a bad stink on both sides of the border—thugs on the American payroll killing in Mexico.[1]

That was a case of bad agents. But even the best agents have to take risks because the very nature of the drug trade sows conspiracy. It is not a crime like a bank heist, where sobbing victims will help the probe and testify against the robbers. In the narcotics trade, billions of dollars spread round among thousands of people. There is no classic victim—only drug takers on the street, who willingly take their dose and haven't a clue about who is moving it. So drug agents have to infiltrate the industry through informants and undercover. They have to get into the espionage game.

After two and a half years flipping smugglers at the border, DEA officers saw that Daniel had huge potential. He had a perfect profile for undercover work south of the Rio Grande: Mexican, tough, street-smart, an ex-marine, and with a proven track record. So they sent him to the school where agents learn to work undercover—in a two-week course.

"You can't learn shit in two weeks. Not a damn fucking thing. That is just for protocol, and that is just to check to say you have been to it. You learn nothing more than the streets will teach you growing up."

With a license to work undercover, Daniel started going after major international trafficking operations. He didn't care about kilos anymore; he was looking for tons.

Several years into this work, he built up his huge case in Panama. He flew down to Central America's skyscraper paradise, packed with businessmen and criminals from all over the planet, glitzy discos, sparkling casinos, and high-class prostitutes, all in a sweltering tropical climate. Like most big cases, this one started with an informant, a Colombian who inherited a transportation company from his father. The man introduced Daniel to major traffickers, and he built up the relationship from there.

Modern drug traffickers contract a lot of their transportation work out to freelancers. This saves them the hassle of owning so many ships or airplanes and cuts down the number of their own people close to the product. This all helps create the diverse structure of cartels, so much tougher to bring down than all-encompassing organizations.

Daniel posed as one of the freelancers tendering transport services, offering them a price per ton to move cocaine on his ship. That way, the traffickers would put a huge amount of product onto a boat that the DEA was really controlling—and give the agents a pile of their cash. It is a pretty simple sting when you break it down; but it was on an aggressive scale that the cartels hadn't caught onto.

To be convincing, Daniel had to build up his role as freelance drug trafficker, his alter ego. He shows me a photo of himself in that character. He has his long hair with a bandanna tied round it and a wild look in his eyes.

"I created somebody else but very realistic so I didn't fuck it up. The difference between that guy and me"—he clicks his fingers—"it could be me right now. That is the problem. He is a lot like me. I grew up so raw that it is nothing. People ask me, 'Are going to go into your mode?' What mode? I am that fucking guy."

Daniel rented out a huge suite at an old Panama hotel where all the traffickers hung out. He would also go to the best table-dance clubs and let himself be seen throwing money round. It was all part of being convincing. (The DEA footed the bill for his hotel, but the strip clubs came out of his own pocket.) He went back and forth to Panama over several months building relations with the traffickers. He would meet them at flash restaurants. First he met with one, then two, then four. Then one time he sat with eight Colombian traffickers.

"It is a little concerning because that is a lot of eyes looking at you. I broke the ice and talked about a soccer game. I follow a lot of soccer—I like Arsenal and I like Boca Juniors—and then we talked for hours. They are very eager and hungry for money.

"I like things that have an adrenaline rush and that is one of them. Undercover is a rush because you don't know what is going to happen, whether you are going to come back or not."

Daniel was getting close. But the work was taking a toll on him. He began to lose his own identity, to get lost in the world of flash Colombian traffickers with their entourages of beautiful women. Who was he really? The undercover cop or the trafficker? Before going out to meets, he got scared. What if he messed up and let on who he really was? One thing that kept him grounded, he said, was a record by New York producer Moby that contained tracks with deep, melancholy beats.

"I would listen to this song and get extremely hyped up. This is how I found the motivation inside of me to get all my energy and my adrenaline to do what I needed to do. I would take a cab from the hotel room to go and meet with the bad guys, and I knew that I had to go there and win. That is all I had to do. I had to go there and confuse them and convince them that I was who I said I was.

"I never took my eyes off them; never looked down. I was very positive and affirmative with the things that I said. When I looked how I looked then, I would believe me too. I had a very dry look. I spoke very sharp and to the point. I had a look that said, 'If you fuck me, you know we are going to go toe-to-toe.'"

That was when *Miami Vice* hit the cinema; with the same scam he was selling. Watching it, he was tempted to run for his life. But he stuck at it. And thankfully, it seemed the Colombians didn't see the movie.

Finally came the day for the deal. The Colombians bought his story and handed over nearly four tons of cocaine and a suitcase of money. The drugs were put onto a thirty-five-foot cargo vessel used to lay cable on the seabed. It had enough fuel to get to Spain. The Colombians put one guy out to sea with the stash, plus Daniel and the crew. The boat hit the waves. Then—*bang*—the navy seized it. Daniel had taken down drugs worth hundreds of millions on the street.

Panama was hard. But another job left a deeper scar in Daniel—when he pulled the same scam on Mexican drug traffickers.

The sting was set up in a city on the U.S.-Mexico border. Daniel gradually built up connections with a major smuggling operation. He offered them a truck to move drugs into the United States. The idea was to seize the drugs, the money, and to get all the crooks in the warehouse where the truck was going.

Daniel's main contact with the smugglers was a legal student in his midtwenties. The young man was taking part in the trafficking to pay his way through the law school. In six more months, he would receive his credentials. The student fell for Daniel's story and bought the transport services. He had inadvertently put the drugs of his bosses into the hands of the DEA.

The movement of cargo went down, and Daniel got a call from the student. The cartel had taken the student hostage in a house as a ransom for the delivery of the drugs.

"He called me and begged for his life through a phone in a room where I could hear him getting beaten down to his very last breath. We took everything down: we delivered the goods; we arrested the people who were receiving it. But I never saw him [the student] again. They found his car and his wallet on the street."

A few days later, Daniel got a call from the student's parents. They had found their son's phone and seen Daniel's number in it. They were asking for any information to recover their son's body.

"The parents asked if I knew where their kid was so they could give him a decent burial. That really sends it home. It really makes you feel like shit, because what if that was your kid? You have so much love for your kid that you would drag them out of the ground. I think that really set the tone for me, like, 'What the fuck are you doing?' You are killing people. You are setting up people to fail."

Daniel started to feel doubts. He asked for permission to leave under-cover and become a regular agent, at least for the short term. It was a few months after this that I met him for beer and pizza.

"I cut all my hair. I wanted a break. I wanted to change who I was."

DEA agents including Daniel train their Mexican counterparts in anti-drug work. It is part of the Mérida Initiative. Washington has concluded that the key to restoring order in Mexico is to build up the country's law enforcement institutions. The United States can offer decades of drug-fighting experience that has culminated in undercover agents such as Daniel. With help from these American cops, it is hoped, Mexico will be able to hammer the drug cartels.

Within this thinking, Colombia is held up as a success story for Mex-ico to follow. Colombia had weak, corrupt law enforcement in the early 1990s when drug violence and civil war made it the most violent country in the world. However, under Plan Colombia, American money and know-how helped Colombia build a fearsome police and military. The Colom-bian National Police now boasts 143,000 officers and dozens of planes, helicopters, and heavy armaments in a single force. Its antinarcotics divi-sion has a considerable success rate in busting traffickers. To see the fu-ture of Mexican law enforcement, you want to turn to Colombia.

The Colombian National Police bases its antidrug strategy on the DEA's trusted use of informants. In fact, they have enhanced the technique. Large resources are given over to paying informants major rewards so they can become rich for their rest of their lives from a tip-off. The gov-ernment also works to persuade the community that ratting out the bad guys is an honorable rather than dishonorable activity. Following arrests, officials declare, "the government congratulates the brave men who gave information leading to this detention," or a similar line. Snitches are he-roes, it argues, not toads.

I wanted to take a closer look at how Colombia's use of informants works. So on one of my visits to Bogotá, German photographer Oliver Schmieg introduces me to his trusted narc contact in the Colombian

National Police, an agent who goes by the code name Richard. When we call Richard, he says he is actually meeting an informant at that very moment. But don't worry, he says, we can come along and talk to his snitch as well!

We go to the meeting at a police and military club in an upscale Bogotá neighborhood. Such clubs are all over the country and are a perk that helps build morale in the security services. One of the key problems for Mexican police forces is low morale, as well as the bad pay and disastrous casualty rate. In contrast, the Colombian police clubs include swimming pools, soccer grounds, and restaurants. We find Richard sitting at a table drinking coffee. On his right-hand side is a fellow officer; on his left are two informants. We sit down for a cozy get-together: two journalists, two narcs, and two snitches.

Richard is a smooth-operating Colombian cop in his early forties with long black hair and a light brown leather jacket. He makes all of us round the table feel at ease with each other, as if it were an everyday situation. The informant singing like a bird is a skinny, light-skinned crook, wearing grubby jeans. He works in a cocaine laboratory in a part of the Colombian jungle controlled by right-wing paramilitaries. However, he explains, these same gangsters actually buy their cocaine from leftist guerrillas. Richard picks up on the point: "You see, all these bad guys are working together now. It is all about money." Colombia is really fighting a criminal insurgency just like Mexico, he argues, not an ideological one.

Richard coaxes the snitch to describe the whole laboratory setup so that Colombian police can take it down. He asks the informant where the gunmen stand, where the weapons are stashed, where the generator is, what vehicles they have. He needs to know all the information so that there will be no surprises when a team goes in blasting. This is data that you can't get from satellite images. You have to buy it.

The informant says that between sixty to eighty men are around the lab. They use Toyota pickups and have snipers with Kalashnikovs. Richard sketches down the details into a notepad and reports information into a cell phone. A few minutes later, he gets a call and a big smile spreads across his face. "The mission has been authorized," he tells the snitch. "You are on." If everything goes to plan, he says, the informant will get a reward of tens of thousands of dollars.

"In this business, the infomants need enough money to take their whole family and live in a different place. They need to be able to really make their life with what we give them. We can make them have some pride in their work. But the key incentive for them is going to be the money."

But while it might be all about the bottom line, Richard has incredibly amiable relationships with his informants. He laughs and jokes and discusses intimate family matters. Turning round to me, he comments on this sociability.

"You have to be friends with each other in this business because you have to trust each other. If someone is loyal and works well, it is because they trust you. It can be hard for an informant to trust me and for me to trust them. So you have to build that trust."

Richard comes from a rough village in the north of Colombia and joined the police as a way out of poverty. He has now spent twenty-one years on the force, mostly in the antinarcotics division. In this time, he has seen the turnaround in the Colombian security services. The methodical buying of information, he says, is a crucial part of the change. He is one of the best informant handlers in the force. He currently has contact with some two hundred sources.

"The most important thing is intelligence. If you have the sources, if you have the intelligence, then you can get any trafficker on the planet."

The Colombian-style use of snitches is being imported into Mexico on a big scale. While paying informants was for a long time prohibited in Mexico, Calderón's government introduced a major reward system. In 2010 and 2011 such payments were key in locating a string of major traffickers, who were arrested or shot down. This use of snitches is one of the main reasons that the Calderón government has been able to hit so many top targets—to the cheers of American agents. Looking at the future of the Mexican Drug War, the use of informants is likely to increase, making kingpins more vulnerable.

The people with most knowledge about drug operations are the high-level gangster operators: lieutenants, right-hand men, and the capos themselves. So when police arrest these big players, they bleed them for as much information as they can. Then they go ahead and seize more drugloads, labs, and gangsters.

Colombians decided in the 1990s that these arch-criminals posed less threat if they were extradited to the United States. So much of the bleeding of information is done there, in the form of negotiated deals. Top narco-lawyer Gustavo Salazar—who represented Pablo Escobar, some twenty other capos, and fifty of their lieutenants—explained the negotiations to me as we chatted in a Medellín café:

"I deal with these drug lords every day. They are these fearsome gangsters. And then they get arrested and they are like crying children. They are scared. They don't want to be locked up in isolation for the rest of their lives. So they make deals.

"They let the agents know where some of their bank accounts and assets are. And they hand over names and routes of other traffickers. Then they get time in easier prisons or reduced sentences."

Everybody knows that American courts love a plea bargain. And they love seizing assets of drug traffickers. The major players boast accounts with tens of millions of dollars or more.

The deals made by these traffickers have been documented for some time. Among the Colombian gangsters to make such a pact is Andrés López, a capo in the Norte del Valle Cartel. López snitched on other members of his criminal organization, who in turn also snitched. López then wrote a book about it all, called *The Cartel of the Toads*, which was made into a successful television series in Colombia.[2] Apparently released and living in Miami, López then went on to co-write another book and live in the glitzy world of Latin American TV stars, dating some famous Mexican soap beauties.

Mexico has also substantially increased extraditions of kingpins to the United States. The deals developed between Colombian kingpins and American courts are moving to the Mexican capos.

The most high-profile deal has been made by drug lord Osiel Cárdenas, the founder of the Zetas. Osiel was extradited in 2007 and participated in negotiations with American authorities over the following three years. Details of the resulting pact were initially held from the public. But reporting by Dane Schiller of the *Houston Chronicle* uncovered much of the deal. Osiel Cárdenas was not sent to the roasting Colorado desert and locked up with Juan Ramón Matta Ballesteros, inventor of the Mexican trampoline. Instead, Osiel was sent to a medium-security facility in Atlanta, where he can go to meals, the library, and recreation time. Also unlike Matta, he is not serving centuries behind bars. Cárdenas has a release date of 2028. In return, agents seized $32 million in his assets and Cárdenas gave up information about his old drug-trafficking allies. That data is likely behind many major arrests of Zetas in 2010 and 2011.[3]

More such deals are likely to mark the future of the Mexican Drug War. Bargains could be waiting for other Mexican traffickers wanted in the United States, such as Benjamin Arellano Félix or Alfredo Beltrán Leyva, or—if he is ever caught—even Chapo Guzmán himself.

This system has some obvious flaws. When major criminals make deals to get out early, it can be seen as a bad example. It is not such a deterrent when a criminal career ends with the villain dating beautiful soap-opera stars. A long list of drug traffickers have ended up as celebrities.

Asset seizure is also controversial. American agents get to spend dirty drug dollars. They say they are making money for Uncle Sam, but then again, they are also paradoxically reaping the benefits of cocaine and heroin being sold. When agents make money busting traffickers, there is an added incentive to sustain the whole war on drugs.

Nevertheless, once these capos have been extradited and made deals, they are truly out of the game. The greater good, agents argue, is to use them to nail more crooks. That is the central imperative of drug warriors: keep seizing, keep arresting.

However many traffickers that police bust, the good guys still face a fundamental problem: other villains always take their place. This is one of the major criticisms of the drug war—it can't be won. As long there is the cash incentive to smuggle narcotics, some hungry crook is going to do it.

The argument is supported by much historical experience. When Richard Nixon first declared the war on drugs, he spoke in absolute terms, calling for "the complete annihilation of the merchants of death."[4] Four decades later, no one dares show such optimism. The goal has changed to damage control. If we weren't here, drug warriors claim, the situation would be a lot worse.

The Colombian experience is a classic example of this paradox. The Colombian police have got much better at busting traffickers, but good evidence shows that the amount of cocaine coming out of the Andean country has not significantly changed. Police spray crops, bust labs, seize submarines, nail capos. And other villains sow more coca leaves, build more labs, and ship out the new product on speedboats. So what has Colombia really achieved? I put the question to DEA Andean Bureau chief, Jay Bergman, who comes out with a persuasive answer. By hammering traffickers, he says, their power to threaten national security has severely been reduced.

"When you go back to Pablo Ecobar, this guy blew up a passenger plane, police headquarters, funded guerrillas to kill Supreme Court justices, and had the number one Colombian presidential candidate assassinated. Now there is no organization in Colombia that can go toe-to-toe with the government, that can threaten the national security of Colombia. In each successive generation of traffickers there has been a dilution of their power.

"Pablo Escobar lasted fifteen years. The average kingpin here now lasts fifteen months. If you are named as a kingpin here, you are gone. The government of Colombia and the government of the United States will not allow a trafficker to exist long enough to become a viable threat."

In this analysis, drug enforcement can be seen as a giant hammer that keeps on falling. Any gangster that gets too big gets smashed by the hammer. This is known as cartel decapitation, taking out the heads of the gang. The villains are kept in check. But the drug trade does go on, and so does the war.

Soldiers and American agents are using the cartel decapitation tactic in Mexico, taking out kingpins such as the Beard Beltrán Leyva, Nazario el Más Loco Moreno, and Antonio "Tony Tormenta" Cárdenas. It has been an impressive list of hits. But will it hammer Mexican cartels hard enough that they won't be a national security threat? Drug agents argue that is working already. With all the arrests, cartels are getting weaker, they say. The violence is a reaction to the attacks and a sign of desperation by criminals. Mexico simply has to see the struggle through. Maybe they are right.

But the dynamics of Mexican cartels have also developed in distinct ways from Colombia. Mexico has seven major cartels—Sinaloa, Juárez, Tijuana, La Familia, Beltrán Leyva, the Gulf, and the Zetas—so it is hard to decapitate them all at once. When leaders such as Osiel Cárdenas are taken out, their organizations have only become more violent, as rival lieutenants fight to become top dog. Groups such as the Zetas and Familia have also become powerful because of their brand names rather than the reputation of their capos. Even if Zetas leader Heriberto Lazcano, the Executioner, is arrested, the Zetas will likely continue as a fearsome militia.

Whether the cartels will get weaker or not, everybody agrees that Mexico needs to clean up its police to move forward. Different corrupt cops firing at each other and working for rival capos is nobody's vision of progress. Such police reform is of course easier said than done. Mexican presidents have talked about it for years, going through numerous clean-ups and reorganization of forces, only to create new rotten units. A central problem is the sheer number of different agencies. Mexico has several federal law enforcement departments, thirty-one state authorities, and 2,438 municipal police forces.

However, in October 2010, Calderón sent a bill to be approved by Congress that could make a real difference to the police. His controversial proposal was to absorb all Mexico's numerous police forces into one unified authority like the Colombians have. It is a colossal reform with a huge amount of technical problems. But such a reform could be a key factor in pulling Mexico away from the brink. Even if drugs are eventually legalized, a single police force would be a better mechanism to fight other elements of organized crime, such as kidnapping.

The approach has many critics. Some argue it would only streamline corruption. But even that would be a better thing for peace. At least corrupt cops could be on the same side instead of actively gunning each other down. Others argue an all-powerful force would be authoritarian. Maybe. But any such force would still be controlled by democratic government. The spiderweb of different police forces only worked because one party ran everything. In democracy, this arrangement needs reform. If a crucial cause of the breakdown in Mexico has been the fragmentation of government power, then a way forward could be to unify its police under one command. Some of the fundamental problems and core solutions lie in Mexico's institutions.

CHAPTER 14

Expansion

It has been said that arguing against globalization is like arguing against the laws of gravity.

—KOFI ANNAN, SECRETARY-GENERAL OF
THE UNITED NATIONS, 2000

It wasn't poverty that drove Jacobo Guillen to sell crack and crystal in his East Los Angeles neighborhood; he had no problems getting jobs in restaurants and car shops and making enough money to get by. The cause wasn't a broken family either; his parents were together, hardworking and encouraging. He just loved gangbanging.

"I just fucking loved the crazy life. I loved getting high. And I loved being to able to score ten thousand dollars in a couple of hours. And I loved the adrenaline of someone wanting to fight me. I didn't care about anything.

"I've got no one to blame but myself. My brothers and sisters all became doctors and accountants and shit. I'm the only one that fucked up."

Jacobo is paying quite a cost for his mistakes. While he grew up in California, he was born in Mexico, in the state of Jalisco. After he was arrested in L.A. with a bag of crystal, he was incarcerated and then deported. Border agents dropped him off at the Tijuana gate and told him not to come back. He was in a strange land with no money and spoke broken L.A. Spanish. If he had been a foreigner in California, he was even more of a foreigner in Mexico. But he did have one marketabe skill: drug dealing. He was soon on a Tijuana street corner serving up crystal meth.

"Down in Mexico, I really did need to sell drugs to survive. But it was way more fucked-up and dangerous than Los Angeles. There is a real mafia down here to deal with. And some people are really crazy. Right after I got here, someone stabbed me. I survived that and kept on selling and smoking crystal. Then someone tried to shoot me over a deal. I only survived by a miracle—because their gun jammed. That was when I realized I had to stop. I had to get out of the drugs and the gangbanging."

He tells me the story two months after this attempted murder. We are sitting in an evangelical Christian drug-rehab center in Tijuana where he has been drying out. He is twenty-five years old with a crew cut, round, chubby face, and pudgy hands. In the spirit of the Christian rehab, he wears a black T-shirt declaring I GANGBANG FOR JESUS. He also listens to Christian hip-hop and plays me songs from the tiny speakers of his cell phone. Some are in Spanish, but he prefers the English ones, many made by rappers in Los Angeles. Living in Tijuana has made his Spanish improve dramatically, but he still feels more comfortable with English, and his heart is in L.A.

The product of a cross-border culture, Jacobo is one of the many links between the drug-trafficking world of Mexico and the drug-distribution world of the United States. He has sold crystal meth in both Tijuana and Los Angeles. He has also smuggled drugs over the border, walking across the California desert with backpacks full of marijuana. In his trafficking, he has dealt with organized-crime figures on both sides of the line.

But while Jacobo's illustrious career illustrates how these worlds are linked, it also illustrates how those links are tenuous. As he discovered painfully, the rules are different in Mexico from in the United States. Different bosses and organizations hold power on either side of the border. And the attitude of gangsters toward police and government changes radically as soon as you cross the Rio Grande.

These sharp contrasts can help us see what El Narco will look like in the future. A central theme in the outlook for Mexican gangsters is their expansion beyond the borders of Mexico as cartel thugs establish themselves across the western hemisphere and over the Atlantic Ocean. El Narco's destiny, some fear, is to emerge as a global power. But what form will it take in these other countries? Experience shows that cartels are likely to take different forms in the different realms where they take root.

Mexican cartels have certainly grown, in the same logical enlargement that spurs other entities in capitalism. The big fish get bigger, allowing them to make more money and get bigger still. In this way Mexican cartels, after usurping the Colombians as the biggest crime syndicates of the Americas, have crept into a number of countries. Not only are they pushing hard into weak Central American states and going to the south of the hemisphere into Peru and Argentina. There are also reports of their buying power in weak African states, dealing with the Russian mafia, and even supplying drugs to dealers in Liverpool, England (and fathoming their high-pitched Scouser accents). But the expansion that has sparked most worry is growth over the Rio Grande in the United States.

The export of cartel power into the USA is a sensitive issue. The discussion about Mexican cartels' northward push gets pulled, often unfairly, into the flaming American immigration debate. The anti-immigrant brigade talk about Mexican laborers as an invading army; and they see all undocumented workers as potential cartel emissaries, using migrant communities to hide undercover ops. The Mexican Drug War, they say, is a reason to militarize the border. Residents of border states vex about the danger of spillover. If thugs are decapitating in Juárez, they fret, how long before they cut off heads in El Paso? Is the Mexican disease contagious?

Down in Mexico, the argument is reversed. A common complaint by politicians and journalists is that there aren't enough arrests of big players in El Norte. Why haven't we heard of the capos in the United States? they ask. How come some Mexican fugitives live unharmed north of the border? Why has Mexico been goaded into a drug war while narcotics move freely around the fifty states of the union?

Mexican drug cartels certainly operate throughout the United States. Murders clearly linked to these cartels have occurred on American soil. But there has been no major spillover of violence from Mexico to its northern neighbor. As of 2011, after five years of cartel devastation south of the Rio Grande, the war simply hasn't crossed the border.

The numbers bear this out. According to the FBI, the four large U.S. cities with the lowest violent-crime rates are all in border states—San Diego, Phoenix, El Paso, and Austin. While Juárez had more than three thousand murders in 2010, a stone's throw over the river in El Paso, there were just five homicides, the lowest number in twenty-three years. Farther west, the city of Nogales sits over from the Mexican state of Sonora, a key turf of the Sinaloa Cartel, which has seen raging firefights and piles of chopped-up corpses. But in 2008 and 2009, there wasn't a single homicide in Nogales. Overall, crime in Arizona dropped by 35 percent between 2004 and 2009, exactly the same time when the Mexican Drug War exploded.[1]

American lawmen offer an explanation for this oxymoron: themselves. While cartels can overwhelm and buy off chunks of the Mexican police, they gloat, in the United States, criminals avoid the police as much as possible. As Sergeant Tommy Thompson of the Phoenix Police Department says:

"In the United States, the cartels want to move their drugs and make money. Police are a hindrance to this. But the best tactic for gangsters is to try and keep a low profile to get off the police radar. If they commit a murder, the police will be on them. If they attack the policemen themselves, authorities will go crazy. And it is a lot harder in the United States to buy off police officers."

These U.S. lawmen have a good point; no one doubts that American cops are better than Mexicans at keeping crooks in their place. But however hard-nosed and square-jawed the U.S. police are, it is still significant that Mexican cartels have had no major turf wars in the United States. It is their land of milk and honey, after all, where all the dirty drug dollars come from. If capos fight over Ciudad Juárez, why don't they fight over billions spent on their narcotics in New York City?

Following the trail of drugs helps explain why not. DEA agent Daniel tracked shipments of cocaine, heroin, crystal, and marijuana as they crossed into America from Tijuana. He would flip smugglers so he could follow the drugs to warehouses in the United States and on to distribution points. Much of the drugs, he found, would zoom through San Diego and go into houses scattered all over Los Angeles. These warehouses are typically rented homes found with little furniture, piles of drugs, and hoods watching them. From these warehouses in L.A., Daniel found, the drugs could then be taken to anywhere in the United States.

"From L.A. they will break it into segments and then fucking disperse it. It can go to the Midwest, either Minnesota or South Dakota. But it can in fact go all the way from L.A. to New York or Boston or Chicago. Why? Why do you think? Because in L.A., a kilo of cocaine could be eighteen grand. Take it to New York, it is about twenty-five a kilo. That is seven grand profit."

In other words, once in the United States, drugs move by a tangled web of routes all over the country. New York gets kilos of cocaine that have moved through Tijuana, passing through the Arellano Félix Cartel, and also cocaine bricks that have passed through the territory of the Juárez Cartel and the Zetas. Agents do make some maps of these drug corridors, but they look like spaghetti-style knots, and all roads lead to New York City. All the gangs sell their narcotics in the Big Apple, and none try to claim it as their own. It is not anyone's turf, but everyone's turf. And New Yorkers' bottomless appetite for drugs makes a big enough market to sustain this.

Within this web, Los Angeles is a hub, a major redistribution point for drugs. The other major hubs are considered Houston, Texas, and Phoenix, Arizona. These hubs tend to have drugs from the cartels that control the nearby border cities—you find more Tijuana Cartel dope in Los Angeles and more Zeta dope in Houston. But no evidence suggests these cartels have imposed monopolies on these cities. Neither Los Angeles nor Houston has seen significant violence related to cartel warfare in Mexico. Once in America, it seems, traffickers don't care who else is selling. The monopoly, and all the violence, is soaked up on the Mexican side of the border.

One exception to this free-for-all rule could be Phoenix, Arizona, which has seen a rash of drug-related kidnappings in recent years. Some commentators scream this shows the Mexican Drug War is taking root in the United States. In 2008, there were 368 abductions, making Phoenix the kidnapping capital of America.[2] Back in Mexico, rumors say the Sinaloa Cartel has claimed Phoenix as its sole property. The city is just 160 miles from Sonora, which is the core border state controlled by the Sinaloan mafia.

I drive round the seething-hot desert city of Phoenix looking at the homes where the abductions have taken place. Almost all are large bungalows in predominantly Mexican neighborhoods. It is soon revealed that most of the kidnappings aren't about drugs at all—they are about human trafficking. The Sonora-Arizona corridor with its vast desert is the biggest path for undocumented migrants looking for the American Dream. Once they arrive in Phoenix hoping to go out and make their fortunes, the hired smugglers demand an extra $1,000 or so from their families before the migrants are released.

This migrant extortion is a rough game. Victims are often badly beaten until they pay up. Girls describe being raped. It is a traumatic first experience in the United States. But it has nothing to do with the drug trade. Rather it is another symptom of a broken immigration system, in which migrants are given jobs but not papers.

Some of the kidnappings are, however, connected to drugs. Sergeant Tommy Thompson, a chirpy officer in the Phoenix Police Department, says they usually suspect narcotics are involved when the ransom demands are high, ranging from $30,000 to $1 million.

"I know the average person can't get thirty thousand dollars cash together at the drop of a hat, let alone three hundred thousand. And quite often the kidnappers throw in, as part of that ransom, the request for illegal drugs as well.

"Sometimes they will smash in the victim's hands with bricks. But we don't see the violence in Mexico where they are cutting fingers off or cutting hands off."

Sergeant Thompson shows me a house where such a kidnapping took place. The nice-looking brick home has a double garage and a basketball court. The homeowner, a Mexican national, was pulling out of the house one night when gangsters boxed in his car and put a gun to his head. Neighbors saw the kidnapping and called the police. (Authorities hear of many of these abductions from neighbors rather than family members themselves.) Phoenix's special antikidnapping unit then hit the case hard, with masked police storming the neighborhood. Seeing they were being targeted, the kidnappers released the victim and ran for their lives. Even though the victim may have been a drug dealer, Sergeant Thompson says, it is worth the effort to save him.

"The victim came out of this okay and that is the important thing. No matter what these people who are kidnapped are involved in, first and foremost we see them as victims, as human beings.

"Now if the kidnappers fire rounds, those rounds don't discriminate between innocent victims and non-innocent victims and that is where we're concerned. And the bottom line is that it is happening on our streets."

The Phoenix Police Department has thrown a lot of resources into rescuing these drug dealers from kidnappers. Sometimes a hundred officers can be drawn in to bust a victim out of a house. They are absolutely right to hit back hard; it is best to hammer the problem straightaway rather than let it get worse. The Phoenix zero-tolerance approach seems to have borne some fruit. In 2009, kidnappings showed a 14 percent drop. (Although with 318 abductions, it was still concerning.)[3]

However, while they are responding to the problem, neither the Phoenix police nor the DEA can offer much explanation as to why these drug-related kidnappings are happening. One speculation is that freelance gunslingers like to jack drug traffickers. While that may explain some cases, it seems unlikely that rogue crooks would really have the balls to take on traffickers linked to the Sinaloa Cartel. Another theory is that the pressure of enforcement means more loads are captured, so gangsters are kidnapping people to make them pay up for lost drugs. That makes more sense, but seizures at the Arizona-Sonora border have not significantly risen in recent years.

It is telling that the kidnappings mushroomed in 2008, just as Mexican cartels exploded into their civil war. Perhaps they do show the Sinaloa Cartel is trying to assert itself in its principal hub north of the border and make traffickers there pay their taxes. But whatever is happening, it is still on a thankfully more peaceful scale than in Mexico. The number of murders in Phoenix has actually been going down: from 167 in 2008 to 122 in 2009.[4]

Mexican cartels are the biggest importers of narcotics into the United States. They smuggle an estimated 90 percent of the cocaine; the majority of imported marijuana and meth; and a substantial amount of heroin. DEA has acknowleged this in congressional hearings for more than a decade. But less publicized is that Mexican gangsters are also moving further down the distribution ladder. In the last five years, Mexicans have increasingly been selling drugs at the kilo level in cities and towns across the United States. This is borne out by busts of Mexican nationals in possession of wholesale quantities of cocaine bricks, brown heroin, and sparkling crystal, especially in the South. They are also pushing into corners of the country they had never before ventured, from the Great Lakes region to the Midwest. In the days of Matta Ballesteros in the eighties, cocaine wholesale was typically handled by Colombians and Anglo- and African-Americans, but now it is often handled by Mexicans.

This development increases the amount of money flowing into Mexican organized crime and is another factor why the drug war has heated to boiling point south of the border. Mexican gangs have expanded toward both ends of the supply chain, both nearer to the leaf in Colombia and nearer to the nose in America. But in the United States, the creep of El Narco doesn't seem to have had adverse effects. The drug trade stays the drug trade; who cares if the dealer flogging the kilo brick is a white biker, a Jamaican yardie, or a Mexican? It is the same brick of yayo.

The most comprehensive study of Mexican cartel activity across the United States was done by the government's National Drug Intelligence Center in 2009.[5] They compiled data from local, state, and federal police agencies across the United States and used the information to draw a detailed map of El Narco's networks north of the border. The map shows cartel activity in 230 cities and in every state, even Alaska and Hawaii. In two thirds of the cities with a narco presence, the report says, links with specific cartels were found. For example, the Sinaloa Cartel was identified in Nashville and Cincinnati among other places, while the Juárez Cartel was traced to Colorado Springs and Dodge City. In other cities, agents could not say for certain whom the gangsters were working for.

The report sparked alarm about the scope of the Mexican mobs, but it left a lot of questions unanswered. It fails to explain exactly what type of representation cartels have in these cities. And it doesn't make clear how the links back to Sinaloa or Juárez are made. Have agents traced phone calls? Or been given solid info from informants? Or are they are more speculative connections? These answers are needed to make better sense of how deeply entrenched El Narco has become in the United States. Because if the crook serving up blow in Bismarck, North Dakota, just happens to have brought some drugs that once belonged to the Sinaloa Cartel, it is one thing. If he is on the direct payroll of Chapo Guzmán, that is a lot more concerning, signaling that the ruthless techniques employed in Mexico could be used there.

Several ongoing criminal cases offer deeper insight into El Narco's American connection. One of the biggest is in Chicago, home to a booming drug market and a deep-rooted Mexican community. In 2009, a Chicago federal court indicted top Sinaloan Cartel leaders, including Chapo Guzmán, in what the district attorney called "the most significant drug importation conspiracies ever charged in Chicago." The numbers were huge. The indictments said the Sinaloan Cartel smuggled two tons of cocaine a month to the Windy City, bringing it in on tractor trailers to Illinois warehouses. The gangsters had allegedly made $5.8 billion bringing drugs into the region over almost two decades. Forty-six people were indicted. Among them were Sinaloans, such as Chapo Guzmán himself, and a number of Americans, of all races, accused of moving the drugs in Illinois.[6]

At the heart of the alleged conspiracy were Mexican American twin brothers Pedro and Margarito Flores, who were twenty-eight at the time of their arrests in 2009. Chicago detectives say the Flores twins come from a large family with long links to trafficking into Chicago's Little Village and Pilsen neighborhoods. The brothers took over a barbershop and a restaurant, but court documents say they were also the main point men for bringing the Sinaloan narcotics into Chicago.

Problems began when the Sinaloan Cartel was split by civil war in 2008. As Chapo Guzmán and the Beard Beltrán Leyva cut off heads back home in Culiacán, they also bickered over their contacts in Chicago. According to the indictments, both Beltrán Leyva and Chapo put violent pressure on the twins to buy from them rather than their rival. Amid this conflict, DEA agents infiltrated the operation and busted the twins and others in the conspiracy.

What is interesting is how the Sinaloan capos fought over the Flores twins as customers. The Flores brothers bought drugs from the Sinaloans rather than worked for them; they were clients rather than employees. The Flores twins also, according to documents, sold the drugs on rather than paying people to move them. As the indictment says:

"The Flores Crew in turn sold the cocaine and heroin for cash to wholesale customers in the Chicago, Illinois, area, as well as to customers in Detroit, Michigan; Cincinnati, Ohio; Philadelphia, Pennsylvania; Washington, D.C.; New York; Vancouver, British Columbia; Columbus, Ohio; and elsewhere. Wholesale customers in these cities further distributed the cocaine and heroin to other cities, including Milwaukee, Wisconsin."

The conspiracy shows a chain of sale rather than a top-down organization. Chicago gangsters may be working with the Sinaloa Cartel, but they are a separate entity. They play by American crime tactics, which include the odd murder and breaking some bones here and there, rather than Mexican crime tactics, such as massacres of entire families and mass graves. Groups of fifty thugs armed with RPGs and Kalashnikovs have thankfully not been seen anywhere near Chicago. Yet.

Getting down to the street level—the retail of grams of cocaine or ounces of ganja—there is no evidence of any Mexican cartel involvement on American corners. This may sound confusing. Surely, Mexicans are busted selling drugs all over the United States; and surely those drugs have passed through Mexico. That is correct. But Mexican cartels themselves are only interested in the wholesale of narcotics in America. Chapo Guzmán doesn't care about a few grams being sold to a junkie on a street corner in Baltimore; he is busy making billions bringing in drugs by the tons.

This retail drug trade is run by a huge array of people, from college kids selling ganja in their Harvard dorms to gangbangers serving up crack in New Orleans. Like most drug dealers on the bottom rung, they have no idea where their product comes from beyond the local supplier who sells them doggie bags.

Mexicans and Mexican Americans are certainly among this army of street sellers, and their numbers have in recent years increased. Much has been made of migrants selling meth to sustain workers through long shifts at meat factories. Mexicans can be found flogging drugs on corners from San Francisco to Queens. But all evidence suggests they are doing it as part of local gangs or as individuals rather than kicking to or receiving any money from the cartels.

Jacobo Guillen, the pudgy-faced meth addict, sold crystal in East Los Angeles. His experience confirms that El Narco hasn't penetrated to the street level. He had no contact at all with the Mexican cartels, he says. Instead, he worked for the U.S. gang the Mexican Mafia. Despite its name, the Mexican Mafia is entirely north of the border, born and based in American prisons. It is, of course, run by people of Mexican descent. As Jacobo says:

"I sold the crystal and every week I paid money to the Mexican Mafia. If I didn't, I would be in real problems. The bosses of the Mexican Mafia are in prison, but they have reach on the street and can still kill people there.

"When I went down to Mexico, it was completely different. In Tijuana, all of the sellers have to pay up their quota to the cartel. In Mexico, the cartel controls both the traffic and the street selling."

Some people may think this difference is academic. The Mexican Mafia or Sinaloa Cartel are both rabid criminal organizations selling narcotics and committing murder. But the difference is very real. The Sinaloa Cartel is a criminal paramilitary complex that has transformed amid the instability of Mexico; the Mexican Mafia is a prison and street gang nurtured in the realities of America. The Sinaloa Cartel can take out senior police commanders and leave piles of twenty bodies; the Mexican Mafia is involved in jail-yard stabbings and neighborhood shootings with pistols.

Most of the drug violence in the United States is the result of territorial disputes over these street corners. This has an obvious logic: corners are physical turf and are not big enough for two gangs. Killings that have haunted Baltimore, Chicago, Detroit, New Orleans, Los Angeles, and dozens of other cities have roots in fights for this real estate. Countless street gangs have been involved. But the Mexican cartels themselves have not yet been pulled into this melee. Why should they? Their drugs go to whoever wins. The fear is that if Mexican cartels ever did get pulled into American corner politics, it would be cataclysmic.

The nightmare of El Narco stepping into American street-gang warfare is starting to play out—in the Lone Star State, which straddles half of the Mexican border. This spillover has two fronts: the central corridor of El Paso-Juárez, and a thousand miles east near the Gulf of Mexico.

In El Paso, the links between the American streets and Mexican drug lords have been strengthened by the growth of the Barrio Azteca gang. Unlike other Chicano gangs, the Barrio Azteca has forged a powerful bond with Mexican cartels and become a true cross-border organization.

Barrio Azteca was founded by El Paso gang members incarcerated in Texas's high-security Coffield prison in the 1980s. They came together so the inmates from El Paso, known fondly as Chuco Town, could defend themselves against other prison mobs such as the Mexican Mafia, with its roots in California. They socked, stabbed, and strangled the bullies pushing them around and became themselves feared intimidators.

Like the Mexican Mafia, the Barrio Azteca gang spilled out into the street. They taxed dealers, and as members were released, they gained a fearsome reputation for violence on the outside, putting out murder contracts, known as green lights. By the late 1990s, they had more than a thousand members spread among the penitentiaries and Texas cities and made millions of dollars from drugs. Then two crucial developments took place: the Barrio Azteca formed cells over the border in Juárez, and they began to deal directly with the Juárez Cartel.

The growth of El Barrio Azteca south of the Rio Grande is linked to the area's distinctive cross-border community. The urban sprawl of El Paso and Juárez is in many ways one community, with families, friends, businesses—and gangs—straddling the line. To compound this, some Mexicans without papers joined up with Barrio Azteca during jolts in Texas prisons. When they finished their sentences, they would be deported to Juárez, where they would carry on gangbanging. These converts recruited fresh members from Juárez's own burgeoning street gangs and in its state and municipal prisons (where the Barrio Azteca now controls an entire wing).

Barrio Azteca members had long sold drugs moved by the Juárez Cartel. As they grew in power, they forged a much stronger alliance with the cartel. An Azteca member named Diablo even described this deal on U.S. television: "The cartel saw that we were doing a lot over there. So they offered us to, like, become a chapter."[7] He then describes how Barrio Azteca began to buy kilos of cocaine at cheaper rates directly from the cartel, and in return they would smuggle caches of assault rifles south from Texas gun shops. Furthermore, if the Juárez Cartel needed some intimidation or violence in the United States, Diablo says, they would call on the Barrio Azteca.

When the Sinaloa Cartel stormed into Juárez in 2008, the Barrio Azteca was called in to help defend the fort. They are alleged to have participated in some of the most brutal massacres south of the border. As Juárez police investigations are all full of holes, it is impossible to know exactly how many of the six thousand killings in Juárez the Barrio Azteca committed, but the number is considerable.

Virtually all this bloodshed has been kept south of the border. But an increasing number of the victims are American citizens. In his TV interview, Diablo describes how the gang often kidnaps targets in El Paso and drives them south to kill them. A murder in Texas attracts a big investigation; in Juárez it is one more of the ten corpses hitting the streets daily. Mexico has become a killing field for American-reared psychos. Down in Juárez, Diablo goes on, the Barrio Azteca will often torture and murder its victims in front of a cheering crowd of gang members. As Diablo describes:

"We'll have a hole in the ground. We'll throw a bunch of mesquites in there, gasoline. And then beat the shit out of you and then throw you in there and light you on fire. Sometimes you'll be dead. But not all the time. Sometimes they'll light you so they can hear you scream. You can hear them and it smells real bad, like human flesh smells when it's burning. The first time that I seen something like that, I couldn't sleep for a while."

Wonks at the State Department couldn't sleep either when they heard about one ferocious Barrio Azteca attack: in March 2010 the gang murdered three people connected to the U.S. consulate in Juárez. The notorious killings took place minutes apart in separate attacks on two cars leaving a party at a U.S. consulate worker's home. One car contained the husband of a Mexican employee at the consulate; the other an American consulate worker and her husband, who worked in the Texas prison system; she was pregnant, and the couple's first child, a seven-month-old baby, watched her parents die from the back of the car.[8]

The murders sent shock waves through America's diplomatic mission in Mexico, and under pressure, Mexican soldiers swiftly rounded up alleged Azteca hit men. Meanwhile, over the border, FBI agents busted dozens of Barrio Azteca members in El Paso. But despite all the shackled gangbangers, police couldn't get a conclusive explanation for the hit. Was the consulate worker targeted because she was being slow with visas for cartel guys? Or was the husband targeted because he had angered Azteca members in the Texas prison? Or was the attack to send a message to American drug agents? Or was it a mistaken identity?

Whatever the reasons, the message sent home the danger of Barrio Azteca and their alliance with the Juárez Cartel. One major concern for the future is more such cross-border gangs linking cartels to U.S. streets, and of American gangs adopting more of El Narco's brutal tactics.

More than five hundred miles east in Laredo, a different cartel has had the nerve to carry out execution-style hits right on American soil. While most gangsters try not to rock the boat north of the river, the men behind these East Texas killings are from the same psychopathic criminal army that has broken all the rules in Mexico: the Zetas.

The five Zetas murders in Texas came to public attention amid a high-profile trial in 2007. During the hearing, American-born Zetas recruits were heard plotting murders on tapped phones and confessing to their brutal techniques in the dock. Among those convicted was seventeen-year-old gunslinger Rosalio Reta, originally from Houston. A loud, brash teenager with tattoos on his face, Rosalio confessed to joining up with the Zetas when he was just thirteen and carrying out his first murder in the same year. He then says he was trained by former special forces at a Zetas camp in Mexico and carried out a spree of killings on both sides of the border. Agents believe he was involved in some thirty murders, although he was convicted of just two and given a forty-year sentence.[9]

Testimony by Rosalio and others described how the Zetas had set up three-man cells in Laredo and Dallas. Recruits were paid a $500-per-week retainer, and cells were given $10,000 to $50,000 for hits. It certainly paid better than murdering someone in Mexico, but then America has a more lucrative job market. The Zetas recruits were boarded in $300,000 homes and given brand-new cars. Rosalio describes the perks as a great incentive for a teenager from the rough end of town.

The motives for the Zetas' Texas killings are mixed and not fully understood. Confessions say one man was targeted because he was dating a girl that the Zetas boss was interested in—the assassins first messed up and killed the target's brother, then killed the target a few months later. Another victim was a local gang member who somehow angered the Zetas. A third was a hit man who had reportedly defected to the Sinaloans.

The murders were carried out in a similar way to the typical cartel murder in Mexico. The Zetas assassins followed victims and then ambushed them, gunning them down as they drove out of fast-food restaurants or went from their cars to their Laredo homes. The killers were less scandalous than is the norm south of the river, firing a few bullets straight into victims, rather than spraying more than three hundred rounds over the whole street. But they were loud enough for American police. Laredo officers worked with the the DEA and other federal agencies to break up the cells, also busting Zetas on drug and money charges.

Since the resulting trials, no more Zeta hits have been confirmed in Texas, and the overall murder rate is down. Maybe the Zetas have got the message that piling up bodies in America means trouble. Or maybe we just don't know about other killings yet. But if it has happened before, it can certainly happen again. A growth of Zetas cells of assassins in the United States would really be a nightmare.

Poorer, weaker nations have been less successful at containing Mexican cartel violence. In Guatemala, the Zetas have unleashed massacres as bad as in their homeland, especially in the jungle region across Mexico's southern border. The Guatemalan government hit back, declaring martial law in the area in December 2010 and seizing one Zetas training camp with a stockpile of five hundred grenades. But in retaliation, the Zetas have fought pitched battles with the Guatemalan army and are one of the suspects behind a bus bomb that killed seven in Guatemala City in January 2011.

As an army of poor country boys, the Zetas are among their ilk in Guatemala and have been able to recruit plenty of locals to fight for their cause. Not only do these Zetas cells protect drug routes, they also set up their own franchises of drug selling and extortion just as in Mexico. While most legitimate Mexican companies have failed to take advantage of the Central American market, El Narco Inc. has solid international ambitions.

These global goals take Mexican cartels far and wide. Mexican crooks have been spotted as far afield as Australia, Africa, and even Azerbaijan. Often their excursions are to buy ingredients for their drug labs, especially pseudoephedrine and ephedrine for crystal meth. In 2008, a U.N.-sponsored initiative called Operation Ice Block seized forty-six illegal shipments of meth precursors around the globe; half were headed for Mexico. The countries of origin included China, India, Syria, Iran, and Egypt. One shipment of ephedrine nabbed just outside Baghdad was alleged to be headed to Mexican mobsters.[10]

In many cases, the chemical shipments stop first in West Africa before crossing the Atlantic. Impoverished African nations along this old slaving coast are increasingly used as trampolines by international criminals of different stripes; the Colombians also jump on them to bounce cocaine into Europe. Guinea-Bissau—the world's fifth-poorest nation, where there is no central electricity grid and the average wage is a dollar a day—is one of the most notorious captured states. Latin American gangsters can buy the country for peanuts. Powerful governments have yet to make any efforts to defend these nations, and El Narco's growth in these vulnerable corners looms on the horizon.

Bang in between Colombia and Mexico, the sweaty tropical country of Honduras has long been an important stopping point for cocaine. Juan Ramón Matta Ballesteros ran his empire there in the eighties, while the right-wing Nicaraguan contra army, which was partially financed by cocaine, was also trained there. Honduras was dubbed the "banana republic" in a 1904 book by American writer William Sydney Porter about the power of foreign fruit companies. Bananas still dominate the economy, and Honduras stumbles on with half the population in poverty, political instability that produced a 2009 coup, and one of the worst levels of violence on the planet. It is ideal pickings for Mexican cartels.

General Julian Aristides Gonzalez is the Honduran official who most followed the rise of El Narco. A square-jawed military officer, Gonzalez left the army in 1999 to join the National Directorate for the Fight Against Narco-Trafficking and later became its head, a kind of antidrug czar. I spoke to him in December 2009 in his office, amid piles of maps and 140 kilos of seized cocaine sitting beside his desk. He had the rigid manners of a military man, but was one of the frankest and most open Latin American drug officials I had ever talked to. In the last decade, General Gonzalez says, the rising Mexican presence in Honduras has been startling.

"It is like a tidal wave we are trying to stop. We bust criminals and seize tons of cocaine, but they are coming at us with a huge amount of money and strength. We are fighting an uphill battle."

Mexican gangsters, Gonzalez goes on, have bought a huge amount of real estate in Honduras, especially in the vast swathes of jungles, mountains, and coast that are sparsely inhabited. The purchases launder money as well as provide storage and waypoints for cocaine. Gonzalez shows me photos and maps of one such narco estate seized by police. It is an old banana plantation deep in the jungle, complete with colonial hacienda buildings and thousands of acres of land. The mobsters built a concrete runway on the plantation, where they landed airplanes packed with white gold.

Gonzalez's men have busted dozens of such planes. They are mostly light, single-engine aircraft like the ones the Sinaloan cartel uses. But the gangsters also have some bigger planes for multiton cocaine loads. As well as flying out of Colombia, many cocaine planes actually fly from

Venezuela, Gonzalez says. Colombia's leftist FARC guerrillas cross the jungles into Venezuela to run flights, he alleges, which can avoid Colombia's more sophisticated air defenses. Such accusations get into South America's left-right political chasm. Conservatives use the drug issue as a stick to bash Venezuela's leftist leader, Hugo Chávez. The firebrand Chávez retorts that the CIA has been in bed with cocaine traffickers for decades.

But whoever moves the cocaine out of Colombia, it is the Mexicans receiving the billion-dollar bundles. The Sinaloa Cartel has been particularly active in Honduras, Gonzalez says, with rumors that Chapo Guzmán has been in the country. "We heard that he was here from various sources. We tried to zero in, but we were never able to pinpoint him. Maybe he was never here. Maybe he is here right now." Gonzalez smiles. Other gangs have also built up a presence, including the Zetas and even the Bible-bashing head choppers themselves: La Famila. When rival Mexican gangs run into each other in Honduras, Gonzalez says, they start blasting.

Mexican gangsters subcontract local crooks to support their operations, Gonzalez elaborates. To enforce their control over these employees, they "execute" anyone who steps out of line, providing yet another source of bloodshed. Mexican capos also work with Honduras's own sanguine villains, the Mara Salvatrucha and Barrio 18 gangs. The Honduran thugs serve up large amounts of the cartel drugs to the local market, Gonzalez says, while also hiring on as paid assassins. Several massacres committed by the Maras and 18 in recent years are believed to be on orders of the Mexican criminals.

"The Maras are violent anyway—they are a real social problem. But when they get big international organizations behind them like the Mexicans, they are much more threatening. That is the danger we face in the future: the criminals here getting more organized, better armed, and really becoming a problem."

I spoke with General Gonzalez on a Thursday. The next Tuesday, back in Mexico, I got a phone call while having breakfast. Gonzalez had been assassinated. He was taking his seven-year-old daughter to school just after dawn when the *sicarios* came for him. They drove up beside his car on a motorcycle and fired eleven bullets, hitting him seven times.[11]

Prosecutors made no arrests on the murder. It had the hallmarks of Colombian *sicarios*, who typically strike on motorcycles, but who knows?

He had given a press conference on the Monday, reitering his accusations that the FARC flys cocaine out of Venezuela. But he had angered
many people during ten years busting traffickers; back in 2008, he said
he received death threats and didn't know whom they were from.

Despite his danger, he never had bodyguards. His widow, Leslie Portillo, was asked about this at the funeral.[12] Her eyes full of tears, she replied that she had always urged him to protect himself, but he never
responded. "I would say to him, 'Are you not going to have security?' He
replied to me, 'My security is God walking beside me.'"

CHAPTER 15

Diversification

The wickedness of bad men also compels good men to have recourse, for their own protection . . . In such condition, there is no place for Industry because the fruit thereof is uncertain . . . no Society; and which is worst of all, continual fear and danger of violent death; And the life of man, solitary, poore, nasty, brutish, and short.

—THOMAS HOBBES, *LEVIATHAN*, 1651

I watch the video leaked by a police commander to journalists. It gives me nightmares. It is the most disturbing footage I have seen in my life. It is worse than seeing the bodies full of bullets on the concrete; the severed heads on public display; the images of masked Zetas shooting prisoners in the head. It is worse than listening to thugs talk about decapitating victims or listening to the pops of bullets echo down sweltering streets. And there is no actual killing or shooting or cutting up limbs in this film. But there is pure cruelty.

The camera shows a kid sitting cross-legged on a gray carpet in front of a white curtain. He is about thirteen years old and all skin and bone. He is stark naked except for a white bandage covering his eyes and nose, and a cord tying his hands together. His head is bent over and trembling, showing severe suffering. A voice off camera growls, "Start now." The kid talks. His adolescent voice is shaking, signaling a pain way beyond tears.

"Mama. Give them the money now. They know we have the consultancy and three properties over there. Please, or they are going to cut a finger off. And they know where my Aunt Guadalupe lives. Please, now. I want to go, Mama."

The gruff off-camera voice kicks in. "Are you suffering or are you tranquil?"

"*No*. I'm suffering," the kid begs.

Then the beating begins. First the torturer kicks the boy in the head. Then he smacks him with a belt. Then he kicks him hard in the head again. Then he turns the skinny, naked boy around, showing bruises on his back, and beats the wounds with the belt. It is unbearable to watch. The beating goes on and on and on. The kid is begging for mercy and unleashing gasps of pain and saying, "No, no, no." During the beating, the torturer is talking, addressing the mother whom the video is sent to.

"This is what you want, you bitch? This is the beginning of the end, I warn you. It depends on you, how far we are going to go. The next step is a finger. This is what you want? It all depends on you. I want six million pesos."[1]

I can't even begin to comprehend the suffering of this boy's mother or father watching this video. I can't even begin to think about the physical and psychological damage to an innocent thirteen-year-old boy.

Mexico has a strong family culture. Parents often mollycoddle their children more than anything I saw in cold England. A twenty-year-old daughter will go out and her parents will wait in the front room until four A.M. when she comes home. An uncle goes to the hospital with a broken ankle, and within hours twenty family members are gathered outside to see if he is okay. There is so much family love. It is hard to understand how in this same culture some men can show so much cruelty preying on that love. Because that is how kidnapping for ransom functions. It pushes people to give away everything they have worked for to stop the pain against a loved one.

Mexicans also find this cruelty hard to comprehend. When such atrocities are reported on, the stories are always met by rabid responses. After the arrest of one kidnapping gang, for example, the following comments were sent to the Web site of Mexico's bestselling newspaper, *El Universal*.

"A bullet in the head. They are trash that is not worth keeping alive."

"I wish divine power would arrive because it is the only punishment that we can hope for."
"Scum. Hang them up on trees."
"Cut them into pieces and feed them to dogs."

Such calls for violent revenge are highly understandable. People feel frustrated and helpless. Kidnapping for ransom is the cruelest of crimes, and as the Mexican Drug War has raged, the number of abductions has gone through the roof. A government study found that between 2005 and 2010, the number of reported kidnappings of Mexicans had risen by 317 percent.[2] An average of 3.7 abductions were reported every day in 2010, some 1,350 over the year. Anticrime groups say for every kidnapping reported, as many as ten may go unreported because the kidnappers say if the police hear about it, the hostage is going to get hurt. Many, many families have suffered. By several counts, Mexico has become the worst place for kidnappings on the planet.

The timing of this crime explosion is no coincidence. Many thugs linked to drug cartels are directly involved in kidnapping. The most notorious trafficking gang that carries out abductions for ransom is the Zetas. As they clash violently with police and soldiers and protect truckloads of cocaine, they also extort millions from sobbing families. When you have a militia that is so feared and with so many guns, kidnapping is an easy sideline.

But kidnapping is only one of the ways that the Zetas have diversified. They have also branched out into extorting bars and discos; taxing shops; taking money from prostitution rings; stealing cars; robbing crude oil and gasoline; getting money from migrant trafficking; and even pirating their own Zetas-labeled DVDs of the latest blockbuster movies. *Drug-trafficking organization* is no longer a sufficient term for them; they are a *criminal paramilitary complex.*

El Narco's diversification has been rapid and painful for Mexico. As a journalist in Juárez said to me, "Until 2008, the only time we had heard of paying protection was in old American movies of Al Capone. Then suddenly every business in the city is being asked for a quota." Like so many other features of the drug war, the tactic is rapidly copied from cartel to cartel. One month, the Zetas are shaking down businesses; the next month La Familia is reported getting protection money; the following month the Beltrán Leyva organization is extorting. It is a logical progression. When gangsters see what their rivals are getting away with and how much money they are pulling in, they want a piece of the action. The move to diversified crime has become an ominous trend across drug cartels. It points to a gloomy future for Mexican communities.

Organized crime has two basic functions: it can offer a product that legal businesses cannot provide; and it can steal or extort. The first category includes the selling of drugs, prostitution, pirate goods, gambling, guns, immigrant smuggling. The second includes kidnapping, cargo robberies, car theft, bank heists.

The first category is the least destructive for the economy. At least with drugs, prostitutes, or gambling, gangs are selling a product and moving money around. Shakedowns and kidnappings, however, terrorize the community, scare away investors, and burn businesses. The Juarez business association never complained much about tons of narcotics pumping through the city and billions of drug dollars flowing back. But when gangs began to shake down businesses, they called for United Nations blue helmets to come and take charge.[3] Shakedowns hurt them hard in their pockets. On a personal level, the move from drugs to kidnapping and extortion is terrifying for the community and strains the social networks of an already troubled country. You start to fear that anyone—your neigbor, your mechanic, your colleague—could be passing information to a kidnapping gang. It is an environment of fear and paranoia.

Maria Elena Morera is one of the prominent antikidnapping activists that have risen up amid the Mexican crime wave. These activists lead a citizen movement that has tried to break the scourge of abductions and antisocial crime. Up until now they have failed. But they may be key to resolving Mexico's crime problem in the future.

Maria says she never wanted to be a public figure. Born in 1958 of a Catalan family, the tall, blond woman trained as a dentist and spent her life happily pulling out teeth and enjoying a fruitful marriage and three healthy children. Then in 2000, her life was thrown on its head. One day, her husband didn't come home from work. She tried his cell phone but there was no answer, called his office phone but no one had seen him. Then she got the unbearable call—the gruff voice telling her that her worst fears had come true: they had her husband.

"Words can't describe how painful that moment was. It is like when something happens and you can't believe it is real, can't believe that this is happening to you. But it is and you have to try and find strength to face it."

She recounts this experience years later and has told it many times. But it still pains her to discuss it. Her face shows anguish, her voice shudders, and she burns through half a packet of cigarettes as she talks to me. Her nightmare was drawn out. The kidnappers terrorized her husband, a businessman, to push for a multimillion-dollar ransom the family couldn't muster. She was told to get a package by the side of a road. She went to the address and there was an envelope. Inside was her husband's middle finger, cut off from the knuckle. A week later, she was given a second finger; then a third; then a fourth. How can you deal with something like that? I ask her. How can you recover?

She replies slowly, "You can never recover from something like this. It is with you all your life. It changes you. It kills something inside you. I can't imagine the suffering that my husband went through. You feel it is your fault. It burns a hole inside."

Maria did what most people are afraid to do—she went to the police. She pressured them to act, worked with them to trace the calls and follow the gang. After her husband had been a hostage for twenty-seven days, federal agents located him and stormed the house. Several gang members were arrested, including a doctor who had been hired to cut the fingers off. And her husband was free. But he had to go on with his life bearing the scars.

The pain didn't stop there. Her husband was withdrawn and distant and didn't want to go to therapy. Maria found she herself couldn't go back to her normal life. The only thing that made sense to her was to fight against this affliction, save others from suffering the same pain. She joined the group Mexico United Against Crime and became its president. She took testimonies from people who have suffered kidnapping, rape, and violence and hooked them up with psychological help and legal aid. She also collected stats to highlight how bad the problem is. Maria's husband appeared in a commercial to support the campaign. He sits in a white polo shirt facing the camera.

"When my kidnappers cut off my first finger, I felt pain. When they cut off the second, I felt fear. When they cut off the third, it gave me rage. And when they cut off the fourth, I filled with strength to demand of the authorities that they don't lie, that they work, that they save our city of fear. And if their hand trembles, I'll lend them mine."

He holds up his hands close to the camera. His right hand is missing the little finger; the left is missing the little, ring, and middle fingers. The stumps left behind are of varied lengths, painting a picture of cruelty.

Another campaigner, Isabel Miranda de Wallace, took activism a step further. After kidnappers killed her son, Miranda pursued the case until she was authorized by the courts to become its official investigator. After five years, she located all the culprits and saw they were arrested. It was a great achievement, but also highlighted how weak Mexico's justice system is.

The anticrime movement has grown in strength to gain national prominence. It has organized two marches against insecurity, and a quarter of a million people took to the streets each time calling on the government to act. However, some reasons can be identified to explain its lack of effectiveness. First, the movement has been drawn into the bickering of Mexican politicians and been used by some officials to bash others. Mexico's deep class divisions are also a barrier. Some on the left accuse the activists of being rich bourgeoise out of touch with the problems of poor Mexicans. This polarization has weakened Mexican society's resistence to the crime wave.

The biggest problem of all has been the involvement of drug cartels in kidnapping. When abductions first started in the 1990s, it was almost all done by freelance criminals who had nothing to do with the mafia. One such rogue psychopath was Daniel "the Ear Lopper" Arizmendi, a former police detective from the industrial city of Toluca just outside the capital. The long-haired sadist, who looks a bit like Charles Manson, secured various million-dollar ransoms before police locked him away in a secure unit.[4]

Then some gunslingers linked to the mafia started partaking in kidnappings up in Sinaloa. One gang was known as the "finger choppers." They worked with drug growers and smugglers in the Sierra but also kidnapped the families of wealthy ranchers. Their most famous victim was the son of superstar singer Vicente Fernández, who lost two fingers to the mobsters before being liberated for a reported $2.5 million.[5] After a backlash from local businessmen, the Sinaloan Cartel apparently prohibited kidnapping in the region. The punishment for violating the ban: death.

I arrive at one Culiacán murder scene that appears to be cartel justice in action. The corpses of two men are dumped on the side of the road with signs of torture and bullets in their heads. A note sits beside the bodies: DAMN KIDNAPPERS. WHAT'S UP. GET TO WORK. This iron rule has been effective. Sinaloa, the cradle of Mexican drug cartels, has had one of the lowest kidnapping rates in Mexico. The mafia offers itself as protectors of the people, including the rich and middle class.

But while the Sinaloan Cartel prohibits kidnapping in its heartland, gunmen linked to the Sinaloa mob kidnap in other parts of Mexico. In 2007, the feisty magazine *Zeta* ran a story about abductions in Tijuana by the Sinaloan mafia. "For organized crime, the life of people from Baja California is worth very little," the article began, tracing a wave of kidnappings of Tijuana businessmen to the Sinaloan "finger choppers" gang.[6] A local commander of the Sinaloa Cartel was also accused of kidnapping Mennonites from a colony in Chihuahua state.

Such contrasts are typical on Mexico's mafia landscape. In one area, a mob can pose as protectors of the people and administer justice; in another, they can bleed the community. La Familia claims to execute kidnappers in their home state of Michoacán. But over the line in Mexico state, La Familia gunmen are accused of rampant kidnapping to fund their plazas.

Kidnapping spiked to unprecedented levels from 2008 as the Mexican Drug War intensified. Many point to cartels reacting to major seizures and lashing out for other sources of income. The government says this shows gangsters are desperate, on the ropes. But there are also signs that kidnapping simply increased amid the lawless atmosphere generated by so much violence. When federal police are themselves being kidnapped and murdered, there is less hope they can save you or your loved ones.

The original kidnappings in the 1990s targeted the rich, but many of the more recent victims have been middle or lower-middle class. Ransoms are often between $5,000 and $50,000, enough to force middle-class Mexicans to lose their life savings or sell their homes. Doctors, who are very visible, have suffered from rampant kidnappings, as have owners of car shops, engineers, and anyone seen getting a severance payment. People with close relatives making dollars in the United States are often targeted.

The drug traffickers most often accused of kidnapping are the usual baddest of the bad, the Zetas. Kidnapping is one of the basic ways Zetas cells fund themselves. They kidnap on an industrial scale. In cities from the Gulf of Mexico to the Guatemalan border, Zetas cells are said to pore over lists of potential abductees, taking anyone they think can pay up. One businessman who was kidnapped in the city of Tampico in 2010 said he personally knew of fifty cases within a year of the Zetas' taking over the town.

The Zetas have also targeted an even poorer class of victim—Central American migrants. The territory controlled by the Zetas on the east of Mexico is one of the busiest corridors for migrants attempting to reach the United States. The vast majority are from Honduras, El Salvador, and Guatemala, traveling on cargo trains and then switching to buses before swimming over the Rio Grande. It is a tough road to the American Dream, and it often leads to a hellish fate because of the Zetas.

Poor migrants may seem an odd target for a kidnapping. Surely they have no money. That is why they risk their lives migrating. But even poor people have relatives with savings, and the Zetas can often get $2,000 from kidnapping migrants. If you multiply that by ten thousand, you get $20 million—truly kidnapping en masse.

This holocaust has been detailed most thoroughly by Oscar Martinez, a brave Salvadoran journalist who spent a year following his country-men on the dark roads through Mexico, jumping trains with them, sleeping at hostels, and hearing of their terror. Oscar traced the begin-ning of the mass kidnapping to the middle of 2007. But the story was largely ignored for years, Oscar writes, for two reasons: local journalists were threatened with death if they reported on it; and few cared about what was happening to the poorest of the poor.

By 2009, the tragedy at last began to gain attention. Mexico's National Human Rights Commission released a report based on testimonies of mi-grants who had been kidnapped. It estimated a stunning ten thousand had been abducted in six months. The scale was unbelievable.[7] To capture so many migrants, Zetas gunmen kidnap huge groups from trains, buses, or trekking though the bush. They are aided in their mis-sion by their huge network of corruption, especially of municipal police. An army of the poor, the Zetas are particularly adept at flipping rank-and-file police officers.

Zetas then take the mass-kidnapped groups to ranches until they get payments from family members up in the United States or down in Cen-tral America. They usually collect the bounty by money-transfer services such as Western Union. These detention camps exist right up the east coast of Mexico, especially in Tamaulipas state, across the border from Texas, in Veracruz, and in Tabasco.

One such camp was located on the Victoria ranch, near the town of Tenosique in the swampy south. The horror story that played out there is told in detail in testimonies collected by human rights workers. In July 2009, fifty-two migrants were hauled off a cargo train by fifteen armed men. Arriving in the camp, their captors announced, "We are the Zetas. If anyone moves, we will kill them." They selected captives and made them kneel down in front of the group, then smashed their lower backs with a wooden board. This torture method is so common to Zetas that they even have their own verb for it, *tablear.* It causes intense pain, threatens vital organs, and leaves distinct bruises. They also starved victims, suffocated them with bags, and beat them with bats. Captive women were repeatedly raped.

Two migrants managed to escape one night. But a commando went after them into the nearby swamps. The migrants were strangers to the terrain, but the Zetas had local men who knew it like the back of their hand. Both escapees were recaptured and dragged back. The Zetas shot them in the head in front of the rest of the terrified prisoners.

To get a better understanding of this terror, I traveled to a migrant shelter in the southern state of Oaxaca. I soon heard stories from several people who had survived kidnappings, confirming the reach of the tragedy. Among them was Edwin, a forthcoming Afro-Honduran in his twenties with warm eyes and well-kept dreadlocks. Zetas had captured Edwin along with a group of sixty-five migrants in Veracruz state and taken him hundreds of miles in a car until he was stashed in a safehouse in Reynosa, on the border. "The only thing that goes through your head is that you are going to die," he told me, remembering his ordeal. "You think they are going to take you some place and it is all going to end."

Edwin was locked up for four months. His captors fed him just once a day with a hard boiled egg and beans, starving him to his skin and bone. He was finally released after his family wired a ransom of $1,400—a small fortune to them. He said he was scared to attempt the trip through Mexico again, but poverty drove him to do it. "In my country, things are very difficult and I have no option but to risk a journey through here. I hope to God it will be all right."

International human rights groups picked up on the news of the mass kidnappings with Amnesty International describing it as "a major human rights crisis."[8] But governments were still depressingly inactive about it, deriding it as a marginal issue. Until August 2010. Then came the massacre that shocked the world.

The San Fernando massacre is a landmark in the Mexican Drug War. It surely woke up anyone who still doubted the existence of a serious armed conflict south of the Rio Grande. But for those following the mass attacks on migrants, it was a tragedy waiting to happen.

San Fernando began just like all the rest of the mass kidnappings. Zetas gunmen stopped the victims at a checkpoint and abducted them, in this case from two buses. The group featured many of the usual Central Americans, but was atypical in that it also had large numbers of Brazilians and Ecuadorians. The Zetas marched the prisoners to the San Fernando ranch, which is in Tamaulipas state, just a hundred miles from the U.S. border. After a long, hard journey, the migrants were closer than ever to their destination. Then something went wrong, and the Zetas decided to murder everybody.

The pure scale of death shocked the world. The seventy-two corpses were piled haphazardly around the edge of the breeze-block barn, arms and legs twisted over one another, waists and backs contorted. There were teenagers, middle-aged men, young girls, even a pregnant woman. This horror could not be ignored.

How, people gasped, had a massacre, comparable to war crimes, taken place in one of Mexico's most developed regions? San Fernando brought home the erosion of society. In the discussion among Mexicans following the tragedy, one telling word was repeated again and again: *vergüenza*, "shame." How would other nations look at what Mexicans had done to their citizens? And how could Mexicans now condemn the maltreatment of migrants in the United States?

The exact circumstances leading to the mass execution are still unclear. Most details we know came from a nineteen-year-old Ecuadorian who, against all odds, survived the massacre. When the gunmen fired, a bullet went through his neck and out his jaw. He fell down as if dead but was still conscious, and after waiting patiently for hours, he got up and stumbled miles on foot. He passed several people, but they were all too frightened to help him; the terror of cartels has left people scared even to help a dying man. Finally, he reached a military checkpoint. A day later, marines stormed the ranch and found the corpses.[9] However, journalists never a got a full testimony from this survivor. For his own protection, the Ecuadorian was kept at a marine base before being flown back to his homeland. He still fears for his life.

There should have been a relentless investigation into the massacre in Mexico, but it soon turned into a typical botched case. First a prosecutor assigned to it was assassinated. Then a caller phoned police to announce that three dead bodies on the side of the road were men responisble for the massacre. The Zetas, it seemed, had offered their own justice.

As families buried their dead in their homelands, they screamed for answers. What could anyone gain from such an atrocity? Was it a message to others not to resist? Or were all the captured migrants too poor to pay? Or did the prisoners rebel? Or was the Zetas leader at the scene just a total psychopath? Perhaps we will never know.

An even deeper concern is that the massacre is not really isolated. The Salvadoran journalist Oscar Martinez has found countless accounts of migrants who have disappeared on their journey through Mexico. Authorities need to excavate around the ranches used as detention camps, he writes. There could be mass graves, he fears, with thousands of corpses.

The Zetas also use their muscle in less bloody ways to make a buck. Among them is the manufacture of pirate DVDs. The group actually prints up its own versions of blockbuster movies and sells them to market stalls. I see the cover of a Zetas copy of the zombie-slaying action film *Resident Evil*. The sleeve has some grainy photos from the flick with the words PRODUCCIONES ZETA in blue letters in the top left-hand corner. Market-stall owners say they buy them from the Zetas' distributor for ten pesos (eighty cents) a movie. The Zetas demand that the stall owner buy from no other providers. But in return, the Zetas promise protection from any problems with police.

At least in the case of piracy, money moves around the economy rather than leaving it. But cartel involvement is really just to tax a black-market industry that is already there. Mexico has tolerated a colossal informal economy for years. In 2010, the Mexican government estimated close to 30 percent of the workforce was outside of formal employment, neither paying taxes nor receiving benefits.[10] Millions work as street vendors flogging products from stalls by bus stations or on sidewalks. Known as *ambulantes*, the vendors sell many consumer goods brought from the United States without paying tariffs. They also sell millions of pirate CDs, DVDs, and computer games. Whereas an original movie will cost about $20 in Mexico, a pirate copy will cost an average of just $2. One can find anything from the latest episodes of HBO's *The Wire* to films not yet in the theaters. For every ten movies sold in Mexico, the studios estimate, nine are pirate copies. There is a huge market for cartels to tap.

The sex industry has also thrived in Mexico for centuries. Street prostitutes, table-dance clubs, old-style cantina escorts, brothels, and massage parlors are tolerated the length and breadth of the country. There isn't much cartels can add to the industry, except to make owners pay them a quota. It is hard for these owners to say no. One night in Ciudad Juárez, I followed journalists to a bordello whose owner had apparently failed to cough up. Gangsters had firebombed the brothel while it was in full service; a sex worker and the john she was with were carted to a hospital with severe burns.

The rise of cartel extortion in Ciudad Juárez was fast and furious. I drove round the city with José Reyes Ferriz, who was mayor of Juárez from 2007 to 2010, when the rackets came in. Speaking perfect English, the American-educated official described how the extortion mushroomed during a few months in 2008, right as the drug war exploded.

"The criminals first started charging protection at used-car lots, which have always had a certain link to organized crime. Then it started growing to affect bars, pharmacies, and funeral parlors. Then they got money from schools and doctors. Then they just went for everything in sight."

Businesses are often charged relatively small amounts—$400 a month for a bar; $500 for a busy grocery store. We passed several burned-out and boarded-up buildings—places that had failed to pay the quota. Mayor Ferriz sighs.

"It has been terrible for business. But we are overwhelmed at a city level. I had no power to take on the mafia. That is why I invited the army in and gave them power of security in the streets. But they are fighting a tough battle too."

I asked him who is behind the extortion. He gives me a telling answer. The extortion shot up right after he "purified" the police force, firing six hundred corrupt officers, he said. The fired policemen were long suspected of working with the Juárez Cartel and other crimes. Some were later arrested for involvement in extortion rackets. It was a bit like the botched de-Baathification of Iraq. When the American-backed authority fired officials of Saddam Hussein's government, the ex-Baathists joined the insurgency. When Ferriz fired mobbed-up officers in Juárez, the bad cops shook down anything that moved.

Some of those demanding cash in Juarez appear to be opportunistic freelancers. Other times, it appears to be criminals with connections to the cartels, including gangbangers from the Barrio Azteca. For terrified business owners, it is hard to know who the person demanding money is. But with so many murders, it is always safer to pay—or like many in the Juarez middle class, pack up and move to the United States.

In other parts of Mexico, cartels such as the Zetas and La Familia hold a monopoly in their extortion. If any small-time crooks try to step in, the mobs leave their corpses on public display.

While protection rackets terrorize, they can also paradoxically entrench cartels deeper into the community. Diego Gambetta, a leading organized-crime expert at Oxford University, has done extensive research on protection rackets that has produced new thinking about them. His ideas are in his landmark book, *The Sicilian Mafia: The Business of Private Protection*.[11] He explains that the mafia is not just an industry of violence that intimidates. Businesses also willingly pay for protection and the services of muscle to achieve things the state can't. This co-option is one of the reasons that the Sicilian mafia has survived a century of government assaults; a section of the community is in bed with it.

Such a scenario is already playing out in Mexico. Zetas have taxed bars and discos across the Monterrey area. But in the rich Monterrey municipality of San Pedro Garza, disco owners chipped into pay gunmen from the Beltrán Leyva organization to keep the Zetas out. In many ways, the owners fell for a trap—they paid protection to one group to avoid paying protection to another. But they felt the Beltrán Leyva gunmen were the lesser of two evils and became complicit in their crime network. The state can't look after them, the owners said, so they turned to Gambetta's "business of private protection." This business will likely be a big part of El Narco's future.

Shakedowns have plagued societies for centuries. Street gangs in New York's Five Points used to do them; Al Capone infamously extorted half of Chicago; gangbangers in Central America do them. It doesn't take a paramilitary cartel to rattle someone into paying up. Often one psychotic thug with a tattoo on his face will do the trick. Perhaps a few shakedowns in Mexico are not the end of civilization.

However, two factors show cartel extortion in Mexico could be a more serious development. First, the cartels take over shakedowns that Mexico's government itself used to do. Government officials are notorious for rattling bribes out of businesses across the country. If owners don't pay up, bureaucrats can always find a way to shut them down. "Oh, there is no knob on the toilet door, you will have to close temporarily; oh, there is no restaurant menu in braille for blind customers—shut down; oh, the front door is not wide enough—*clausurado!*" The powers of government give officials an excuse to line their pockets regularly—especially at Christmastime.

But as cartels now extort businesses, owners complain they can't pay twice. So cartels make sure they get paid and tell government officials to back off. In most cases, the gangsters are kicking back to these officials. The frightening implication is that as El Narco takes over the government's role as extortionist, it becomes even more of a shadow state, the real muscle and power behind the facade of elected officials.

The second worrying factor about cartel extortion is that criminals are ambitious enough to go after heavy industry. In Michoacán, a mine owner I interviewed said that he has to pay off the cartel. In return for his payments, the gangsters offered to go after any extortionists on building sites he owned over in Mexico City. Gangsters also tax the Michoacán timber industry and help loggers ignore restrictions on deforesting.

Over in the east, the Zetas tax Mexico's most vital natural resource: oil. Mexico's black gold is owned by the government monopoly Petróleos Mexicanos or Pemex. But police investigations found the Zetas used high-tech drills and rubber hoses to siphon oil out of pipelines and put it on stolen tanker trucks. In some cases, stolen oil has been taken into the United States and sold at cut-rate prices to Texans. In 2009, a former president of a Houston oil company pleaded guilty to buying stolen Mexican petroleum. Stealing oil can be highly dangerous. In December 2010, oil thieves are alleged to have puntured a pipeline in Puebla state, sparking an explosion that sent fireballs down the streets of a local town, incinerating houses and killing thirty people.

Zetas have also been accused of various kidnappings and murders of Pemex union reps. One Pemex worker at the central offices says the violence is part of the cartel muscling in on the union's ill-gotten gains, such as taking bribes for getting people well-paid oil jobs.

This oil money is no small change. In 2009 to 2010, the pipeline hijacking was said to cost Pemex $1 billion.[12] That is only the tip of the iceberg. Pemex is one of the world's biggest oil companies, with total sales worth $104 billion in 2010.[13] Black gold is even bigger than drugs.

All this has deadly implications. When crime groups fight over the spoils of heavy industry and government skim, the stakes for Mexico go up. The Mexican Drug War could escalate to a broader civil war over the country's natural and financial resources. Imagine a scenario in which paramilitary squads are securing oil installations and mines and fighting off enemies trying to seize them. Such a conflict could draw in hundreds of thousands of people and have a devastating human cost.

Prophecies of civil war may sound alarmist. But few predicted thirty-five thousand dead in a drug war. When warlords are unleashing private armies throughout the countryside, the possibility of a wider war has to be taken seriously. The criminal insurgency might dig Mexico into an even bigger hole. We worry about fifteen thousand killings in a year, but imagine the implications if there were fifty thousand. Policy makers and citizens should not allow the drug-war fire to keep getting bigger and more ferocious—we have to find ways to put out the flames.

CHAPTER 16

Peace

I heard almost exactly the same phrase twice: once in Culiacán, Sinaloa; once in Ciudad Juárez. The first time it came from Alma Herrera, the elegant fifty-year-old mother whose innocent son had been shot dead when he went to fix the brakes of the family car. We were talking about all the murder and injustice in Culiacán, how normal citizens feel helpless against the power of these mafias and corrupt police, soldiers, and politicians. How they feel so useless when their children are held by kidnappers or filled with bullets before they have celebrated their eighteenth birthday. How they feel impotent in the face of gunmen taking the lives of whomever they want, whenever they want. Then she said the phrase that stuck in my mind:

"We need a Superman to come here and save us, to clean up this city, to take out the bad guys."

It may sound ridiculous. It is something out of simplistic D.C. comics and Hollywood films, the idea of a caped crusader flying through the sky, deflecting bullets and grabbing villains by the scruff of their neck. But amid such frustration and desperation, her hope is completely understandable, if unrealistic. Culiacán is grimmer than Gotham City in its worst depictions. They don't stick heads on sticks in Gotham City.

Up in Ciudad Juárez, I heard the notion again in a song—or rather a rap. The rapper goes by the name Gabo and is part of a new school of Mexican-border hip-hop that criticizes rather than celebrates gang life and violence. Gabo was letting loose with his lyrics on a sidewalk outside a nightclub while I filmed with a TV crew. His verse was also about the frustration one feels living in neighborhoods plagued by cartel assassins and corrupt cops. Then he dropped a stanza that struck another chord in my mind.

Peace *will be the last word we hear,*
Where is Superman or Jesus Christ?
Come out of the sky and fight this,
Sorry, God, I am no atheist,
I am just tired of what I live, feel, and see.

Again, feeling utterly impotent, one turns to a greater power. Where is the man in a tight, blue-and-red suit or a crown of thorns to emerge from the clouds? It is a comprehendible wish.

Unfortunately, no supermen or messiahs are going to zap away the Mexican Drug War. No magic wands will make it all better. The solution is in flawed, greedy, evasive, confused, deceitful human beings. It is in the same humans who have created the problem in the first place, made El Narco grow slowly but surely by buying its drugs, selling it guns, laundering its money, taking its bribes, paying its ransoms. And it is in the same flawed politicians from Washington to Mexico City who have pushed policies that don't work, left kids stuck in a corner with no hope, and let killers get away with murder.

The way out doesn't involve one improved policy in one country, but a group of improved policies in Mexico, the United States, and beyond. Even though El Narco is a criminal insurgency, soldiers are only a small part of this solution. America and Europe have to wake up and confront the drug money and guns we spew out. The debate cannot conveniently be tucked away any longer. Estimated Mexican drug profits over the last decade total more than quarter of a trillion dollars. Giving psychopathic cartels another quarter of a trillion dollars in the next decade should not be acceptable. Would we accept foreigners throwing such money at insurgent militias in our countries?

But even if the demons of the drug trade are magically vanquished, Mexico has to confront its own deep problems. The country is struggling with a historical transition: the old world of the PRI has died; the new democracy hasn't yet been built. The nation has to find the architects to construct it. It has to make a real police force that will not tolerate an innocent child's being kidnapped and having his life destroyed; and it has to offer more hope to teenagers than grabbing Kalashnikovs, making fast dollars, and dying before they reach manhood.

Peace has to come one day, but a lot more corpses will come first. And these bodies will not all be safely south of the Rio Grande.

North of the border in California, some say they have a solution to the violent drug trade in light green plants reared with electric lights and sold in cookie jars. Walking around a square mile in Los Angeles, you can pass twenty medical-marijuana stores with names including Little Ethiopia, Herbal Healing Center, Green Cross, Smokers, Happy Medical Centers, La Kush Hemporium, and the Natural Way. Stepping through the door of one, you pass a receptionist asking for your doctor's prescription to smoke bud—a script that can be for illnesses from cancer, paralysis, and Alzheimer's to feeling stressed (who isn't?). You then pass to a room packed with jars of goodies with such names as Purple Kush, Super Silvers, God's Gift, Strawberry Cough, Granddaddy, and Trainwreck. The California indoor plants are usually purer and lighter colored than Mexican weed, showing a yellow-green tinge. Patients can take their medicine to the comfort of their own home and smoke their sorrows away in stinky clouds. And nobody gets gunned down by ski-masked hoods with AKs.

Drug policy reformists say these shops are a glimpse of the future. The grass is grown in America, smoked legally in America, and taxed in America. No dollars are spent on busting it, and no drug money goes to cartel militias in Mexico. El Narco, some say, may be resistant to a million army rounds, but it can be slain by the dreaded L-word—legalization. So we get into that toxic, contentious, prohibited, muddled, and crucially needed argument—the legalization debate.

Right as the Mexican Drug War rages, the debate is reaching the second great flux in its history. The first came in the seventies, with the Jimmy Carter White House. Legalization advocates, including various doctors, got into key government positions, their papers got play, their ideas gained currency. States began to decriminalize marijuana and cocaine was viewed in the media as a happy-go-lucky party drug. Reformers thought they had won the debate. They were wrong. In the eighties, America lashed back against narcotics with a vengeance, and in the nineties the drug war went on steroids. The crack epidemic broke out, celebrities died of overdoses, and lots of middle-class parents got concerned about lots of middle-class kids on smack, speed, and sensimilla. In the early 1990s, surveys found large numbers of Americans thought drugs were the number one problem the country faced. The media was packed with stories of crack babies, cracked-up gangbangers, and nice white kids turning into demons on drugs.

But that was two decades ago. The pendulum has swung back again. For now. Most people don't even list drugs in their top ten of America's problems. The economy is most people's priority, and terrorism, immigration, crime, religion, abortion, gay marriage, and the environment all spark more concern than narcotics. Meanwhile, drug-policy reformers have emerged strengthened with propositions to decriminalize, spread medical use, and finally fully legalize marijuana. Proposition 19 to legalize cannabis in California narrowly missed passing, getting 46.5 percent in the 2010 vote. Activists are determined it will pass in 2012. And if not, in 2014. Or 2016. They can just keep on going.

The policy-reform movement is also enjoying a surge in Latin America, where a number of top politicians are joining a chorus singing for change. In February 2009, former Mexican president Ernesto Zedillo, former Colombian president César Gaviria (who oversaw the killing of Pablo Escobar), and former Brazilian president Fernando Cardoso signed a landmark document calling for a U-turn on policy. The report, which they presented with the intention of kick-starting a movement, stated in unambiguous terms:

"The war on drugs has failed. And it's high time to replace an ineffective strategy with more humane and efficient drug policies . . .

"Prohibitionist policies based on eradication, interdiction, and criminalization of consumption simply haven't worked. Violence and the organized crime associated with the narcotics trade remain critical problems in our countries. Latin America remains the world's largest exporter of cocaine and cannabis and is fast becoming a major supplier of opium and heroin. Today, we are further than ever from the goal of eradicating drugs.

"The first step in the search for alternative solutions is to acknowledge the disastrous consequences of current policies. Next, we must shatter the taboos that inhibit public debate about drugs in our societies."[1]

The paper caused a whirlwind across the continent. But typical of the drug debate, this was a salvo from former rather than current presidents. Questioning the righteousness of the war on drugs has long been seen as a terminally toxic vote loser. Until politicians get out of office.

Another retired head of state who joined the movement to legalize was Vicente Fox. I went to see him on his ranch to talk about his new-found cause. He looked decidedly less stressed than when in office, relaxing on his large estate in jeans and a T-shirt. Asked why his position had swung round, he explained that the situation itself has changed, with the problem of violence now a far worse cost for Mexico.

I was surprised by how radical his views were on reform. He didn't just want to decriminalize but spoke of full-on legalization and taxation of the entire narcotics industry. He envisions the marijuana growers up in the Sierra Madre raising their weed as legal farmers. Mexican marijuana could be like its tequila industry, supporting some rural barons and known by drunks (or stoners) the world over. He added that it was a shame Prop 19 failed in California, as it would have been a huge first step. Speaking in his usual baritone voice, the former president went on:

"Prohibition didn't work in the Garden of Eden. Adam ate the apple. And Al Capone and Chicago are the biggest example of prohibition not working. When they legalized alcohol, that got rid of the violence.

"The damage Mexico is paying for prohibition now is getting exponentially worse. It is affecting investment and tourism. Is it destroying hotels and restaurants and nightclubs in the north of the country. I see important businessmen leaving the country and going to San Antonio or Houston or Dallas.

"But it is not just a loss of income. It is the loss of tranquillity. In the collective psychology, there is fear in the country, and when you have an atmosphere of disharmony, no human being can make the best of themselves. This cost is not worth paying.

"You also have to think that the responsibility of drugs is with the consumer. It is the family that has to give information and educate. We can't pass that responsibility to the government. The government has to respond urgently to our security. They have to make sure our children get home safe and healthy, that they don't get caught up in a shoot-out."

Fox touches on the central points raised for years by the drug-policy reformists in the United States: that drug prohibition hasn't stopped drug taking; that it creates organized crime with catastrophic consequences; and that the whole idea of a government telling you what to put in your body is illogical.

Arguments for legalization have filled whole books, and this doesn't intend to be another one. This is a book about El Narco and the Mexican Drug War. Most people have already made up their minds about legalization. But the debate is crucial to understanding the future of El Narco, because how drug-policy reform plays out will have epic consequences in Mexico.

The growing policy-reform movement is a broad church. It includes everyone from ganja-smoking Rastafarians to free-market fundamentalists and all in between. There are socialists who think the drug war hurts the poor, capitalists who see a business opportunity, liberals who defend the right to choose, and fiscal conservatives who complain America is spending $40 billion a year on the War on Drugs rather than making a few billion taxing it.[2] The movement can't agree on much other than that the present policy doesn't work. People disagree on whether legalized drugs should be controlled by the state, by corporations, by small businessmen, or by grow-your-own farmers, and on whether they should be advertised, taxed, or just handed out free in white boxes to addicts.

Powerful groups are lined up against reform. Certain Christians and religious-driven organizations believe drugs are immoral and that it is our duty to fight their use. This fundamental force has driven the drug war since Opium Commissioner Hamilton Wright railed against pink poppies in 1908, and its influence on American thinking should not be underestimated. Many in the drug-fighting establishment also stand firmly in their trenches. The DEA doesn't want to lose its $2.3 billion budget, and soldiers who have dedicated their lives can't stand the idea that struggle has been in vain. Plenty of well-meaning agents firmly believe narcotics are a scourge we have to fight with force. Finally, there is the same group that has provided the impetus for politicians to call the battle cry all along: the concerned middle class. Being hard on drugs is seen as a vote winner for a reason: parents are genuinely concerned about the issue.

Outside America, voices add to the drug-war camp. The United Nations treaties demand that all signatories pursue prohibitionist policies and are made in a hard way to change. Supporting this conservative position are officials from countries as far afield as Italy, Russia, Iran, Nigeria, and China, who are all convinced that the line on prohibition cannot be broken. If California did legalize marijuana, it would not only contravene American federal law, it would also violate the UN treaty. It would be a legal can of worms.[3]

As the calls for drug reform rise, those in the drug-war camp raise their tone. They claim that drug legalization would be a catastrophe. Even if we did legalize marijuana, they say, how could we ever legalize cocaine, heroin, and meth? One report wildly speculated cocaine use would rise tenfold. If you think things are bad now, they say, imagine the chaos if drugs were legal. There would be psychopathic, gun-toting crackheads on every corner. It would be hell on earth. El Narco would have won.

Despite these immense challenges, several factors are making the drug-policy reform movement stronger than ever. The most important is historical experience. With modern mass drug use beginning in the 1960s, we have had more than four decades to watch its trends. Tellingly, laws do not appear to be the underlying factor determining the amount of drug use. Holland for example has had liberal drug laws, but has lower drug use than the United Kingdom with stricter laws. Portugal had one of the lowest drug-use rates in Europe when it had strict laws, and even lower rates following the decriminalization of all drugs in 2001. The main achievement of this change was to save money and reduce HIV infections.

The United States continues to have some of the highest drug use in the world while maintaining a generally prohibitionist policy. But the types of drugs used have changed over the decades. Powder cocaine was trendy and popular in the seventies, crack exploded in the eighties, ecstasy gained strength in the nineties, and crystal meth had its notorious star turn at the dawn of the new millennium. These changes seem more to do with fashions and transforming social environments than laws and any success at stopping supply. The argument that legalizing drugs would create a catastrophic wave of users isn't backed by facts.

Drug use in Latin America, including Mexico, is much lower than in the United States, but has substantially risen in the last two decades, giving Latin American countries their own problems with addicts and street-corner battles. Judging from historical experience, drug use is likely to rise in these countries whatever governments do. Drugs are part of globalization and modern consumer societies. This will create even more income for El Narco and make policy reform more urgent.

Advocating legalization of drugs is by no means saying that drugs are good. Everyone agrees that heroin is a dastardly scourge. Reformers argue, however, that the best way to control narcotics is to get them in the open and regulate them. Meanwhile, the billions of dollars spent trying to prohibit narcotics could be spent on prevention campaigns and rehabilitation. Most people who use drugs are not problematic addicts, just as most who drink are not sick alcoholics. But addicts give the most resources to organized crime and cause the gravest damage to their families and communities. Rehabilitation workers say most of those who suffer compulsive drug use have other problems: child abuse, poverty, neglect. They need help. Criminalizing them normally aggravates rather solves their tribulations.

Meanwhile, the hard-core crime associated with drugs is not caused by the narcotics themselves; it is precisely because they are illegal. People kill over street corners because they are fighting over the wealth of the black-market trade, not because they smoked spliffs. Mexican gangsters don't cut off their rivals' heads because they are tripping on psychedelics. They go beyond the pale because so much money is involved.

Policy-reform advocates envision a bright future in which the international community comes to terms with the use of narcotics in the modern world in a legal sphere. This would finally destroy trafficking mafias, who would by definition not be able to exist. There would be no more street-corner beefs, shoot-outs over shipments, executions of pushers who haven't paid their quota, drug money going to the Barrio Azteca, Sinaloa Cartel, Medellín Cartel, Zetas, La Familia, Cosa Nostra, or Jamaican yardies, cocaine fights in Brazilian favelas, or cartel hits on drug czars nor any other drug-related bloodshed in grimy corners all over the globe.

This vision has long been derided as utopian, classified as a nonstarter. But it is rapidly gaining strength with new converts from U.S. Internet billionaires to Latin American peasants. This momentum gives reform advocates a feeling of a snowball effect, a sense that history is on their side. As French poet Victor Hugo said, "Nothing is more powerful than an idea whose time has come."

Then again, many activists felt like that in the seventies. Overconfidence can be dangerous. The pendulum could always swing back.

The biggest policy change so far has been the decriminalization of drug use. Governments who take this course still keep narcotics illegal, but will not punish—or at least not give jail time—to anyone found possessing personal amounts. This has already been done in thirteen U.S. states regarding marijuana, and in Holland and Portugal. In the last two years, it has also gained ground in the front-line states of Latin America. Argentina's supreme court ruled marijuana possession was not a crime, and Colombia and Mexico itself have decriminalized the personal use of almost all narcotics. In Mexico's law, approved in 2009, anyone caught with two or three joints, about four lines of cocaine, or even a little bit of meth or heroin can no longer be arrested, fined, or imprisoned.[4] However, police will give them the address of the nearest rehab clinic and advise them to get clean. The law was approved on the argument that police had to prioritize going after bigger, more violent criminals. They certainly have plenty of those.

The Mexican law was an important landmark, especially considering the reaction of the United States. Back in 2006, the Mexican Congress had approved an almost identical law. But the Bush White House went ballistic and put pressure on President Fox, who vetoed it. In contrast in 2009, the Obama White House was notably mum about the issue, and Calderón signed it. This reaction was not missed across Latin America and could signal a longer-term change of direction both in Washington and southern-hemisphere capitals. Another notable point was that the Mexican law had no immediate effect on drug use on the street. No fourth graders rushed out of school to try heroin, no sudden explosion of kids on crack occurred. Long term, of course, this could be a different story. But from a policy point it breaks the argument that the world will immediately stop turning if drugs are decriminalized. Fear of the unknown world of tolerated drugs has long been a factor driving the debate.

However, while decriminalization saves police money and stops punishing addicts, opponents are right to point out that it does nothing to stop organized crime. While drug use is effectively legal, trafficking and selling is still in the shadows. We will likely have to deal with this painful contradiction for many years ahead.

California's Prop 19 doesn't mess with these contradictions, but advocates a step into a new realm, legalized marijuana. The 2010 version proposed that anyone over twenty-one should be able to possess up to an ounce of weed for personal use, smoke in his or her own home, and grow it in greenhouses. Ganja would be sold by licensed dealers, with medical-marijuana stores providing a concrete example of what this would look like; you just wouldn't need the doctor's prescription. The debate will rage again in 2012, with most arguments over the health of California kids and public finances. (Advocates say the state could make some $1.4

billion in tax revenues annually from ganja.) But others will be watching it closely hundreds of miles south of the border, in the marijuana fields of the Sierra Madre.

Everyone agrees that legalized weed in the United States would have an effect on El Narco in Mexico. The question is how much. We keep getting back to the base problem that since the drug trade is illegal, we don't know how much Mexico produces, or what crosses the border, or even how many Americans smoke weed. But we try to guess. These guesses on how much weed Mexico sells America vary wildly, from a whopping $20 billion at the top end to $1.1 billion at the bottom.

The top figures came after the drug czar's office back in 1997 multiplied some estimated yields of Mexican marijuana crops based on plane sightings and other factors. It then multiplied these yields with American street prices and came up with an astronomical figure with a lot of zeros. It was even more than Mexicans made from cocaine. The office thus concluded that the Mexican mobs make 60 percent of their income from weed. A similar figure was produced again when the Mexican government estimated that cartels grew a whopping 35 million pounds of ganja a year and multiplied it by the American street costs (of about $525 a pound)—to produce the $20 billion. This number floated around in the media in the run-up to the Prop 19 vote.

The Rand Corporation then came up with its own study before the California referendum.[5] The report launched an attack on the high-end figures, saying they should not be taken seriously. "Legalization advocates seize on such figures to complement their traditional arguments," it states. It goes on to rightly show the immense problems with estimates and how all the numbers we are dealing with are dubious. But then the report makes its own guesstimates, involving lot of funny-looking equations with a's and b's and long numbers. Getting back into the confused territory of guessing how much weed stoners put in each joint (0.39 grams by one measure), it looks at data dividing wasters into four groups—from casual users to chronic smokers (of the Chronic). After more bells and whistles, it concludes that Mexican traffickers make just $1.1 billion to $2 billion in the entire American marijuana market and only 7 percent of that comes from California. Its conclusion: voting for Prop 19 won't affect Mexican drug violence.

That deduction is highly questionable. The most concrete source, seizures, shows that tons of Mexican cartel grass go directly into California. Mexico made its biggest marijuana seize since the eighties right over the California border, in Tijuana, in 2010 (two weeks before the Prop 19 vote). It was 134 metric tons, or 295,000 pounds of the psychedelic leaves! It is so much grass, it was carried in a whole convoy of trucks and soldiers filled a parking lot with it. The pressure-packed bundles in yellow, red, green, gray, and white reached the sky. It made a hell of a bonfire. The grass would have been worth about $100 million on California streets. In apparent reaction to the loss, a cartel massacred thirteen addicts in a rehab center. It was one life for each ten tons of ganja.[6]

If cartels murder over the marijuana traffic into California, it is obviously a serious market. And that was only one seizure. California's border patrol and customs also seize hundreds of tons of cannabis every year.

Mexican marijuana heading into California also moves on to other American states. If California did legalize the herb, there would be a perplexing patchwork: you would have grass produced legally in Cali sold illegally in other states; Mexican weed imported unlawfully into San Diego and selling over the counter in Los Angeles; and a whole array of other confused combinations. And it would be bizarre for Mexican soldiers to seize a truck of ganja in Tijuana if it was openly being sold in dispensaries a few miles over the border.

Policy-reform advocates, of course, see California as a first step. Once it is shown to work there, the policy could be followed in New Mexico or Washington State. Eventually, the whole union might legalize. And if the United States legalized marijuana, Mexico would inevitably legalize its own farmers and transporters. Campesinos in the Sierra Madre could get out of the drug trade and into a legitimate business; it would be one more Mexican crop such as coffee, tequila agave, or avocados.

You can argue forever with fuzzy figures about the size of this industry. But even if you believe the lowest estimates, Mexico's marijuana trade to the United States is in the billions. If it was legalized, this would take these billions away every year from organized crime. That is more financial damage than the DEA or Mexican armed forces have achieved in a decade.

Taking Mexico's marijuana business out of the black market would clearly mean less money spent on Kalashnikovs and paying child assassins. But whatever happens in drug-policy reform, cartel militias are not going to disappear overnight. Gangs such as the Zetas and Familia will keep fighting over any illegal drugs on the market as well as going on with their extortion, kidnapping, human smuggling, and their portfolio of other crimes. They are a threat that Mexico must confront.

Some analysts fear calling these groups insurgents because they fear counterinsurgency tactics. Armies battling rebel groups have caused human rights tragedies from Algeria to Afghanistan. Mexican soldiers have already committed widespread human rights abuses, and if they get schooled in a real anti-insurgency campaign, their record could get even worse. This is a real fear.

But the Mexican Drug War is already completely militarized. While the Mexican government refuses to concede it is fighting an insurgency, it uses a completely military strategy against cartel militias, battling them with the army, marines, and units of federal paramilitary police. Protesters march to condemn the abuses of soldiers; but they also protest how the government is failing to protect them from gangsters. Often these two points are protested in the same marches. That is the central problem for Calderón and whoever follows him. He is damned if he uses the army; and he is damned if he doesn't.

Realistically, no president is going to completely withdraw the military while groups such as the Zetas maintain their current strength. How can any government permit squads of fifty men with automatic rifles, RPGs, and belt-driven machine guns to steam through villages? It has to challenge them. And only the military has the capacity to go toe-to-toe with Zetas black commandos.

However, the government could certainly refine this strategy. The army, or particularly the marines, have been successful in strikes on cartel bosses such as when they blew away Arturo "the Beard" Beltrán Leyva in the apartment block. But soldiers also waste a lot of time raiding random houses without intelligence, harassing civilians on the street, and manning checkpoints on dark country roads. Nervous soldiers have shot dead many of their innocent victims at these checkpoints. The military needs to be used for the heavy stuff. The intelligence has to be gathered by civilian agents who really know how to collect it, or the American desperado agents who collect much of it anyway; and daily policing has to be handled by police.

The marines are already being reorganized as the elite strike force for these type of operations. As WikiLeaks cables show, they are the Mexican force most respected by American officials. In a December 2009 cable, then American ambassador Carlos Pascual praised the marines for their work killing the Beard and some Zetas leaders, while scolding the army, who, he said, had failed to act on American intel.

"The successful operation against ABL [Arturo Beltrán Leyva] comes on the heels of an aggressive SEMAR [marines] effort in Monterrey against Zeta forces and highlights its emerging role as a key player in the counternarcotics fight. SEMAR is well-trained, well-equipped, and has shown itself capable of responding quickly to actionable intelligence. Its success puts the army in the difficult position of explaining why it has been reluctant to act on good intelligence and conduct operations against high-level targets."[7]

The ambassador also revealed (thanks to WikiLeaks) that the marine unit that led the operation had been "extensively trained" by the U.S. Northern Command, the Pentagon's joint operations center in Colorado. Other cables elaborated on American doubts about the Mexican army and recommended more training with U.S. forces. John Feeley, the deputy chief of mission for the U.S. embassy in Mexico City, wrote a scathing assessment of Mexico's military capacities in January 2010. He called the armed forces "parochial and risk averse," said they were "incapable of processing information and evidence," and called the defense minister, General Galvan, "a political actor." It was quite different from America's public line, and quite embarrassing for Feeley when it flashed up on the Internet. Feeley's solution: more training with the United States as well as the Colombians.[8]

America will invariably continue to train Mexican troops, and building up elite units that take out the worst gangsters and commandos is a good thing. But Mexico also has to work on paying these elite units decently and keeping their loyalty so they don't desert and become more mercenaries. The modern marine core is better trained and more experienced than Arturo Guzmán Decena was when he went over to the Zetas. If a crew of marines ever deserted, it would be an awesome threat. While the U.S. trains Mexicans, the use of American forces themselves should be kept firmly off the agenda. It looms as a likely disaster, provoking nationalist resentment and pulling U.S. troops into a quagmire.

Americans do need to step up their efforts to help improve the Mexican police. A long-term solution to Mexico's security problems is training real cops—and not just gangsters in uniform who let criminals get away with murder. Whether it is a single national force or separate agencies, the quality of officers has to be vastly improved. This is a generational project, not something that will miraculously happen in one or five or even ten years. The police ranks have to be trained and improved and monitored and cleaned out and trained again . . . As well as help from American police, support of Latin American police is crucial, as these corps deal with a more similar culture and circumstances. The Colombian National Police is obviously touted, but other forces have gained respect and good clearance rates in Latin America, including police in Nicaragua—Central America's poorest country, but one of its safest.

Dealing with Mexico's mountain of unsolved murders and crimes now seems an insurmountable task. So police have to prioritize. Busting small-time drug dealers is a never-ending mission that gets bodies in cells but doesn't stop the drug trade or violence. Meanwhile, kidnapping for ransom is the most heinous antisocial crime of all and should not be tolerated one inch. In front of Mexico's wave of abductions, this should be the number one priority.

The good news about kidnapping is that it can be stopped (unlike the drug trade). This point was brought home to me by former Colombian president César Gaviria. In an interview, the former premier described Colombia's experience with the scourge of kidnapping in the nineties and what Mexico can learn from it.

"Kidapping is a problem of bad policing. Because good police can always catch kidnappers. The bad guys have to expose themselves by getting in contact with the family and getting money from them. And that allows you to trace them. If the success rate of kidnappings goes down radically, that makes it a much less profitable business.

"And unlike drug traffickers, there are not that many kidnappers. If you lock away a single gang of kidnappers, you can affect the amount of abductions; if you hit five gangs, you can make a real change."9

In Colombia, Gaviria went on, police aggressively went after abductors and drastically changed the situation. It went from the worst kidnapping rate in the world to being the ninth on the list (with Mexico being on top, followed by Iraq and India). Most of the kidnappings that still take place in Colombia are in war-wracked corners of countryside. Kidnappings for ransom in the capital, Bogotá, have been reduced to close to zero.

Mexico needs a similar hands-on strategy to fight kidnappings. Gaviria suggested a federal antikidnapping unit to handle every case. (In the current mess, some kidnappings in Mexico are handled by *federales* and others by state cops, whom victims fear going to in case they are part of the gang.) If a carefully watched federal unit achieved a high clearance rate, it would inspire others to trust in them rather than to pay ransoms. Once victims start consistently turning to police rather than paying the bounties, kidnapping ceases to be a growth industry.

Even if Mexico's police force is transformed, bad barrios are going to keep churning out killers. When teenagers are out of school, from broken homes, in violent gangs, with no jobs, harassed by soldiers, with no hopes for the future, and struggling even to get enough to eat, they will keep turning to the mafia. Every politician promises better job opportunities, and these are easier said than delivered. But ways exist to fix broken communities even with limited resources.

The Mexico City government instigated a scholarship program to stop kids from dropping out of high school. If they could keep up a certain grade average, they would get a token monthly allowance to help them get by. The program was wildly popular, with fifty thousand drawing from it. Mexico City authorities say this is one of the key reasons the capital has kept a violent crime rate akin to U.S. cities rather than falling to the devastating levels of Juárez or Culiacán. These fifty thousand poor kids are off the streets and not working as hawks, hustlers, or hit men. Why isn't such a program instituted across the whole of Mexico? Sometimes a little bit of investment in teenagers is cheaper than locking them up when they go down the wrong path. (It costs 125 pesos a day to hold a prisoner, but 23 pesos a day to keep a kid in school.)[10]

Sometimes all kids need is more attention. Sandra Ramirez is a social worker in Ciudad Juárez's westside slums, home to many cartel foot soldiers. She works in the Casa center, which offers guidance as well as art, music, and computer workshops and a place to hang out. On a baking-hot day, a few dozen kids are jumping around on skateboards and sitting in the shade strumming on guitars. Sandra, who grew up in the barrio and used to work in an assembly plant, labors hard with each kid to steer him or her away from a life of crime.

"One boy I am working with is fourteen years old and just studied in elementary school. His mother uses drugs and he doesn't live with her. He told me that a car came by with some guys he hadn't seen before. And they offered him five hundred pesos [$40] a week, a cell phone, and work. And all he had to do is to stand at a post and keep watch. And there are hundreds of cases like this in Juárez, hundreds. Nobody else has come to offer him anything. Nobody but them."

The young boy is on a knife edge, and Sandra and the Casa social center are all that is keeping him from falling. Another older teenager at the center shows off his art, a painting of his neighborhood in surreal form, the people blurred, immersed in fog. On one side is a sanguine depiction of mafia bosses, on the other a sadistic-looking soldier. The barrio kids are stuck in the middle. It is a grim image, but the artist says he got rid of a lot of stress painting it—and discovered a bright artistic talent. When people start finding something of worth in themsleves, they are pulled away from the street and crime.

Sandra and Casa have saved the lives of dozens of kids, but only a couple of centers like that exist, while miles more westside slums have nothing. The Casa center, which relies on donations from NGOs or the government, has actually lost funding during the very time the drug war has exploded and it is most needed. Perhaps more of the Mexican budget that gives politicians some of the highest salaries in the world—or even a tiny fraction of the $1.6 billion of the Mérida Initiative giving Mexico Black Hawks—could be used to fund centers in the slums. Social workers are better than soldiers at helping neglected teenagers.

In other countries, two mafia capitals have been regenerated by inspired leadership. One is Palermo, Sicily, home of the most famous mafia of all. The city was long notorious for cutthroats and thieves. However, when former university professor Leoluca Orlando saved two terms as mayor in the eighties and nineties, he oversaw a renaissance, restoring 150 endangered buildings, constructing parks, and lighting dark streets. Crucially, he instigated programs to engage citizens, including schoolchildren, to help maintain these assets and take pride in their community. These may not be traditional crime-fighting methods, but the crime rate went down drastically.[11]

Over the pond in Medellín, Colombia, long-haired mathematician Sergio Fajardo took over as mayor in 2004 and took the ideas of Orlando further. He poured city resources into building high-tech cable cars up the mountains into the Medellín slums (*comunas*) and hired world-famous architects to construct public buildings, including an eccentric-shaped library and the best music conservatory in the city. It made the middle class travel into the *comunas*, many for the first time. During his term in office, homicides went down drastically. Visiting Medellín, I asked Fajardo if such regeneration could possibly take place in a city as ugly as Juárez.

He replied swiftly, "It has to be done. We have no other options. The government has a responsibility to do it. I see it like a mathematical problem. How can you readdress the social inequalities? It is simple. The most beautiful buildings have to be in the poorest areas."

Critics point out that Fajardo was not the only reason for the decline in Medellín's murder rate. He also benefited from a strong mafia godfather, Diego Murillo, alias Don Berna, who kept assassins in check through his Office of Envigado. Anyone who wanted to kill had to get permission or be killed themselves. Even from prison, Don Berna could broker peace in his empire. But when he was extradited to the United States in 2008, the office broke into two and a turf war pushed Medellín's murder rate back up.

In 2010, civic leaders, including a well-known priest and a former guerrilla, went to meet with mafia leaders in a Medellín prison and brokered a new truce between them. It was a controversial move, talking to gangsters. But it seemed to have an immediate result in the lowering of deaths on the street. The civic leaders did not have the official backing of the government and did not offer the mafia anything in return. It was simply a plea: "For the good of the community, can you stop murdering each other in broad daylight?"

Calls for truces could also bring relief to Mexico's murder capitals. Asking for peace is not sanctioning organized crime, it is just appealing to gang leaders to stop killing. The United States uses such tactics in its penitentiaries, actively working with prison gangs to broker truces. Some gang leaders will listen to these pleas—they themselves do not want to see their own family murdered. You don't need to talk to the mafia godfathers in their palaces, but the low-level street-gang affiliates have an interest in their community. The bloody turf wars and sky-high murder rates do not help defeat the mafia; they just create an insecure atmosphere in which crime prevails.

Mexico also has a challenge to heal the wounds of the many who have lost family in the bloodshed. The increasing number of drug-war orphans need help or they will turn into an even more lost generation seeking bloody revenge. Other conflict-scarred countries have created national programs for victims. In some cases orphans or widows need financial help; but in many cases the need is psychological.

Families of victims help themselves now by sharing their pain. In Culiacán, a group of men and women meet to talk about the suffering from losing their loved ones. Many are mothers. They can never let go of burying their sons, but can at least feel that others suffer like them.

Alma Herrera, the mother whose son was shot in the car shop, takes me to meet a grieving friend one evening. We go to a park in the center of Culiacán, where old men rest their weary feet, children play by fountains, and young couples flirt on benches, sowing the seeds of their own marriages and families. The light in Sinaloa just before dusk looks beautiful, a rich, bright blue filling the streets.

Alma's friend is a forty-year-old woman called Guadalupe. She lost her eldest son, Juan Carlos, who was gunned down by police. She clutches a huge photo of him, a handsome twenty-three-year-old staring upright at the camera. The police had gone after somebody else in the neighborhood, she said, and Juan Carlos was shot down in the cross fire. She sobs hard, uncontrollably, as she tells the story. She gave birth to him when she was just seventeen, carried him in her womb, changed his nappies, watched his first steps, took him to school . . . and then kissed his corpse.

Guadalupe carries a three-month-old baby with her. The infant sleeps as she sobs and tells her story, then wakes up for milk, then sleeps again. I ask his name. "Juan Carlos," she says. It is the same name as that of her firstborn who was gunned down. This is a new son for the one that was lost. His mother has put hope in the fresh blood to grow up and make a better world than the one that killed his brother. We have to put our hope there too.

Acknowledgments

Foreign journalists wouldn't get one inch into covering the Mexican Drug War without the work and help of Mexican journalists and academics who labor day in and day out under incredibly difficult conditions. I am continually impressed by the professionalism and generosity of my Mexican colleagues. Thanks especially to those below. I also want to give special thanks to all the people who agreed to be interviewed for this book and told their own stories of crime, tragedy, and survival—often at a personal risk. As well as those mentioned in the text, dozens of other interviewees have helped shape the narrative. They include many agents from the ATF, DEA, FBI, PGR, federal police and Mexican army, members of Congress, lawyers and activists, as well as many gang members, smugglers, drug addicts, and a fair few drunks.

Mexico City: Diego Osorno, Alejandra Chombo, Daniel Hernández, Alejandro Almazán, Luis Astorga, José Reveles, John Dickie, Marcela Turati, Alfredo Corchado, Dudley Althaus, Guillermo Osorno, Gustavo Valcarcel, Mark Stevenson, Eduardo Castillo, Wendy Perez, Laurence Cuvilliert, Matthieu Comin, Jonathan Roeder, Jason Lange, José Cohen, José Antonio Crespo, Lorenzo Meyer, Federico Estevez, Ciro Gómez Leyva, Alejandro Sánchez, Alberto Najar. Enrique Marti, Jorge Barrera, Marco Ugarte, Olga Rodriguez, Louis Loizides.
Sinaloa: Fernando Brito and *El Debate de Sinaloa*, Fidel Duran, Javier Valdez (and the staff of El Guayabo), Ismael Bohorquez, Froylan Enciso, Vladimir Ramírez, Raul Quiroz, Barbara Obeso, Cruz Serrano, Emma Quiroz, Bobadilla, Arturo Vargas and everyone from *La Locha*, Elmer

Mendoza, Lizette Fernández, Francisco Cuamea, Manuel Insunza, Socorro Orozco, Mercedes Murillo.

The Rest of Mexico: Miguel Perea, Justino Mirando, Francisco Castellanos, Magdiel Hernández, José Maria Álvarez, Vicente Calderón, Victor Jaime, Victor Clark, Luis Perez, Martha Cazares, Miguel Turriza, Jorge Machuca, Jorge Charez.

Central and South America: Alfredo Rangel, Oliver Schmieg, John Otis, Wenceslau Rodriguez, Juan Carlos Llorca, Lourdes Honduras, Mery Carcamo, Kenya Torres, Noe Leiva, Karla Ramos, Gustavo Duncan, Otilia Lux.

The United States: Michael Marizco, Mike "Mad Dog" Kirsch, Elijah Wald, Chris Shively, Darlene Stinston, Dane Schiller, Jim Pinkerton, Tracey Eaton, Tim Padgett, Howard Chua, Tony Karon, Stephanie Garlow, Mark Scheffler, Tomás Mucha, Charles Sennot, Jorge Mujica, George Grayson, Rob Winder.

A big special thanks to agent Katherine Fausset and publisher Pete Beatty for believing in this book and making it happen. I wouldn't have got anywhere without them. Or without my parents. Or my wife, Myri, who has put up with my covering drug traffickers for the last decade. Thank you.

Books

The literature on Latin American trafficking is almost as jumbled as the drug trade itself. It includes breathtaking investigations, profound academic studies, accounts by American agents, scrawling by semiliterate gangsters and wonderful novels—which are often the safest way to tell the dark story. I have tried to read everything printed on Mexican gangsters, but it is hard to keep up with the flurry of books on El Narco that have come out of Mexico in recent years. One that stands out is *El Cártel de Sinaloa* by Diego Osorno, which among other things put the diaries of godfather Miguel Ángel Félix Gallardo into our hands. The books of José Reveles, Julio Scherer, Ricardo Reveles, Javier Valdez, and Marcela Turati have also been crucial to build up the complicated big picture.

The older work of Jesús Blancornelas's still shines, especially his landmark volume *El Cártel: Los Arellano Félix, la mafia más poderosa en la historia de America Latina*. Among Mexican academics, or narco-ologists, the undisputed champion remains Luis Astorga. I find his books *El Siglo de las Drogas* and *Drogas Sin Fronteras* especially useful. The wave of narco-fiction includes great novels by Élmer Mendoza and Alejandro Almazán, while the most famous is *La Reina del Sur* by Spaniard Arturo Pérez-Reverte.

Books in English on the Mexican drug trade have been more sporadic. *Desperados* by Elaine Shannon is a jewel for historic context, telling the tale of DEA agents in the 1980s, while Terrence Poppa's *Drug Lord* offers a compelling account of traffickers themselves in the period. Charles Bowden has authored a series of influential books on the issue, and *Down By The River* gave me great context on the Salinas era. Among American academics, John Bailey and George Grayson are some of the most renowned Mexican-ologists. I also found anthropologist Howard

Campbell's *Drug War Zone* very useful for its interviews with traffickers on the U.S. side of the border. For Mexico in general, *Distant Neighbors* by Alan Riding holds up after three decades. Andres Oppenheimer's *Bordering on Chaos* and Julia Preston and Samuel Dillion's *Opening Mexico* also helped me piece together the turbulent transition to democracy in the 1990s.

I found many books on organized crime in other countries helpful in deciphering Mexico. *McMafia* by Misha Glenny offers great insight into the Russian mafia and how organized crime has mushroomed globally since the end of the Cold War. Roberto Saviano's classic, *Gomorrah*, is useful in identifying criminal systems rather than just crime families. *Confesiones de un paraco* by José Gabriel Jaraba helped me understand the growth of Colombian paramilitaries and their parallels with Mexico. *Cocaine* by Dominic Streatfield gives a wonderfully written history of the drug itself. But one of the best crime journalists of all time writes on the New York mob. Nicolas Pileggi's classics, *Goodfellas* (originally called *Wiseguy*) and *Casino*, show that books on organized crime can be rigid with the facts and still read like novels.

Notes

Chapter 1: Ghosts

1. Comparison of FBI homicide statistics with Mexico City's PGJDF homicide statistics.

2. Report entitled *Joint Operating Environment 2008* by the Virginia-based United States Joint Forces Command.

3. The phrase *smoke and mirrors* to describe the drug war was most famously used in the classic by Dan Baum, *Smoke and Mirrors: The War on Drugs and the Politics of Failure* (New York: Little, Brown, 1996).

4. Database released in December 2010 by Mexico's Public Safety Department (Secretaria de Seguridad Publica) on deaths connected to organized crime.

5. Mexico's 2010 census counted 112,332,757 residents.

6. Count of police deaths was first given by Public Safety Secretary Genaro García Luna on August 7, 2010, and updated in December 2010.

7. The International Monetary Fund in 2010 counted Mexico's GDP at $1.004 trillion, the fourteenth-biggest economy in the world.

8. Forbes list of the world's billionaires (2010).

Chapter 2: Poppies

1. The crossroads described is in the village of Santiago de los Cabelleros, municipality Badiraguato, Sinaloa.

2. The family home of Joaquin Guzmán is in the village of La Tuna, municipality Badiraguato, Sinaloa.

3. My Sinaloan history was helped by the work of Sergio Ortega, *Breve Historia de Sinaloa* (Mexico City: Fondo de Cultura Economica, 1999).

4. The Treaty of Guadalupe was signed on February 2, 1848, in Guadalupe Hidalgo, Mexico. The new territory boundaries are described in Article 5, beginning, "The boundary line between the two Republics shall commence in the Gulf of Mexico, three leagues from land . . ."

5. The first detailed study on opium receptors was published in March 1973 by Candace Pert and Solomon H. Snyder.

6. David Stuart, *Dangerous Garden: The Quest for Plants to Change Our Lives* (London: Frances Lincoln Limited, 2004), 82.

7. Lo-shu Fu, *A Documentary Chronicle of Sino-Western Relations* (Tucson: Association for Asian Studies by the University of Arizona Press, 1966), 1:380.

8. The reference was in the government study *Geografía y Estadistica de la Republica Mexicana*, cited by Luis Astorga, *El Siglo de Las Drogas: El narcotráfico, del Porfiriato al nuevo milenio* (Mexico City: Plaza & Janés, 2005), 18.

9. The photograph described is of an opium den in Malinta Street, Manila, Philippines, and can be found in the Library of Congress, Washington, DC, Prints and Photographs, LC-USZ62-103376.

10. Edward Marshall, "Uncle Sam Is the Worst Drug Fiend in the World," *New York Times*, March 12, 1911.

11. Edward Huntington Williams, "Negro Cocaine 'Fiends' New Southern Menace," *New York Times*, February 8, 1914.

12. Document was sent by F. E. Johnson, Agent in Charge, September 16, 1916, cited by Luis Astorga, *Drogas sin Fronteras: Los Expedientes de una guerra permanente* (Mexico City: Grijalbo, 2003), 17.

13. Report filed by G. S. Quate, Deputy Collector of Department of Treasury, January 15, 1918, cited by Astorga, *Drogas sin Fronteras*, 20.

14. "Customs Agents in Gun Battle With Runners," *El Paso Times*, June 16, 1924.

15. Manuel Lazcano, *Vida en la Vida Sinalense*, ed. Nery Cordova (Culiacán, Mexico: self-published, 1992), 38–39.

16. Ibid., 40.

17. "Todavia No Han Logrado Aprehender a 'La Nacha,'" *El Continental*, August 22, 1933.

18. Vargas Llosa said the oft-quoted phrase in 1990 during a debate with Mexican writer Octavio Paz organized by *Vuelta* magazine.

19. Journalist Alan Riding writes a chapter on this metaphor in his classic work *Distant Neighbors: A Portrait of the Mexicans* (New York: Knopf, 1985).

20. Lazcano, *Vida*, 207.

21. Ibid., 202.

22. The letter from Anslinger to journalist Howard Lewis is cited in Astorga, *Drogas sin Fronteras*, 138–39.

23. Lazcano, *Vida*, 207.

Chapter 3: Hippies

1. The marijuana smoking of Diego Rivera and other Mexican artists is described in the work of muralist David Alfaro Siquieros, *Me llamaban el Cornelazo* (Mexico City: Biografías Gandesa, 1977).

2. Details of the Coronado Company case can be found in the court document, *The United States vs. Donald Eddie Moody*, 778 F.2d 1380, September 4, 1985.

3. Elaine Shannon, *Desperadoes: Latin Drug Lords, U.S. Lawmen and the War American Can't Win* (New York: Viking, 1988), 33.

4. Oval Office Tape, May 13, 1971, between 10:32 A.M. and 12:20 P.M.

5. G. Gordon Liddy, *Will: The Autobiography of G. Gordon Liddy* (New York: St Martin's Press, 1980), 134.

6. Richard Nixon speech, September 18, 1972.

7. Richard Nixon, Executive Order 11727—Drug Law Enforcement, July 6, 1973.

8. One of the first comprehensive reports of the Sicilia Falcon case was in a German article, "Die gefährlichen Geschäfte des Alberto Sicilia," *Der Spiegel*, May 9, 1977). The case is also elaborated in detail through the work of James Mills, *Underground Empire* (New York: Dell Publishing Company, 1985).

9. The jailhouse book of Sicilia Falcon was entitled *El Túnel de Lecumberri* (Mexico City: Compañia General de Ediciones, circa 1977).

10. José Egozi is registered in Cuban Information Archives as a participant in the Bay of Pigs invasion. His code number was R-537. R-710.

11. Luis Astorga, *El Siglo de las Drogas* (Mexico City: Plaza & Janés, 2005), 115.

12. Shannon, *Desperadoes*, 63.

13. Fabio Castillo, *Los Jinetes de la Cocaina* (Bogotá: Editorial Documentos Periodisticos, 1987), 18–21.

14. CIA Declassified Docs, *Mexico: Increases in Military Antinarcotics Units* (declassified October 1997).

15. A vivid account of the plaza system in the 1970s is offered in Terrence Poppa, *Drug Lord: The Life and Death of a Mexican Kingpin* (New York: Pharos Books, 1990).

Chapter 4: Cartels

1. The phrase *banana republic* was coined in the 1904 book *Cabbages and Kings* by American writer O. Henry.

2. The early cocaine trade is well documented by the utmost authority on the issue, Paul Gootenberg, in *Andean Cocaine: The Making of a Global Drug* (Chapel Hill: University of North Carolina Press, 2003).

3. Interview of George Jung from prison with PBS *Frontline* (2000).

4. Pablo Escobar dressed up as Pancho Villa in an iconic photo, in which he wears a Mexican sombrero and ammunition belts. The photo is reprinted in James Mollison, *The Memory of Pablo Escobar* (New York: Chris Boot, 2009).

5. Documents from U.S. 9th Circuit Court of Appeals, *U.S.A. vs. Matta Ballesteros*, No. 91-50336.

6. Billy Corben, *Cocaine Cowboys* (Miami: Rakontur, 2006).

7. Michael Demarest, "Cocaine: Middle Class High," *Time*, July 6, 1981.

8. Official homicide statistics from Miami-Dade Police Department.

9. Photos of Félix Gallardo were published by his son on the Web site http://www.miguelfelixgallardo.com until the site was supended.

10. The infamous marijuana farm was on the El Bufalo ranch, near Jiménez and Camargo, Chihuahua, raided in November 1984.

11. Documents from U.S. 9th Circuit Court of Appeals, *U.S.A. vs. Matta Ballesteros*, 91-50165 (argued and submitted January 4, 1993).

12. The prison diary was passed by Félix Gallardo to his son and published in Diego Osorno, *El Cartel de Sinaloa* (Mexico City: Grijalbo, 2009), 207–57.

13. The seizure was in Yucca, Arizona, on November 27, 1984.

14. *U.S.A. vs. Matta Ballesteros*, No. 91-50336.

15. This incident is retold in Elaine Shannon, *Desperadoes* (New York: Viking, 1988), 213–14.

16. The Ronald Reagan speech was broadcast live on September 14, 1986.

17. The full version of the *Dark Alliance* series, along with dozens of files of audio and documentary evidence, has been rehosted on the Web site http://www.narconews.com/darkalliance/drugs/start.htm.

18. The *Senate Committee Report on Drugs, Law Enforcement and Foreign Policy* is also known as the Kerry Report, as Senator John F. Kerry chaired the committee that prepared it.

19. *CIA Report on Cocaine and the Contras*, paragraph 35. The report was released in 1998, during the attempted impeachment of Bill Clinton, burying the news that some basic truths of *Dark Alliance* were conceded.

20. The violence was reported in detail in B. Esteruelas, "Cinco muertos en una manifestación frente a la embajada norteamericana en Honduras," *El Pais*, February 23, 1988.

Chapter 5: Tycoons

1. All the ballad lyrics quoted throughout the book are my own translations. If I don't do the poetry justice—sorry!

2. Jesús Blancornelas, "Death of a Journalist," *El Andar* (Fall 1999).

3. Official figures from the Office of the United States Trade Representative.

4. Diego Osorno, *El Cartel de Sinaloa* (Mexico City: Grijalbo, 2009), 184–85.

5. Jesús Blancornelas, *El Cartel: Los Arellano Félix, la mafia mas poderosa en la historia de America Latina* (Mexico City: Plaza & Janés, 2002), 46.

6. Ibid., 48.

7. Report entitled *Amado Carrillo-Fuentes*, from Operational Intelligence Unit of El Paso Intelligence Center, marked "DEA Sensitive."

8. The hunt for Pablo Escobar is related in great detail in Mark Bowden, *Killing Pablo: The Hunt for the World's Greatest Outlaw* (New York: Penguin, 2001).

9. The Swiss Police investigation was headed by Valentin Roschacher and the report compiled in 1998. It is detailed in Tim Golden, "Questions Arise About Swiss Report on Raúl Salinas's Millions," *New York Times*, October 12, 1998.

10. Tim Padgett and Elaine Shannon, "La Nueva Frontera: The Border Monsters," *Time*, June 11, 2001.

11. Blancornelas, *El Cartel*, 237.

12. Ibid., 243–44.

13. Ibid., 284.

14. Jesús Blancornelas in interview with Guillermo López Portillo for Televisa in 2006.

Chapter 6: Democrats

1. Fox made the notorious comment at a news conference in Puerto Vallarta, May 13, 2005.

2. I counducted the interview with Vicente Fox in San Francisco del Rincón, November 25, 2010.

3. The quote was from ABC's *Nightline*, July 3, 2000, transcribed from the original recording courtesy of ABC's Mexico City bureau.

4. José Reveles, *El Cartel Incómodo: El Fin de los Beltrán Leyva y la Hegemonía del Chapo Guzmán* (Mexico City: Random House Mandadori, 2010), 57–71.

5. A series of love letters from Joaquin "Chapo Guzmán" were published to much fanfare in Julio Scherer Garcia, *Maxima Seguridad: Almoloya y Puente Grande* (Mexico City: Nuevo Siglo Aguilar, 2001), 21–28.

6. This anecdote is also discussed in Diego Osorno, *El Cartel de Sinaloa* (Mexico City: Grijalbo, 2009), 193.

7. Many articles exploring links between the federal government and Sinaloa Cartel have been published in Mexico's bestselling newsmagazine, *Proceso*, among other places.

8. Juan Nepomuceno, also known as the Padrino de Matamoros, was a huge figure for more than half a century. In old age, he gave an interview with Sam Dillon, "Matamoros Journal; Canaries Sing in Mexico, but Uncle Juan Will Not," *New York Times*, February 9, 1996.

9. The quote is from the manual *Handling Sources*, of the U.S. army, which has been redistributed by School of Americas Watch NGO.

10. Details of these attacks are included in the Zapatista (EZLN) communiqué entitled *Sobre el PFCRN, La Ofensiva Militar del Gobierno, los actos terroristas y el nombramiento de Cammacho* (January 11, 1994).

11. The text of the conversation was released by an agent in the Agencia Federal de Investigación (AFI).

12. The DEA agent was Joe DuBois and FBI agent was Daniel Fuentes.

13. The meeting was first reported by Mexican journalist Alberto Najar, who obtained an intelligence document from the PGR. It was later supported by testimonies of protected witnesses handled by federal agents.

14. The described mass killing took place in Nuevo Laredo, October 8, 2004.

15. Sources have quoted different towns as the birthplace of Lazcano, but evidence points to Hidalgo towns near the state border with Veracruz, where he has sponsored at least two churches.

16. The killing of Nuevo Laredo police chief Alejandro Dominguez took place on June 8, 2005.

17. Bradley Roland Will, aged thirty-six, was shot dead on October 27, 2006, in Oaxaca city. At least two other people were killed in gun battles in Oaxaca city on the same day.

18. Fox made the comments on his blog, August 9, 2010.

Chapter 7: Warlords

1. Felipe Calderón, *El Hijo Disobediente: Notas en Campana* (Mexico City: Aguilar, 2006), 16.

2. First presidential debate, April 25, 2006.

3. I covered this for the AP agency in stories such as Ioan Grillo, "Thousands of Mexican troops ordered to arrest smugglers, burn marijuana and opium fields," Associated Press, December 12, 2006.

4. Felipe Calderón made the comments at a Defense Department installation in Mexico City, February 10, 2007.

5. The initial Mérida Initiative agreement was for $1.6 billion over the fiscal years 2008 to 2010. The aid has continued beyond, with President Obama requesting $334 million in funding in Mexico in 2011.

6. Mexico's federal security budget approved for 2011 included $4.7 billion for the Defense Department (Sedena), $1.46 billion for the navy and marines (Semar), $2.8 billion for the Public Security Department (SSP), and $5.76 billion for the Federal Attorney General's Office (PGR)—a total of $14.72 billion.

7. Édgar Valdéz's statement was taken and filmed by agents from the Public Safety Department (SSP) and released to the press.

8. One metric ton of cocaine is one thousand kilo bricks, or 1 million gram wraps.

9. The narco message was displayed on blankets in several cities across Mexico on February 12, 2010.

10. Paquiro, "Breve Tumba-Burros Culichi Inglés para Corresponsales (de Guerra)," *La Locha*, September 2008.

11. Arturo Beltrán Leyva was killed on December 16, 2009. Information about the shooting is detailed in a classified State Department memo, later released by WikiLeaks, entitled "Mexico Navy Operation Nets Drug Kingpin Arturo Beltrán Leyva" (created December 17, 2009).

12. The Mexican government's own homicide count compared to census figures found a murder rate in Ciudad Juárez of 191 per 100,000 residents in 2009, rising to 229 per 100,000 in 2010. According to FBI statistics, New Orleans was the most violent U.S. city in 2009 with 52 homicides per 100,000 residents.

13. This estimate of ten thousand Zeta members was given by a member of CISEN, Mexico's spy agency, in a meeting with foreign journalists in 2010.

14. Mexico's National Human Rights Commission, or Comisión Nacional de los Derechos Humanos, reported at a news conference in Mexico City,

November 22, 2010, it had more than a hundred files on civilians killed by police and soldiers.

15. Undersecretary of the Army Joseph Westphal made the comments at the University of Utah's Hinckley Institute of Politics, February 8, 2011.

Chapter 8: Traffic

1. The seizure statistics were provided by the Department of Homeland Security, which incorporates both the Border Patrol and Ports of Entry.

2. From the 2010 *World Drug Report* published by the United Nations Office on Drugs and Crime.

3. Border Patrol agents discovered the twenty-four-hundred-foot tunnel in Otay Mesa in January 2006. It remains the longest such tunnel discovered to date.

4. The survey is entitled "National Survey on Drug Use & Health."

5. The surveys, entitled "What America's Users Spend on Illegal Drugs, 1988–2000," were prepared for the Office of National Drug Control Policy (drug czar's office) by private consultants.

6. Petróleos Mexicanos (Pemex) Annual Report 2009.

7. Bank of Mexico figures based on electronic and bank transfers of small amounts.

8. Public Safety Secretary Genaro García Luna made the statement during a speech to the National Governors Conference in Puerto Vallarta, August 7, 2010.

9. Jason Lange, "From Spas to Banks, Mexico's Economy Rides on Drugs," Reuters, January 22, 2010.

10. The blacklist is entitled "List of Specially Designated Nationals and Blocked Persons" and is released by the Office of Foreign Assets Control of the Department of the Treasury.

11. Written in *World Drug Report 2009*, by the United Nations Office on Drugs and Crime.

12. The interview was given to AP in New York in May 2007 and finally released in July 2007 after the AP attempted to corroborate sensitive information. The delay triggered conspiracy theories in the Mexican media.

Chapter 9: Murder

1. A detailed chapter on El Gitano is in Diego Osorno, *El Cartel de Sinaloa* (Mexico City: Grijalbo, 2009), 95–109.

2. José González, *El Negro del Negro Durazo: La biografia criminal de Durazo, escrita por su Jefe de Ayudantes* (Mexico City: Editorial Posada, 1983), 22.

3. Tabio Castillo, *Los Jinetes de la Cocaina* (Bogotá: Editorial Documents Periodisticos, 1987), 11.

4. Homicide statistics by Colombia's National Institute of Legal Medicine and Forensic Science.

5. Police shot dead Pablo Escobar in Medellín on December 2, 1993.

6. The Colombian youth unemployment figure of 22 percent—about double the overall unemployment rate—was from March 2010, when I conducted the interview.

7. The song "Oficio Pistolero" is by *norteño* band Grupo Cartel.

8. The scandal of prisoners going out to commit murders was broken on July 25, 2010, causing a political firestorm.

9. Mexico's 2010 census counted 1,328,000 residents in the municipal boundaries of Ciudad Juárez.

10. From the government-funded study *Todos Somos Juárez, Reconstruyamos La Ciudad* (Ciudad Juárez: Colegio de la Frontera Norte, March 2010), 4.

11. The maxium sentences for minors vary according to Mexican states and ages, with nowhere allowing more than five years. In Morelos state, those under sixteen can only be sentenced to three years, a fact that gained public attention following the December 2010 arrest of fourteen-year-old alleged killer Edgar Jimenez, alias El Ponchis.

Chapter 10: Culture

1. From the first recorded Robin Hood rhyme in the fifteenth century.

2. Édgar "the Barbie" Valdéz's statement was taken and filmed by agents from the Public Security Department (SSP) and released to the press.

3. Vicente T. Mendoza, *El Romance Español y El Corrido Méxicano: Estudio Comparativo* (Mexico City: Universidad Nacional Autónoma de México, 1939), 219.

4. Américo Paredes, *With His Pistol in His Hand* (University of Texas Press, 1958), 3.

5. Sam Quinones, *True Tales from Another Mexico: The Lynch Mob, the Popsicle Kings, Chalino and the Bronx* (Albuquerque: University of New Mexico Press, 2001).

6. The murder of Valentín Elizalde took place in Reynosa on November 25, 2006.

7. The tomb of Valentín Elizalde is in the Sinaloan town of Guasave.

Chapter 11: Faith

1. Cardinal Norberto Rivera of Mexico City wrote one statement conceding and condemning the widespread use of narco alms in the parish newspaper *Desde la Fe*, October 31, 2010.

2. The words are from the song "Corrido a Malverde" by Julio Chaidez.

3. Before the Spanish conquest of 1521, Mexico City was known as Tenochtitlán and included the modern-day historic center, with Tepito and other neighborhoods on the outskirts.

4. Actress and dancer Niurka Marcos, originally from Cuba, married actor Bobby Larios in a ceremony headed by David Romo in February 2004.

5. Romo's church was registed with the Interior Ministry (Gobernación) as Iglesia Católica Tradicional México-EEUU. Gobernación annulled the registration in April 2007.

6. The life and death of Jonathan Legaria is also told in detail in Humberto Padgett, "Vida, Obra y Fin de Padrino Endoque, el ahijado de la Santa Muerte," *Emeequis*, September 1, 2008.

7. The corpses were found in the state of Yucatán, August 28, 2008. The three alleged perpertrators of the killings were arrested in nearby Cancún, September 2, 2008.

8. Mictecacihuatl is also known as Catrina and is represented by a skull figure, similar to La Santa Muerte.

9. The gangsters carried out the notorious atrocity in the town of Uruapan, September 6, 2006.

10. John Eldredge, *Wild at Heart: Discovering the Secret of a Man's Soul* (Nashville: Thomas Nelson, 2001).

11. Armando Valencia Cornello, alleged to be a powerful kingpin in Michoacán, was arrested on August 15, 2003.

12. Published in *La Voz de Michoacán*, November 22, 2006.

13. Servando Gómez, alias La Tuta, phoned up host Marcos Knapp live on the program *Voz y Solución*, July 15, 2009.

14. Nazario Moreno was allegedly shot dead in Apatzingán on December 9, 2010. He was forty years old.

Chapter 12: Insurgency

1. *Breaking Bad*, produced by Vince Gilligan, Series 2, Episode 7, April 19, 2009.

2. Alejandro Almazán, *Entre Perros* (Mexico City: Grijalbo Mandadori, 2009).

3. John P. Sullivan and Adam Elkus, "Cartel v. Cartel: Mexico's Criminal Insurgency," *Small Wars Journal*, January 26, 2010.

4. Report entitled *Joint Operating Environment 2008* by the Virginia-based United States Joint Forces Command.

5. Clinton made the comments at the Council on Foreign Relations in Washington, September 8, 2010.

6. *Merriam-Webster's Collegiate Dictionary*, 11th ed., 2003.

7. Statement by Mexico's Foreign Relations Department, February 9, 2011.

8. Eric Hobsbawm, *Primitive Rebels: Studies in Archaic Forms of Social Movement in the 19th and 20th Centuries* (Manchester: Manchester University Press, 1959).

9. Stephen Metz, "The Future of Insurgency," *Strategic Studies Institute*, December 10, 1993.

10. The interrogation of Marco Vinicio Cobo was undertaken by military intelligence following his arrest on April 3, 2008, in Salina Cruz, Oaxaca.

11. Servando Gómez, alias La Tuta, phoned up host Marcos Knapp live on the program *Voz y Solución*, July 15, 2009.

12. Gunmen killed PRI candidate Rodolfo Torre on June 28, 2010. His brother took over his candidacy and was elected governor of Tamaulipas.

13. Front-page editorial in *El Diario de Juárez*, September 19, 2010.

14. The interrogation of Miguel Ortiz was conducted by members of the Secretaria de Seguridad Pública, Mexico's Public Saftey Department.

15. The attack on Minerva Bautista took place on the outskirts of Morelia, April 24, 2010.

16. The training video of alleged members of La Resistencia was released in February 2011.

17. Numbers released by Mexico's Defense Department (Sedena).

18. Report entitled *Combating Arms Trafficking* released by the U.S. embassy in Mexico City, May 2010.

19. The bust took place in Laredo, Texas, May 29, 2010.

20. Nick Miroff and William Booth, "Mexican drug cartels' newest weapon: Cold War–era grenades made in U.S.," *Washington Post*, July 17, 2010.

21. Marines shot dead Ezequiel Cárdenas in Matamoros on November 5, 2010.

22. From report entitled *Advisory: Explosives Theft by Armed Subjects* released by United States Bomb Data Center, February 16, 2009.

23. The confession of Noe Fuentes was released by the Public Safety Department following his arrest in Juárez on August 13, 2010.

24. The corpses were found in the state of Yucatán, August 28, 2008.

Chapter 13: Prosecution

1. The first scandal broke in 2005, with reporting led by Alfredo Corchado in the *Dallas Morning News*. The second scandal broke in 2009 and was reported by various news organizations.

2. Andrés López, *El Cartel de los Sapos* (Bogotá: Planeta, 2008).

3. Details of Cárdenas's case were revealed in a series of stories published by Dane Schiller in the *Houston Chronicle* in 2010.

4. Richard Nixon speech, September 18, 1972.

Chapter 14: Expansion

1. From *FBI Uniform Crime Reports*, 2004–10.

2. Figure provided by the Phoenix Police Department.

3. Ibid.

4. Ibid.

5. National Drug Intelligence Center, *Cities in Which Mexican DTO's Operate Within the United States*, April 11, 2008, updated in *National Drug Threat Assement 2009*, January 2009.

6. Indictment from U.S. District Court, Northern District of Illinois, Eastern Division, *United States of America v. Arturo Beltrán Leyva*.

7. From excellent documentary *Blood River: Barrio Azteca*, Series 5, Episode 4, History Channel's Gangland series, released June 18, 2009.

8. The attacks on the consulate officials took place in Ciudad Juárez, March 13, 2010.

9. Revealed in court case and reiterated in appeal documents entited *Rosalio Reta v. State of Texas*, from the 49th Judical District Court, Texas, filed March 3, 2010.

10. From report entitled *Precursors and chemicals frequently used in the*

illicit manufacture of narcotic drugs and psychotropic substances, by the International Narcotics Control Board, February 19, 2009.

11. General Julian Aristides Gonzalez was shot dead in Tegucigalpa on December 8, 2009.

12. The funeral took place in in Tegucigalpa on December 9, 2009.

Chapter 15: Diversification

1. Six million pesos was worth approximately $500,000 in 2011.

2. Study released by Mexico's lower chamber of Congress (Cámara de Diputados) based on official figures, September 7, 2010.

3. The heads of Juárez's Chamber of Commerce and Assemby Plant Association publicly called for UN intervention in November 2009. UN officials said they would need direct pleas from Mexico's federal government.

4. Daniel Arizmendi was arrested in Naucalpan, Mexico State, on August 17, 1998. He is serving a maximum fifty-year sentence.

5. Vicente Fernández later said that he offered to transplant his own fingers to his son, but a doctor advised against it.

6. Rosario Mosso Castro, "Secuestradores Vienen de Sinaloa," *Zeta* (2007 edition 1721).

7. Comisión Nacional de Derechos Humanos, *Informe especial sobre los casos de secuestro contra migrantes*, June 15, 2009.

8. Amnesty International, *Mexico: Invisible Victims. Migrants on the Move in Mexico*, April 28, 2010.

9. The survivor made contact with the marines on August 23, 2010. The massacre is believed to have taken place on August 21 or August 22.

10. From government study *Encuesta Nacional de Ocupación y Empleo Instituto Nacional*, released by Instituto Nacional de Estadística y Geografía (Inegi), August 13, 2010.

11. Diego Gambetta, *The Sicilian Mafia: The Business of Private Protection* (Cambridge: Harvard University Press, 1993).

12. Estimates provided by Pemex.

13. Pemex yearly report for 2010, March 1, 2011.

Chapter 16: Peace

1. Zedillo, Gaviria, and Cardoso put their arguments in a document entitled *Drogas y democracia: Hacia un cambio de paradigma*, February 11, 2009.

2. Estimate from a paper by Harvard professor Jeffery Miron and New York University's Katherine Waldock, *The Budgetary Impact of Ending Drug Prohibition* (Cato Institute, 2010).

3. The treaties include the United Nations Convention Against Illicit Traffic in Narcotic Drugs and Psychotropic Substances of 1988, the Convention on Psychotropic Substances of 1971, and the Single Convention on Narcotic Drugs of 1961.

4. Mexico's law decriminalizing possession of small quantities of narcotics was enacted on August 20, 2009.

5. Rand Corporation, *Legalizing Marijuana in California Will Not Dramatically Reduce Mexican Drug Trafficking Revenues*, October 12, 2010.

6. The marijuana was seized on October 18, 2010. The recovering addicts were shot dead on October 24.

7. Classified State Department memo, later released by WikiLeaks, "Mexico Navy Operation Nets Drug Kingpin Arturo Beltrán Leyva" (created December 17, 2009).

8. Classified State Department memo, later released by WikiLeaks, "Scene-setter for the Opening of the Defense Bilateral Working Group" (created January 29, 2010).

9. Interview I conducted with Gaviria in Mexico City on February 22, 2010.

10. Figure was given to reporters by Mexico City education secretary Mario Delgado on December 6, 2010.

11. Leoluca Orlando was mayor of Palermo from 1985 to 1990 and 1993 to 2000.

Index

abductions. *See* kidnappings
Ábrego, Juan Garcia, 87
Absolut ad, 22
Acapulco, 41–42, 106, 112
Acapulco Gold, 41–42
addiction, 9, 25, 281
Afghanistan, 39, 70
Africa, 255–56
African Americans, 27–28
Aguilar, Carlos, 52
Airmobile Special Forces Group (GAFE), 96
AK-47s, 53–54, 215
alcohol prohibition, 31–32, 95
Almada, Mario, 172
Almazán, Alejandro, 203
Althaus, Dudley, 100
American Civil War, 11
Among Dogs (Almazán), 203
Annan, Kofi, 10, 241
Anslinger, Harry, 36, 43–44
anticrime movement, 262–65
Anti Drug Abuse Act, 68
anti-insurgency tactics, 96, 205, 285
antikidnapping activists, 262–65
AR-15 assault rifles, 215
Arellano Félix, Benjamin, 80–81, 88, 94
Arellano Félix, Francisco, 81
Arellano Félix, Ramón, 80–81, 86–88, 94
Arellano Félix brothers, 75, 79–81, 86–88, 93, 95, 117
Argentina, 282
Arizmendi, Daniel (Ear Lopper), 4, 264
Arizona, 22
    crime in, 244
    gun shops in, 216–17
    Phoenix, 243, 245–47
arrests, 115. *See also* prosecutions
Artist Assassins, 2, 166–67

assassinations. *See also* murders
    in drug war, 121–23, 126–27
    in mid-twentieth century, 154–55
    of officials, 103–04, 212
assassins
    gatilleros, 154–55
    sicarios, 155–68
    training camps for, 212–13
    in U.S., 254–55
assault rifles, 215–16
asset seizures, 238
Astorga, Luis, 13, 30
ATF. *See* Bureau of Alcohol, Tobacco, and Firearms (ATF)
Austin, Texas, 243
Australia, 255
Avilés, Pedro, 50
Azerbaijan, 255
Aztecs, 20–21, 40

balloon effect, 50
banana republic, 57, 256
Banda Guasaveña, 170, 182–83
Banda music, 182–83
Barrio 18 gang, 257
Barrio Azteca, 2, 166–67, 251–53, 271
barrios, 164–66, 288
Barron, David, 87
Bautista, Efrain, 39–42, 53–54, 105, 173
Bautista, Minerva, 212
Bay of Pigs, 47
Beatles, 38
Bejar, José Egozi, 47
Beltrán Leyva, Arturo (the Beard), 37, 100, 106, 118, 249
    death of, 19, 126–27
    tomb of, 186
    turf wars and, 116–17, 121–23

Bergman, Jay, 63–64, 81–83, 138, 238
Bias, Len, 68
black market, 269–70
black tar, 45
Blanco, Griselda, 62–63
Blancornelas, Jesús, 13, 74–76, 78, 80–81, 86–88
Blog del Narco, 220
Blow (film), 42
Bonanza Marimbera, 49–50
bootleggers, 31–32, 95
border crossings, 142–43
border seizures, 137
border towns, 29, 31, 142
born-again Christians, 2–3
Boys Town, 101
Boyz N the Hood (film), 56
Brazil, 5
Breaking Bad (TV series), 202–03
bribes, 84, 97–98, 272
buchones, 8, 180
Bureau of Alcohol, Tobacco, and Firearms (ATF), 214–17
burros, 139–43
Bush, George, 63, 109–10
Bush, George W., 114, 215

caciques, 35
Cahita, 20
Calderón, Felipe, 6–7, 10, 93, 94, 107, 108, 282
    background of, 111–12
    election of, 112
    Fox compared with, 110
    Mexican Drug War and, 109–30, 149, 222
    physical appearance of, 112
    presidency of, 109–30
    swearing in of, 109–10
Calderón, Luis, 110
Calderoni, Guillermo González, 77–78
California, 276, 282–84
Calles, Plutarco Elias, 34
Camarena, Enrique "Kiki," 56, 66–68, 72
Cancún, 6, 11
cannabis. *See* marijuana
Cantú, Esteban, 30–31
capitalism, 10, 77, 81, 243
Capone, Al, 31, 271
capos. *See also specific names*
    extraditions of, 113, 237
    motivations of, 206–08
    plea bargains with, 237–38
    prosecution of, 226

spending by, 83–84, 173
summits by, 78
car bombs, 217–19
Cárdenas, Cuauhtémoc, 76–77
Cárdenas, Ezequiel, 217
Cárdenas, Lázaro, 35, 76
Cárdenas, Osiel, 94, 95, 97–100, 113, 237
Cardoso, Fernando, 277
Carillo Fuentes, Vicente, 117
Caro Quintero, Rafael, 64, 67
Carrillo Fuentes, Amado, 79, 87
cartels. *See* drug cartels
cartel warfare, 10, 94, 98–99, 104–06, 206–07
Carter, Jimmy, 50, 51, 63, 276
Casa social center, 288–89
cash, movement of, 147–48
Castro, Fausto "Tano," 169–70
Castro, Fidel, 47
casualties. *See also* murders
    civilian, 123–26, 129, 161, 218, 219
    in Mexican Drug War, 10–11
Catholic Church, 110, 187–88, 190, 193, 195
Central America. *See also specific countries*
    Cold War and, 68–70
Central American migrants, kidnapping of, 266–69
Central Intelligence Agency (CIA), 47–48, 51, 58, 68–70
Chávez, Hugo, 257
Chiapas, 10, 127–28
Chicago, 248–50
Chihuahua, 51, 174
Chile, 58
China, 25, 208, 255
Chinese immigrants, 25–26, 28–30, 32–33
Christians, born-again, in prison, 2–3
cinema, 172–73
Ciudad Juárez, 2, 4, 33, 95, 127, 163–64, 202–03, 252–53, 274–75
civilians, killed in drug war, 123–26, 129, 161, 218, 219
civil war, 29, 117, 209, 273
Clinton, Bill, 77, 85, 215
Clinton, Hillary, 7, 129, 204
Cobo, Marco Vinicio, 207
cocaine, 8–9, 280
    busts, 115
    cartels, 56–63
    CIA and trafficking of, 68–70
    confiscated, 134–35
    effects of, 59
    price of, 59–60, 83
    processing of, 137–38
    profits from, 59–60, 65, 137–39

taste of, 135
trafficking in, 56–60, 62–68, 82–83, 256–57
use of, 27–28, 59, 145–46
U.S. market for, 58–60
Cocaine Cowboys (film), 62
codeine, 24
Coffield Prison, 251
Coke, Christopher "Dudus," 5
Cold War, 68–70, 82
Colombia, 4, 7, 20, 39
assassins from, 156–61
cocaine trafficking in, 58–60, 62–68, 138
drug cartels in, 61–63, 81–83
law enforcement in, 234–36, 287
marijuana cultivation in, 49–50
Mexico compared with, 204–05, 209
U.S. aid to, 114–15
violence in, 56
Colombian Civil War, 209
commercial insurgencies, 206
communism, 51, 68
communist guerrillas, 5, 9, 68
contra rebels, 58, 68–71, 256
Coronado Company, 42
Coronel, Ignacio "Nacho," 186
corporations, 81
corridos, 173–85
corridos enfermos, 179
corruption, 34, 35, 52–53, 84, 104, 118, 239–40
Cortés, Hernán, 21
counter-cultural revolution, 44
counterinsurgency campaigns, 205, 285
coups, 57, 256
crack, 56, 68, 69, 276–77
crime
drugs and, 44
in Mexico, 85, 86
in U.S., 243–44
criminal insurgency, 116–17, 202–22
criminals
former policemen turned, 4
vs. insurgents, 11
uprisings by, 5
Cristero War, 110
crops, destruction of, 19
crop spraying, 49
cross-border culture, 242, 252
cross-border trade, 77
crystal meth, 20, 150, 255
Cuba, 47, 58, 208
Cuban immigrants, 62
Cuidad Juárez, 29, 117
Culiacán, 20, 49–50, 117, 119–26, 133–35, 274
culture, 8, 169–85

Dallas, 95
Dante, Sergio, 13
Dark Alliance (Webb), 69
DEA agents
training of Mexican counterparts by, 234
undercover, 225–34
use of informants by, 230–31
deal making, 236–38
decapitations, 4, 106, 112
decriminalization, of narcotics, 281–84
Delgado, Americo, 13
Democratic Revolution Party, 107
democratic transition, in Mexico, 10, 89–92, 97–98
Desperados (Shannon), 66
Díaz, Porfirio, 22–23, 29, 35, 189, 190
disappeared, the, 51, 97–98
Dominguez, Alejandro, 13, 103
Dorados (Golden Ones), 154
drug ballads, 173–85
drug busts, 225–40
drug cartels, 55–72. *See also* drug smugglers;
El Narco
cocaine, 56–63
Colombian, 43, 57–63, 81–83
concept of, 60–61
demise of, 4
diversification by, 259–73
emergence of, 56–61
expansion, into U.S., 241–55
expansion of Mexican, 81–84
extortion by, 207–08, 270–73
flourishing of, 10
as insurgents, 202–22
leadership of, 239–40
in Mexico, 64–68, 78–84
motivations of, 203
recruitment by, 163–66
truce between, 115–16
violent tactics of, 61–62, 79–81, 86
Drug Enforcement Administration (DEA).
See also DEA agents
Camarena murder and, 66–68
Cárdenas and, 98–99
creation of, 43, 46
Falcon case and, 46–48
legalization movement and, 279
Operation Condor and, 49–52
drug legalization, 108, 276–86
drug market
profits from, 43, 59–60, 65, 137–39, 275, 283
in U.S., 244–45, 250–51
drug policy reform, 276–86

drugs
  confiscated, 133–35, 137
  decriminalization of, 281–84
  methods of hiding, 143–44
  retail sale of, 250–51
  transport of, 135, 244–45
drug smugglers, 3, 4, 7–8, 142–43
  busts of, 229–30, 233–34
  Chinese, 28–30, 32–33
  early, 18, 25–26, 32–34
  extraditions of, 113, 236–38
  female, 144–45
  freelance, 231–33
  ingenuity of, 142–44
  prosecution of, 61, 225–40
  spotting, at border, 229
  stories of, 139–42
drug trafficking. *See also* Mexican drug
    industry
  business of, 135–36
  CIA and, 68–70
  cocaine, 56–60, 62–68, 82–83, 137–39,
    256–57
  corruption and, 52–53
  early, 18, 28–29, 32–34
  evolution of, in Nuevo Laredo region,
    94–104
  expansion of Mexican, 81–85, 241–58
  Fox policies on, 91–94
  growth of, 35–37
  involvement of officials in, 118
  marijuana, 40–43
  on Mexican-U.S. border, 29, 82
  U.S. efforts to halt, 29–31, 44–48, 83, 244
drug use, 8–9
  by Americans, 145–47, 280
  in Latin America, 280
  by Mexicans, 85–86
  in sixties, 38–39, 42–43
drug-war orphans, 290–91
drug warriors, 27, 36, 82–83
Drummond, John, 65
Duran, Fidel, 120–21
Durango, 3, 39
Durazo, Arturo, 155

East India Company, 25
economy
  Mexican, 85, 147
  of Mexico, 11
ecstasy, 8
Egypt, 255
ejecuciones, 154
El Barrio Bravo, 192

Eldredge, John, 197
Elizalde, Valentín (Golden Rooster), 169–70,
  182–85
Elkus, Adam, 204
El Narco, 7–12. *See also* drug cartels; Mexican
    drug industry
  diversification by, 259–73
  future of, 242–43
  as insurgency, 202–22
  international expansion of, 242–58
  religion of, 186–201
  spread of, 88
  in U.S., 242–55
El Negro. *See* Matta Ballesteros, Juan Ramón
  (El Negro)
El Paso, Texas, 243–44, 251, 252
El Salvador, 5, 102
El Veracruz, 33
encobijado, 81
Escadon, Iran, 139–42
Escobar, Pablo, 4, 20, 60, 61, 82–83, 156, 157,
  238–39
Esternberg, Isaac Guttnan, 155
ETA, 11, 205
Europe, 83
evangelicalism, 2
executions, 154. *See also* assassinations
explosives, 217–19
extortion, 105, 207–08, 261–68, 270–73
extraditions, 113, 236–38

Fabrique Nationale 5.7 pistols, 216
failed states, 10, 208–09
Fajardo, Sergio, 289–90
Falcon, Alberto Sicilia, 46–48, 58–59, 63
family culture, 260
FARC, 70, 257, 258
fashion, 8
Federal Bureau of Narcotics (FBN),
  36, 43
Federation, 20
Feeley, John, 286
Félix, Héctor, 76
Félix Gallardo, Miguel Ángel, 64–65, 67,
  77–78
female mobsters, 33–34
female smugglers, 144–45
Fernández, Vicente, 264
Ferriz, José Reyes, 270–71
feuds, 39, 54
Fierro, Rodolfo, 29
.50-caliber guns, 217
First Command, 5
Flores, Margarito, 249

Flores, Pedro, 249
Florida, 62–63, 82
folk saints, 188–93
Forcelli, Peter, 215–16
Fox, Vincente, 9, 10, 150
    Calderón compared with, 110
    Cárdenas and, 99–100
    drug policy of, 91–94, 113–14
    election of, 89–92
    legalization movement and, 278
    Mexican Drug War and, 102
    presidency of, 89–108
    retirement of, 108
France, 45
free trade, 4, 9, 75, 77, 151
"Fríjol," 163–65, 167–68
front companies, 148–49
Fuentes, Carillo, 201
Fuerzas Especiales de Arturo (FEDA), 106

Gabo, 274–75
GAFE. See Airmobile Special Forces Group
    (GAFE)
Gallardo, Miguel Ángel Félix, 4
Gambetta, Diego, 271
gangs, 2, 164–66, 251
ganja. See marijuana
Garcia, Teodoro, 117
gatilleros, 154–55
Gaviria, César, 277, 287
Giancana, Sam, 47
globalization, 4, 75, 241
Godfather, The (films), 171–72
godfathers, 171–73. See also capos
Goldbaum, David, 30
Golden Triangle, 19
Gómez, Sergio, 184
Gómez, Servando (La Tuta), 197, 202, 207, 211
González, Jaime (the Hummer), 184
González, Jesús, 189–90
González, José, 155
Gonzalez, Julian Aristides, 13, 256–58
"Gonzalo," 1–4, 79, 161–63
Gorbachev, Mikhail, 91
government corruption, 118
Gravano, Salvatore "Sammy the Bull," 56
grenades, 217, 219
Grupo Cartel del Sinaloa, 152, 179–82
Guadalajara, 50, 64–65
Guadalajara Cartel, 20, 57, 64–68
Guatemala, 105, 106, 128, 213, 244
Guerrero, 39, 40
guerrillas, 51, 53, 56, 68, 206
Guillen, Jacobo, 241–42, 250–51

Guinea-Bissau, 255–56
Gulf Cartel, 61–62, 87, 95, 100, 105, 113, 128.
    See also Zetas
Gulf War, 228
Gulf War syndrome, 228
gummers, 23, 48
gun lobby, 213–14, 216
gun trade, 213–17
"Gustavo," 156–61
Gutiérrez Rebollo, Jesús, 91, 97–98
Guzmán, Édgar, 121–22
Guzmán, Joaquin "Chapo," 37, 78–80, 100, 117,
    126, 257
    assassination of son of, 121–22
    escape of, 92–94
    indictment of, 248–49
    net worth of, 136
    protection of, 118
    whereabouts of, 19
Guzmán Decena, Arturo, 95–98, 99

Hamas, 11
Handling Sources (manual), 96
Hank, Jorge, 76
Harrison Narcotics Act, 28, 29, 58
hashish, 8
Hendix, Jimi, 39
Hernandez, Zulema, 92
heroin, 8, 9
    addiction, 25
    crackdown on, 44, 45
    early trade in, 33–34, 37
    effects of, 24
    profits from, 43
Herrera, Alma, 123–26, 274, 291
Herrera, César, 124–25
Herrera, Cristóbal, 124
Hidalgo, Miguel, 174
hippies, 38–39, 42–43
Hobbes, Thomas, 259
Hobsbawm, Eric, 206
Holland, 280, 282
homicides. See murders
Honduras, 56, 57, 68, 71, 102, 138, 256–57
Houston, 95, 245
Houston Chronicle, 100–101
Hugo, Victor, 281
human trafficking, 245–46
Humaya Gardens, 186–87

illegal immigrants, 243, 245–46
immigration debate, 243
Immigrations and Customs Enforcement, 230
India, 208, 255

indigenous rights, 10
industrialization, 23
inflation, 85
informants, 30, 46, 66, 96, 226, 230–31, 234–38
Institutional Revolutionary Party (PRI), 9, 10,
    34–35, 50–53, 76–77, 90, 91, 104
insurgents, 11, 50–51, 53, 116–17, 202–22, 285
international expansion, by Mexican drug
    cartels, 241–55
Iran, 255
Irish Republican Army (IRA), 11, 205
Italian mafia, 19, 20

Jacobo, César, 179–82
Jalisco, 39
Jamaica, 5
Jasso, Ignacia (La Nacha), 33–34
Jesuit missionaries, 21
Joplin, Janis, 39
journalists, 74–76, 119–21, 220
Juárez, 77, 86
Juárez Cartel, 2, 75, 79, 166, 207, 218, 252
Juárez School of Improvement, 163
Jung, George, 42–43, 59
"Just Say No" campaign, 8

Kaczynski, Theodore, 56
Kaibil commandos, 105
Kaibiles, 106
Kalashnikov, Mikhail, 53–54
Kalashnikov rifles, 53–54, 215, 216
Kelley, Jerry, 49
kidnappings, 94, 128–29, 161–62, 245–47,
    259–68, 287–88

La Esmeralda (ship), 115
La Familia Cartel, 112, 172, 187–88, 196–201, 207
    extortion by, 208
    in Honduras, 257
    kidnappings and, 265
    organizational structure of, 211
    Ortiz and, 209–12
    political influence of, 206
    tactics of, 106
La Nacha, 33–34
Laredo, 253–55
La Resistencia, 212
Lazcano, Heriberto (Executioner), 102–05,
    128, 239
Lazcano, Manuel, 32–33, 35, 36
leftist insurgents, 50–51, 53, 114
legalization movement, 108, 276–86
Legaria, Jonathan (Comandante Pantera),
    193–94

Lehder, Carlos, 43, 60
Libros en Cristo, 2
Liddy, G. Gordon, 44
Lins, Paulo, 13
Llosa, Mario Vargas, 35
Loaiza, Rodolfo, 154
López, Andrés, 237
López Obrador, Andrés Manuel, 107–09
Los Angeles, 241–42, 244, 245
Los Herederos de Sinaloa, 184
Los Tigres del Norte, 64, 175–76
Lugo, Conrado, 178–79
Luna, Garcia, 147

M67 grenades, 217
Madrazo, Roberto, 112
mafia. See organized crime
mafia capitalism, 10
Malverde, Jesús, 188–91
Mandela, Nelson, 89
Mara Salvatrucha, 5, 257
Marcos, Subcomandante, 10, 96–97
Maria Costa, Antonio, 149
marijuana
    in California, 276, 282–84
    campaigns against, 43–44
    Colombian, 49–50
    cultivation of, 19, 39–42, 65
    legalization of, 277, 282–84
    medical, 276, 282–83
    poisonous, 49
    profits from, 283
    smoking, 38–39
    smuggling of, 42–43
    U.S. demand for, 42–43
    use of, 43
    Zetas and, 105–06
marines, 285–86
Martinez, Oscar, 266, 269
Matamoros, 29
Matta, Ramón, 57
Matta Ballesteros, Juan Ramón (El Negro),
    56–61, 63–72, 256
Mayans, 10, 21
Mazatlán, 20
Medellín, Colombia, 20, 155, 289–90
Medellín Cartel, 43, 57–58, 60–63, 157
media coverage, of Mexican Drug War,
    100–101, 107, 119–21, 220
medical marijuana, 276, 282–83
Medina Mora, Eduardo, 116
Méndez, José de Jesús, 197
Mendoza, Vincent T., 174
Mérida Initiative, 114–15, 234

Mermelstein, Max, 59
Mesopotomia, 25
Metz, Steven, 206
Mexicali, 29
Mexican-American War, 21–22
Mexican culture, 169–85
Mexican drug enforcement
    during Calderón's administration, 112–16
    during Fox administration, 91–94, 113–14
    Operation Condor, 49–53
Mexican drug industry. *See also* drug cartels;
    El Narco
    as business, 135–36
    cartels and, 55–72, 81–84
    changes in, 3–5
    corruption and, 52–53
    growth of, 35
    international expansion of, 241–58
    money from, 146–48
    reorganization of, 78
    size of, 136–37
    workers in, 139–43
    worth of, 146–47
Mexican Drug War
    beginnings of, 10, 94–108
    Calderón presidency and, 109–30, 149
    casualties in, 10–11
    in Culiacán, 117, 119–26
    cultural impact of, 169–85
    importance of understanding, 5
    as insurgency, 202–22
    intensification of, 116–19
    kidnappings in, 259–68
    media coverage of, 100–101, 107, 119–21, 220
    militarization of, 285–86
    Nuevo Laredo battle in, 94–104
    prosecutions in, 225–40
    San Fernando massacre, 268–69
    tactics in, 94, 106, 210–12, 219–22
    violence of, 4–11, 19, 48–49, 106–09, 115–17,
        119, 121–29, 152, 202–03, 217–22, 252–53
    ways to peace in, 274–91
Mexican immigrants, 243
Mexican journalists, 13, 74–76
Mexican Mafia, 250–51
Mexican military, 95–98
    drugs confiscated by, 133–35
    U.S. training of, 286
    war on drugs and, 113–15, 119, 128–29,
        285–86
Mexican mud, 24, 34, 45
Mexican prisons, 2–3, 162
Mexican Revolution, 19, 29, 40
Mexicans, drug use by, 85–86

Mexican-U.S. border
    business along, 75
    guarding of, 216
    shutdown of, 44–45
    trafficking on, 29, 82, 142–43
Mexico
    black market in, 269–70
    ceded territory of, to U.S., 21–22
    cocaine smuggling through, 63–68
    compared with Colombia, 204–05, 209
    crime in, 85, 86
    criminal insurgency in, 202–22
    decriminalization in, 282
    democratic transition in, 9–10, 89–92,
        97–98
    economy of, 11, 85, 147
    as failed state, 10, 208–09
    under Fox, 89–108
    history of, 21–23
    industrialization in, 23
    internal disorder in, 21–22, 29, 108, 129–30
    politics in, 9, 35, 114
    reforms needed in, 275–76
    U.S. aid to, 114–15
    wars between U.S. and, 21–22
Mexico City, 288
Mexico United Against Crime, 263
Miami, 62–63
Miami Vice (film), 225, 233
Michoacán, 112–13
migrants, kidnapping of, 266–69
migration, to U.S., 22.91, 243
military coups, 57, 256
military dictators, 9
Millán, Édgar, 122
Mills, Barry Byron, 56
mining industry, 208, 272
missionaries, 21
money laundering, 148–51, 256
Montoya, Pedro de, 21
Moreno, Nazario, 188, 197–201, 211
Morera, Maria Elena, 262–64
Morocco, 39
morphine, 24, 36
mothers, of murdered children, 123–26
"the movement," 8
Munday, Mickey, 59, 62
murders, 2, 152–68
    by assassins, 154–68
    decrease in, 116
    in drug war, 119, 121–26
    increase in, 100, 107, 116
    in Mexico, 243–44, 252–53
    in Miami, 62–63

murders (continued)
  of officials, 11, 103–04, 212
  of police, 94, 103–04, 106, 116, 122, 152–54,
    207, 210–11
  in Tijuana, 86
  in U.S., 244, 253–55
  of U.S. citizens, 252–53
Murillo, Diego (Don Berna), 157, 158, 290
music, 8, 170–71, 173–85
musicians, 169–70, 173–85

narco alms, 187
narco-cinema, 172–73
narcocorridos, 8, 170–71, 173–85
narcocultura, 170–85
narcos, 48, 78, 100
narcotics. See drugs
Narcotics Board, 29
narco videos, 220–21
National Action Party, 90, 107, 110
Nepomuceno, Juan, 95
New York City, 245
Nicaragua, 56, 58, 68, 71, 287
Night of the Iguana (film), 42
Nixon, Richard, 38, 43–46, 114, 238
Nogales, 29, 244
Noriega, Manuel, 56, 71
North American Free Trade Organization
    (NAFTA), 4, 75, 77
Northeast Mexico, 95. See also Nuevo
    Laredo
Northern Alliance, 70
Nuevo Laredo, 29, 117
Nuevo Laredo turf war, 94–104

Oaxaca, 39, 108, 114, 127–28
Obama administration, 7, 112, 129–30, 214,
    216, 282
Office of Envigado, 157
officials
  American, 98–99
  attacks on, 116, 122
  bribery of, 272
  corrupt, 52–53
  involvement of, in drug trade, 118
  murdered, 11, 103–04, 212
offshore tax havens, 149
oil industry, 208, 272–73
Operation Clean House, 118
Operation Condor, 49–53, 64–65, 114
Operation Cooperation, 45
Operation Ice Block, 255
Operation Intercept, 44–45
Operation Michoacán, 112–13

Operation Secure Mexico, 102
opium, 17–37
  addiction, 25
  bans on, 25
  buying of, by U.S. government, 35–36
  consumption of, 27
  early drug trafficking in, 18, 32–37
  effects of, 23–25
  history of, 25–26
  increase in, 35
  poppy cultivation, 19, 23, 26
  prohibition of, 26–27
  smuggling of, 25–31
  Turkish production of, 45
opium dens, 26
Opium Wars, 25
Organization of Petroleum Exporting
    Countries (OPEC), 60
organized crime. See also drug cartels
  commercial hubs for, 20
  impact of, on those involved, 3, 8
  management of, 10
  role of government in, 84
Orlando, Leoluca, 289
orphans, 290–91
Ortiz, Francisco, 88
Ortiz, Miguel, 209–12
outlaws, idealization of, 171–72
overdoses, 9

Palenque, 6
Palermo, Italy, 20, 289
Palma, Hector "Whitey," 113
PAN, 111
Panama, 56, 138, 225, 231
paramilitary hit squads, 94, 98, 99, 104–06,
    206–07
  ex-soldiers in, 213
  training camps for, 212–13
  weapons for, 213–15
paraquat, 49
Paredes, Américo, 175
Pascual, Carlos, 285–86
Pemex, 272–73
Pensamientos (Moreno), 198–99
Pershing, John, 101
Peru, 58
peso crisis, 85
Petróleos, 272
Phoenix, 243, 245–47
Pinkerton, Jim, 100
pirated DVDs, 269–70
Plan Colombia, 114–15, 234–36
planes, 138, 256–57

plaza system, 53
plea bargains, 237–38
Poland, 89
police
  abuses by, 50
  attacks on, 11, 94, 103–04, 106, 116, 122, 207, 210–11
  Colombian, 234–36, 287
  combining, under one authority, 240
  corrupt, 52–53, 77–78, 104, 147, 239–40
  involvement of, in drug war, 103–04
  kidnapping cases and, 287–88
  murders of, 152–54
  training of Mexican, 234, 286–87
  turned criminals, 4
  U.S., 244
  working with mafia, 162, 210–11, 218–19
political candidates, attacks on, 207
political reforms, 275–76
political violence, 108
politicians
  corrupt, 107–08
  involvement of, in drug trade, 30–31, 39–40, 52–53, 84
politics, 9
  corruption in, 35
  of drug war, 114
  of prohibition, 27
poppies. See also opium
  cultivation of, 17–18, 23, 26
  history of, 25–26
Porter, William Sydney, 256
Portugal, 282
Posadas Ocampo, Juan Jesús, 80
presidential elections, 76–77, 90–91, 107–08
PRI. See Institutional Revolutionary Party (PRI)
prisons
  born-again Christians in, 2–3
  crimes committed from, 162
  escapes from, 162
  gangs in, 2
  Mexican, 2–3, 162
  Supermax, 55–56
profits
  from cocaine, 59–60, 65, 137–39
  from drugs, 43, 275
  from marijuana, 283
prohibition
  alcohol, 31–32
  origins of, 26–28
Prohibition era, 31–32, 95
Proposition 19, 277, 282–83

prosecutions, 225–40
  deal making in, 236–38
  use of informants in, 230–31, 234–38
prostitution, 270
protected witnesses, 46, 72
protection rackets, 270–71. See also extortion
pseudoephredrine, 150, 255
psychological warfare, 96

Al Qaeda, 106, 205, 213
Qing Dynasty, 25

race riots, 33
racism, 26–28, 32–33
Racketeer Influenced and Corrupt Organizations Act (RICO), 61
Ramirez, Sandra, 165–66, 288–89
Rattenbury, John, 133
Reagan, Ronald, 63, 65–66, 68, 82, 114
recreational drug use, increase in, 39–40
Reefer Madness (film), 43–44
Reid, Richard, 56
religion, 8, 186–201
Reta, Rosalio, 254
retail drug trade, 250–51
Reveles, José, 92
Reynosa, 29
Reynoso, Jorge, 172
RICO laws, 61
Rio Grande, 2
Rivera, Diego, 40
Roberts, Jon, 59
rock music, 38–39, 175
Rogers, Don, 68
"Rolando," 101–02
Roman Catholic Church. See Catholic Church
Romero, Enriqueta, 192
Romo, David, 192–93
Russian mafia, 144–45
Rwanda, 11

Salazar, Gustavo, 61, 236–37
Salinas, Carlos, 35, 77, 84
Salinas, Raúl, 84, 91
Salvador (film), 9
Sánchez, Rosalino "Chalino," 176–77
San Diego, 87, 243, 244
San Fernando massacre, 268–69
San Miguel de Allende, 6
Santa Marta Gold, 49–50
Santa Muerta (Holy Death), 191–96
Santana, Carlos, 175
Scarface (film), 56, 172, 227
Scherer, Julio, 92

Schiller, Dane, 237
Schmeig, Oliver, 155–56, 234–35
scholarship programs, 288
School of the Americas, 96
Schwarzenegger, Arnold, 109–10
Second World War, 35–36, 53–54
security issues, in Mexico, 21–22
SEMAR, 286
serial murderers, 2
Serrano, Irma, 47
SETCO, 69–70
sex industry, 270
Sgt. Pepper's Lonely Hearts Club Band
    (Beatles), 38
shakedowns. *See* extortion
Shannon, Elaine, 66
shrines, 188–95
sicarios, 155–68
Sicily, 19, 20
Sierra Madre Occidental, 19, 20
Sinaloa, 19–21, 23
    drug wars in, 48–49
    early drug trafficking in, 28–29, 35–37
    leftist insurgents in, 51
    marijuana cultivation in, 39–42
    Operation Condor in, 49–50
    poppy cultivation in, 26
Sinaloa Cartel, 2, 19–20, 79, 93, 100–102, 104,
    106, 113–17, 251
    business of, 208
    in Honduras, 257
    kidnappings and, 264–65
    officials involved in, 118
    Phoenix and, 245, 247
    in U.S., 248–50
    war among, 117–18, 119–26
Sinaloan tribes, 20–21
sixties, 38–39, 42–43
smack, 8
Small Wars Journal, 204
snuff videos, 220–21
soldiers
    abuses by, 285
    bribes to, 97–98
    drug enforcement and, 50, 92
    gunfights with, 18
    involvement of, in drug trade, 97
    involvement of, in paramilitary, 98, 213
    training of Latin American, by U.S., 96
Solórzano, Eduardo, 133–34
Sol Records, 177–78
Somalia, 11, 208
South Africa, 89
South Florida Task Force, 63

Soviet Union, 4, 10
Spanish conquistadors, 21
state capture, 209
straw purchases, 216
street races, 140–41
Sullivan, John, 204
Summer of Love, 38–39
Supermax prison, 55–56
Syria, 255

Taliban, 70
Tamaulipas, 6
Tegucigalpa, Honduras, 58, 71
Teloloapan, 41–42
Tepito, 192
tequila, 31
terrorism, 203, 219–22
Texas, 22, 95, 174, 251, 253–55
thalamus, 24
Thompson, Tommy, 244, 246
Tierra Blanca, 48–49
Tierra Caliente, 196–97, 200
Tijuana, 29, 42, 73–77, 85–86, 95, 112–13, 117,
    250–51, 265
Tijuana Cartel, 75, 79–81
timber industry, 272
tombs, 186–88
Torre, Rodolfo, 207
torture, 4, 67, 266–68
tourism, 6, 11
Tovex, 218
Traffic (film), 86
traffickers. *See* drug smugglers
training camps, 212–13
transporters, freelance, 231–33
trap cars, 143
Treaty of Guadalupe, 22
truces, 115–16, 290
tunnels, 143
turf wars, 94–104, 127, 139, 244, 290
Turkey, 39, 45
Twitter, 220

United Nations, 279
United States
    1960s in, 38–39
    aid from, 114–15
    cocaine market in, 58–60
    decriminalization in, 281–84
    demand for marijuana in, 42–43
    drug market in, 244–45, 250–51
    drug use in, 145–47, 280
    drug violence in, 251, 253–55
    expansion of drug cartels into, 241–55

foreign diplomacy of, 31
gun trade and, 213–17
involvement of, in countering insurgency, 204
Mérida Initiative and, 114–15
Mexican migration to, 22, 91, 243
Mexican territory ceded to, 21–22
Prohibition era, 31–32
training of Mexican troops by, 286
wars between Mexico and, 21–22
Uon, J., 30
U.S. drug enforcement, 29–31
  Colombians and, 83
  Falcon case and, 46–48
  Operation Cooperation, 45
  Operation Intercept, 44–45
  success of, 244
U.S. drug policies
  Harrison Narcotics Act, 28, 29
  under Nixon, 43–46
  origins of, 26–28
U.S. embassy, burning of Honduran, 71
U.S. government, buying of opium by, 35–36
U.S. officials, 98–99

Valdemar, Hugo, 195
Valdés, Rodolfo (Gitano), 154
Valdéz, Édgar (Barbie Doll), 116, 126, 173
Valencia, Armando, 94, 197
Valens, Ritchie, 175
Valero, Luis, 87
Venezuela, 257, 258
victims, 290–91
Vietnam War, 11
Villa, Pancho, 3, 19, 29, 60, 205
Villegas, Elizabeth, 167
violence
  anti-Chinese, 32–33
  cartels and, 61–62, 79–81, 86
  in Colombia, 56
  feuds and, 39, 54
  gang, 164–67
  in Honduras, 257
  of Mexican Drug War, 4–11, 19, 48–49, 102–09, 115–19, 121–29, 152, 202–03, 217–22, 252–53
  during Mexican Revolution, 29
  in Miami, 62–63
  between narcos, 79–80
  political, 108
  as retaliation, 207
  in U.S., 251, 253–55

Walesa, Lech, 89
Walker, Art, 175
Wallace, Isabel Miranda de, 264
Wang Si Fee, 30
War of Independence, 21
war on drugs. See also Mexican Drug War
  failure of, 5
  funding of, 18
  under Nixon, 43–46
  perpetual nature of, 238–39
  politics of, 114
  under Reagan, 63–66, 68–70
war on terror, 205
weapons smuggling, 47, 213–17
Webb, Gary, 69
Web sites, 220
West Africa, 255–56
Westphal, Joseph, 129–30
whiskey, 31
WikiLeaks, 129, 285, 286
Wild at Heart (Eldredge), 197
withdrawal effects, 25
Wright, Hamilton, 27, 279

Yaqui tribe, 22–23
Ye Gon, Zhenli, 149–51
Yeltsin, Boris, 91
Yousef, Ramzi, 56
youth programs, 288–89

Zambada, Ismael "the Mayo," 78, 79, 117, 118, 170–71
Zapata, Emiliano, 198, 205
Zapata, Haime, 130
Zapatista rebels, 93, 96–97
Zedillo, Ernesto, 85, 90–91, 277
Zeta (magazine), 76, 86, 88
Zetas, 94, 99–106, 112, 115–17, 198, 239, 285
  extortion by, 207–08, 272–73
  in Guatemala, 255
  in Honduras, 257
  as insurgents, 207
  kidnappings by, 261, 266–69
  organizational structure of, 211
  piracy by, 269–70
  spread of, 127–28
  tactics of, 128, 221–22
  training camps of, 212–13
  in U.S., 253–55
Zuaques, 21

A Note on the Author

Ioan Grillo has reported on Latin America since 2001 for international media, including *Time* magazine, CNN, the Associated Press, *PBS News-Hour*, the *Houston Chronicle*, CBC, and the *Sunday Telegraph*. He has covered military operations, mafia killings, and cocaine seizures, and has discussed the drug war with two Mexican presidents, three attorneys general, and the U.S. ambassador. A native of England, he lives in Mexico City. *El Narco* is his first book.